Wake Up, Sleeping Beauty

5

MEGUMI
MORINO

CONTENTS

Characters

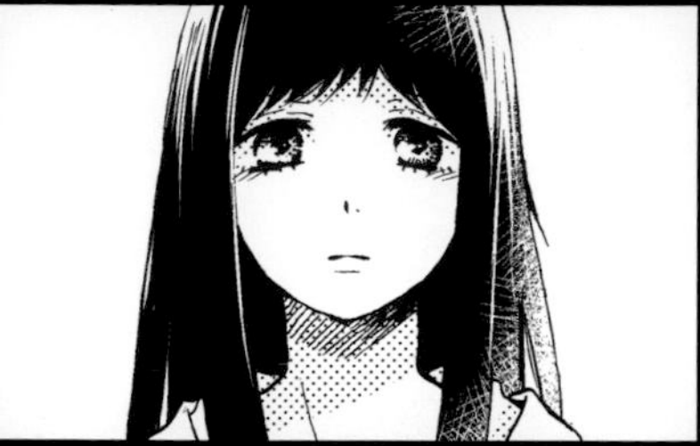

Shizu Karasawa

The only child of Testu's wealthy employers. She is prone to possession by spirits of the dead, and has been forbidden from leaving her house.

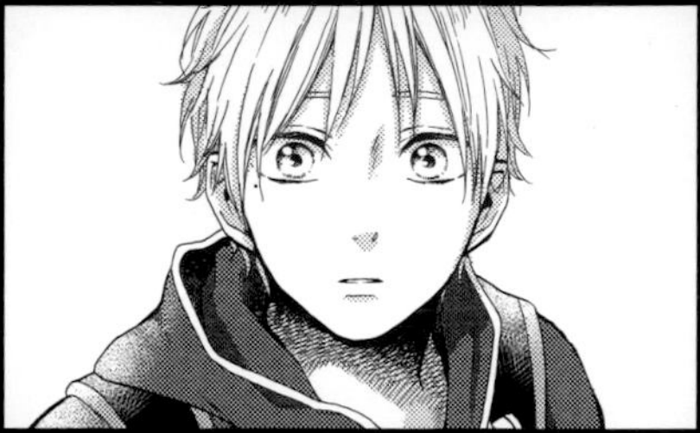

Tetsu Misato

A third-year in high school. Due to personal circumstances, he dove into a part-time job to save up money. He is nimble with his hands, and is afraid of ghosts.

Spirits Inside Shizu

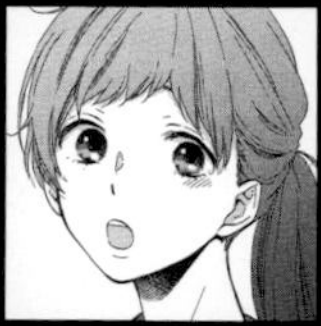

Haru

A caring, athletic man.

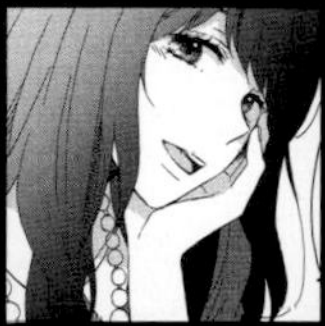

Mirei

Loves fashion, hates cleaning.

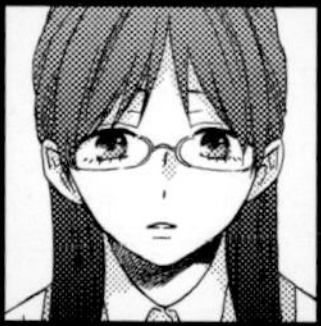

Shinobu

Shizu's great-grandfather. Enjoys gardening.

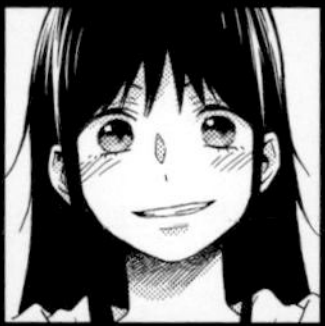

Kanato

A boy's spirit who only recently took up residence in Shizu's body.

Tetsu's Family

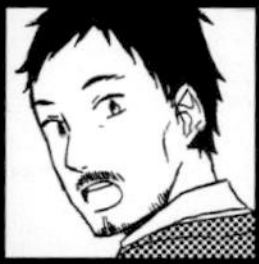

Father

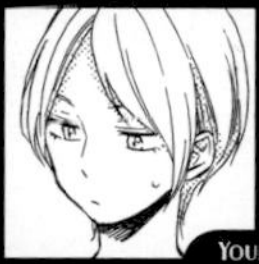

Ryō

Younger Sisters

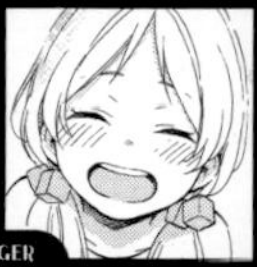

Suzu

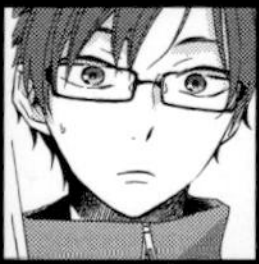

Chihiro Ueno

Tetsu's childhood friend. Soccer Club captain.

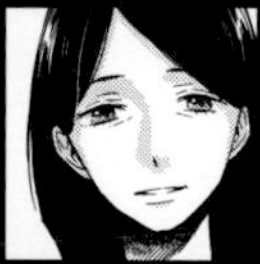

Sanae Karasawa

Shizu's mother.

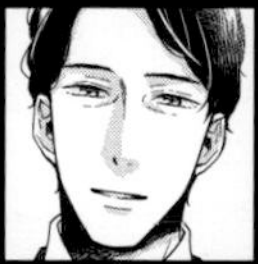

Takashi Karasawa

Shizu's father.

Story

Tetsu works as a housekeeper at the Karasawa Estate—the rumored "Haunted House on the Hill." One day, he meets Shizu, the mysterious girl who lives alone in the outbuilding. He is drawn to her sad smile, but when he meets her again, she has changed so dramatically it's as if she's a different person. Tetsu initially thinks Shizu has multiple personality disorder and continues to work hard to be her friend. However, after a frightening incident, he learns that she is susceptible to being possessed by spirits. After striking a deal with Shizu's mother, Tetsu decides to keep working with Shizu. As the two spend more time together, Shizu experiences new emotions and begins to come into her own identity, and it compells Tetsu to see her for the woman she is. One day, Shizu's father comes home from a trip overseas and decides to ship her off to a hospital. Tetsu rescues her from the mansion and they run away together, but...?!

Wake Up,
Sleeping
Beauty

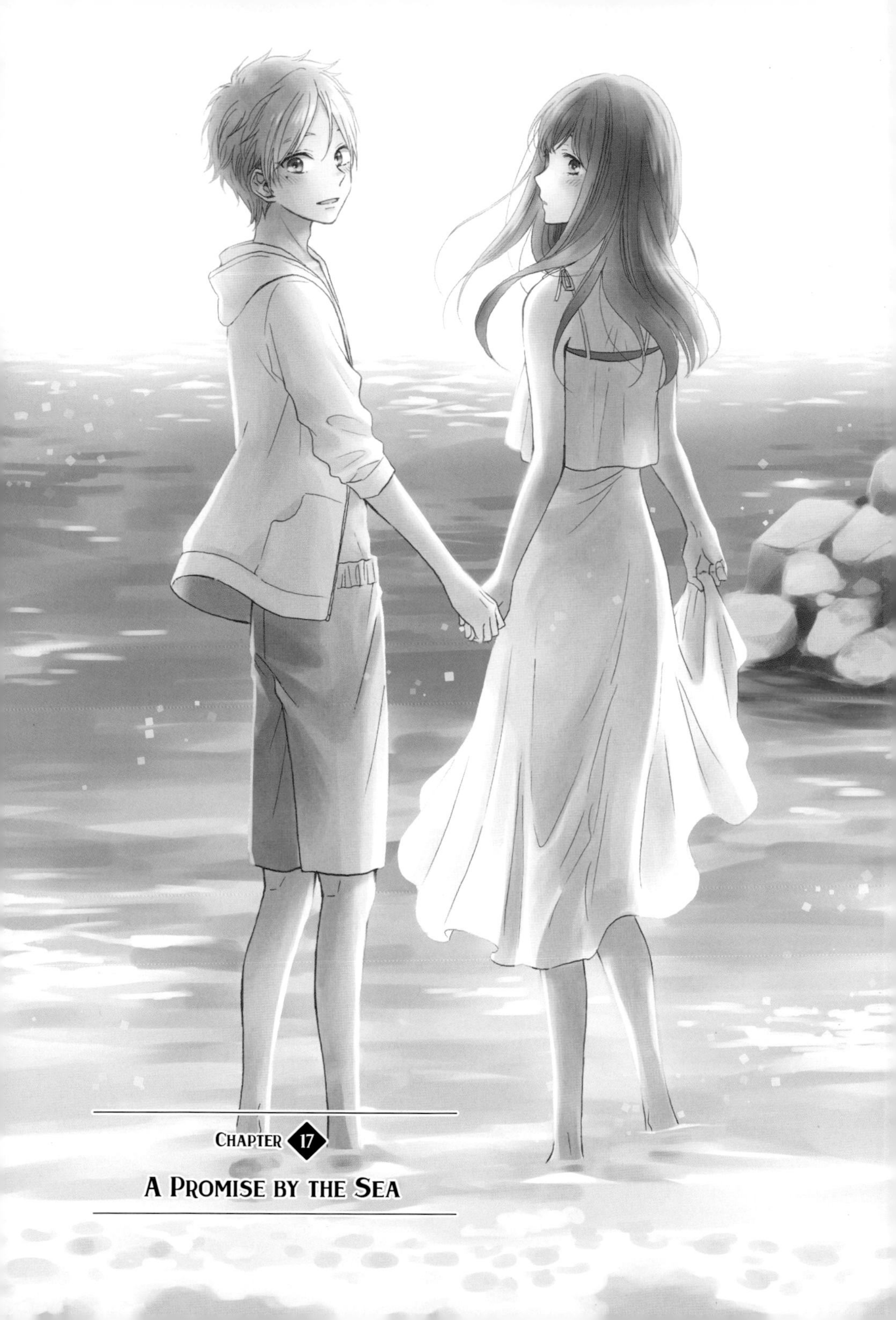

Chapter 17

A Promise by the Sea

Spirits I've met:
- Haru-san   • Shinobu-san
- Mirei-san   • Kanato

Notes on Shizu-san's Possession

- Shizu-san gets possessed when she is not conscious (sleeping, fainted, etc.).
- Shizu-san cannot do anything beyond her physical abilities.
- When a spirit takes over for a long time, it takes a toll on Shizu-san's health.

- Shizu-san's personal memories and experiences
  & everything that happens while someone else is in her body
    → Shared among everyone inside her body.
- Shizu-san does remember what happens when someone else is controlling her body.

- To force a spirit out of Shizu-san's body
    → Give her a physical or mental shock to wake her up.

- When someone who is haunted by another spirit is near
  Shizu-san, Shinobu-san and the others couldn't get near her

- What if the spirit inside her refuses to leave?

- When Shizu-san wants badly enough to take over,
  apparently the spirit inside her will be driven out.

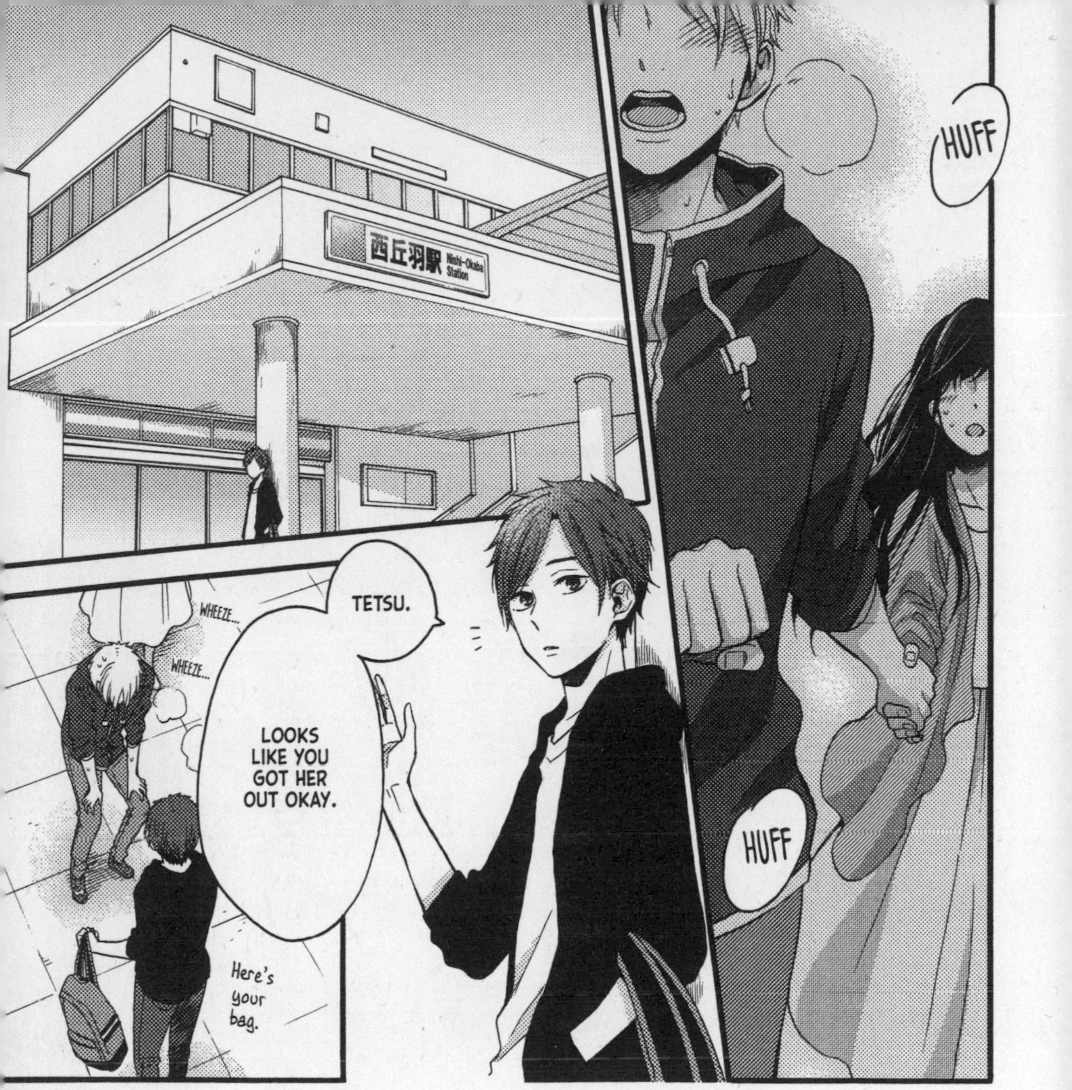
HUFF
HUFF
西丘羽駅 Nishi-Okaba Station
TETSU.
LOOKS LIKE YOU GOT HER OUT OKAY.
WHEEZE...
WHEEZE...
Here's your bag.

Wake Up, Sleeping Beauty

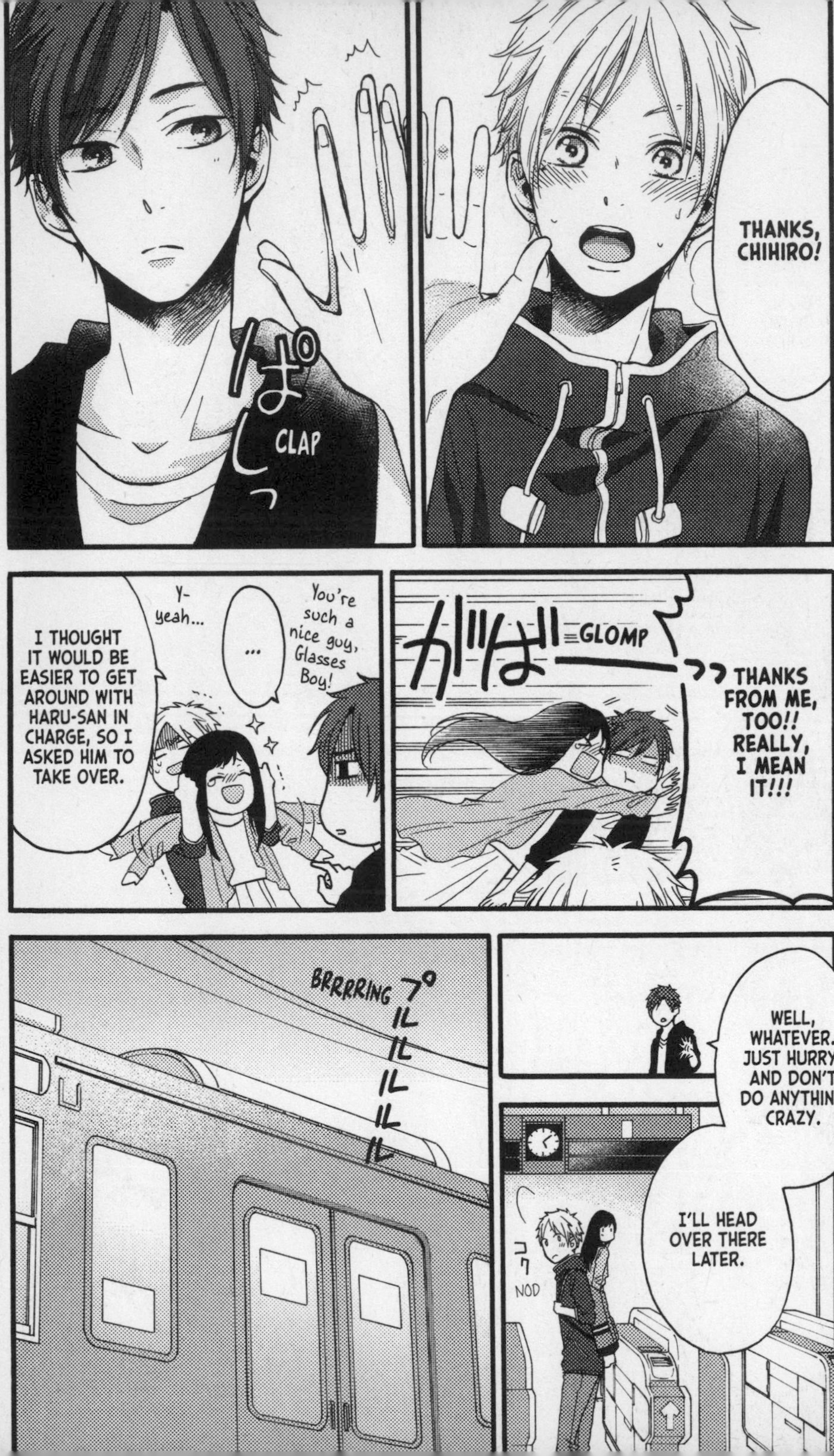
THANKS, CHIHIRO!
ぱしっ
CLAP
がばー
GLOMP
THANKS FROM ME, TOO!! REALLY, I MEAN IT!!!
You're such a nice guy, Glasses Boy!
...
Y-yeah...
I THOUGHT IT WOULD BE EASIER TO GET AROUND WITH HARU-SAN IN CHARGE, SO I ASKED HIM TO TAKE OVER.
WELL, WHATEVER. JUST HURRY. AND DON'T DO ANYTHING CRAZY.
I'LL HEAD OVER THERE LATER.
コク
NOD
BRRRRING
プルルルルル

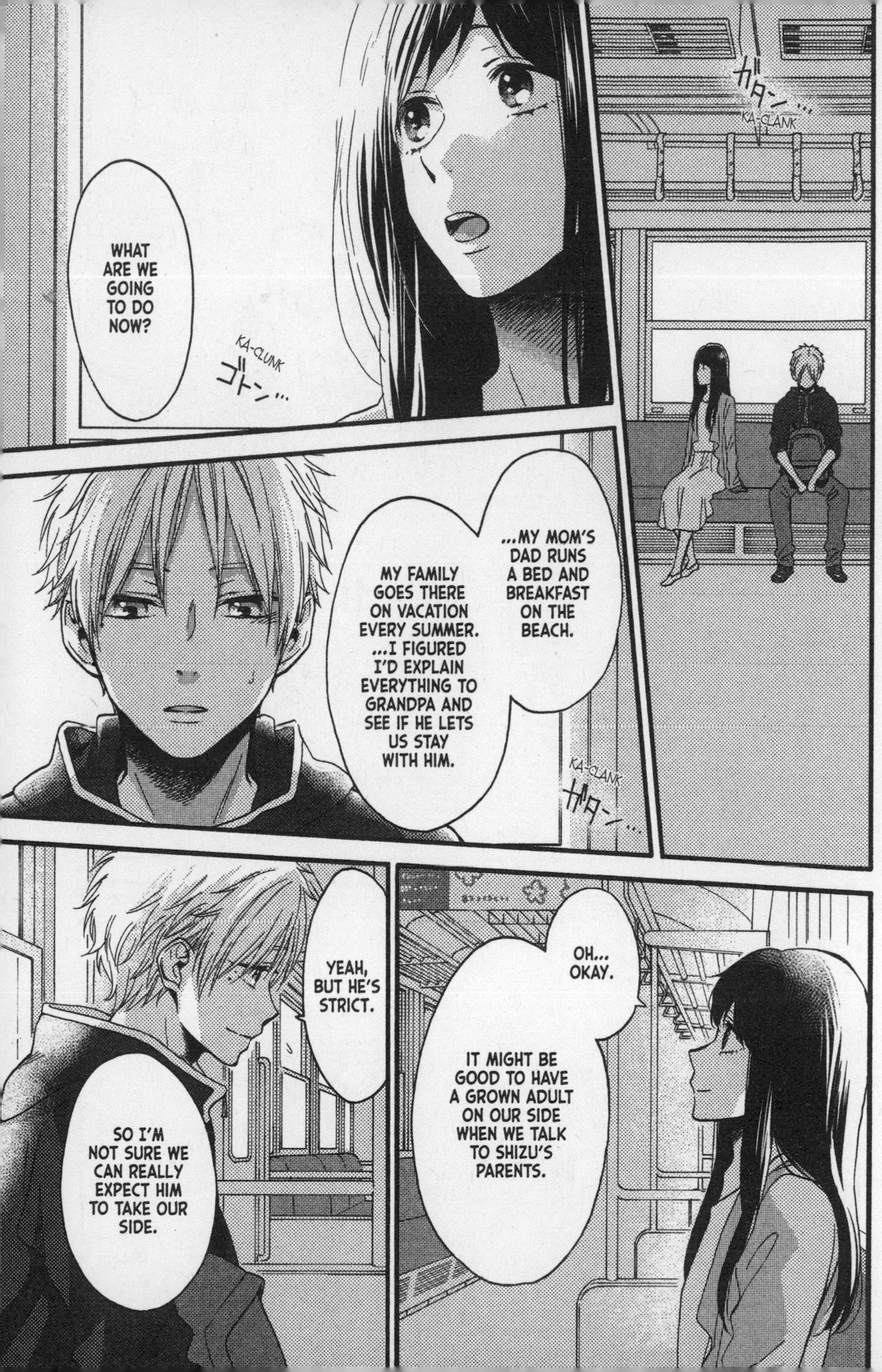
ガタン…
KA-CLANK
WHAT ARE WE GOING TO DO NOW?
KA-CLANK
ゴトン…
...MY MOM'S DAD RUNS A BED AND BREAKFAST ON THE BEACH.
MY FAMILY GOES THERE ON VACATION EVERY SUMMER. ...I FIGURED I'D EXPLAIN EVERYTHING TO GRANDPA AND SEE IF HE LETS US STAY WITH HIM.
KA-CLANK
ガタン…
OH... OKAY.
IT MIGHT BE GOOD TO HAVE A GROWN ADULT ON OUR SIDE WHEN WE TALK TO SHIZU'S PARENTS.
YEAH, BUT HE'S STRICT.
SO I'M NOT SURE WE CAN REALLY EXPECT HIM TO TAKE OUR SIDE.

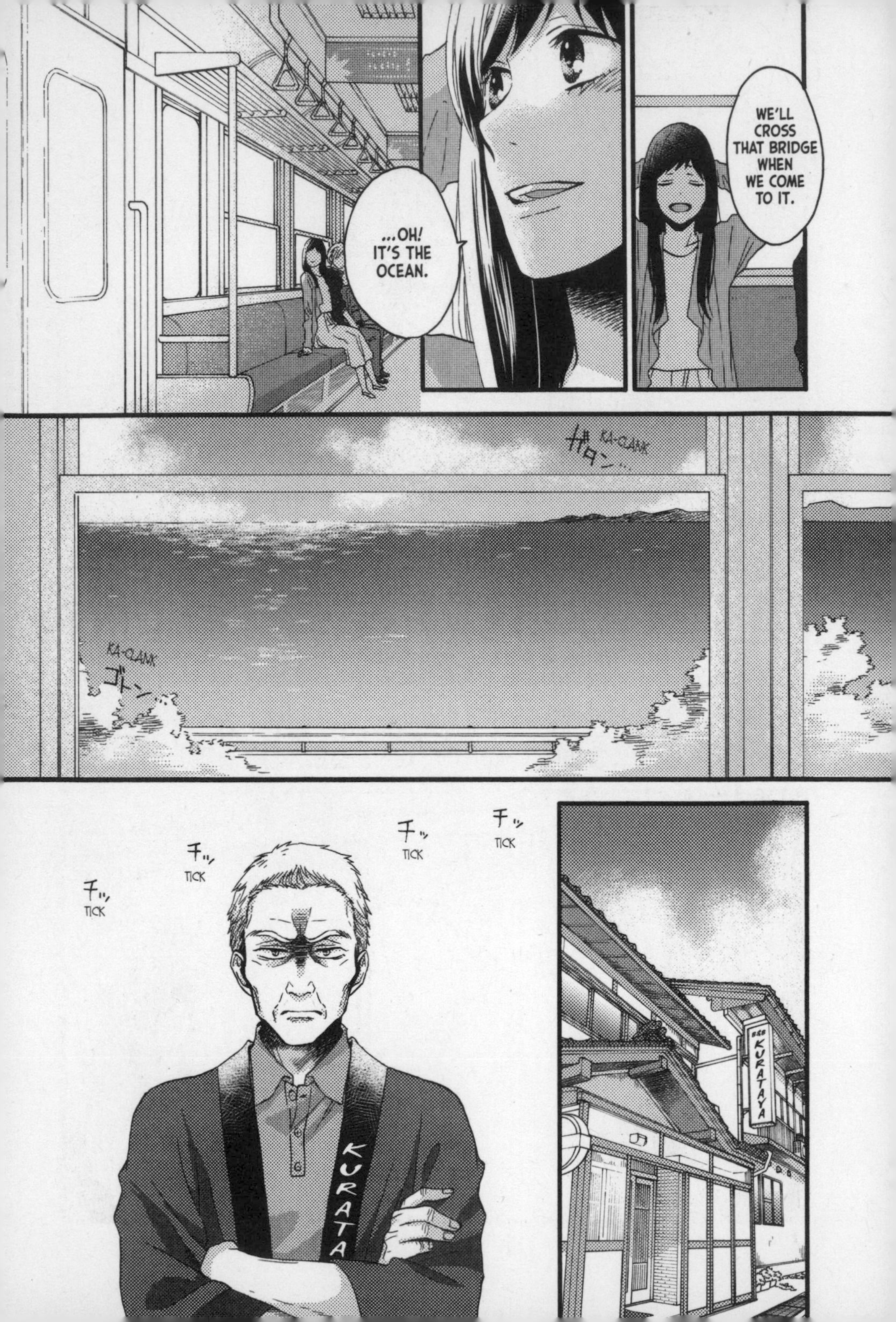

WE'LL CROSS THAT BRIDGE WHEN WE COME TO IT.
...OH! IT'S THE OCEAN.
ガタン
KA-CLANK
ゴトン
KA-CLANK
KURATAYA
チッ
TICK
チッ
TICK
チッ
TICK
チッ
TICK
KURATA

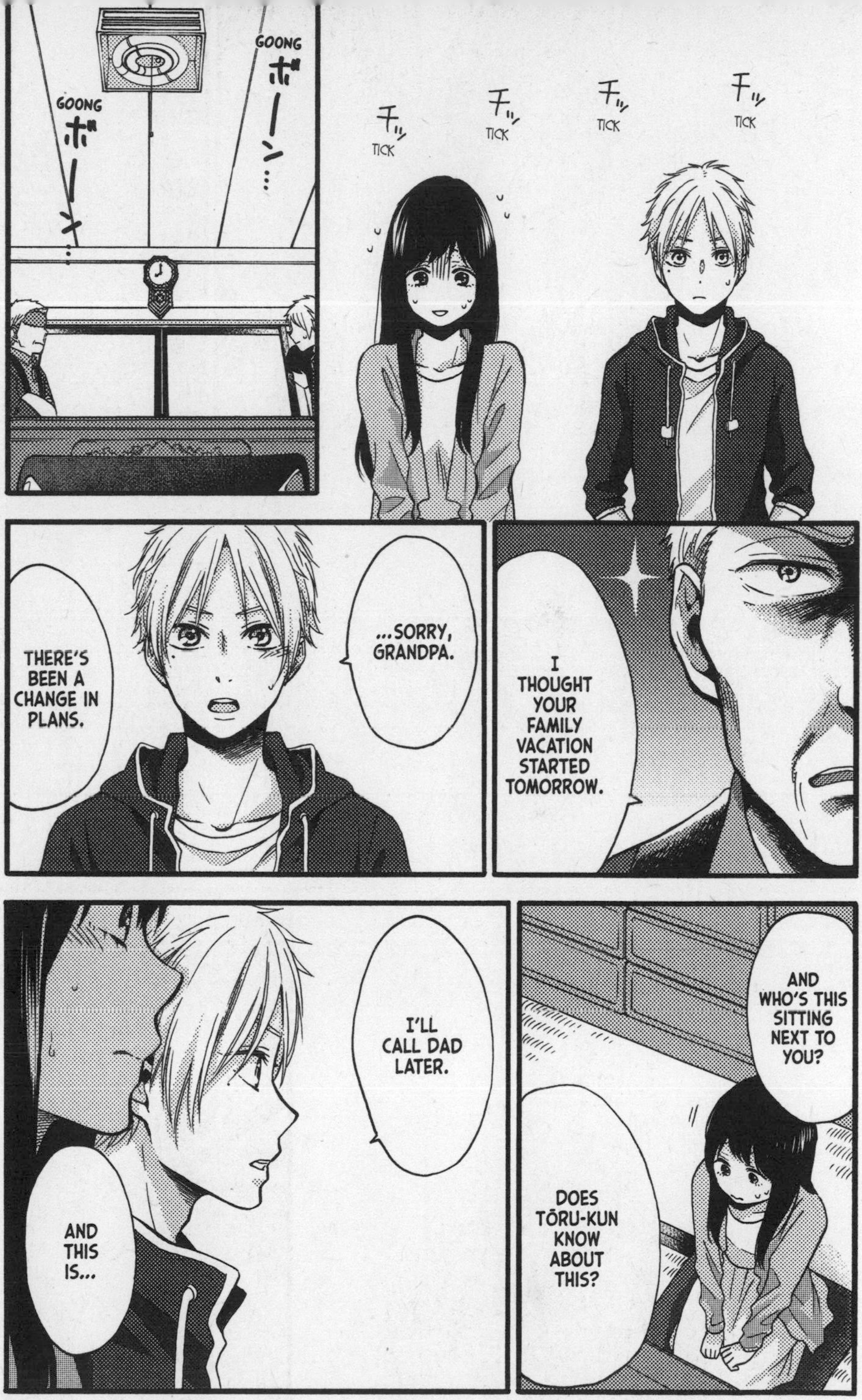

チッ TICK
チッ TICK
チッ TICK
チッ TICK
GOONG ボーン…
GOONG ボーン…
I THOUGHT YOUR FAMILY VACATION STARTED TOMORROW.
...SORRY, GRANDPA.
THERE'S BEEN A CHANGE IN PLANS.
AND WHO'S THIS SITTING NEXT TO YOU?
DOES TŌRU-KUN KNOW ABOUT THIS?
I'LL CALL DAD LATER.
AND THIS IS...

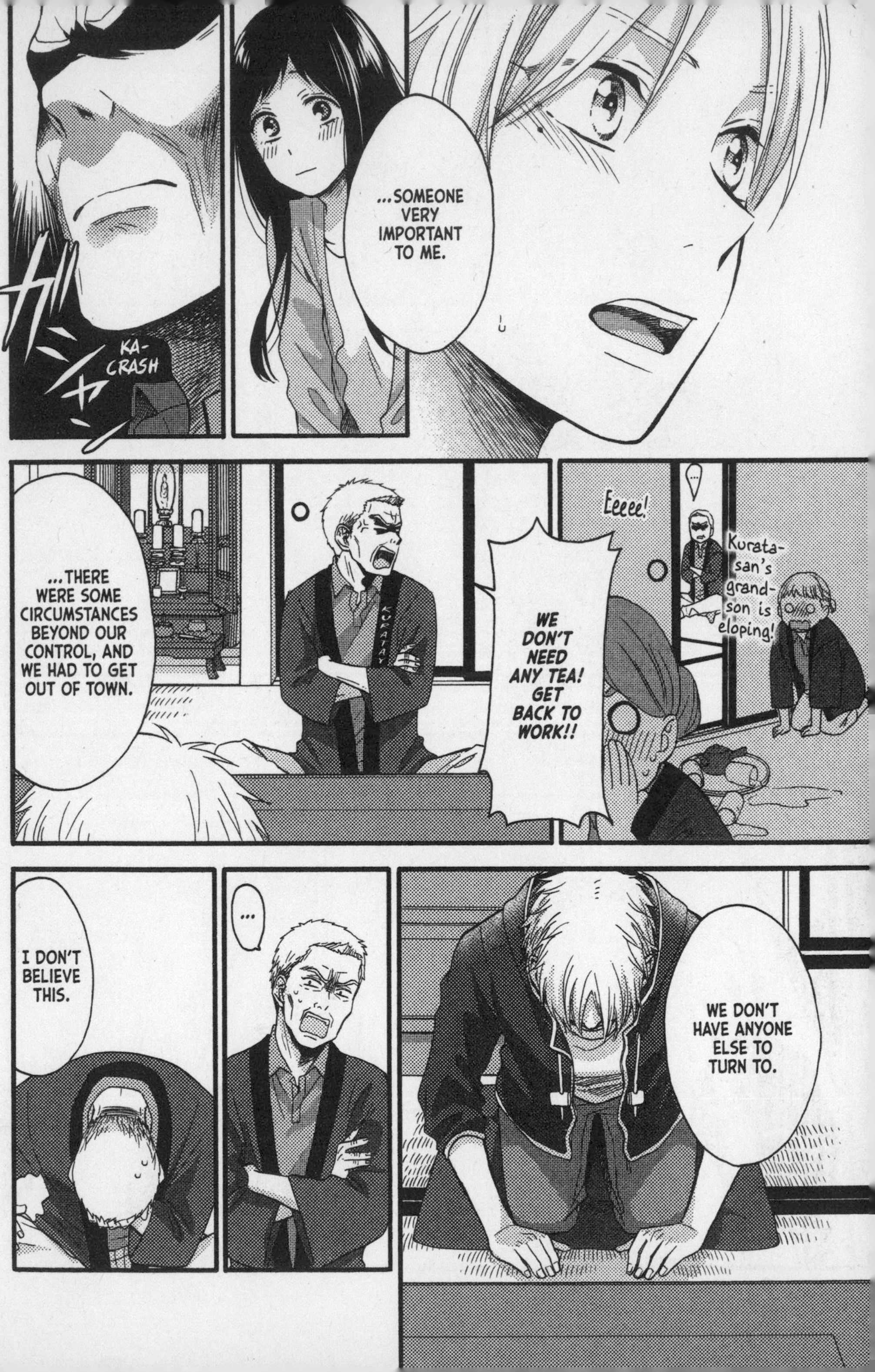
...SOMEONE VERY IMPORTANT TO ME.
KA-CRASH
...
Eeeee!
Kurata-san's grand-son is eloping!
WE DON'T NEED ANY TEA! GET BACK TO WORK!!
...THERE WERE SOME CIRCUMSTANCES BEYOND OUR CONTROL, AND WE HAD TO GET OUT OF TOWN.
WE DON'T HAVE ANYONE ELSE TO TURN TO.
...
I DON'T BELIEVE THIS.

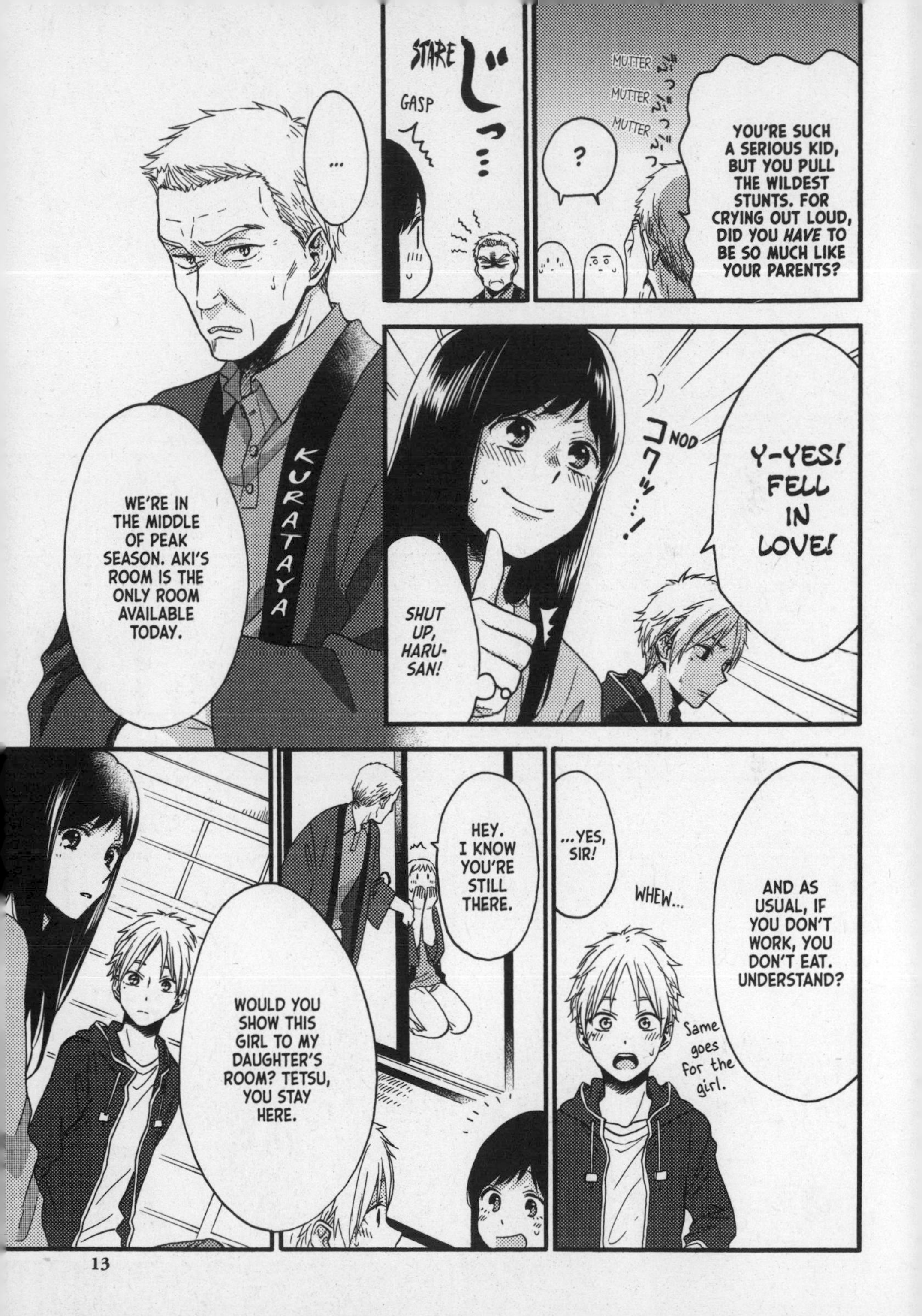
MUTTER
MUTTER
MUTTER
?
YOU'RE SUCH A SERIOUS KID, BUT YOU PULL THE WILDEST STUNTS. FOR CRYING OUT LOUD, DID YOU *HAVE* TO BE SO MUCH LIKE YOUR PARENTS?
STARE
GASP
Y-YES! FELL IN LOVE!
NOD
SHUT UP, HARU-SAN!
...
KURATAYA
WE'RE IN THE MIDDLE OF PEAK SEASON. AKI'S ROOM IS THE ONLY ROOM AVAILABLE TODAY.
AND AS USUAL, IF YOU DON'T WORK, YOU DON'T EAT. UNDERSTAND?
Same goes for the girl.
WHEW...
...YES, SIR!
HEY. I KNOW YOU'RE STILL THERE.
WOULD YOU SHOW THIS GIRL TO MY DAUGHTER'S ROOM? TETSU, YOU STAY HERE.

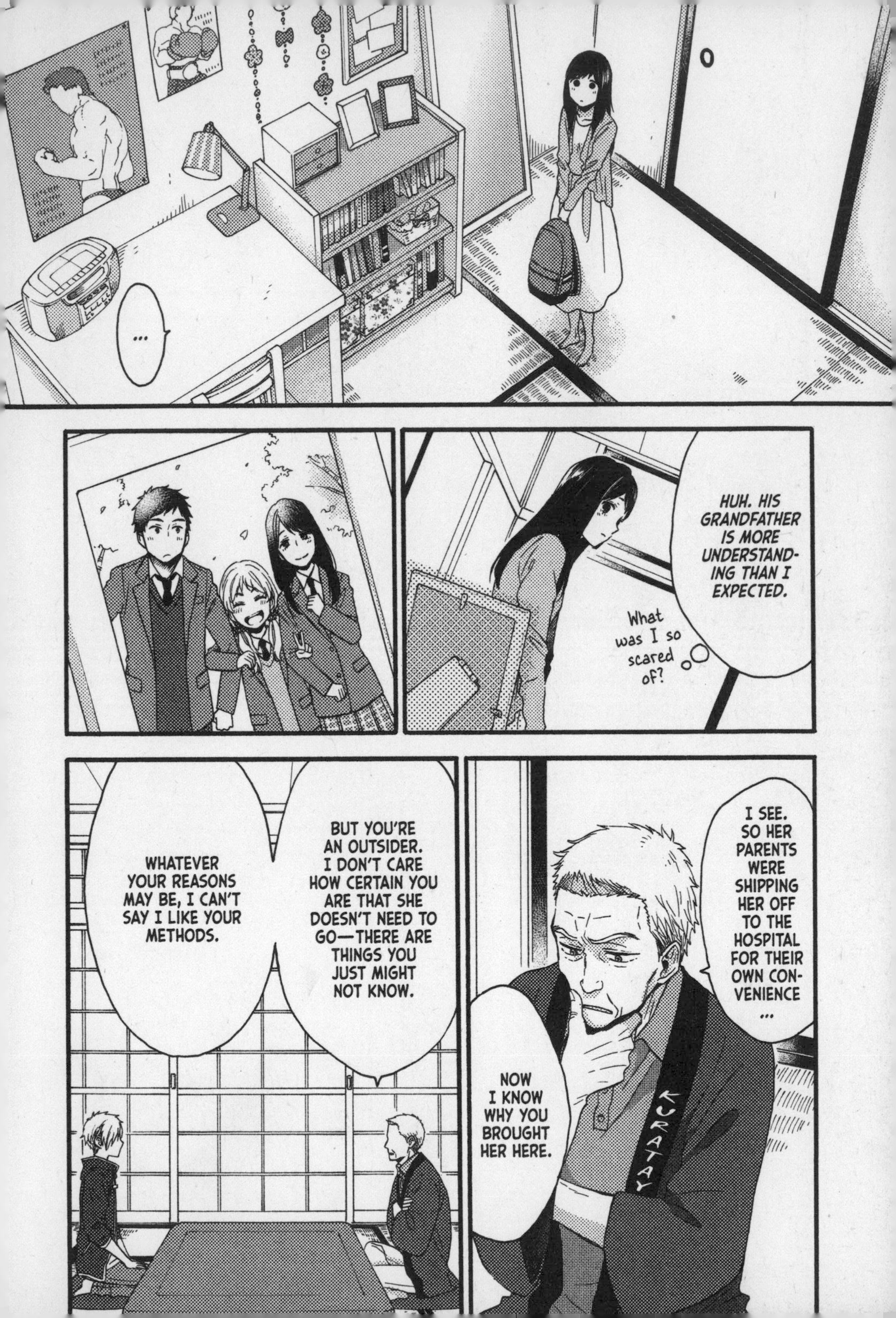
...
HUH. HIS GRANDFATHER IS MORE UNDERSTAND-ING THAN I EXPECTED.
What was I so scared of?
I SEE. SO HER PARENTS WERE SHIPPING HER OFF TO THE HOSPITAL FOR THEIR OWN CON-VENIENCE ...
NOW I KNOW WHY YOU BROUGHT HER HERE.
KURATAY
BUT YOU'RE AN OUTSIDER. I DON'T CARE HOW CERTAIN YOU ARE THAT SHE DOESN'T NEED TO GO—THERE ARE THINGS YOU JUST MIGHT NOT KNOW.
WHATEVER YOUR REASONS MAY BE, I CAN'T SAY I LIKE YOUR METHODS.

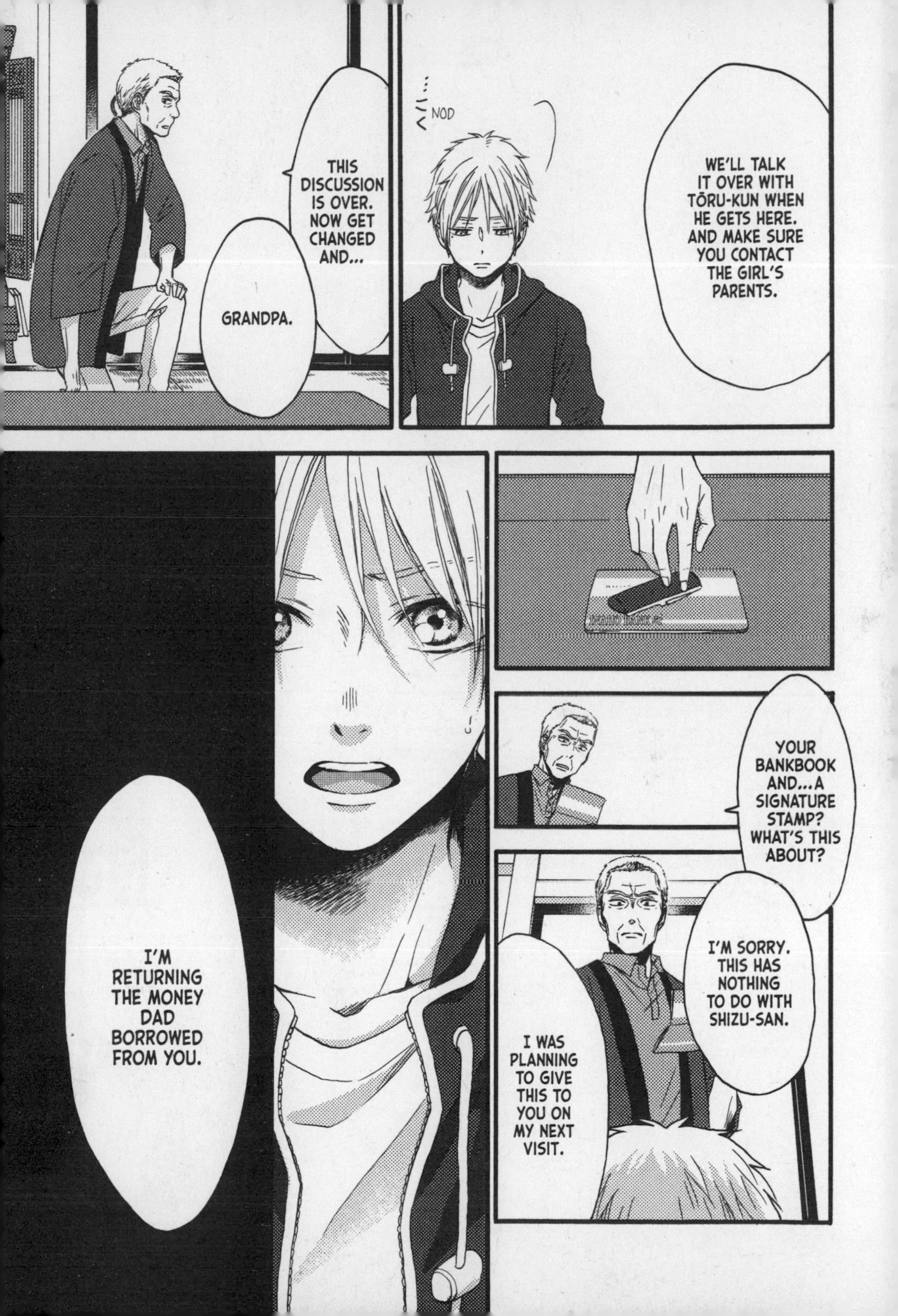
WE'LL TALK IT OVER WITH TŌRU-KUN WHEN HE GETS HERE. AND MAKE SURE YOU CONTACT THE GIRL'S PARENTS.
NOD
THIS DISCUSSION IS OVER. NOW GET CHANGED AND...
GRANDPA.
INAHO BANK
YOUR BANKBOOK AND...A SIGNATURE STAMP? WHAT'S THIS ABOUT?
I'M SORRY. THIS HAS NOTHING TO DO WITH SHIZU-SAN.
I WAS PLANNING TO GIVE THIS TO YOU ON MY NEXT VISIT.
I'M RETURNING THE MONEY DAD BORROWED FROM YOU.

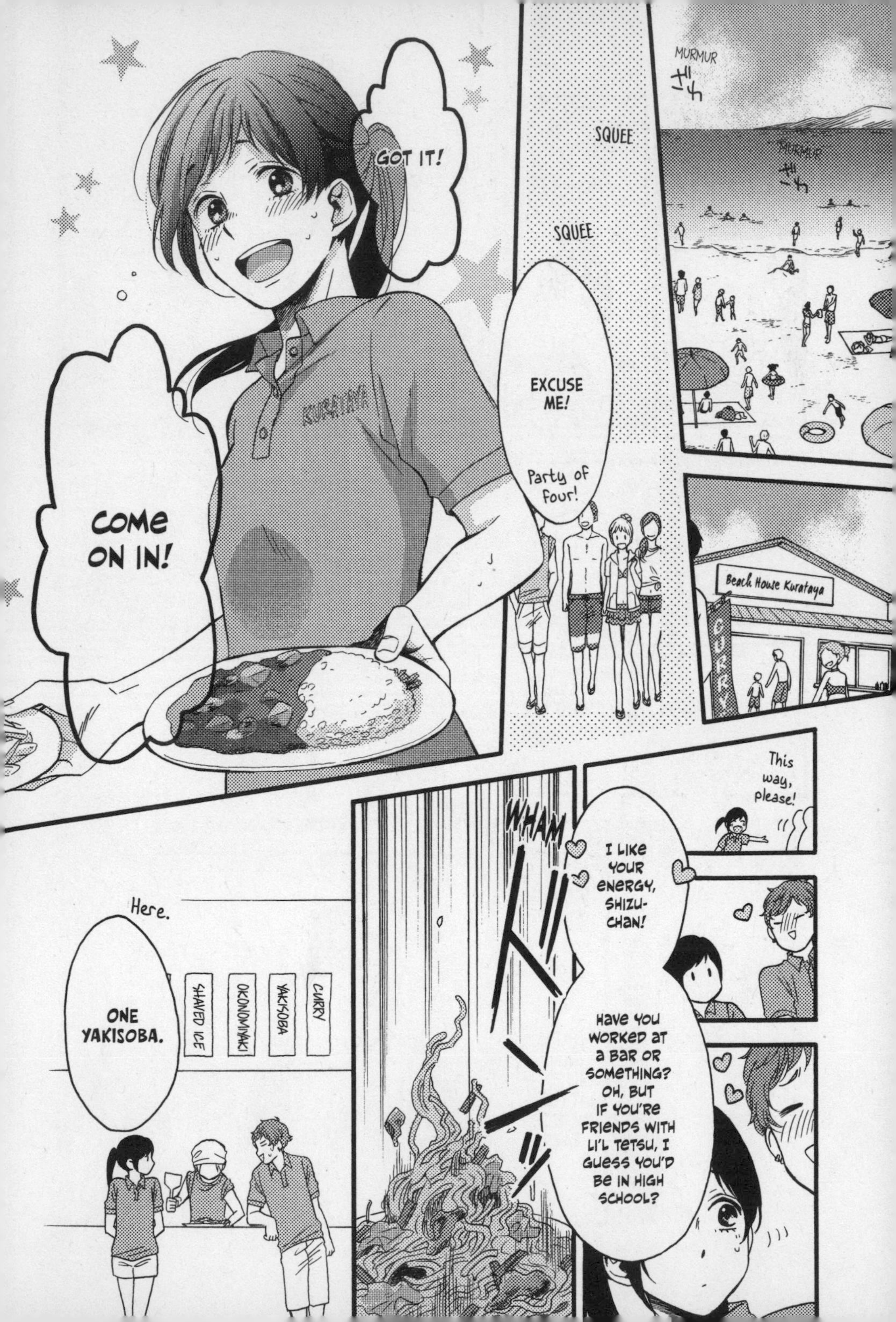
MURMUR
MURMUR
Beach House Kurataya
CURRY
SQUEE
SQUEE
EXCUSE ME!
Party of four!
GOT IT!
COME ON IN!
This way, please!
I LIKE YOUR ENERGY, SHIZU-CHAN!
HAVE YOU WORKED AT A BAR OR SOMETHING? OH, BUT IF YOU'RE FRIENDS WITH LI'L TETSU, I GUESS YOU'D BE IN HIGH SCHOOL?
WHAM
Here.
ONE YAKISOBA.
CURRY
YAKISOBA
OKONOMIYAKI
SHAVED ICE

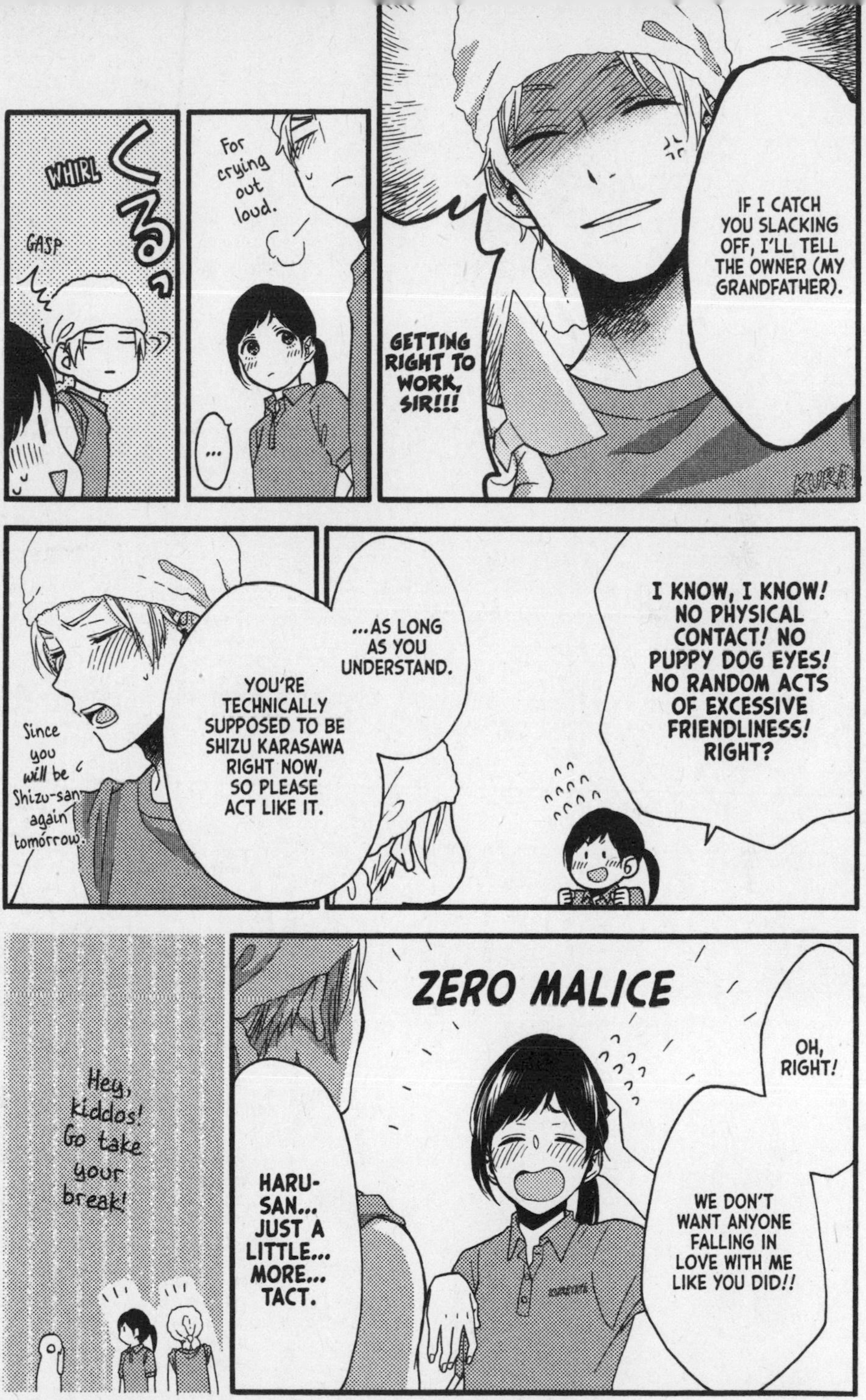
IF I CATCH YOU SLACKING OFF, I'LL TELL THE OWNER (MY GRANDFATHER).
GETTING RIGHT TO WORK, SIR!!!
KURA
For crying out loud.
...
WHIRL
くるっ
GASP
I KNOW, I KNOW! NO PHYSICAL CONTACT! NO PUPPY DOG EYES! NO RANDOM ACTS OF EXCESSIVE FRIENDLINESS! RIGHT?
...AS LONG AS YOU UNDERSTAND.
YOU'RE TECHNICALLY SUPPOSED TO BE SHIZU KARASAWA RIGHT NOW, SO PLEASE ACT LIKE IT.
Since you will be Shizu-san again tomorrow.
ZERO MALICE
OH, RIGHT!
WE DON'T WANT ANYONE FALLING IN LOVE WITH ME LIKE YOU DID!!
HARU-SAN... JUST A LITTLE... MORE... TACT.
Hey, kiddos! Go take your break!

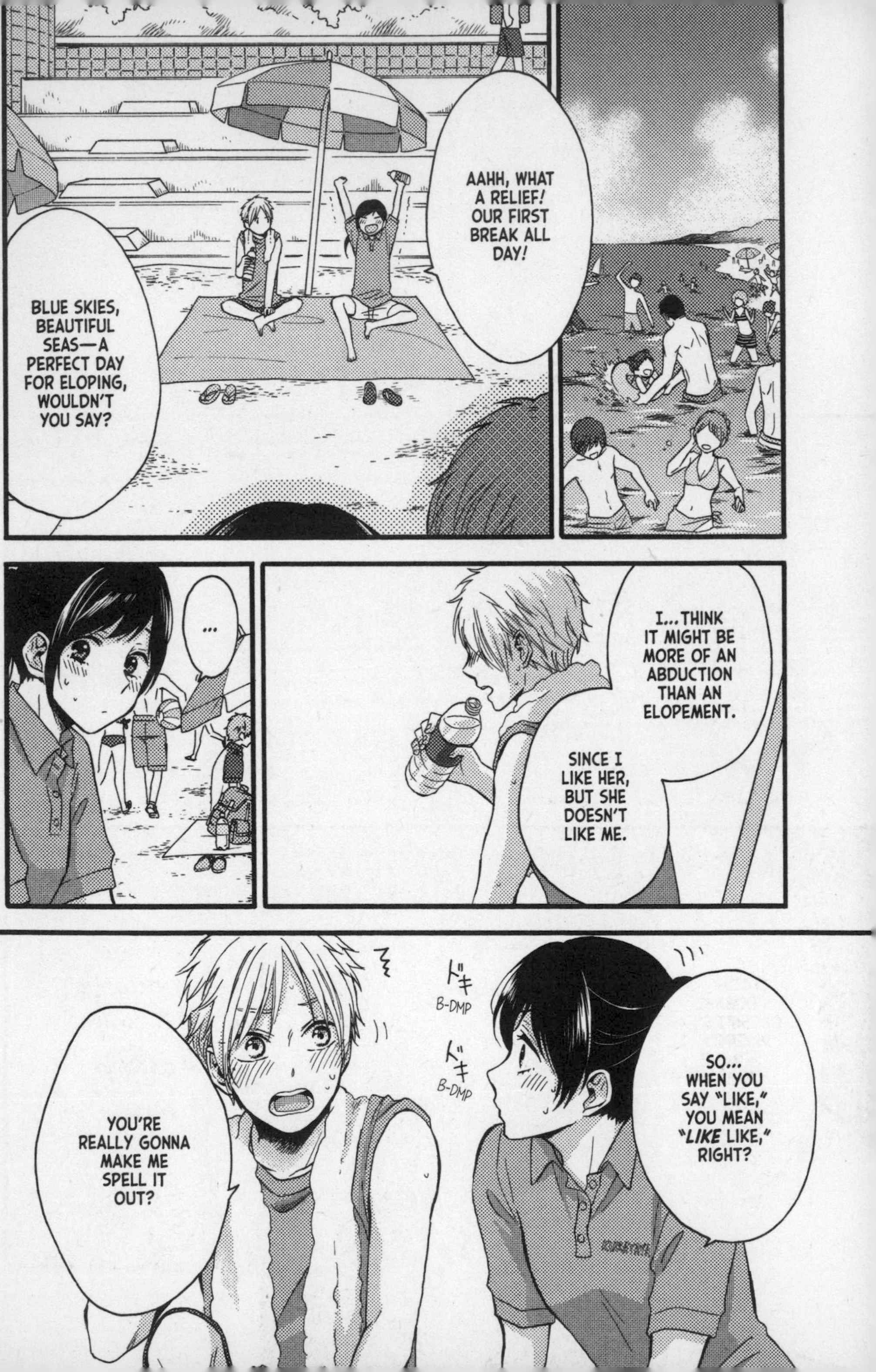
AAHH, WHAT A RELIEF! OUR FIRST BREAK ALL DAY!
BLUE SKIES, BEAUTIFUL SEAS—A PERFECT DAY FOR ELOPING, WOULDN'T YOU SAY?
I...THINK IT MIGHT BE MORE OF AN ABDUCTION THAN AN ELOPEMENT.
SINCE I LIKE HER, BUT SHE DOESN'T LIKE ME.
...
SO... WHEN YOU SAY "LIKE," YOU MEAN "LIKE LIKE," RIGHT?
ドキ B-DMP
ドキ B-DMP
YOU'RE REALLY GONNA MAKE ME SPELL IT OUT?

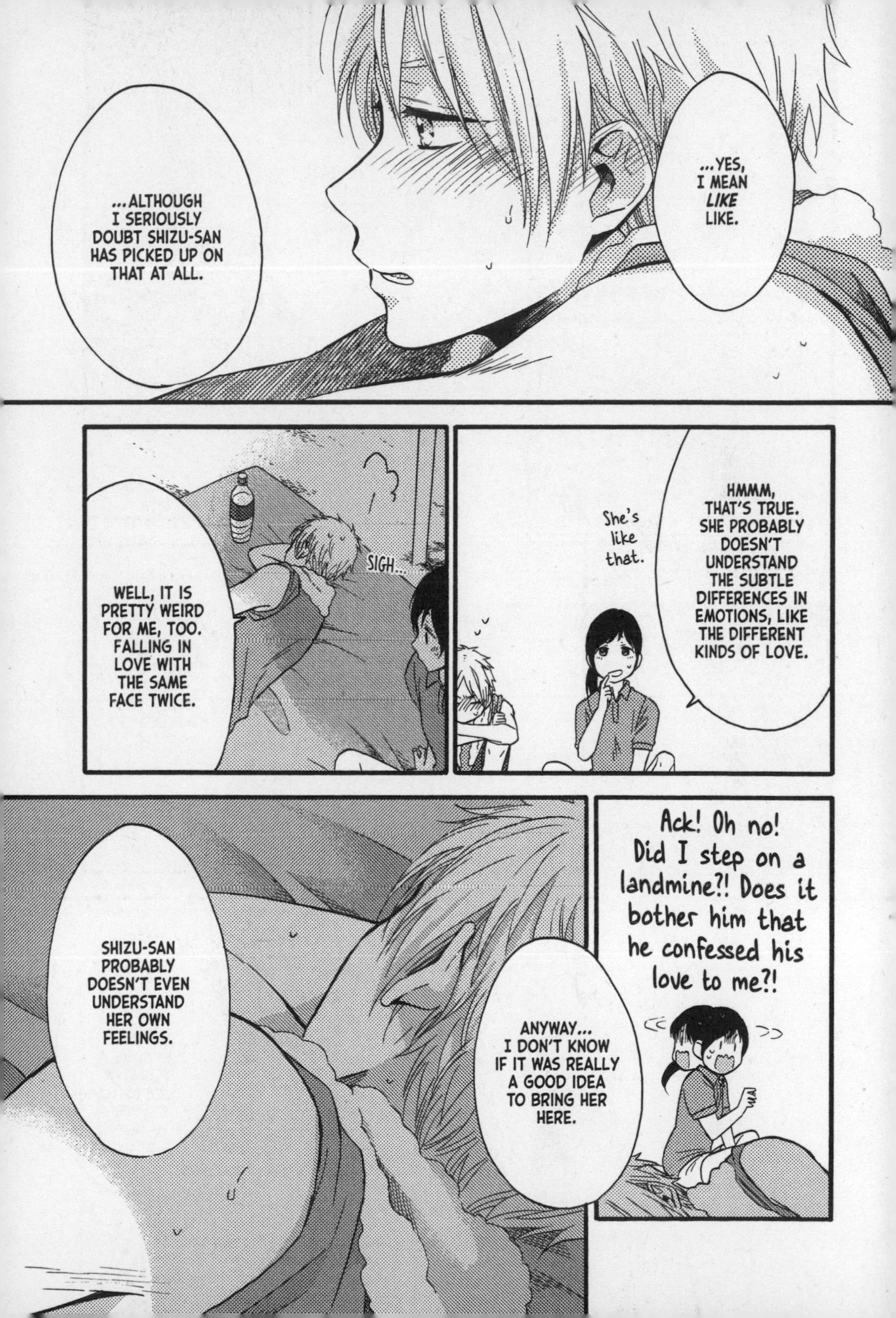
...YES, I MEAN *LIKE* LIKE.
...ALTHOUGH I SERIOUSLY DOUBT SHIZU-SAN HAS PICKED UP ON THAT AT ALL.
HMMM, THAT'S TRUE. SHE PROBABLY DOESN'T UNDERSTAND THE SUBTLE DIFFERENCES IN EMOTIONS, LIKE THE DIFFERENT KINDS OF LOVE.
She's like that.
SIGH...
WELL, IT IS PRETTY WEIRD FOR ME, TOO. FALLING IN LOVE WITH THE SAME FACE TWICE.
Ack! Oh no! Did I step on a landmine?! Does it bother him that he confessed his love to me?!
ANYWAY... I DON'T KNOW IF IT WAS REALLY A GOOD IDEA TO BRING HER HERE.
SHIZU-SAN PROBABLY DOESN'T EVEN UNDERSTAND HER OWN FEELINGS.

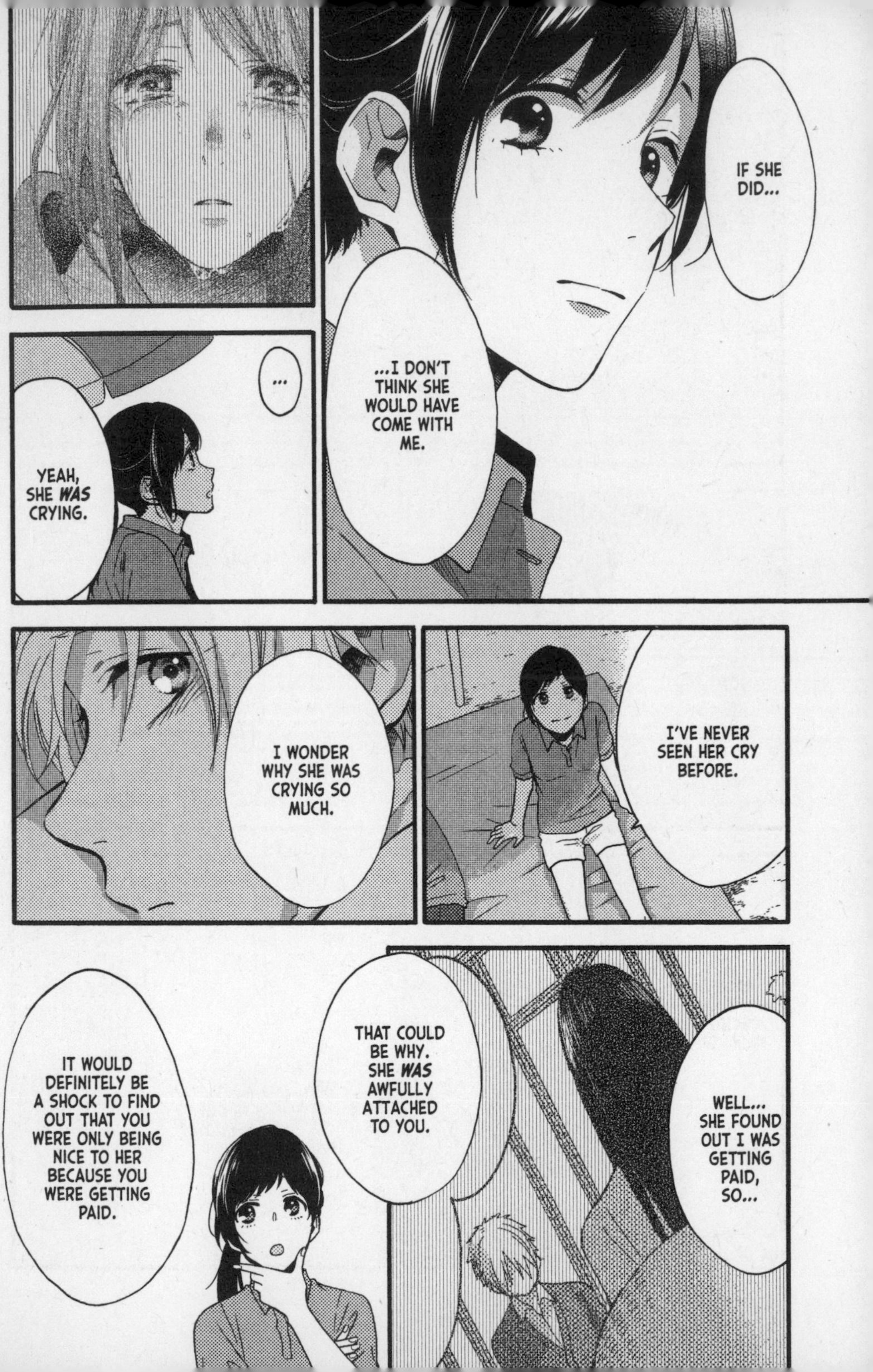
IF SHE DID...
...I DON'T THINK SHE WOULD HAVE COME WITH ME.
...
YEAH, SHE *WAS* CRYING.
I'VE NEVER SEEN HER CRY BEFORE.
I WONDER WHY SHE WAS CRYING SO MUCH.
WELL... SHE FOUND OUT I WAS GETTING PAID, SO...
THAT COULD BE WHY. SHE *WAS* AWFULLY ATTACHED TO YOU.
IT WOULD DEFINITELY BE A SHOCK TO FIND OUT THAT YOU WERE ONLY BEING NICE TO HER BECAUSE YOU WERE GETTING PAID.

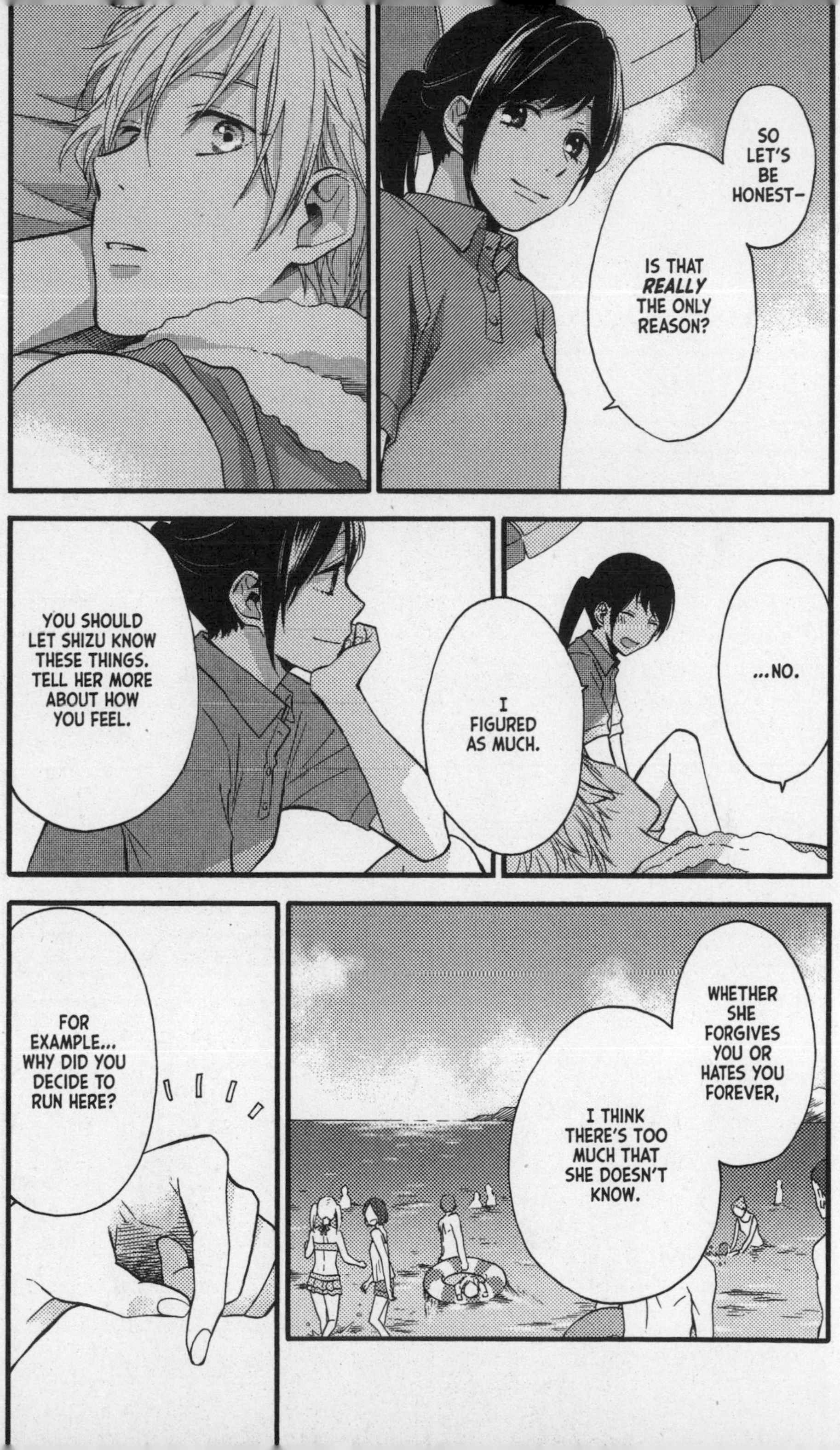
SO LET'S BE HONEST—
IS THAT *REALLY* THE ONLY REASON?
...NO.
I FIGURED AS MUCH.
YOU SHOULD LET SHIZU KNOW THESE THINGS. TELL HER MORE ABOUT HOW YOU FEEL.
WHETHER SHE FORGIVES YOU OR HATES YOU FOREVER,
I THINK THERE'S TOO MUCH THAT SHE DOESN'T KNOW.
FOR EXAMPLE... WHY DID YOU DECIDE TO RUN HERE?

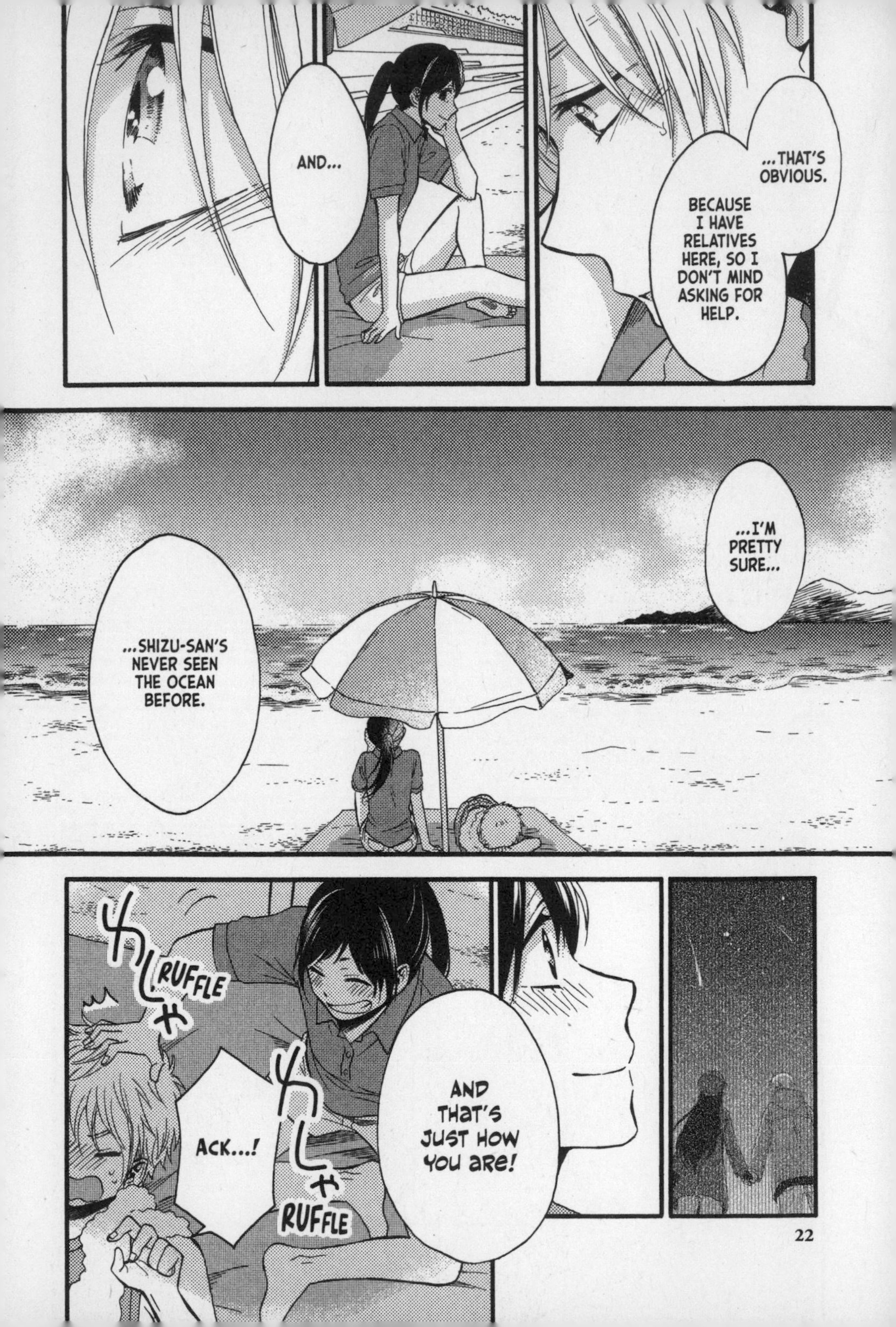
...THAT'S OBVIOUS.
BECAUSE I HAVE RELATIVES HERE, SO I DON'T MIND ASKING FOR HELP.
AND...
...I'M PRETTY SURE...
...SHIZU-SAN'S NEVER SEEN THE OCEAN BEFORE.
AND THAT'S JUST HOW YOU ARE!
RUFFLE
RUFFLE
ACK...!

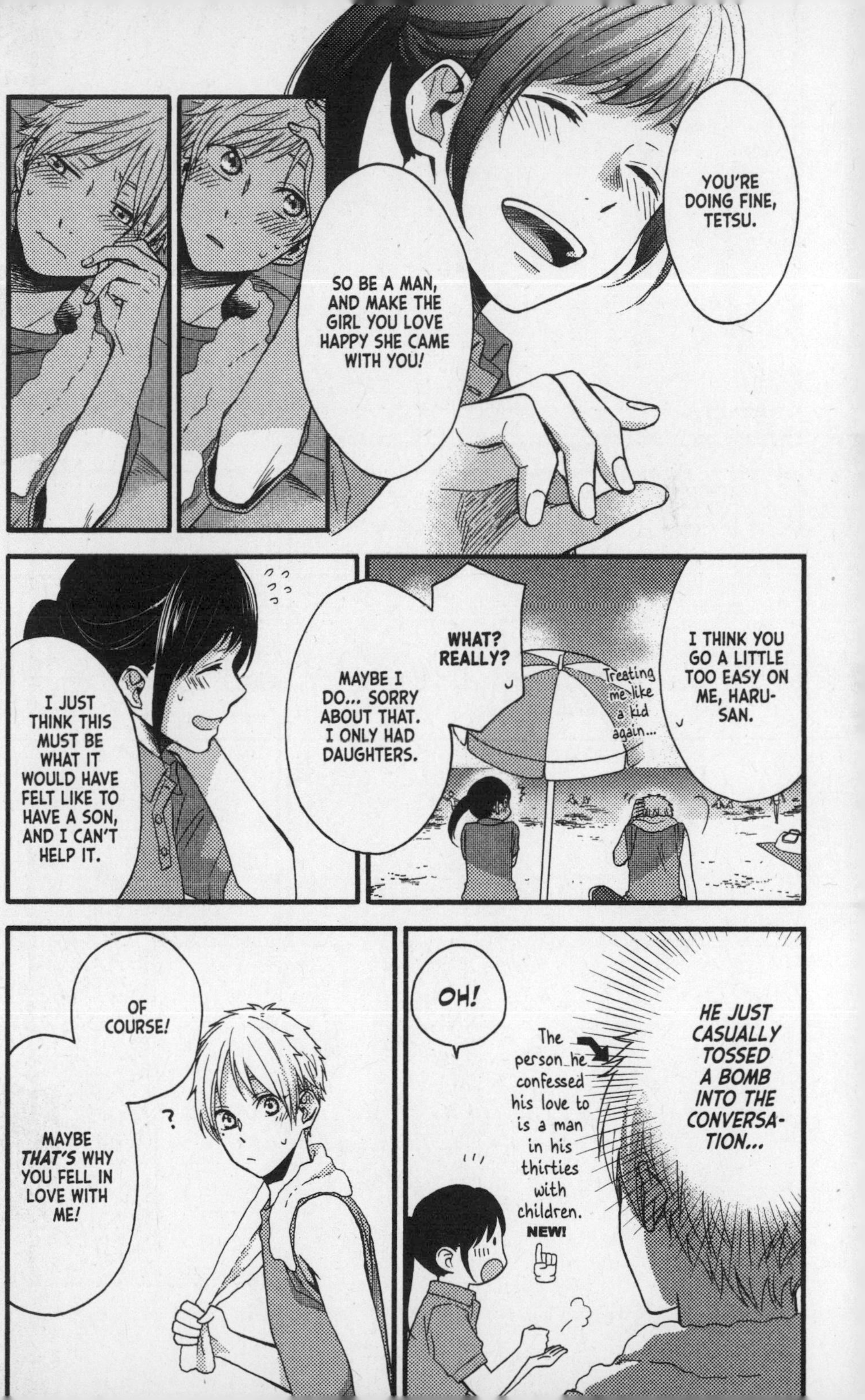
YOU'RE DOING FINE, TETSU.
SO BE A MAN, AND MAKE THE GIRL YOU LOVE HAPPY SHE CAME WITH YOU!
I THINK YOU GO A LITTLE TOO EASY ON ME, HARU-SAN.
Treating me like a kid again...
WHAT? REALLY?
MAYBE I DO... SORRY ABOUT THAT. I ONLY HAD DAUGHTERS.
I JUST THINK THIS MUST BE WHAT IT WOULD HAVE FELT LIKE TO HAVE A SON, AND I CAN'T HELP IT.
HE JUST CASUALLY TOSSED A BOMB INTO THE CONVERSATION...
The person he confessed his love to is a man in his thirties with children.
NEW!
OH!
OF COURSE!
?
MAYBE *THAT'S* WHY YOU FELL IN LOVE WITH ME!

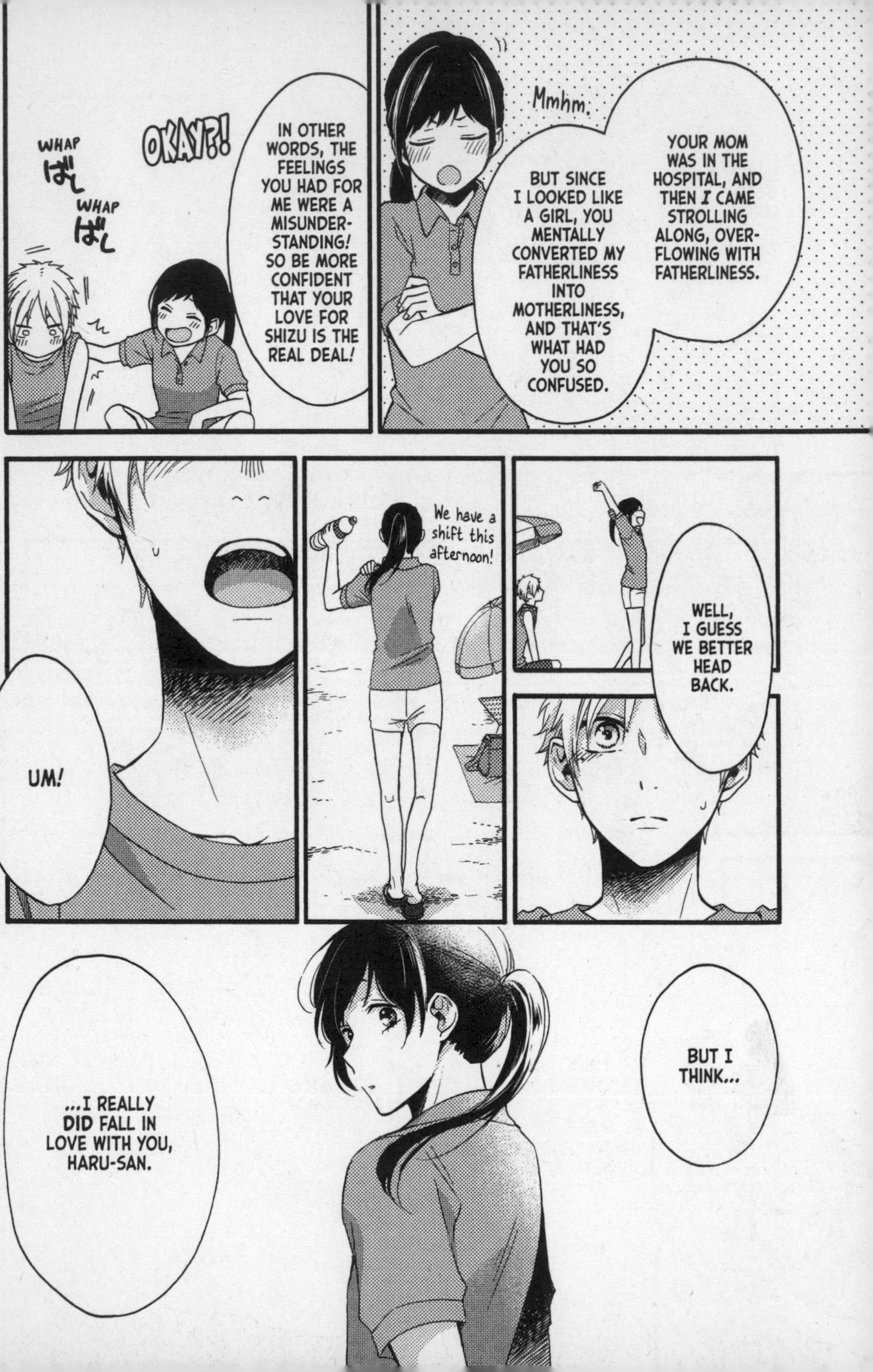
Mmhm.
YOUR MOM WAS IN THE HOSPITAL, AND THEN *I* CAME STROLLING ALONG, OVER-FLOWING WITH FATHERLINESS.
BUT SINCE I LOOKED LIKE A GIRL, YOU MENTALLY CONVERTED MY FATHERLINESS INTO MOTHERLINESS, AND THAT'S WHAT HAD YOU SO CONFUSED.
IN OTHER WORDS, THE FEELINGS YOU HAD FOR ME WERE A MISUNDER-STANDING! SO BE MORE CONFIDENT THAT YOUR LOVE FOR SHIZU IS THE REAL DEAL!
OKAY?!
WHAP ばし
WHAP ばし
WELL, I GUESS WE BETTER HEAD BACK.
We have a shift this afternoon!
UM!
BUT I THINK...
...I REALLY DID FALL IN LOVE WITH YOU, HARU-SAN.

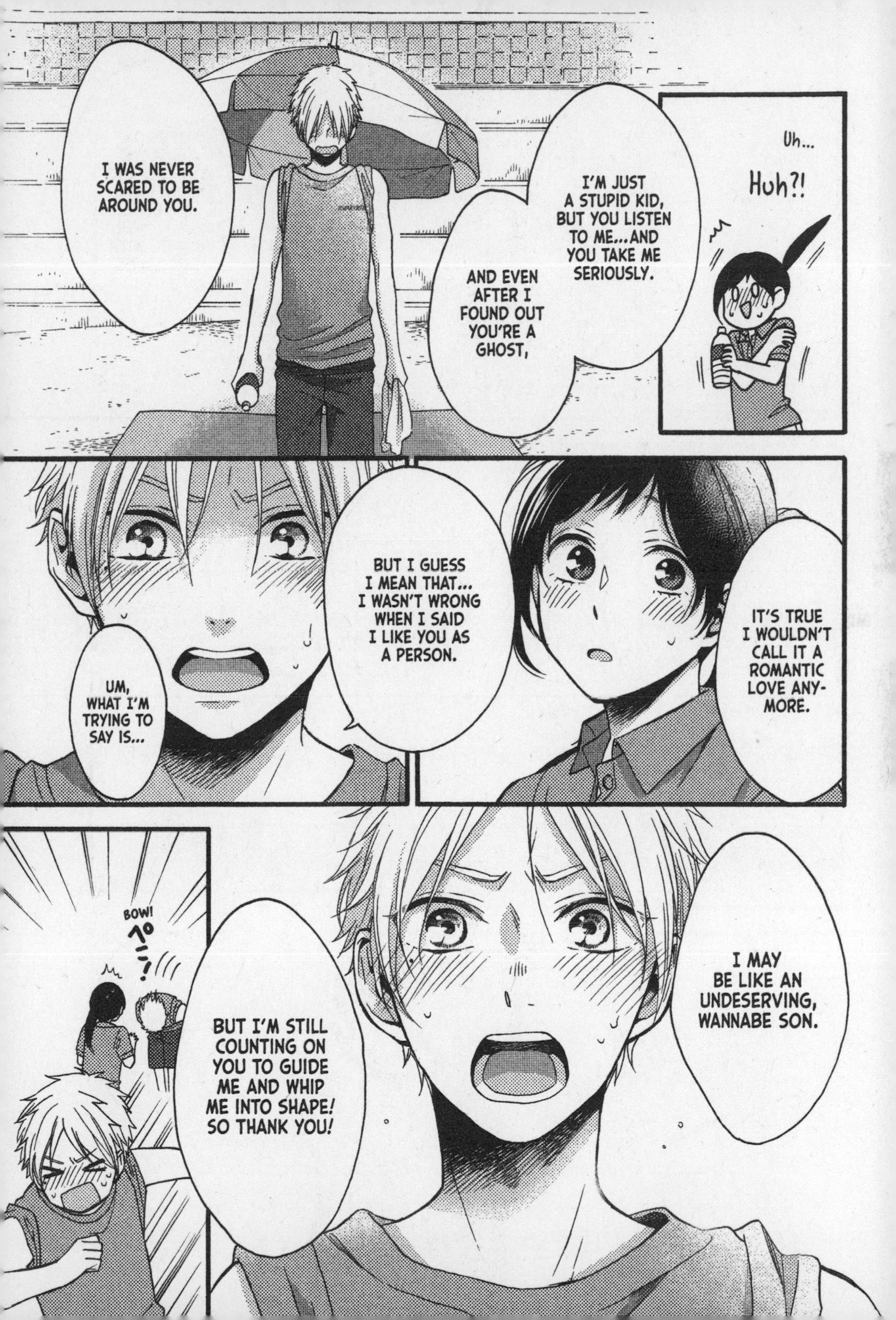
Uh...
Huh?!
I'M JUST A STUPID KID, BUT YOU LISTEN TO ME...AND YOU TAKE ME SERIOUSLY.
AND EVEN AFTER I FOUND OUT YOU'RE A GHOST,
I WAS NEVER SCARED TO BE AROUND YOU.
IT'S TRUE I WOULDN'T CALL IT A ROMANTIC LOVE ANY-MORE.
BUT I GUESS I MEAN THAT... I WASN'T WRONG WHEN I SAID I LIKE YOU AS A PERSON.
UM, WHAT I'M TRYING TO SAY IS...
I MAY BE LIKE AN UNDESERVING, WANNABE SON.
BUT I'M STILL COUNTING ON YOU TO GUIDE ME AND WHIP ME INTO SHAPE! SO THANK YOU!
BOW!

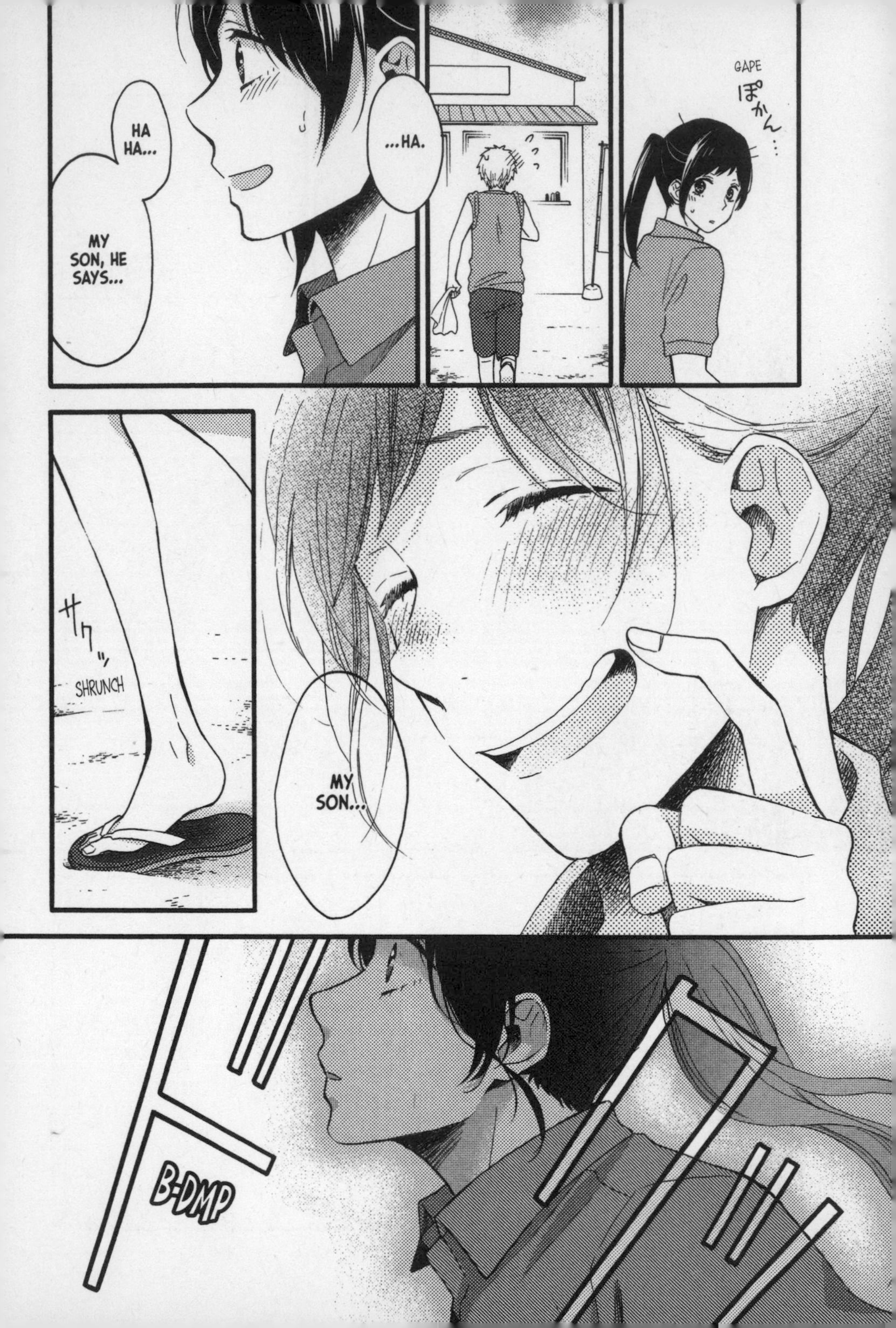
GAPE
ぽかん…
...HA.
HA HA...
MY SON, HE SAYS...
MY SON...
サクッ
SHRUNCH
B-DMP

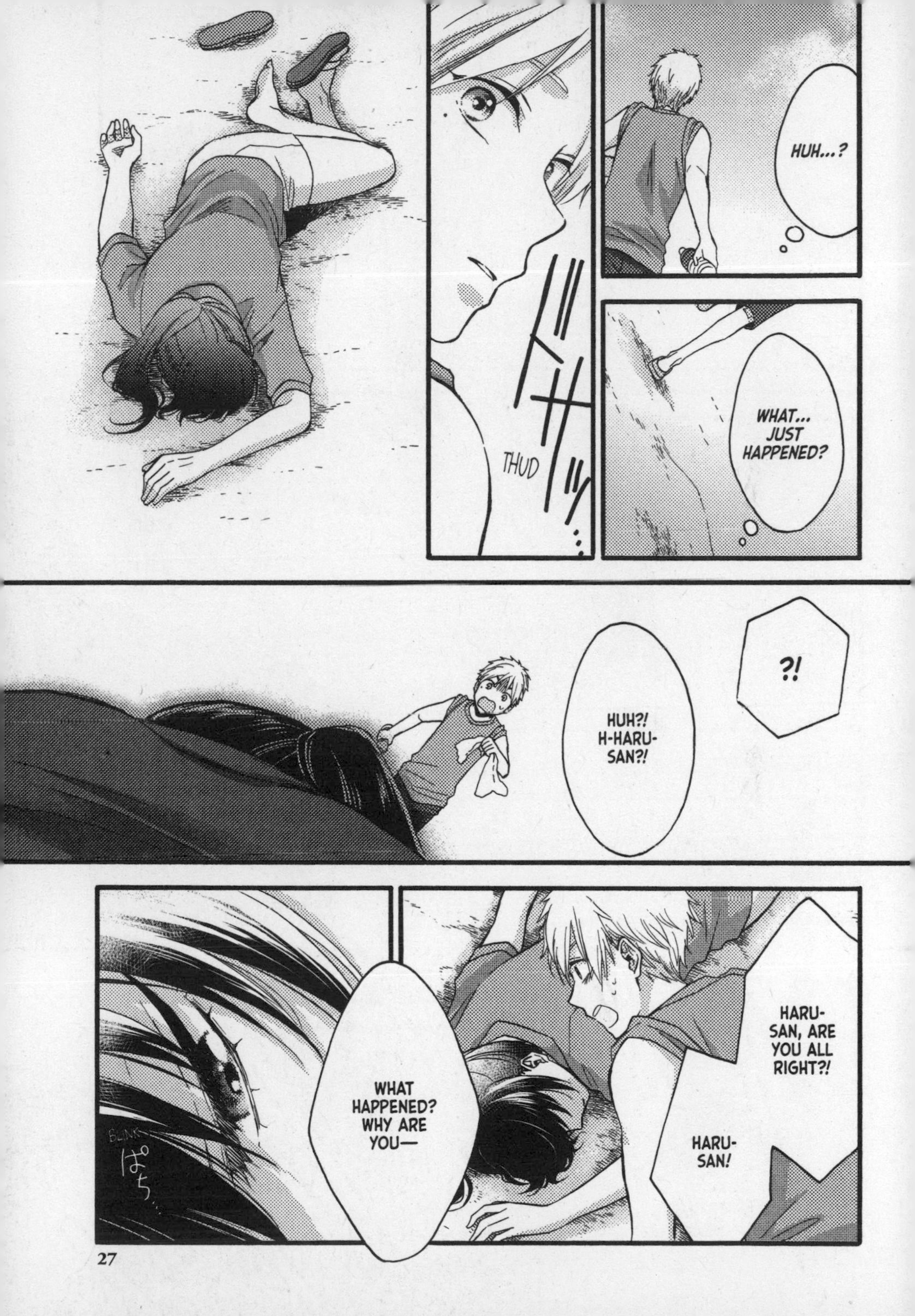
HUH...?
WHAT... JUST HAPPENED?
THUD
?!
HUH?! H-HARU-SAN?!
HARU-SAN, ARE YOU ALL RIGHT?!
HARU-SAN!
WHAT HAPPENED? WHY ARE YOU—
BLINK
ぱち...

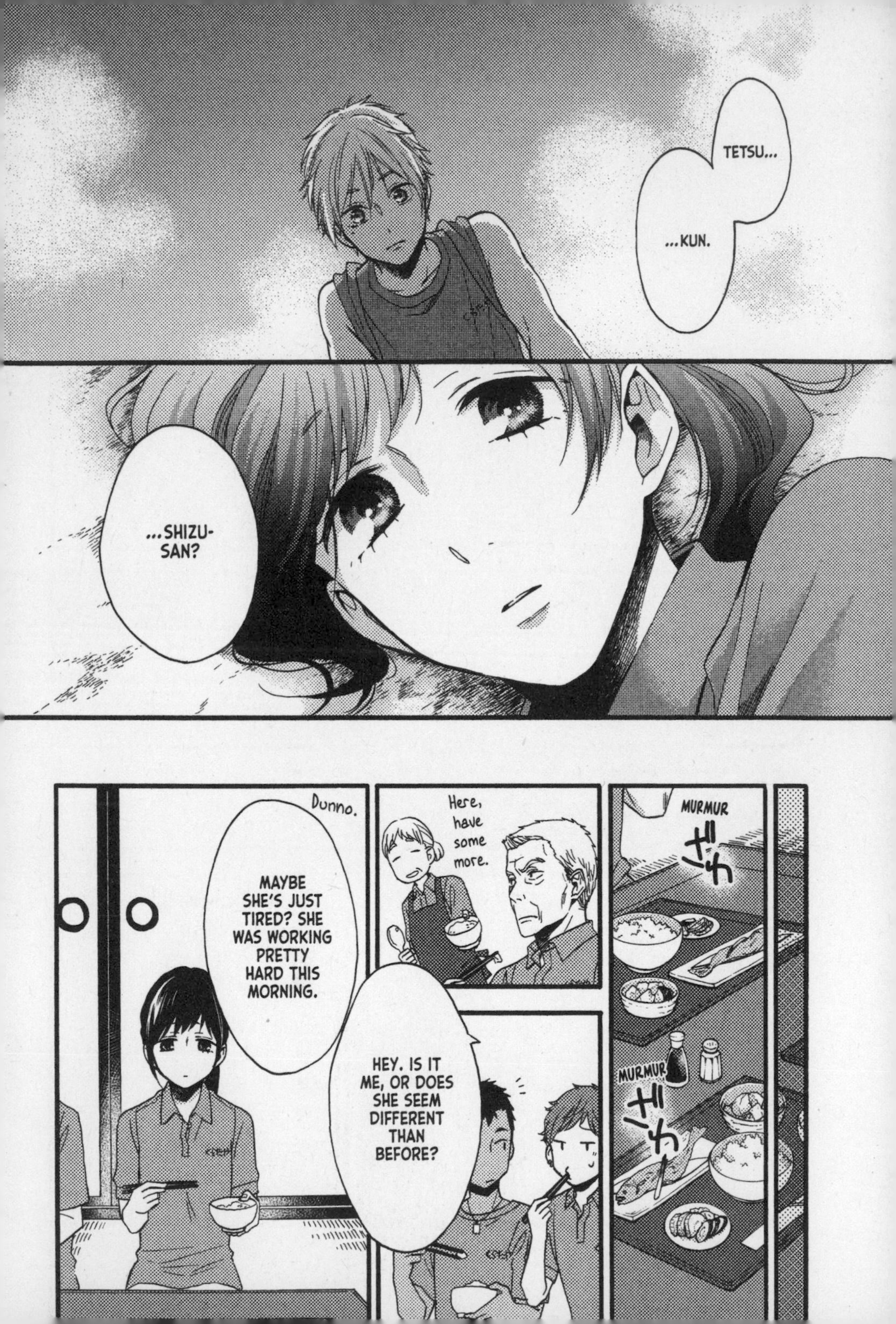
TETSU...
...KUN.
...SHIZU-SAN?
MURMUR
MURMUR
Here, have some more.
HEY. IS IT ME, OR DOES SHE SEEM DIFFERENT THAN BEFORE?
Dunno.
MAYBE SHE'S JUST TIRED? SHE WAS WORKING PRETTY HARD THIS MORNING.

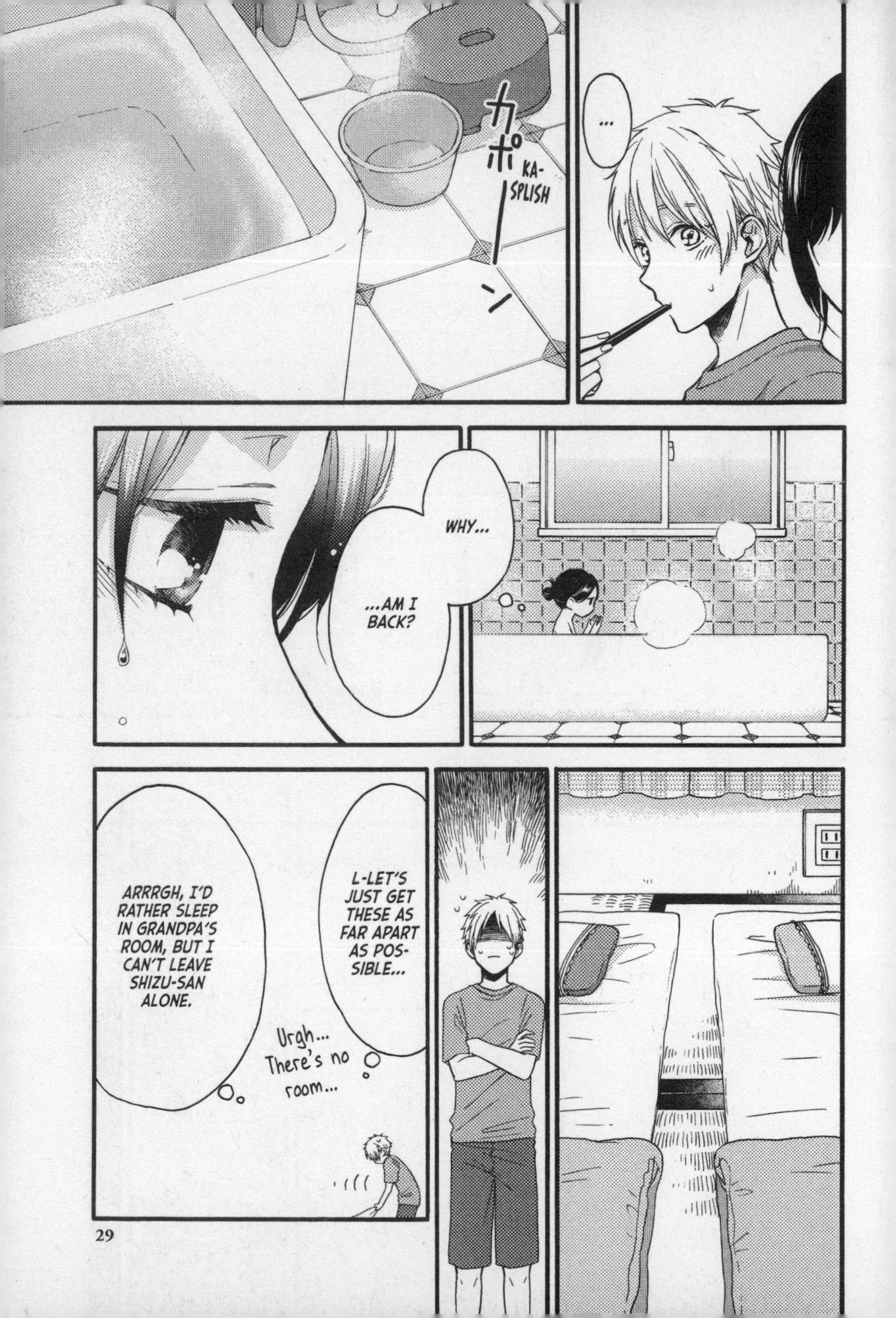

...
KA-SPLISH
WHY...
...AM I BACK?
L-LET'S JUST GET THESE AS FAR APART AS POS-SIBLE...
ARRRGH, I'D RATHER SLEEP IN GRANDPA'S ROOM, BUT I CAN'T LEAVE SHIZU-SAN ALONE.
Urgh... There's no room...

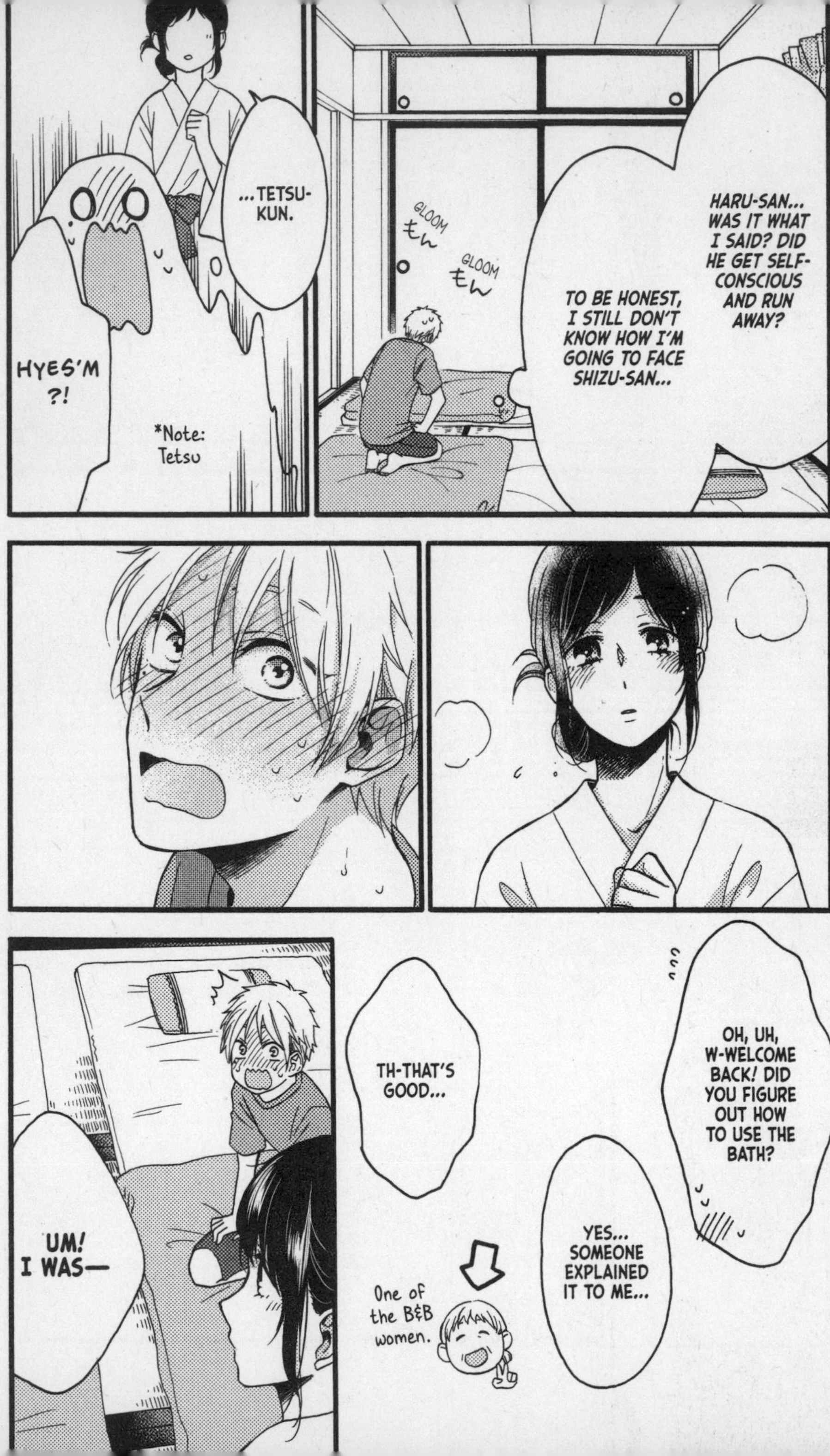
HARU-SAN... WAS IT WHAT I SAID? DID HE GET SELF-CONSCIOUS AND RUN AWAY?
TO BE HONEST, I STILL DON'T KNOW HOW I'M GOING TO FACE SHIZU-SAN...
GLOOM もん
GLOOM もん
...TETSU-KUN.
HYES'M ?!
*Note: Tetsu
OH, UH, W-WELCOME BACK! DID YOU FIGURE OUT HOW TO USE THE BATH?
YES... SOMEONE EXPLAINED IT TO ME...
One of the B&B women.
TH-THAT'S GOOD...
UM! I WAS—

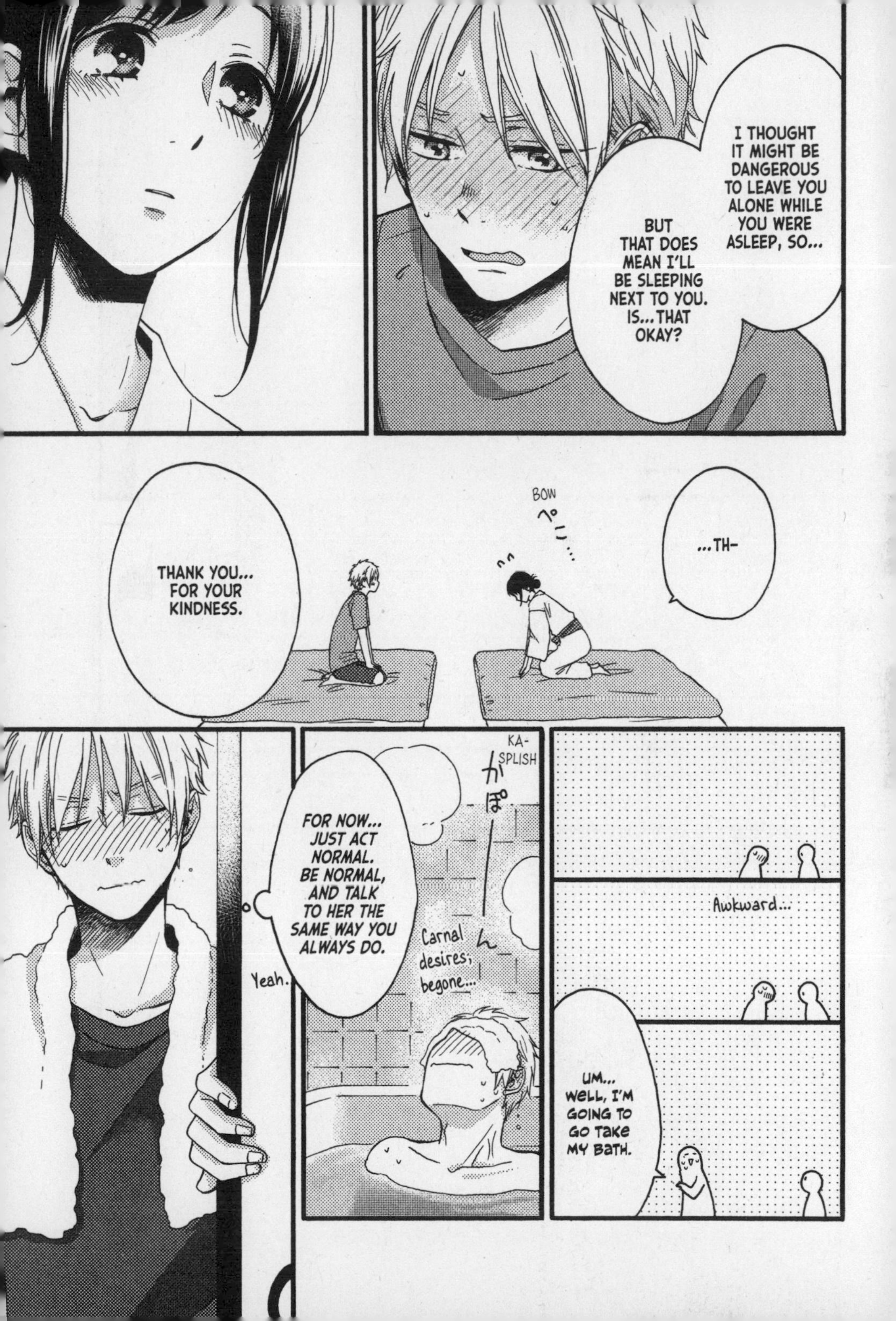
I THOUGHT IT MIGHT BE DANGEROUS TO LEAVE YOU ALONE WHILE YOU WERE ASLEEP, SO...
BUT THAT DOES MEAN I'LL BE SLEEPING NEXT TO YOU. IS...THAT OKAY?
...TH-
BOW
ぺこ…
THANK YOU... FOR YOUR KINDNESS.
Awkward...
UM... WELL, I'M GOING TO GO TAKE MY BATH.
KA-SPLISH
がぽーん
Carnal desires, begone...
FOR NOW... JUST ACT NORMAL. BE NORMAL, AND TALK TO HER THE SAME WAY YOU ALWAYS DO.
Yeah.

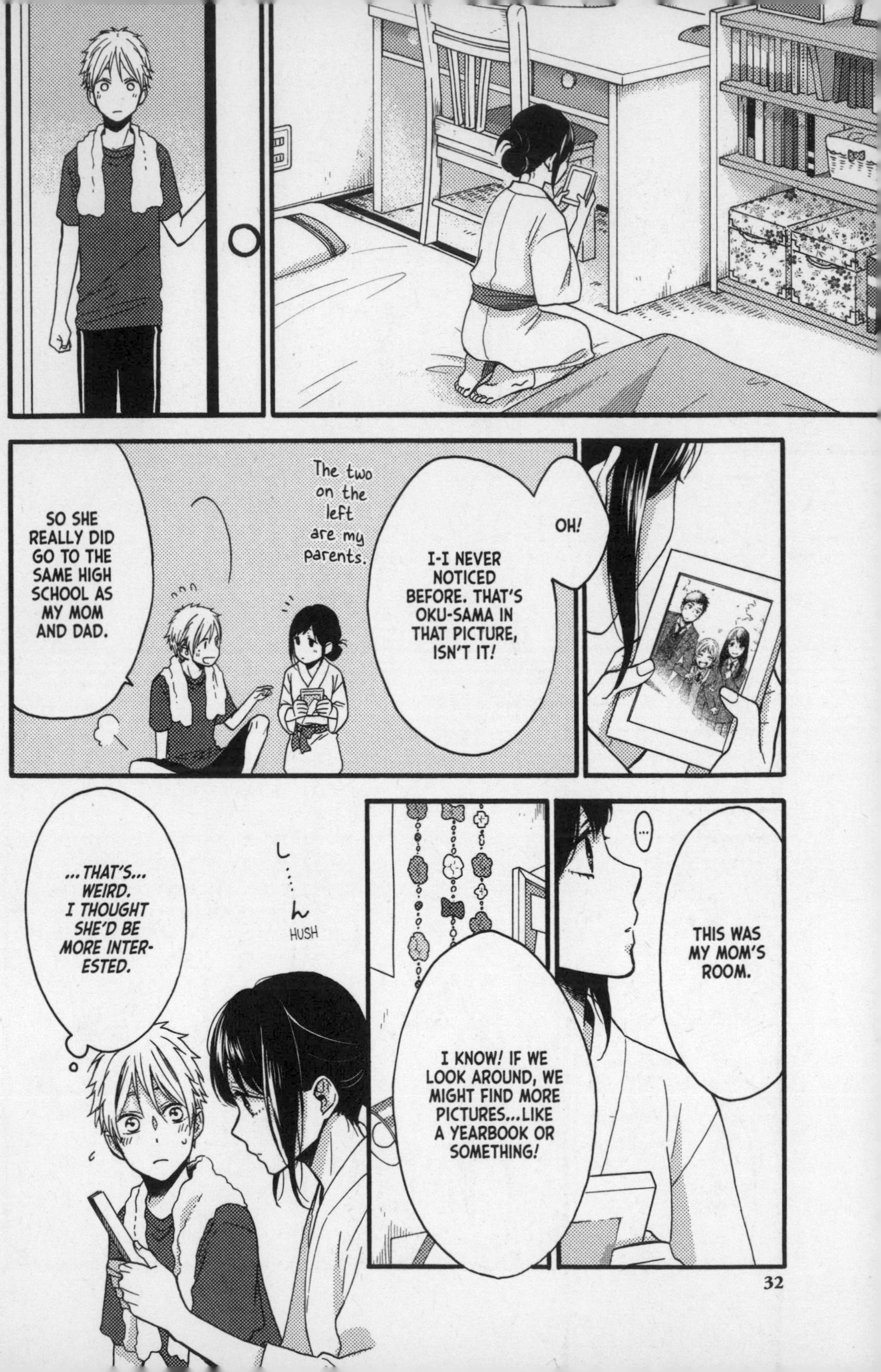
OH!
I-I NEVER NOTICED BEFORE. THAT'S OKU-SAMA IN THAT PICTURE, ISN'T IT!
The two on the left are my parents.
SO SHE REALLY DID GO TO THE SAME HIGH SCHOOL AS MY MOM AND DAD.
...
THIS WAS MY MOM'S ROOM.
I KNOW! IF WE LOOK AROUND, WE MIGHT FIND MORE PICTURES...LIKE A YEARBOOK OR SOMETHING!
し…ん
HUSH
...THAT'S... WEIRD. I THOUGHT SHE'D BE MORE INTER-ESTED.

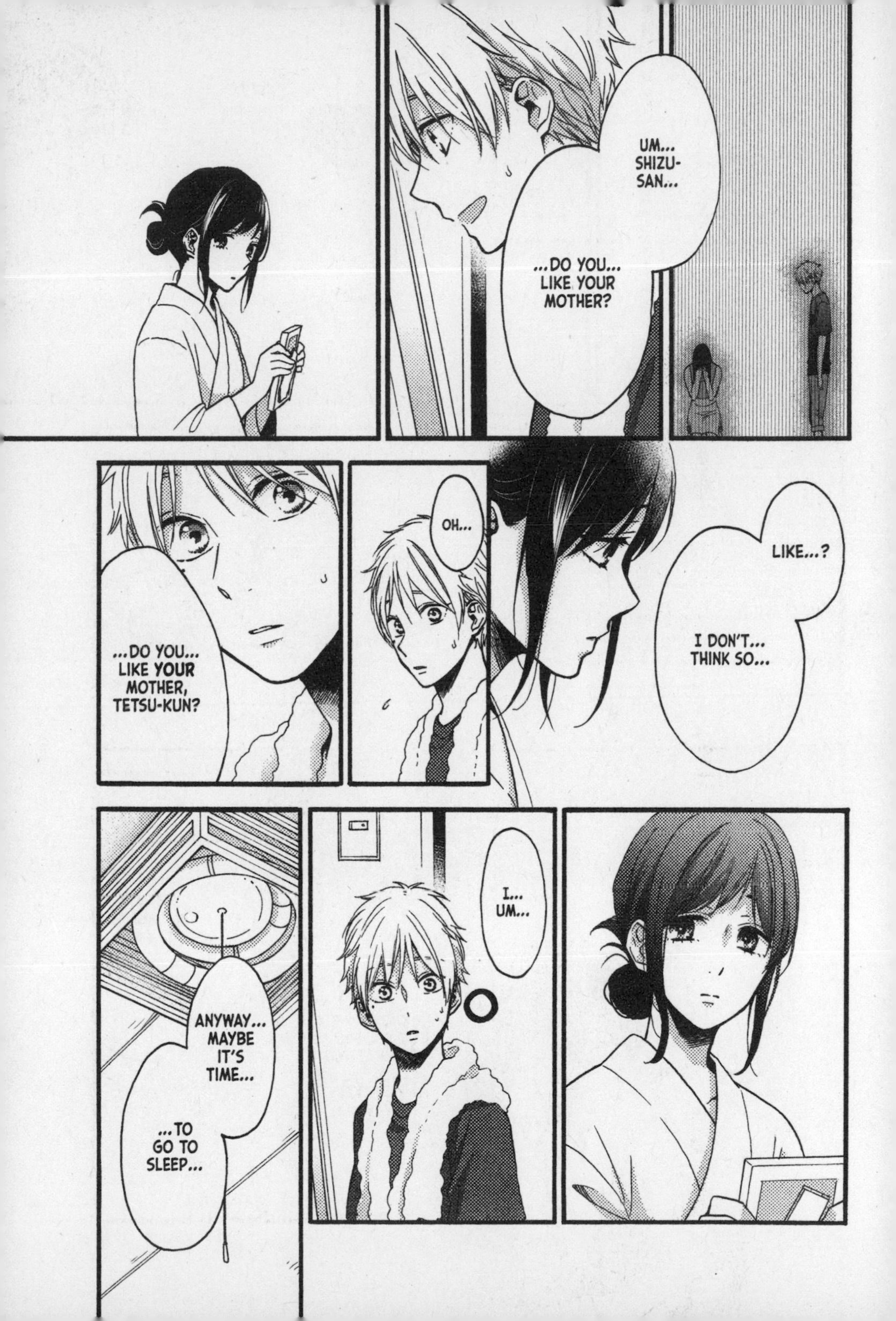
UM... SHIZU-SAN...
...DO YOU... LIKE YOUR MOTHER?
LIKE...?
I DON'T... THINK SO...
OH...
...DO YOU... LIKE YOUR MOTHER, TETSU-KUN?
I... UM...
ANYWAY... MAYBE IT'S TIME...
...TO GO TO SLEEP...

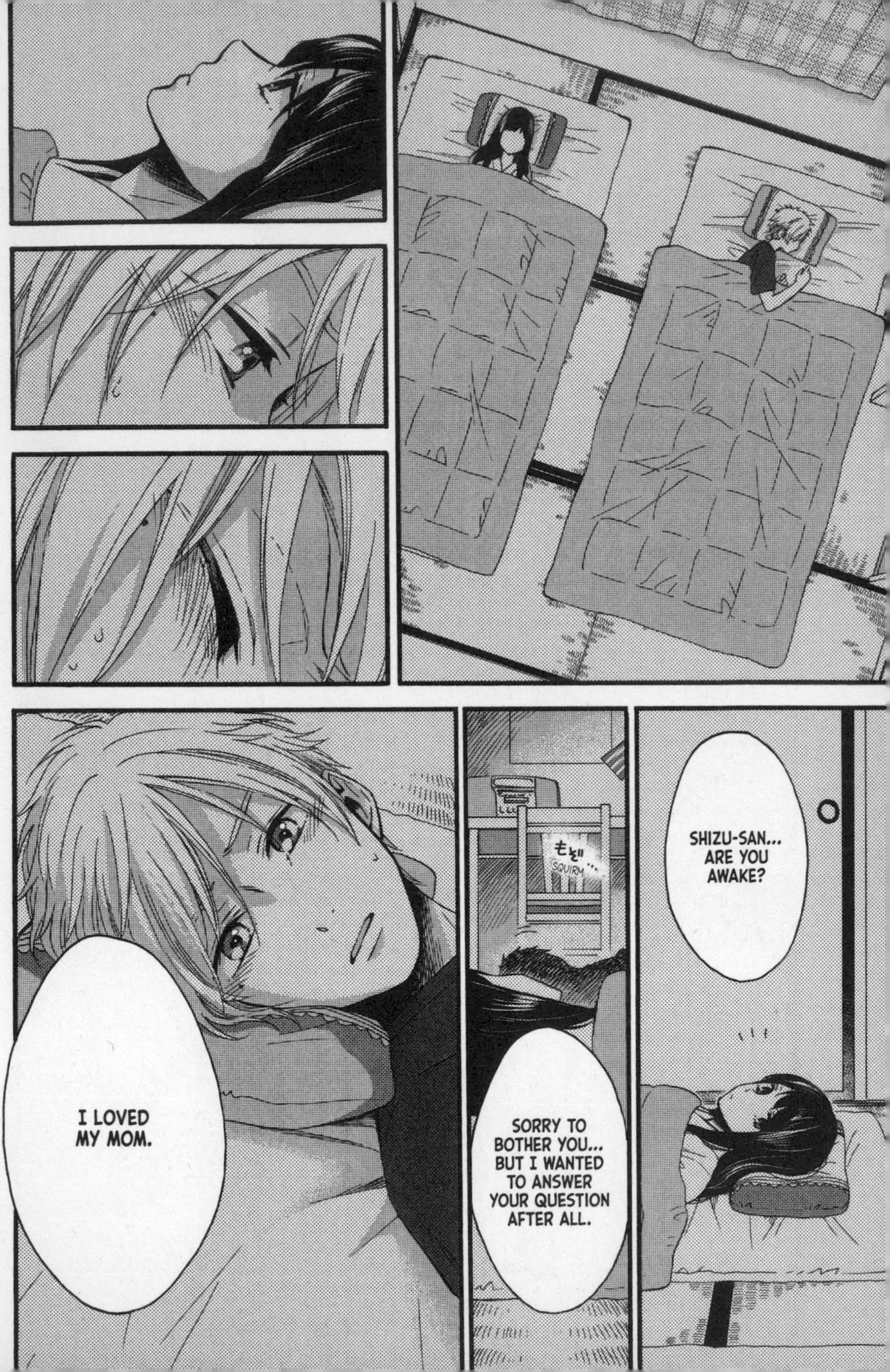
SHIZU-SAN... ARE YOU AWAKE?
もぞ...
SQUIRM
SORRY TO BOTHER YOU... BUT I WANTED TO ANSWER YOUR QUESTION AFTER ALL.
I LOVED MY MOM.

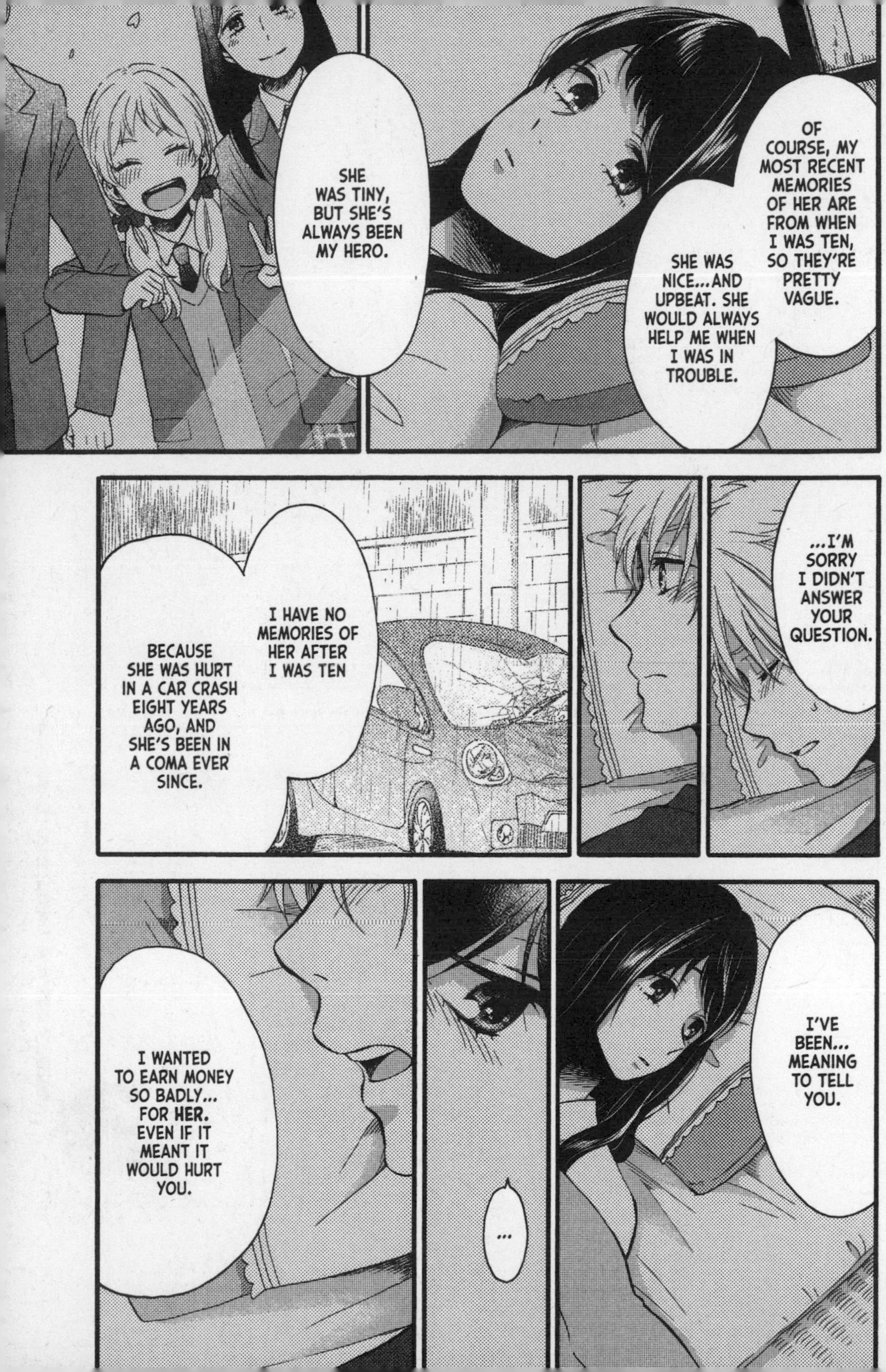
OF COURSE, MY MOST RECENT MEMORIES OF HER ARE FROM WHEN I WAS TEN, SO THEY'RE PRETTY VAGUE.
SHE WAS NICE...AND UPBEAT. SHE WOULD ALWAYS HELP ME WHEN I WAS IN TROUBLE.
SHE WAS TINY, BUT SHE'S ALWAYS BEEN MY HERO.
...I'M SORRY I DIDN'T ANSWER YOUR QUESTION.
I HAVE NO MEMORIES OF HER AFTER I WAS TEN
BECAUSE SHE WAS HURT IN A CAR CRASH EIGHT YEARS AGO, AND SHE'S BEEN IN A COMA EVER SINCE.
I'VE BEEN... MEANING TO TELL YOU.
...
I WANTED TO EARN MONEY SO BADLY... FOR HER. EVEN IF IT MEANT IT WOULD HURT YOU.

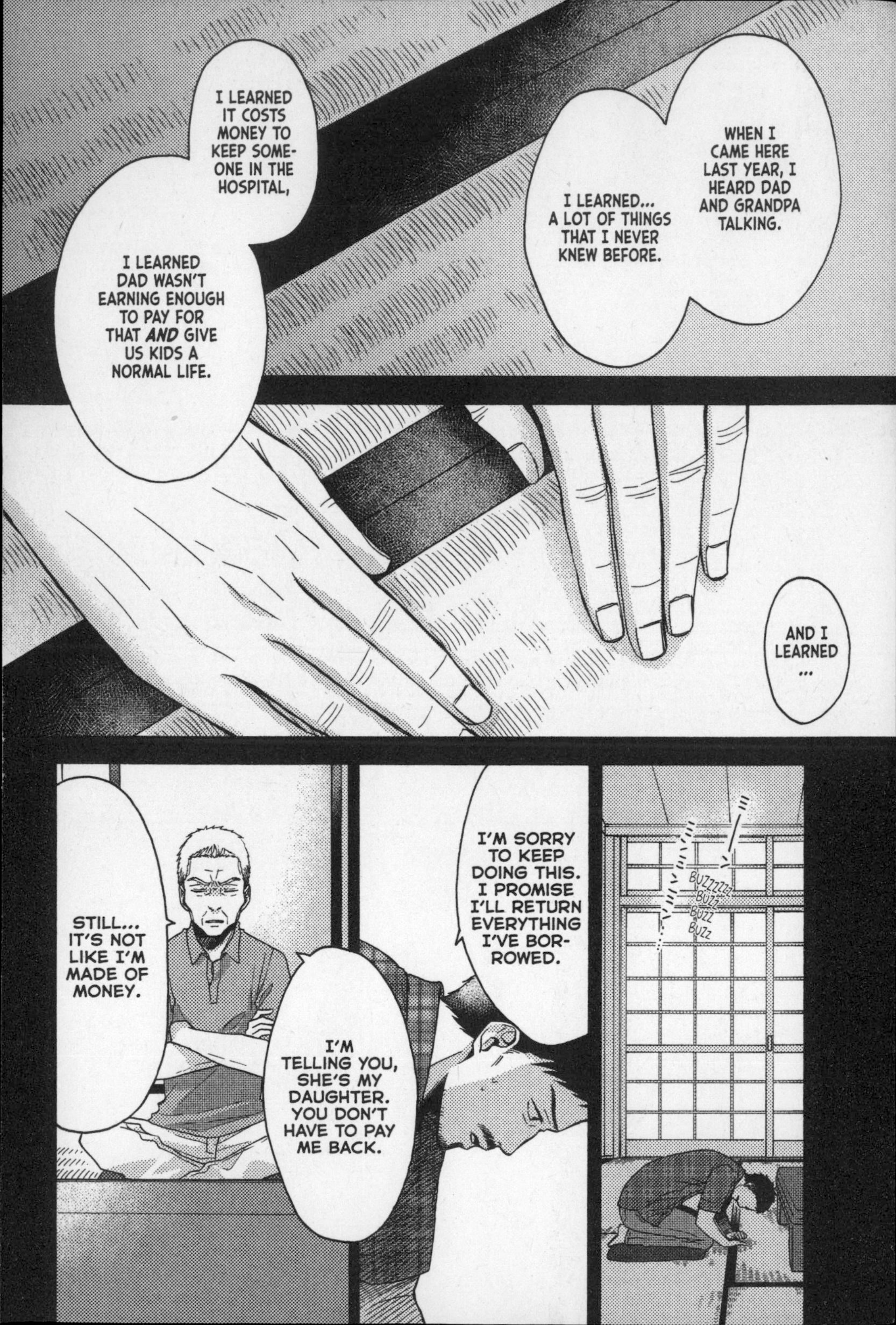
WHEN I CAME HERE LAST YEAR, I HEARD DAD AND GRANDPA TALKING.
I LEARNED... A LOT OF THINGS THAT I NEVER KNEW BEFORE.
I LEARNED IT COSTS MONEY TO KEEP SOME-ONE IN THE HOSPITAL,
I LEARNED DAD WASN'T EARNING ENOUGH TO PAY FOR THAT *AND* GIVE US KIDS A NORMAL LIFE.
AND I LEARNED ...
BUZZZZZ BUZZ BUZZ BUZZ
I'M SORRY TO KEEP DOING THIS. I PROMISE I'LL RETURN EVERYTHING I'VE BOR-ROWED.
I'M TELLING YOU, SHE'S MY DAUGHTER. YOU DON'T HAVE TO PAY ME BACK.
STILL... IT'S NOT LIKE I'M MADE OF MONEY.

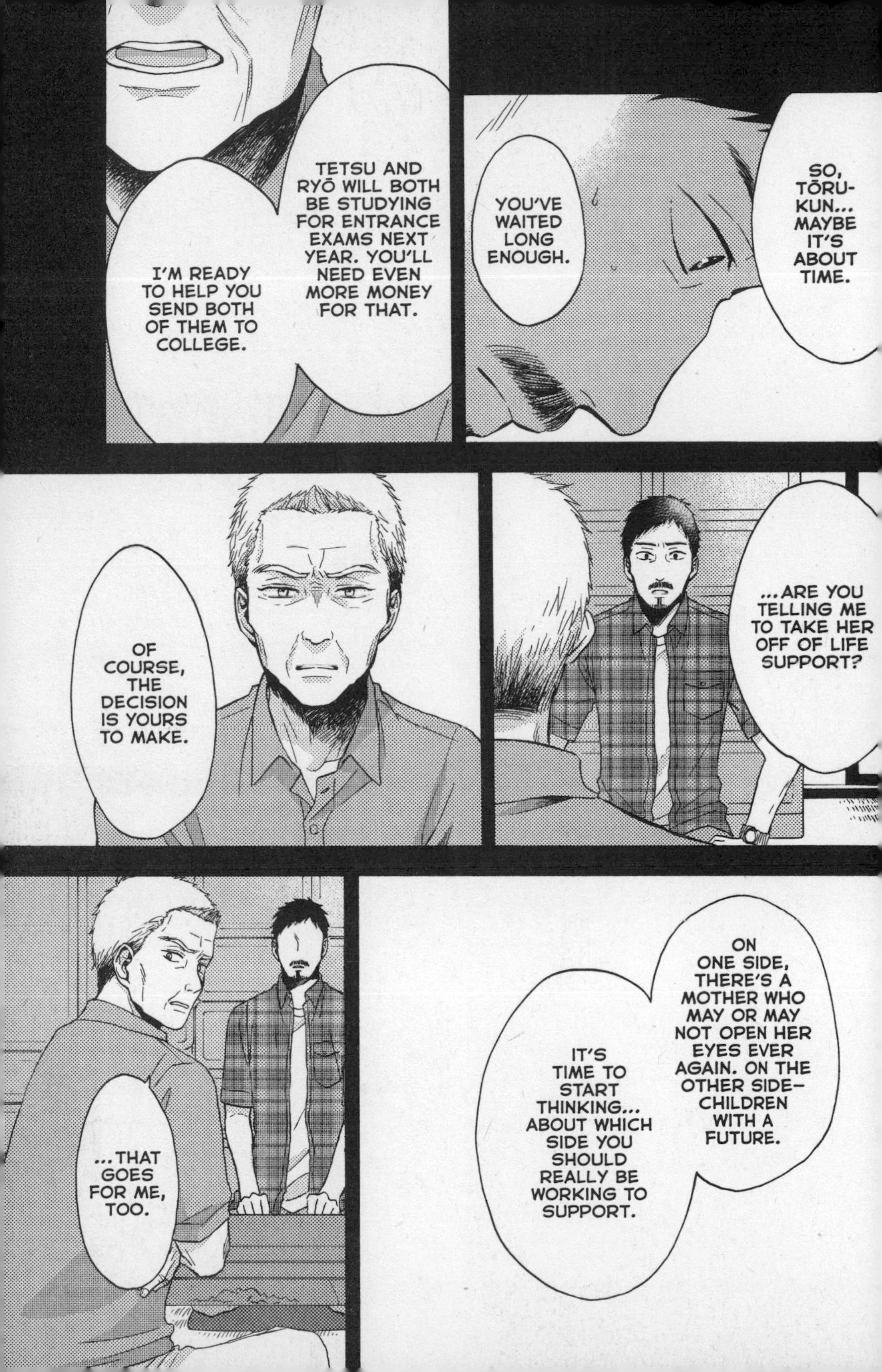
SO, TŌRU-KUN... MAYBE IT'S ABOUT TIME.
YOU'VE WAITED LONG ENOUGH.
TETSU AND RYŌ WILL BOTH BE STUDYING FOR ENTRANCE EXAMS NEXT YEAR. YOU'LL NEED EVEN MORE MONEY FOR THAT.
I'M READY TO HELP YOU SEND BOTH OF THEM TO COLLEGE.
...ARE YOU TELLING ME TO TAKE HER OFF OF LIFE SUPPORT?
OF COURSE, THE DECISION IS YOURS TO MAKE.
ON ONE SIDE, THERE'S A MOTHER WHO MAY OR MAY NOT OPEN HER EYES EVER AGAIN. ON THE OTHER SIDE—CHILDREN WITH A FUTURE.
IT'S TIME TO START THINKING... ABOUT WHICH SIDE YOU SHOULD REALLY BE WORKING TO SUPPORT.
...THAT GOES FOR ME, TOO.

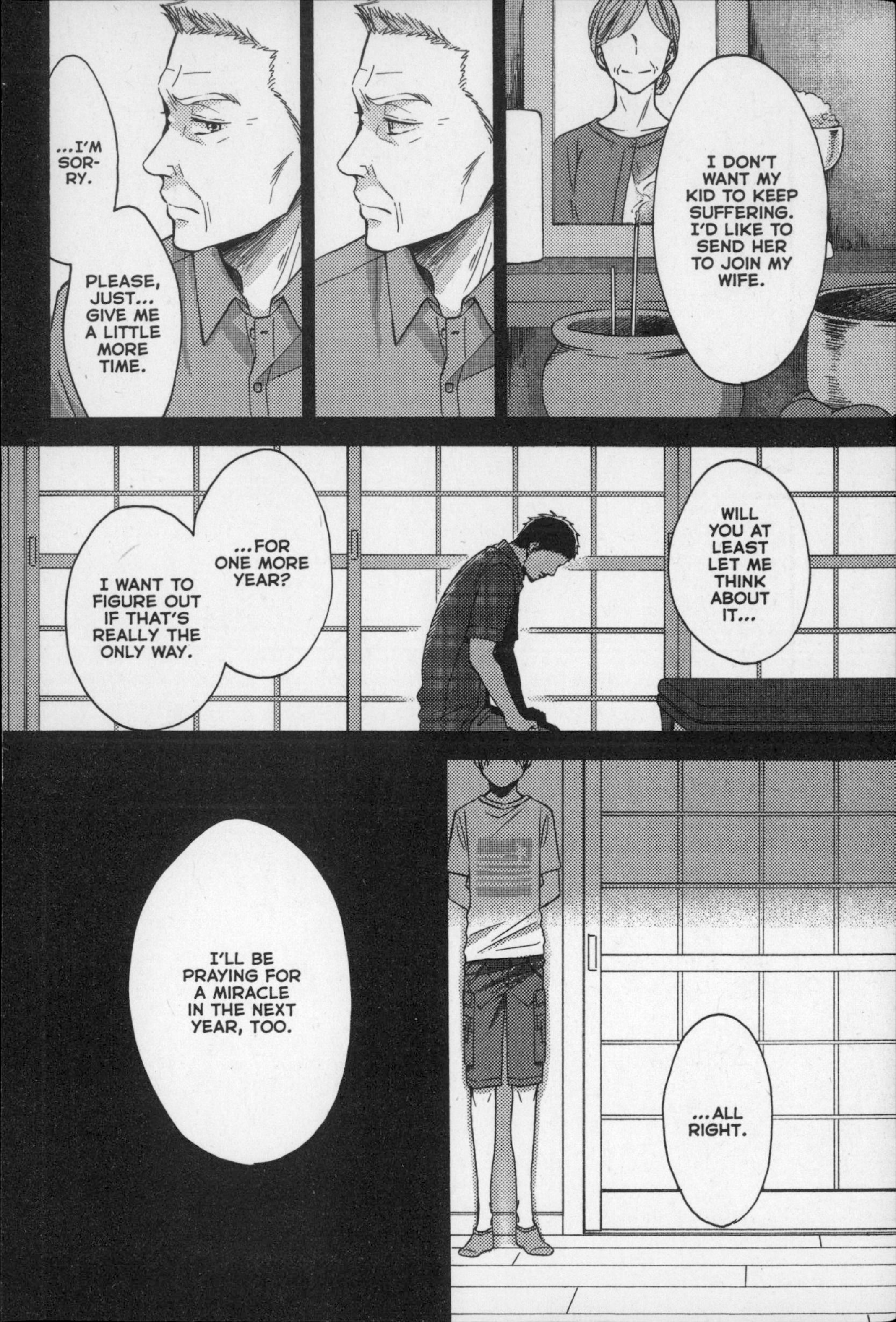
I DON'T WANT MY KID TO KEEP SUFFERING. I'D LIKE TO SEND HER TO JOIN MY WIFE.
...I'M SORRY.
PLEASE, JUST... GIVE ME A LITTLE MORE TIME.
WILL YOU AT LEAST LET ME THINK ABOUT IT...
...FOR ONE MORE YEAR?
I WANT TO FIGURE OUT IF THAT'S REALLY THE ONLY WAY.
...ALL RIGHT.
I'LL BE PRAYING FOR A MIRACLE IN THE NEXT YEAR, TOO.

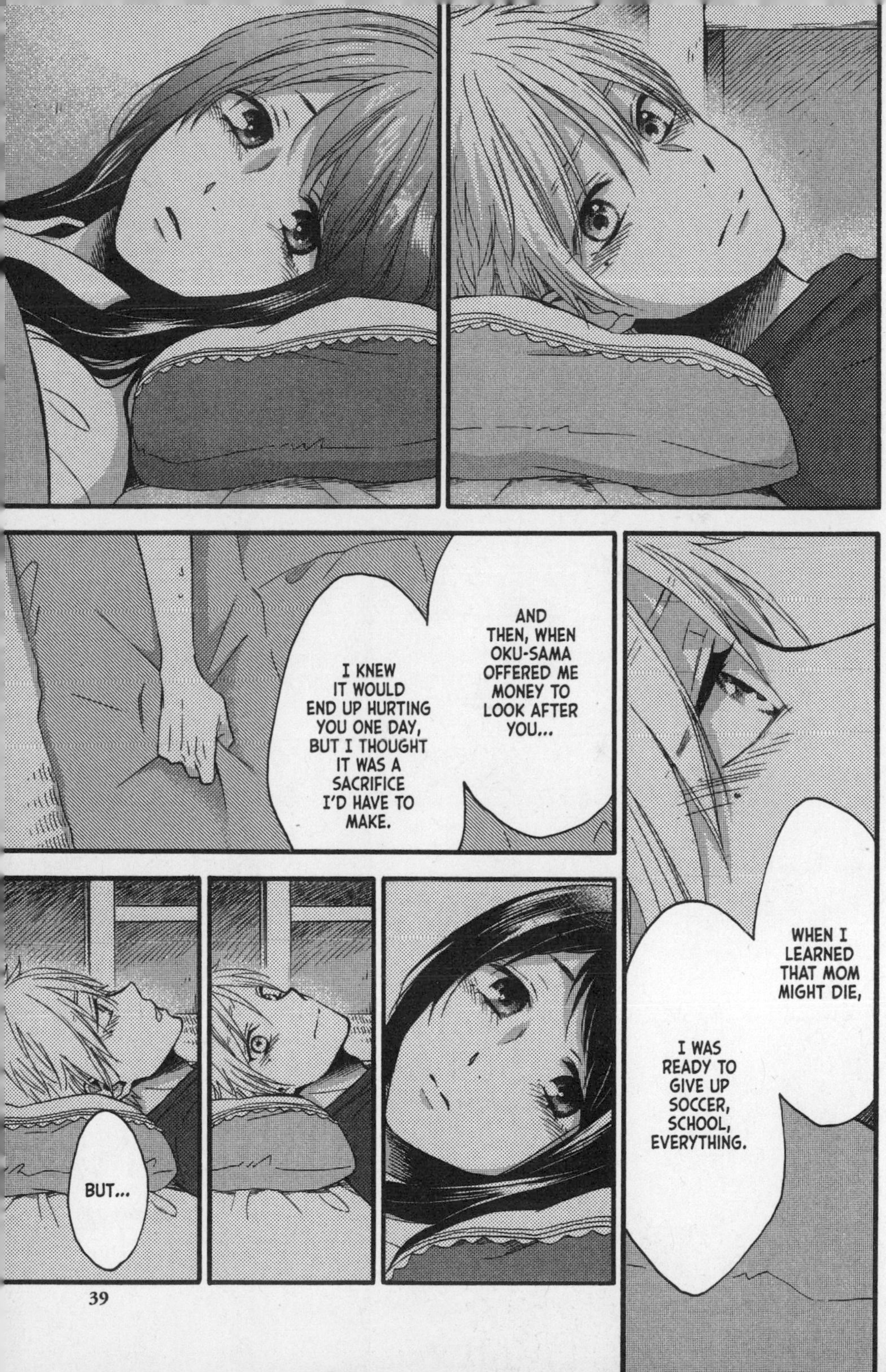
WHEN I LEARNED THAT MOM MIGHT DIE,
I WAS READY TO GIVE UP SOCCER, SCHOOL, EVERYTHING.
AND THEN, WHEN OKU-SAMA OFFERED ME MONEY TO LOOK AFTER YOU...
I KNEW IT WOULD END UP HURTING YOU ONE DAY, BUT I THOUGHT IT WAS A SACRIFICE I'D HAVE TO MAKE.
BUT...

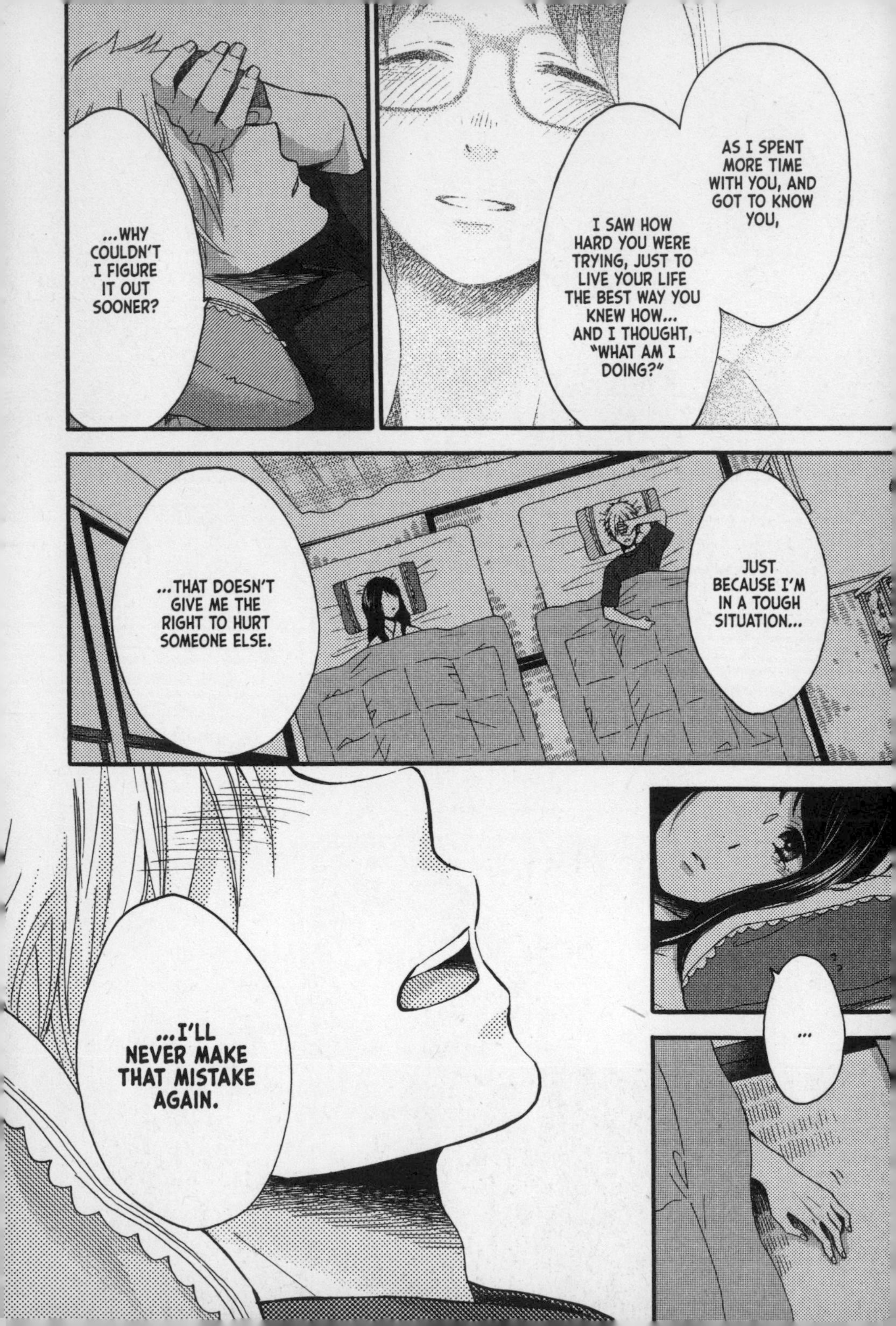
AS I SPENT MORE TIME WITH YOU, AND GOT TO KNOW YOU,
I SAW HOW HARD YOU WERE TRYING, JUST TO LIVE YOUR LIFE THE BEST WAY YOU KNEW HOW... AND I THOUGHT, "WHAT AM I DOING?"
...WHY COULDN'T I FIGURE IT OUT SOONER?
JUST BECAUSE I'M IN A TOUGH SITUATION...
...THAT DOESN'T GIVE ME THE RIGHT TO HURT SOMEONE ELSE.
...
...I'LL NEVER MAKE THAT MISTAKE AGAIN.

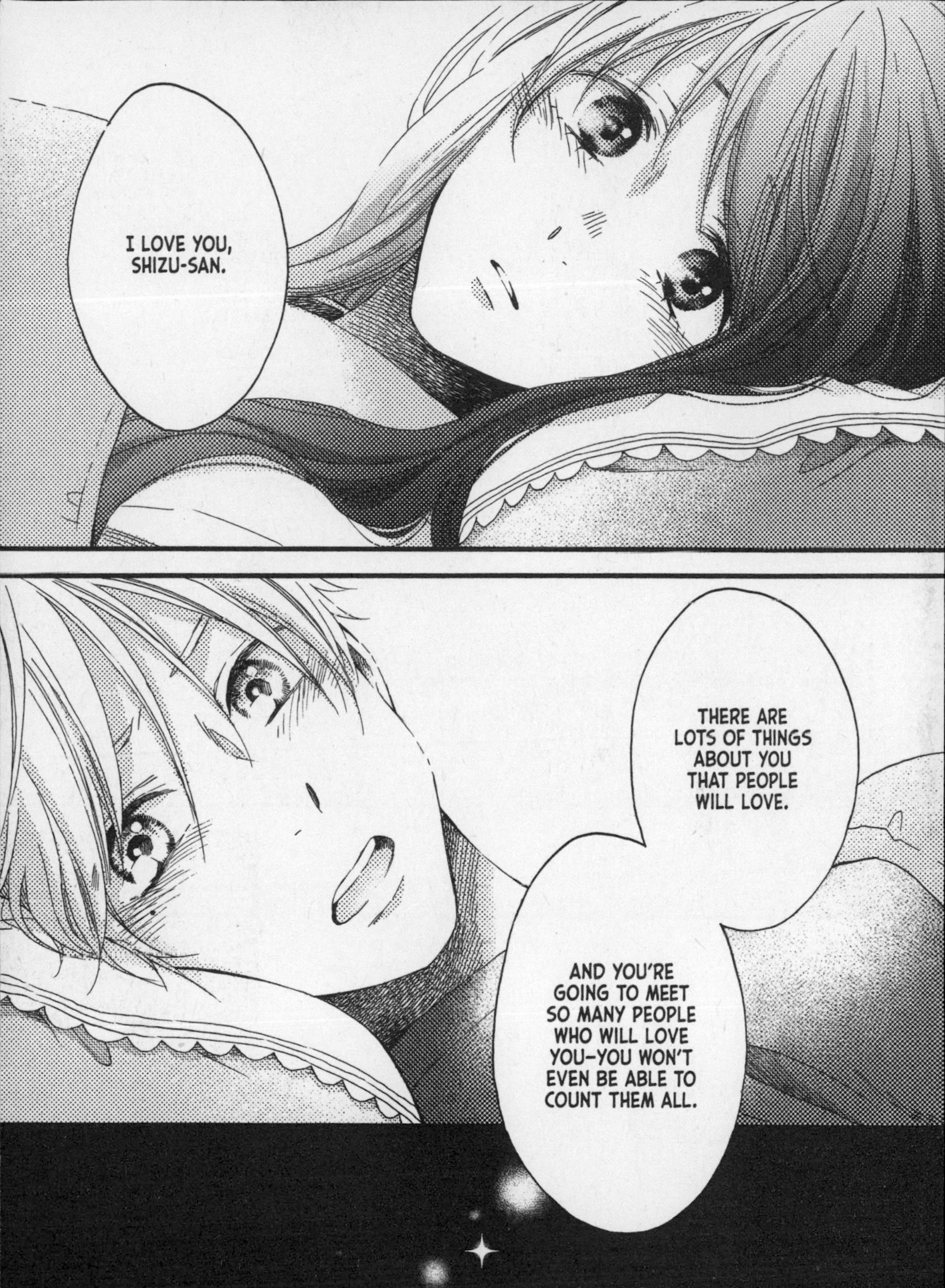
I LOVE YOU, SHIZU-SAN.
THERE ARE LOTS OF THINGS ABOUT YOU THAT PEOPLE WILL LOVE.
AND YOU'RE GOING TO MEET SO MANY PEOPLE WHO WILL LOVE YOU—YOU WON'T EVEN BE ABLE TO COUNT THEM ALL.

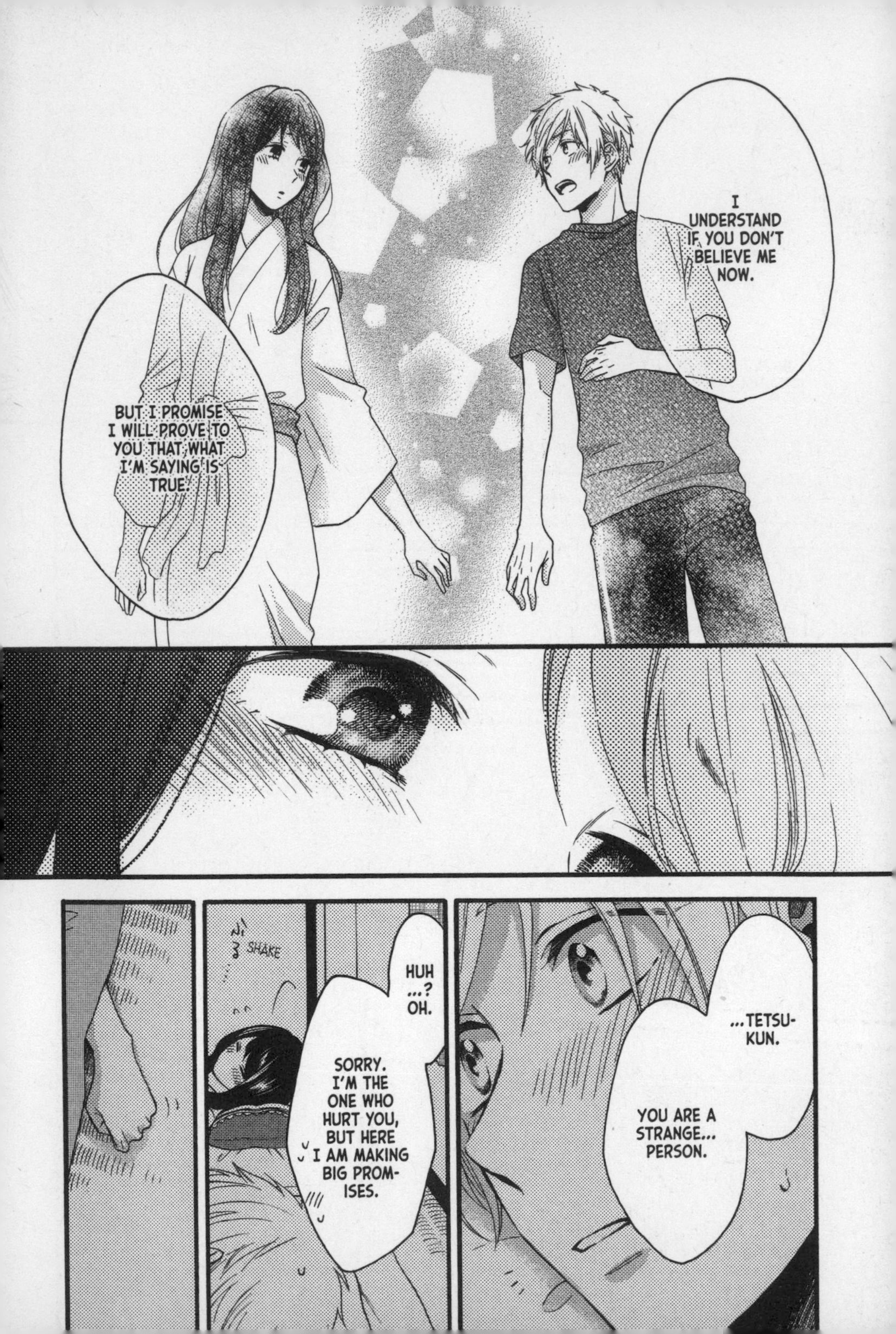
I UNDERSTAND IF YOU DON'T BELIEVE ME NOW.
BUT I PROMISE I WILL PROVE TO YOU THAT WHAT I'M SAYING IS TRUE.
...TETSU-KUN.
YOU ARE A STRANGE... PERSON.
SHAKE
HUH ...? OH.
SORRY. I'M THE ONE WHO HURT YOU, BUT HERE I AM MAKING BIG PROMISES.

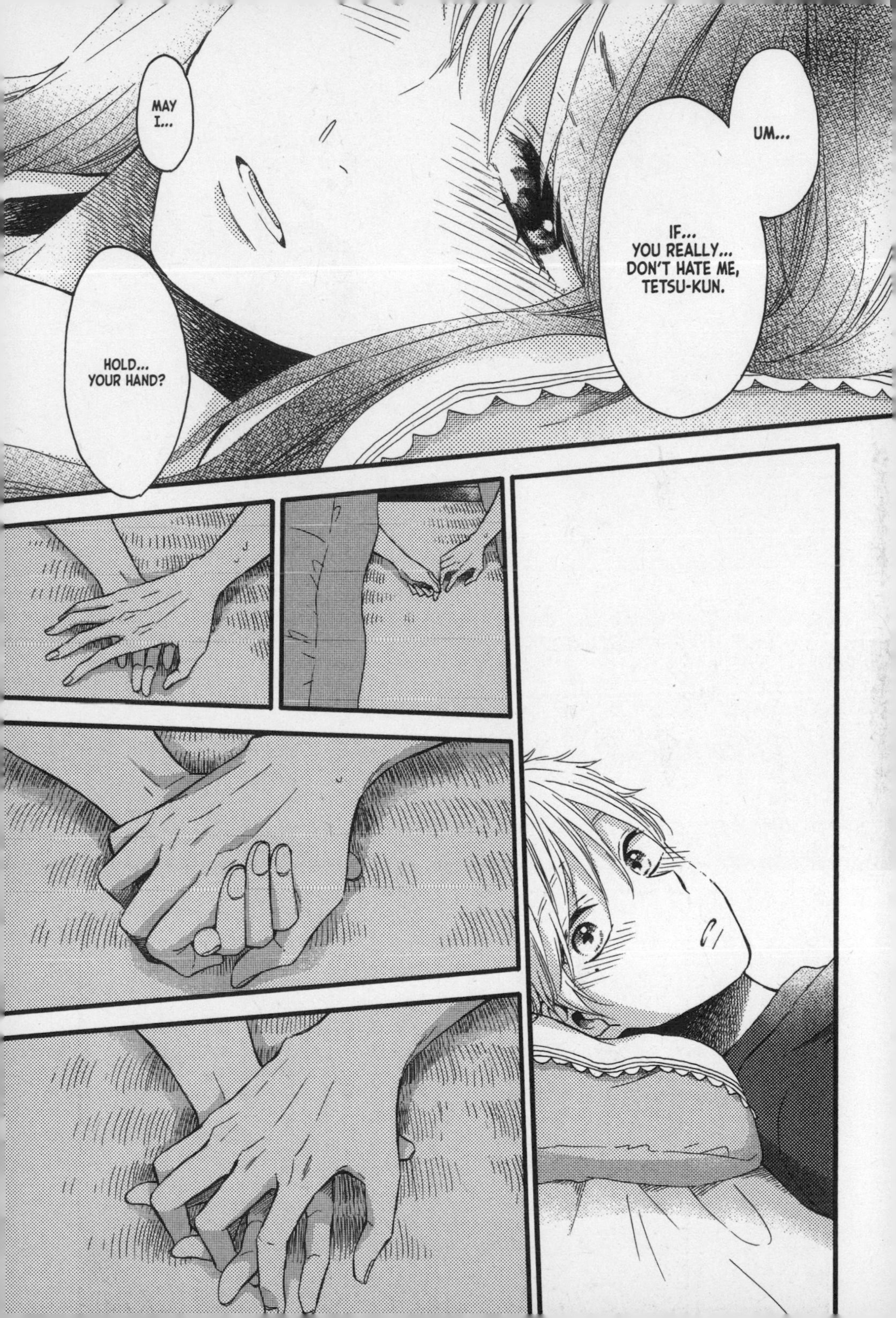
UM...
IF... YOU REALLY... DON'T HATE ME, TETSU-KUN.
MAY I...
HOLD... YOUR HAND?

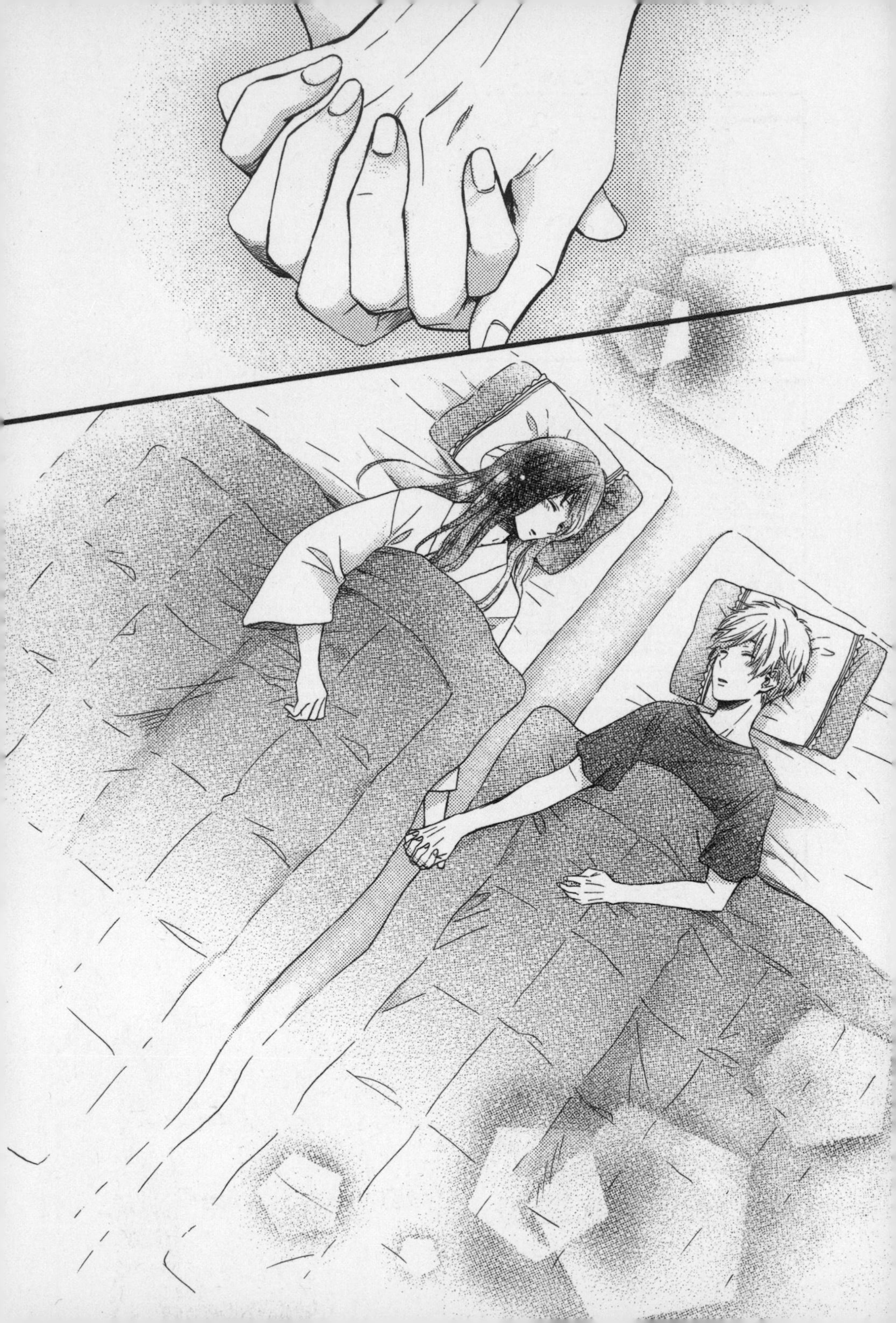

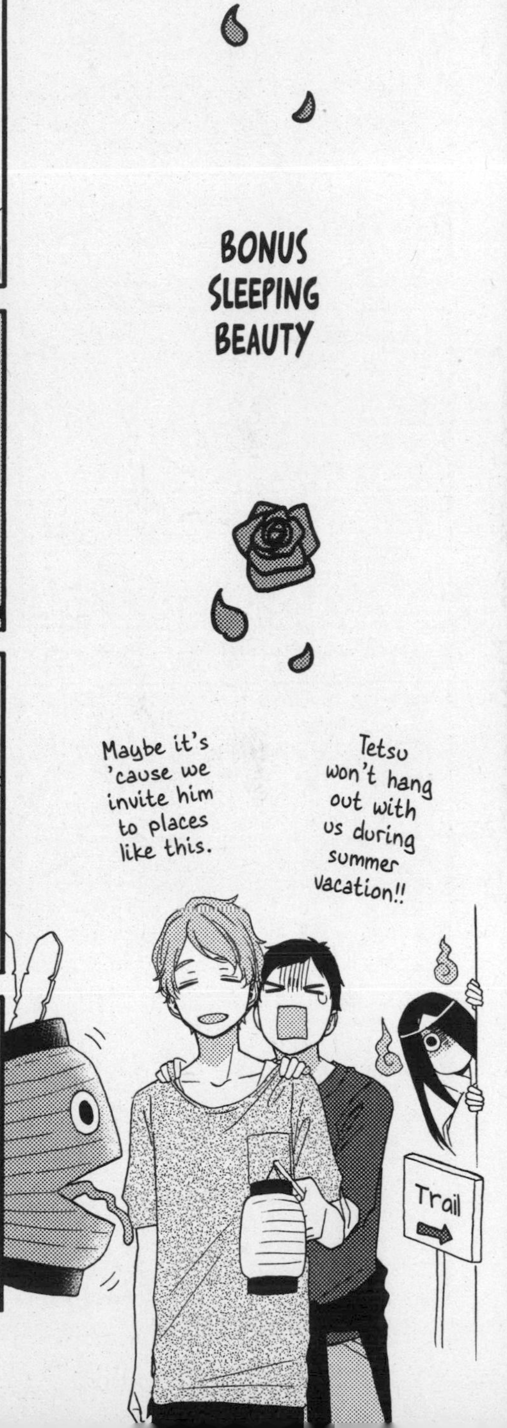
BONUS
SLEEPING
BEAUTY
Tetsu won't hang out with us during summer vacation!!
Maybe it's 'cause we invite him to places like this.
Trail

NIGHT AT KURATAYA

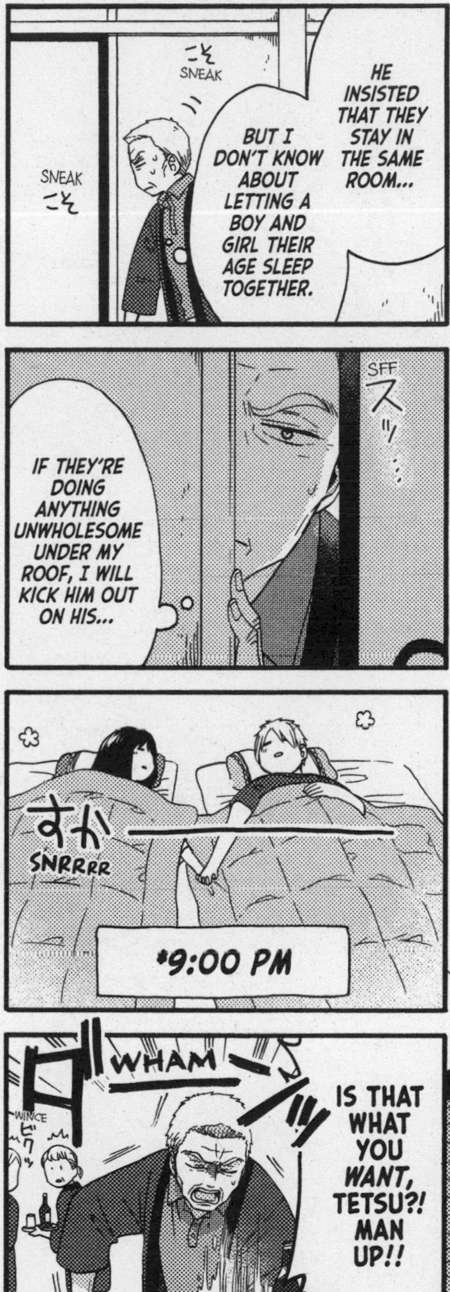
こそ
SNEAK
こそ
SNEAK
HE INSISTED THAT THEY STAY IN THE SAME ROOM...
BUT I DON'T KNOW ABOUT LETTING A BOY AND GIRL THEIR AGE SLEEP TOGETHER.
スッ…
SFF
IF THEY'RE DOING ANYTHING UNWHOLESOME UNDER MY ROOF, I WILL KICK HIM OUT ON HIS...
すか
SNRRRR
*9:00 PM
WHAM
IS THAT WHAT YOU WANT, TETSU?! MAN UP!!
ビク
WINCE

MEANWHILE, AT THE UENO HOME

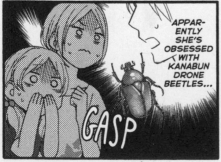

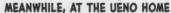

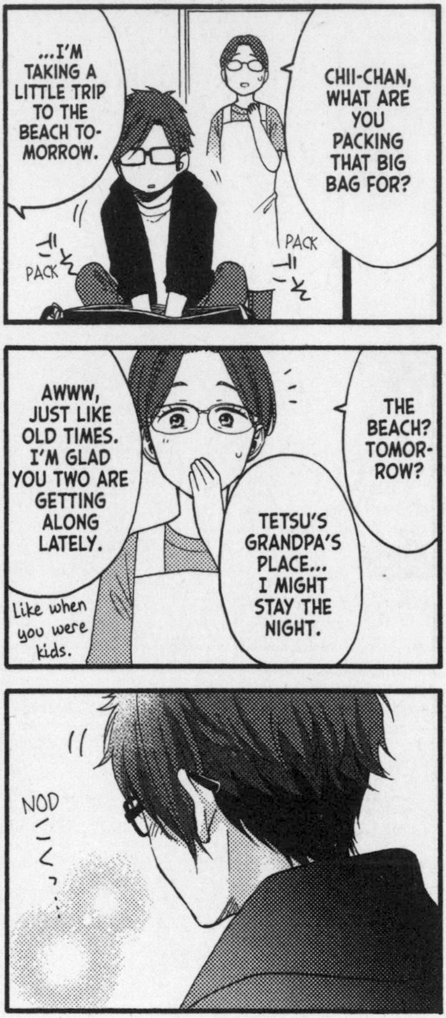
CHII-CHAN, WHAT ARE YOU PACKING THAT BIG BAG FOR?
...I'M TAKING A LITTLE TRIP TO THE BEACH TOMORROW.
PACK
PACK
THE BEACH? TOMORROW?
TETSU'S GRANDPA'S PLACE... I MIGHT STAY THE NIGHT.
AWWW, JUST LIKE OLD TIMES. I'M GLAD YOU TWO ARE GETTING ALONG LATELY.
Like when you were kids.
NOD
SQUEEEEEZE
STAY AS MANY NIGHTS AS YOU NEED TO.
MOM.... I CAN'T... BREATHE...

MEANWHILE, AT THE MISATO HOME

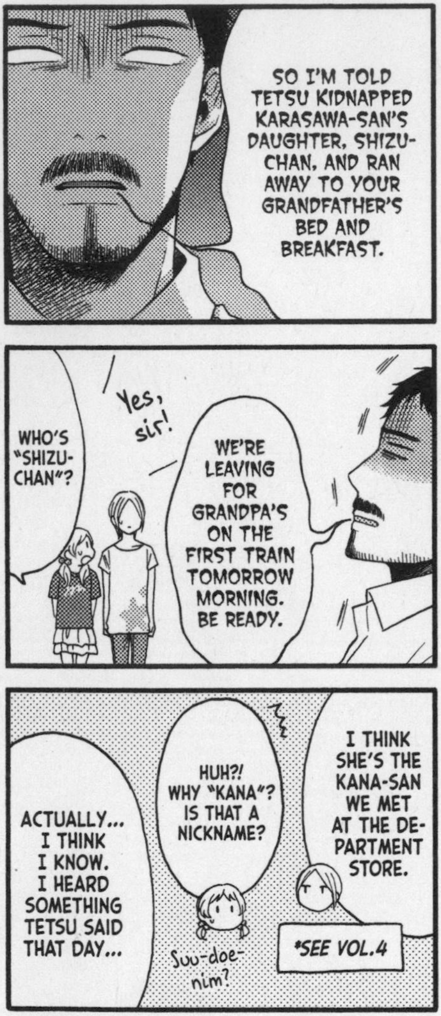
SO I'M TOLD TETSU KIDNAPPED KARASAWA-SAN'S DAUGHTER, SHIZU-CHAN, AND RAN AWAY TO YOUR GRANDFATHER'S BED AND BREAKFAST.
WE'RE LEAVING FOR GRANDPA'S ON THE FIRST TRAIN TOMORROW MORNING. BE READY.
Yes, sir!
WHO'S "SHIZU-CHAN"?
I THINK SHE'S THE KANA-SAN WE MET AT THE DEPARTMENT STORE.
*SEE VOL.4
HUH?! WHY "KANA"? IS THAT A NICKNAME?
Suu-doe-nim?
ACTUALLY... I THINK I KNOW. I HEARD SOMETHING TETSU SAID THAT DAY...
APPARENTLY SHE'S OBSESSED WITH KANABUN DRONE BEETLES...
GASP

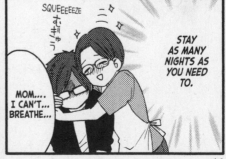

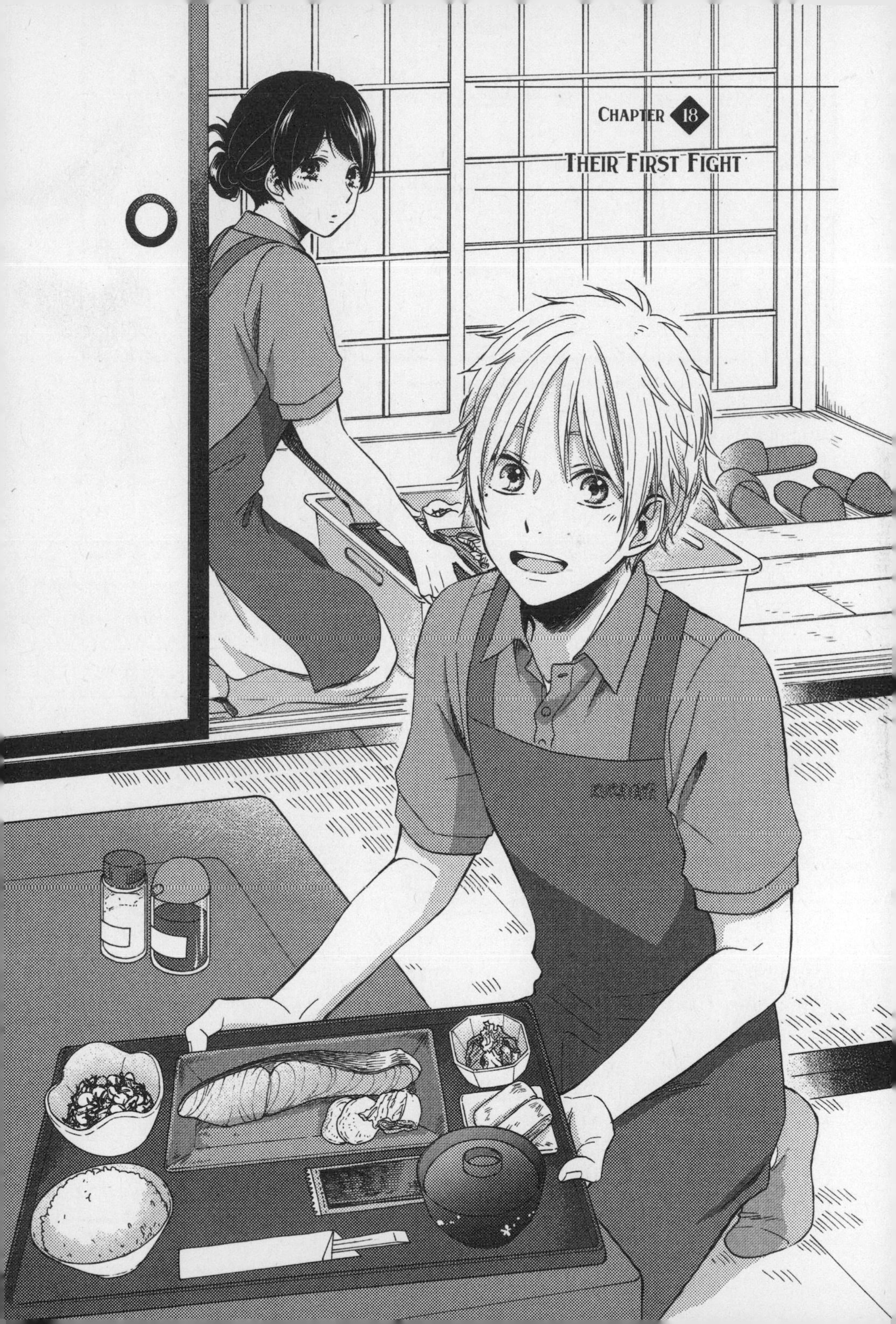
Chapter 18
Their First Fight

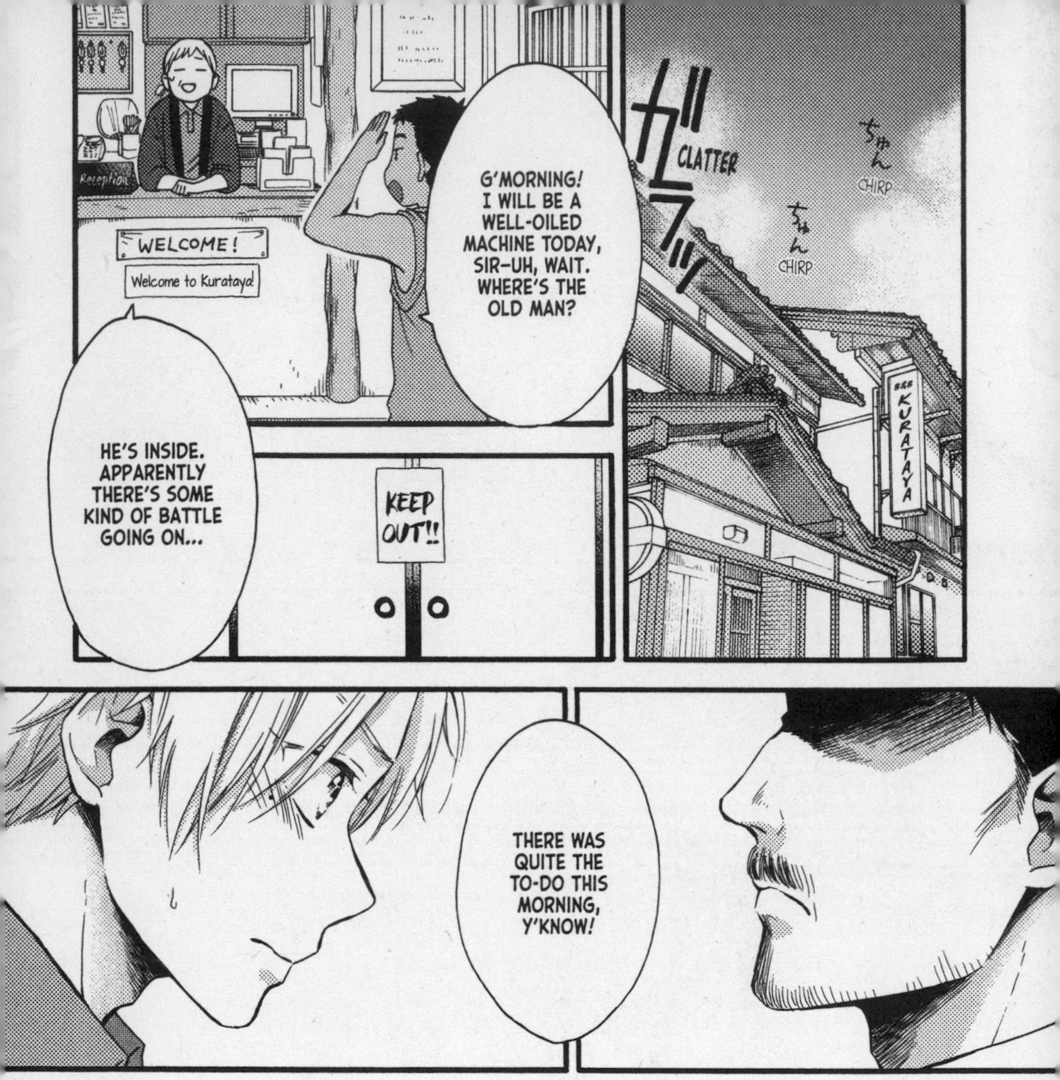

CLATTER
ちゅん
CHIRP
ちゅん
CHIRP
KURATAYA
Reception
WELCOME!
Welcome to Kurataya!
G'MORNING! I WILL BE A WELL-OILED MACHINE TODAY, SIR—UH, WAIT. WHERE'S THE OLD MAN?
HE'S INSIDE. APPARENTLY THERE'S SOME KIND OF BATTLE GOING ON...
KEEP OUT!!
THERE WAS QUITE THE TO-DO THIS MORNING, Y'KNOW!

Wake Up, Sleeping Beauty

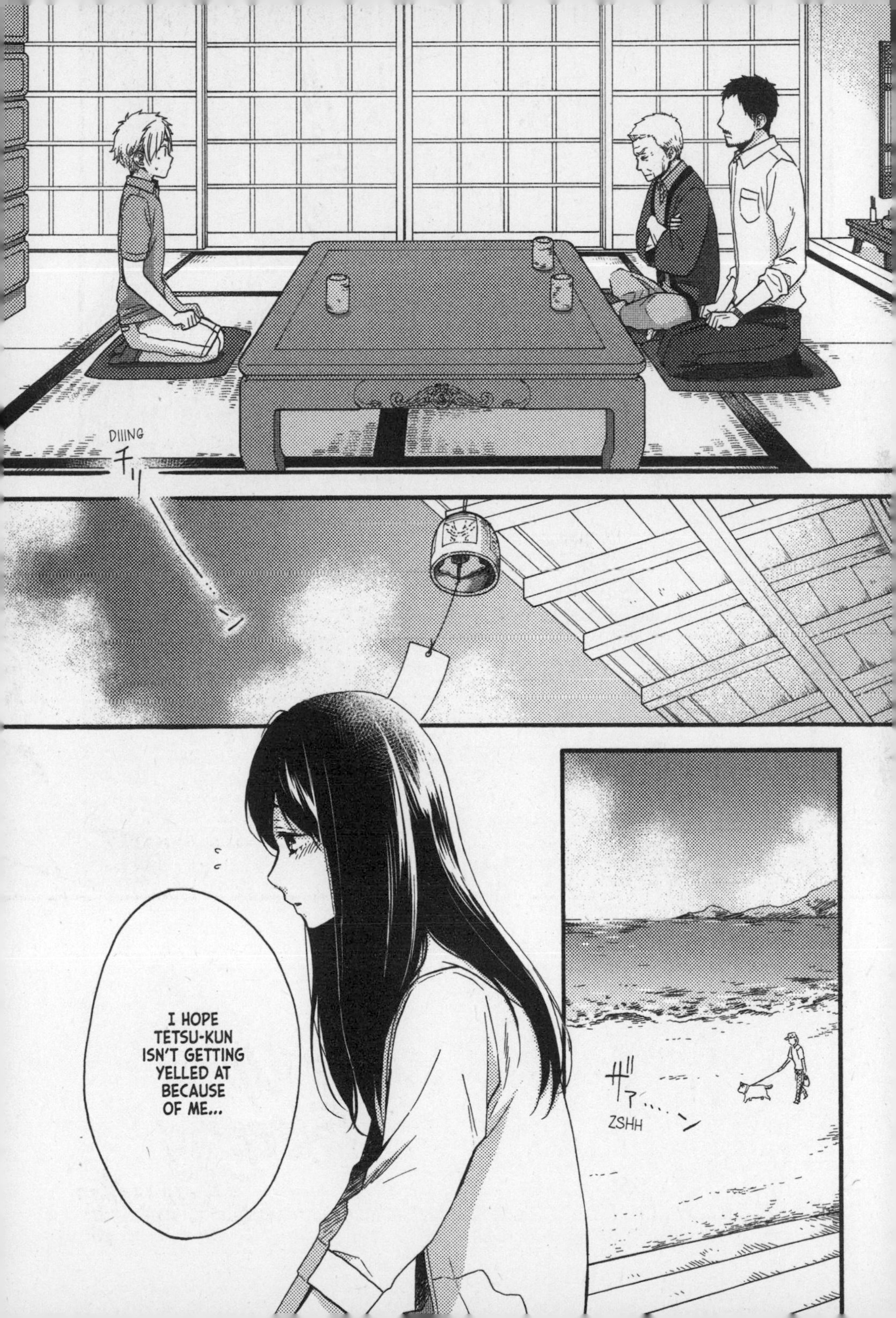
DIIING
チリ
ザァ……ン
ZSHH
I HOPE TETSU-KUN ISN'T GETTING YELLED AT BECAUSE OF ME...

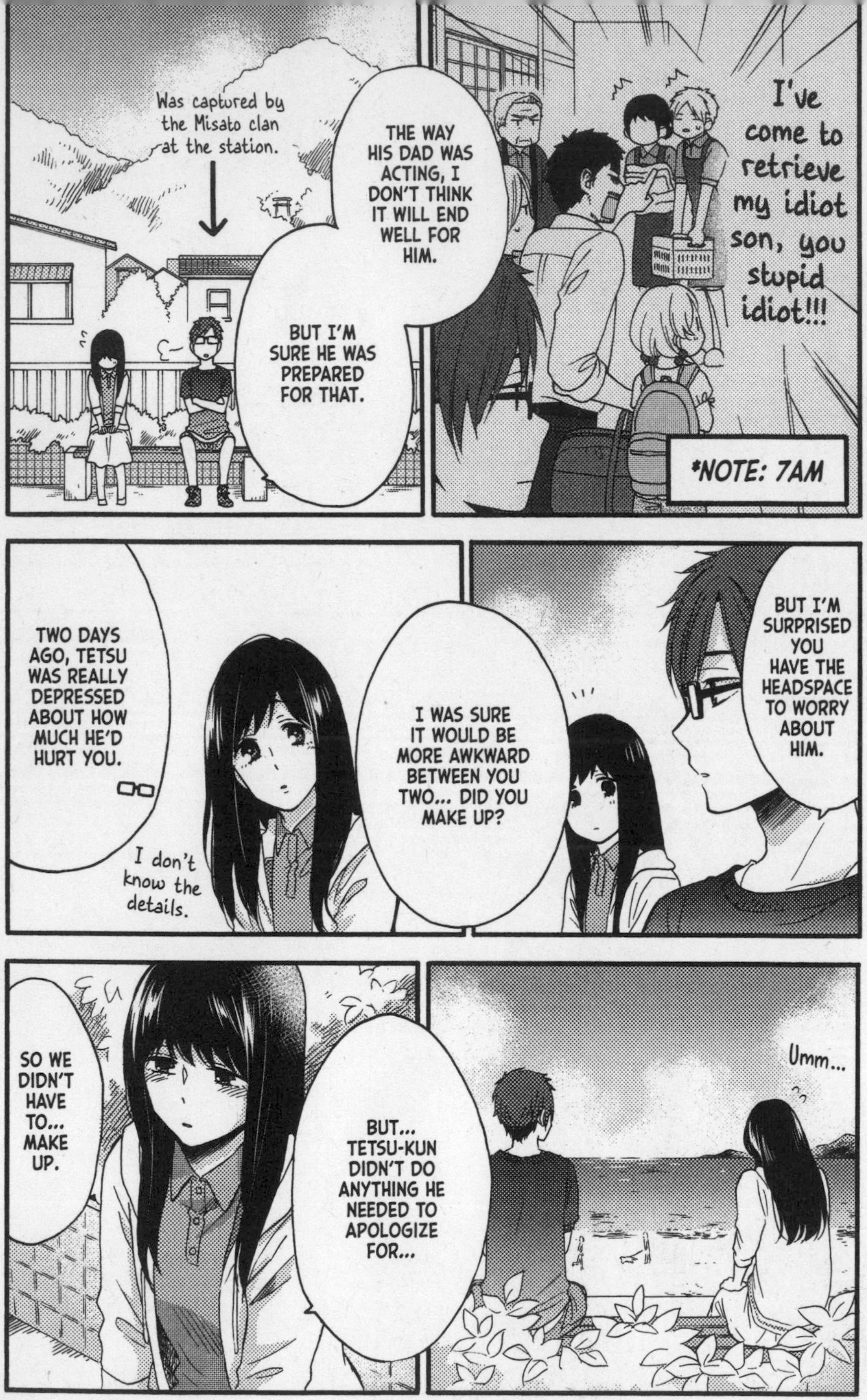
I've come to retrieve my idiot son, you stupid idiot!!!
*NOTE: 7AM
THE WAY HIS DAD WAS ACTING, I DON'T THINK IT WILL END WELL FOR HIM.
Was captured by the Misato clan at the station.
BUT I'M SURE HE WAS PREPARED FOR THAT.
BUT I'M SURPRISED YOU HAVE THE HEADSPACE TO WORRY ABOUT HIM.
I WAS SURE IT WOULD BE MORE AWKWARD BETWEEN YOU TWO... DID YOU MAKE UP?
TWO DAYS AGO, TETSU WAS REALLY DEPRESSED ABOUT HOW MUCH HE'D HURT YOU.
I don't know the details.
Umm...
BUT... TETSU-KUN DIDN'T DO ANYTHING HE NEEDED TO APOLOGIZE FOR...
SO WE DIDN'T HAVE TO... MAKE UP.

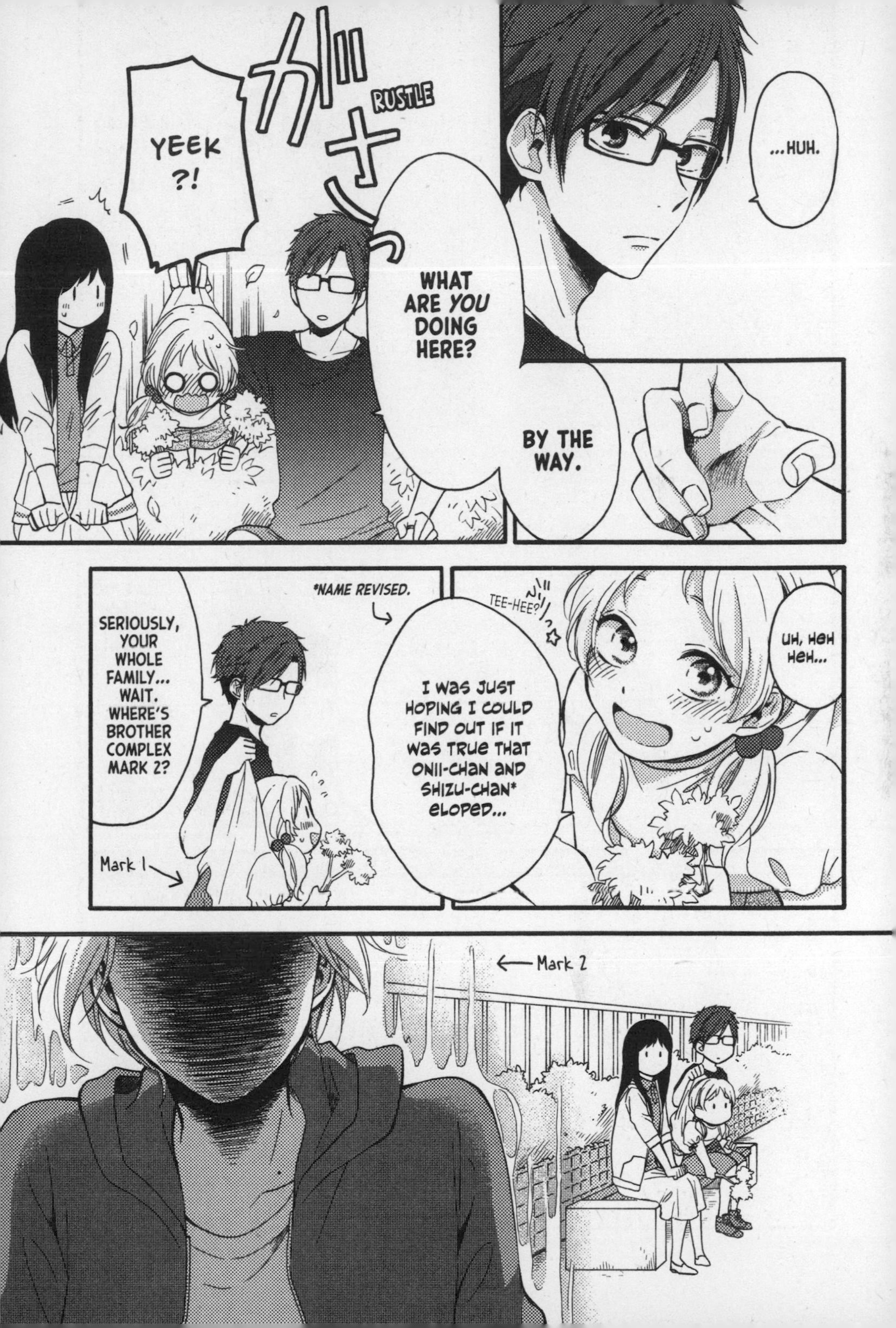
...HUH.
WHAT ARE YOU DOING HERE?
BY THE WAY.
RUSTLE
YEEK ?!
UH, HEH HEH...
TEE-HEE?
I WAS JUST HOPING I COULD FIND OUT IF IT WAS TRUE THAT ONII-CHAN AND SHIZU-CHAN* ELOPED...
*NAME REVISED.
SERIOUSLY, YOUR WHOLE FAMILY... WAIT. WHERE'S BROTHER COMPLEX MARK 2?
Mark 1
Mark 2

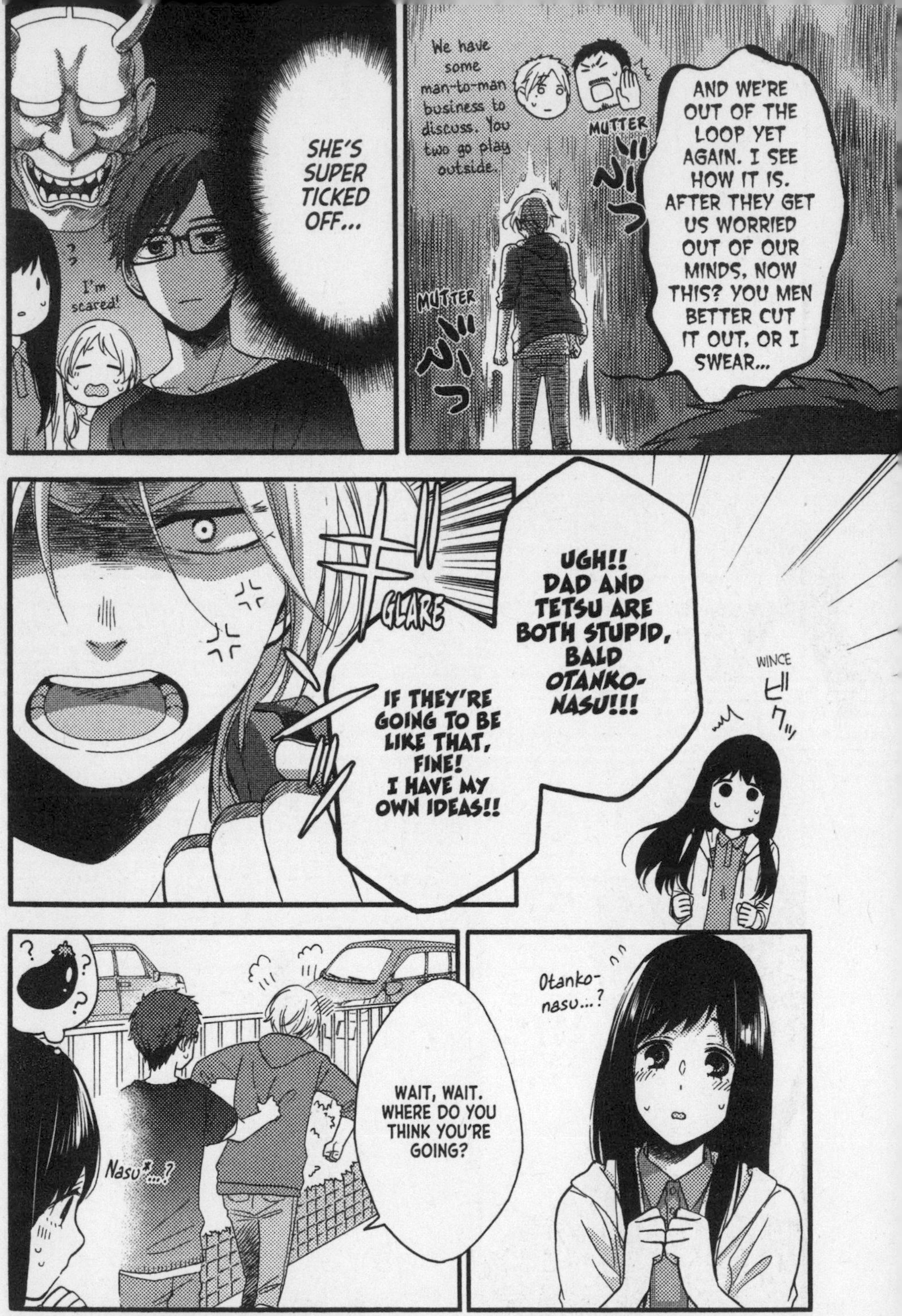
We have some man-to-man business to discuss. You two go play outside.
MUTTER
AND WE'RE OUT OF THE LOOP YET AGAIN. I SEE HOW IT IS. AFTER THEY GET US WORRIED OUT OF OUR MINDS, NOW THIS? YOU MEN BETTER CUT IT OUT, OR I SWEAR...
MUTTER
SHE'S SUPER TICKED OFF...
I'm scared!
UGH!! DAD AND TETSU ARE BOTH STUPID, BALD OTANKO-NASU!!!
IF THEY'RE GOING TO BE LIKE THAT, FINE! I HAVE MY OWN IDEAS!!
GLARE
WINCE
Otanko-nasu...?
WAIT, WAIT. WHERE DO YOU THINK YOU'RE GOING?
Nasu*...?

*OTANKO-NASU IS SLANG FOR CALLING SOMEONE STUPID. NASU IS THE JAPANESE WORD FOR EGGPLANT.

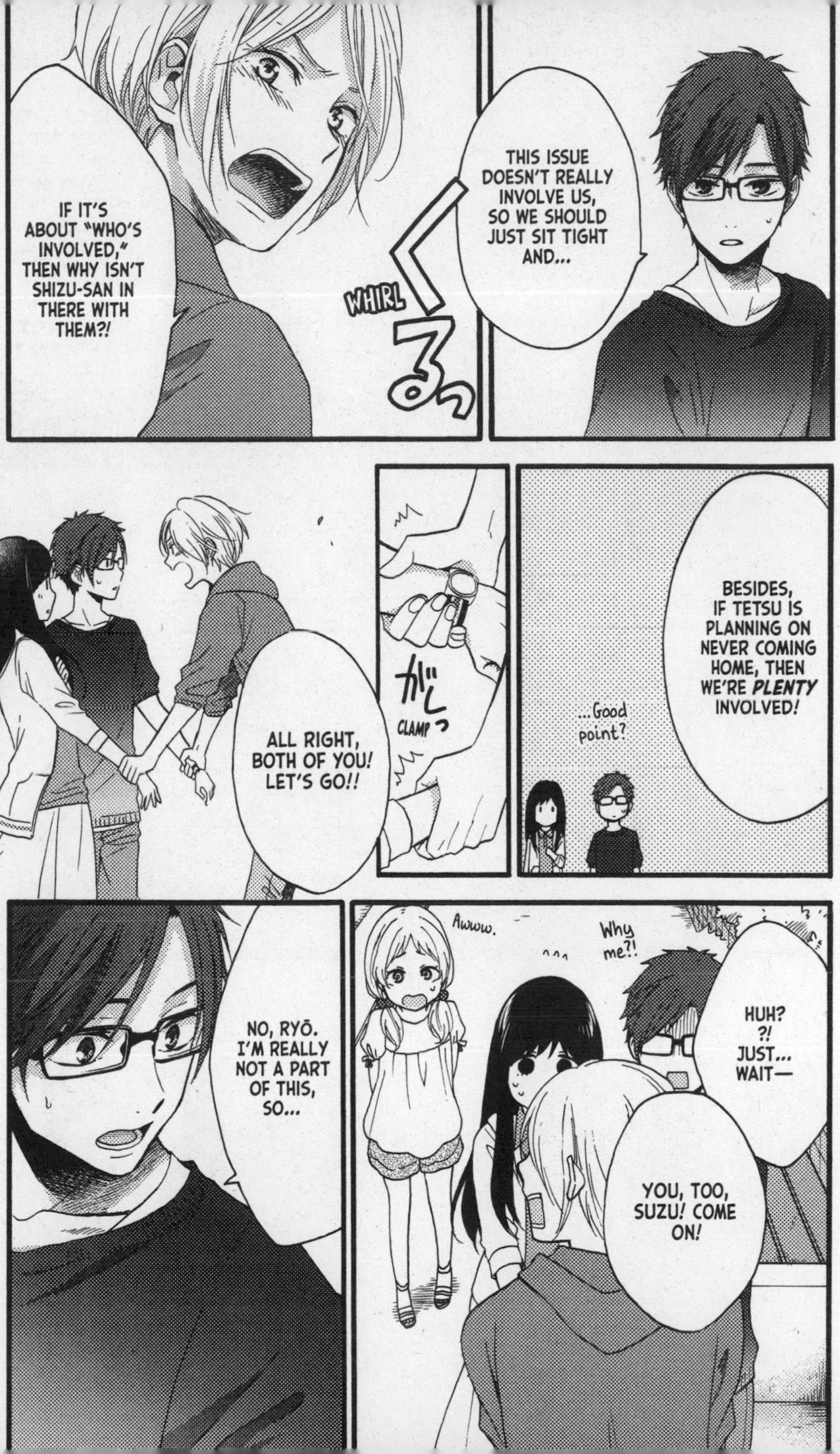
THIS ISSUE DOESN'T REALLY INVOLVE US, SO WE SHOULD JUST SIT TIGHT AND...
WHIRL
IF IT'S ABOUT "WHO'S INVOLVED," THEN WHY ISN'T SHIZU-SAN IN THERE WITH THEM?!
BESIDES, IF TETSU IS PLANNING ON NEVER COMING HOME, THEN WE'RE *PLENTY* INVOLVED!
...Good point?
CLAMP
ALL RIGHT, BOTH OF YOU! LET'S GO!!
Awww.
Why me?!
HUH? ?! JUST... WAIT—
YOU, TOO, SUZU! COME ON!
NO, RYŌ. I'M REALLY NOT A PART OF THIS, SO...

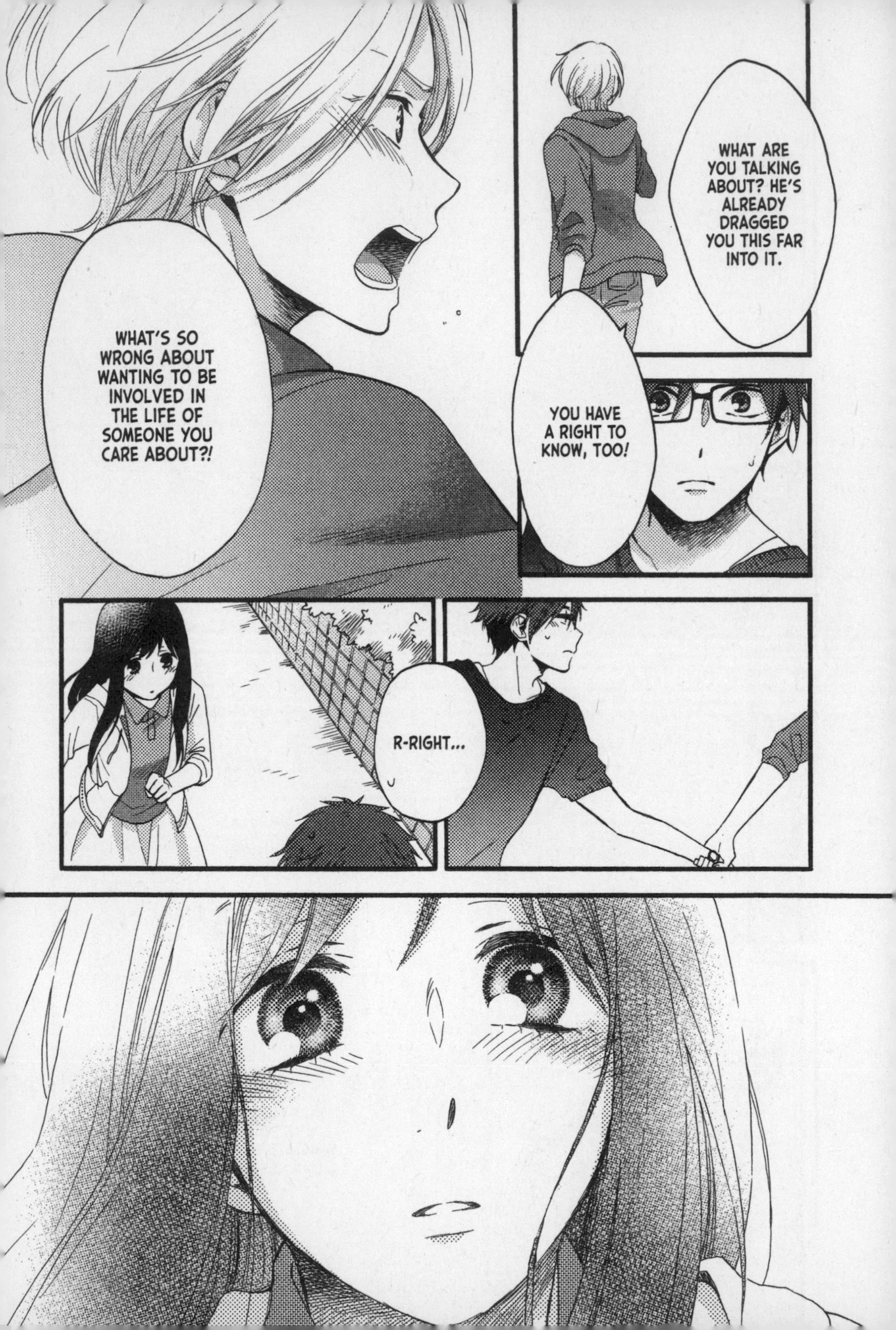
WHAT ARE YOU TALKING ABOUT? HE'S ALREADY DRAGGED YOU THIS FAR INTO IT.
YOU HAVE A RIGHT TO KNOW, TOO!
WHAT'S SO WRONG ABOUT WANTING TO BE INVOLVED IN THE LIFE OF SOMEONE YOU CARE ABOUT?!
R-RIGHT...

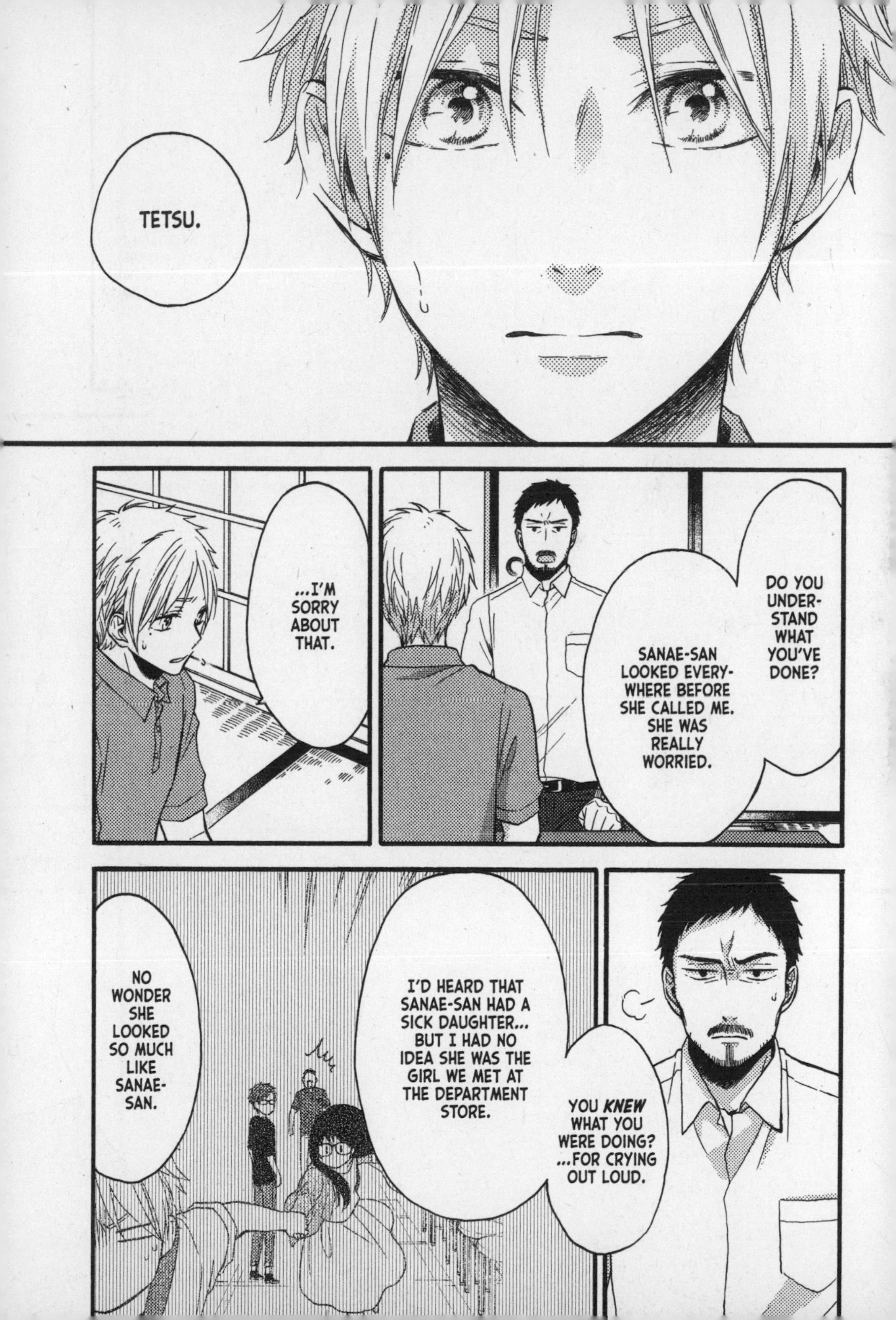
TETSU.
DO YOU UNDERSTAND WHAT YOU'VE DONE?
SANAE-SAN LOOKED EVERYWHERE BEFORE SHE CALLED ME. SHE WAS REALLY WORRIED.
...I'M SORRY ABOUT THAT.
YOU *KNEW* WHAT YOU WERE DOING? ...FOR CRYING OUT LOUD.
I'D HEARD THAT SANAE-SAN HAD A SICK DAUGHTER... BUT I HAD NO IDEA SHE WAS THE GIRL WE MET AT THE DEPARTMENT STORE.
NO WONDER SHE LOOKED SO MUCH LIKE SANAE-SAN.

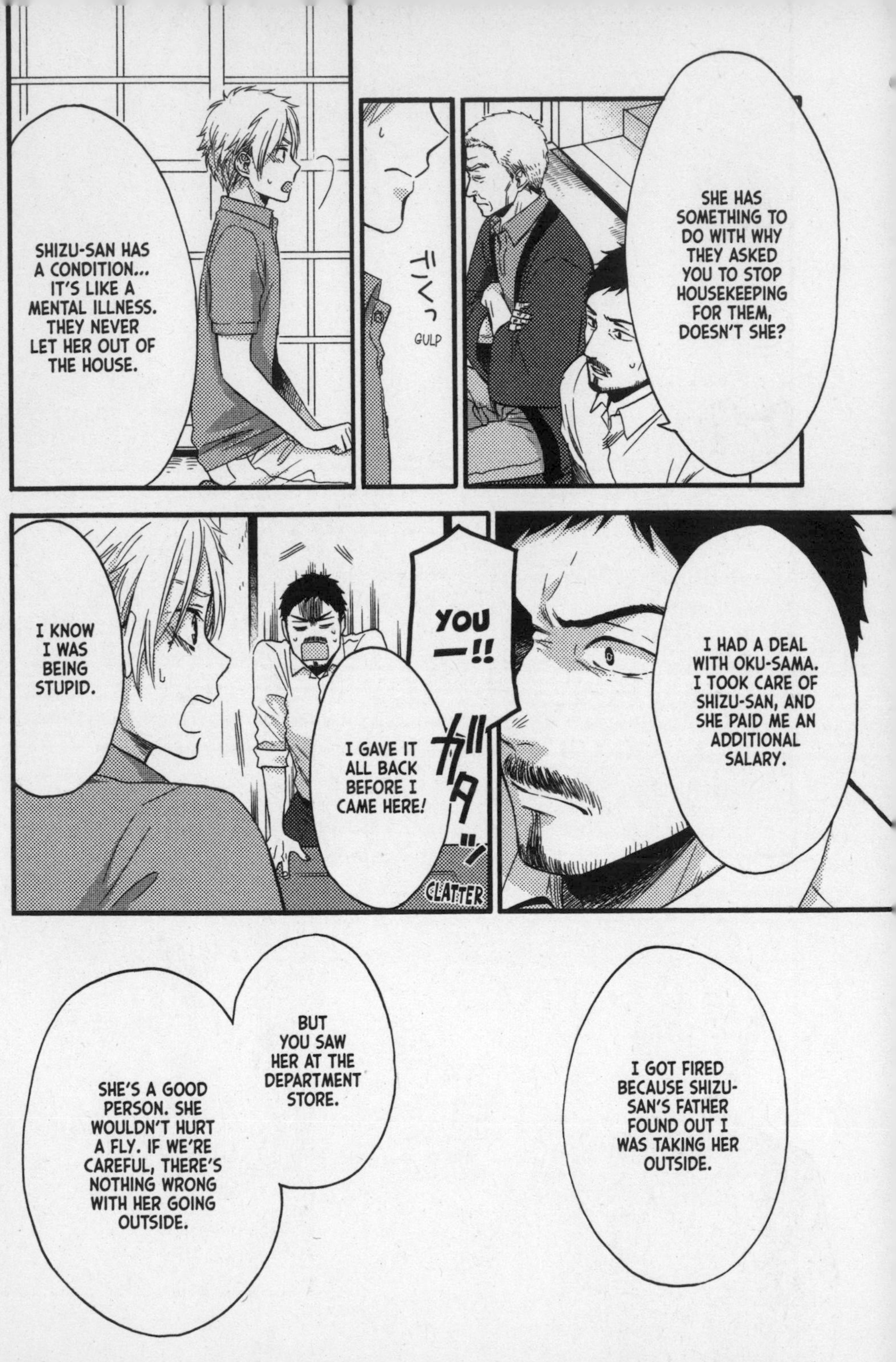
SHE HAS SOMETHING TO DO WITH WHY THEY ASKED YOU TO STOP HOUSEKEEPING FOR THEM, DOESN'T SHE?
GULP
SHIZU-SAN HAS A CONDITION... IT'S LIKE A MENTAL ILLNESS. THEY NEVER LET HER OUT OF THE HOUSE.
I HAD A DEAL WITH OKU-SAMA. I TOOK CARE OF SHIZU-SAN, AND SHE PAID ME AN ADDITIONAL SALARY.
YOU—!!
I GAVE IT ALL BACK BEFORE I CAME HERE!
CLATTER
I KNOW I WAS BEING STUPID.
I GOT FIRED BECAUSE SHIZU-SAN'S FATHER FOUND OUT I WAS TAKING HER OUTSIDE.
BUT YOU SAW HER AT THE DEPARTMENT STORE.
SHE'S A GOOD PERSON. SHE WOULDN'T HURT A FLY. IF WE'RE CAREFUL, THERE'S NOTHING WRONG WITH HER GOING OUTSIDE.

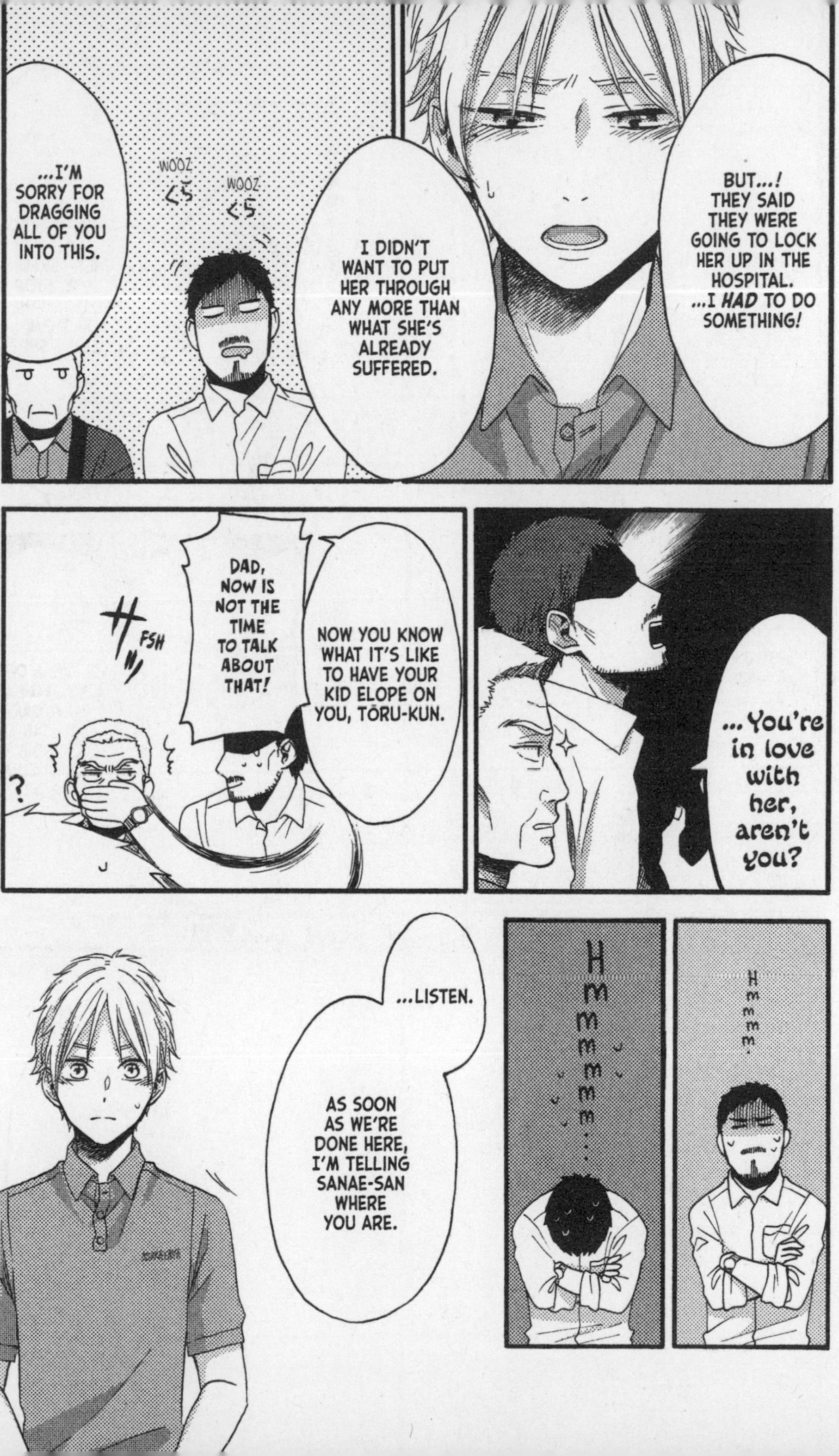
BUT...! THEY SAID THEY WERE GOING TO LOCK HER UP IN THE HOSPITAL. ...I HAD TO DO SOMETHING!
I DIDN'T WANT TO PUT HER THROUGH ANY MORE THAN WHAT SHE'S ALREADY SUFFERED.
WOOZ くら
WOOZ くら
...I'M SORRY FOR DRAGGING ALL OF YOU INTO THIS.
...You're in love with her, aren't you?
NOW YOU KNOW WHAT IT'S LIKE TO HAVE YOUR KID ELOPE ON YOU, TŌRU-KUN.
DAD, NOW IS NOT THE TIME TO TALK ABOUT THAT!
FSH
?
Hmmmm.
Hmmmmm...
...LISTEN.
AS SOON AS WE'RE DONE HERE, I'M TELLING SANAE-SAN WHERE YOU ARE.

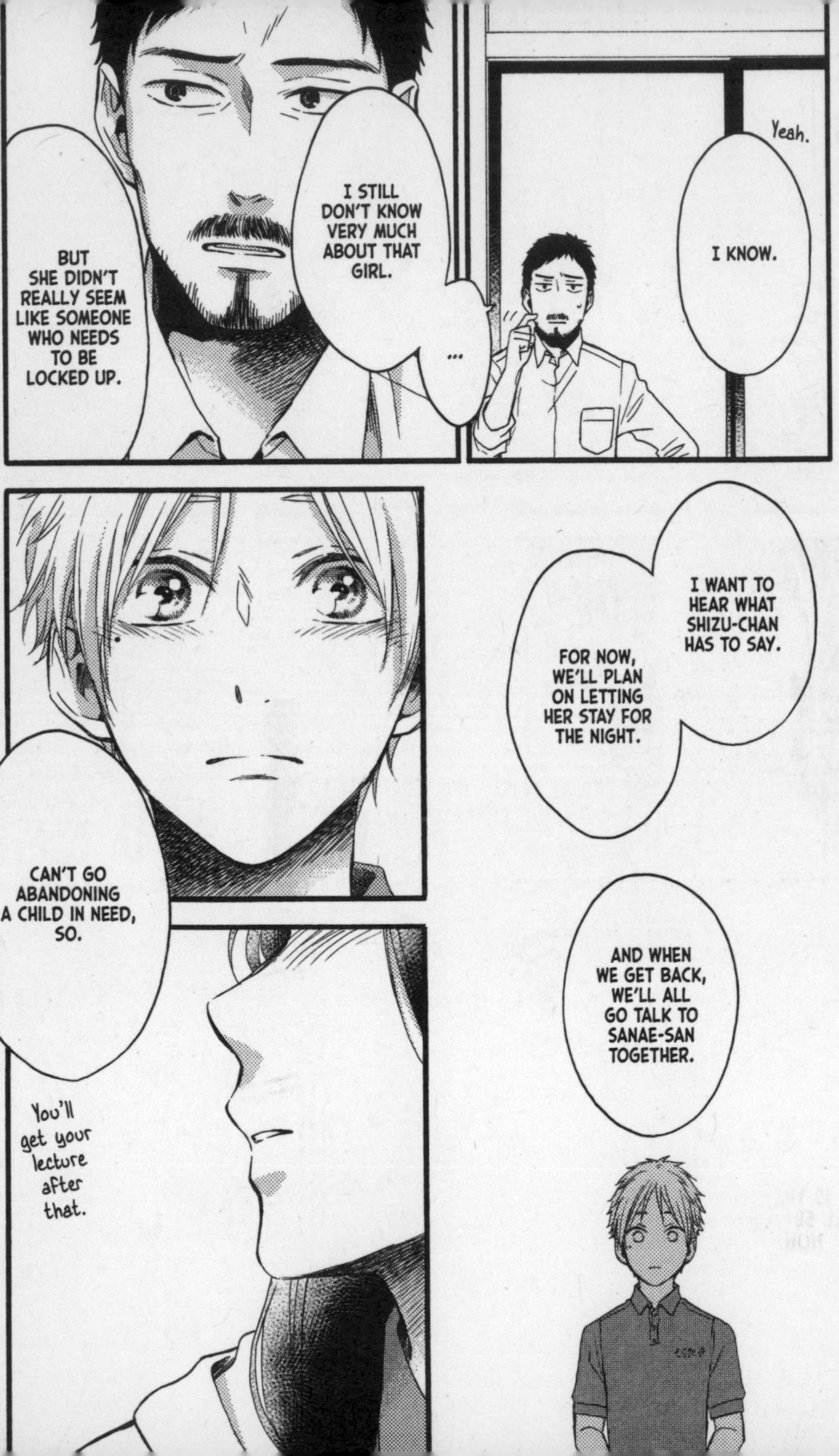
Yeah.
I KNOW.
I STILL DON'T KNOW VERY MUCH ABOUT THAT GIRL.
...
BUT SHE DIDN'T REALLY SEEM LIKE SOMEONE WHO NEEDS TO BE LOCKED UP.
I WANT TO HEAR WHAT SHIZU-CHAN HAS TO SAY.
FOR NOW, WE'LL PLAN ON LETTING HER STAY FOR THE NIGHT.
AND WHEN WE GET BACK, WE'LL ALL GO TALK TO SANAE-SAN TOGETHER.
CAN'T GO ABANDONING A CHILD IN NEED, SO.
You'll get your lecture after that.

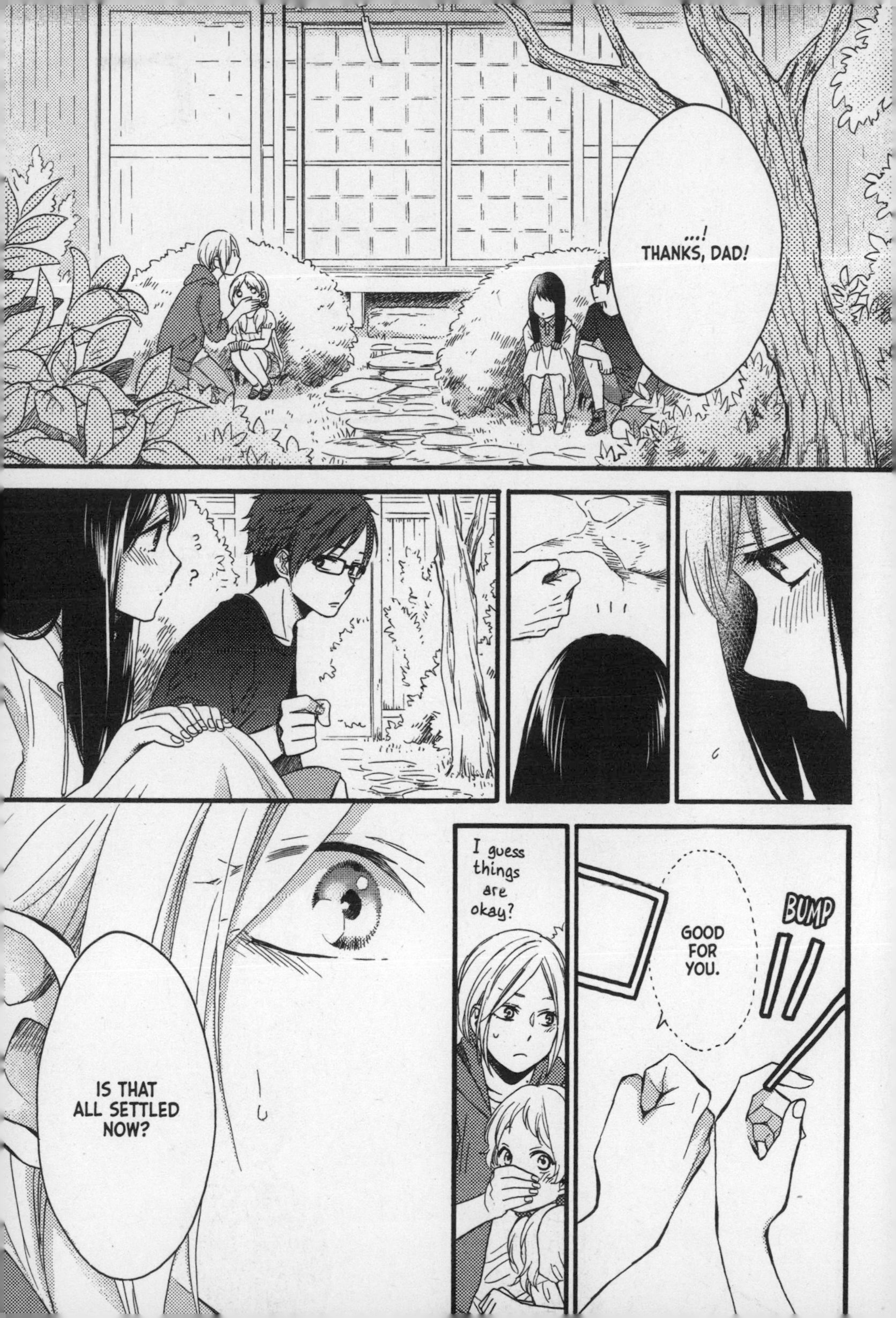
...!
THANKS, DAD!
GOOD FOR YOU.
BUMP
I guess things are okay?
IS THAT ALL SETTLED NOW?

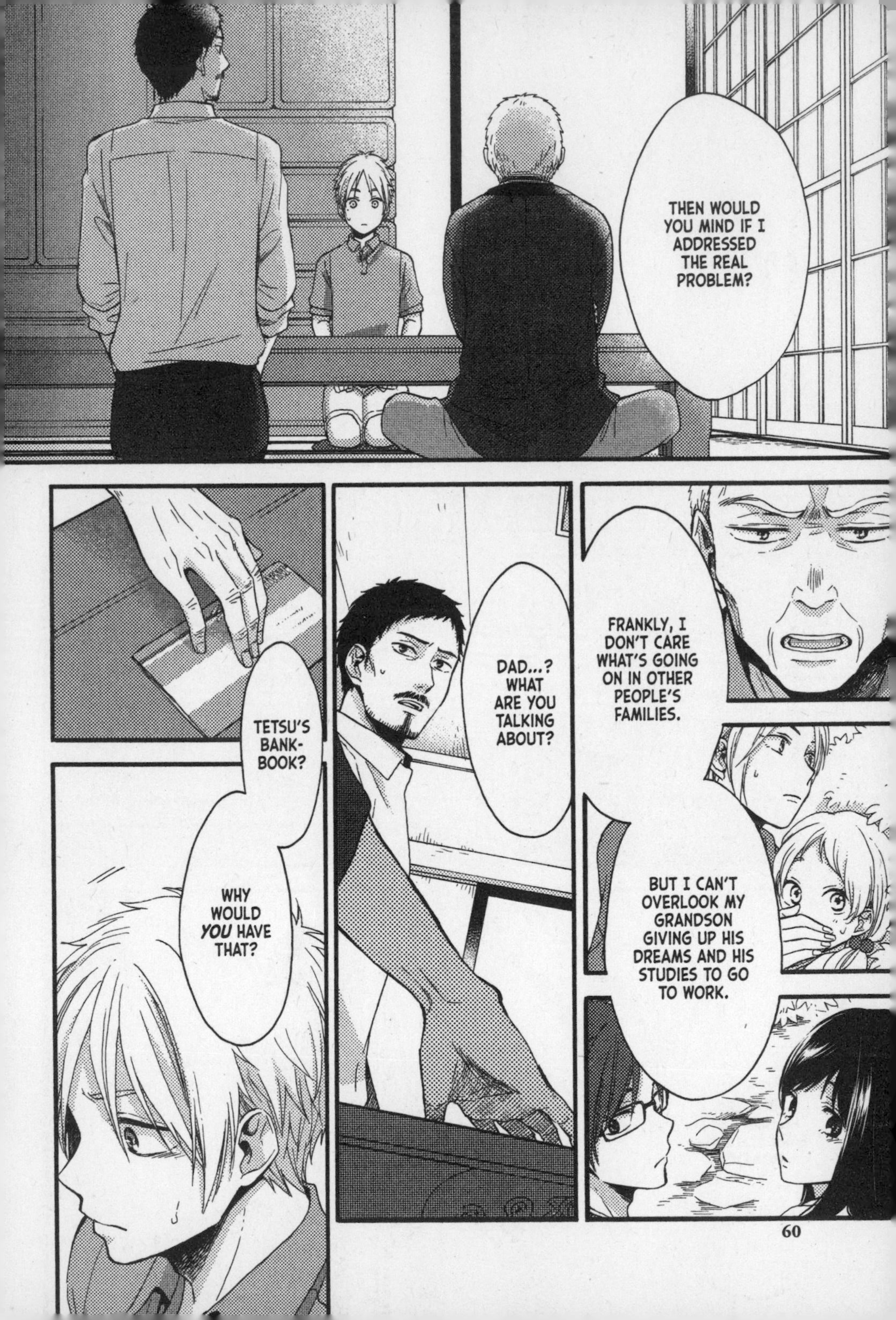
THEN WOULD YOU MIND IF I ADDRESSED THE REAL PROBLEM?
FRANKLY, I DON'T CARE WHAT'S GOING ON IN OTHER PEOPLE'S FAMILIES.
BUT I CAN'T OVERLOOK MY GRANDSON GIVING UP HIS DREAMS AND HIS STUDIES TO GO TO WORK.
DAD...? WHAT ARE YOU TALKING ABOUT?
TETSU'S BANK-BOOK?
WHY WOULD *YOU* HAVE THAT?

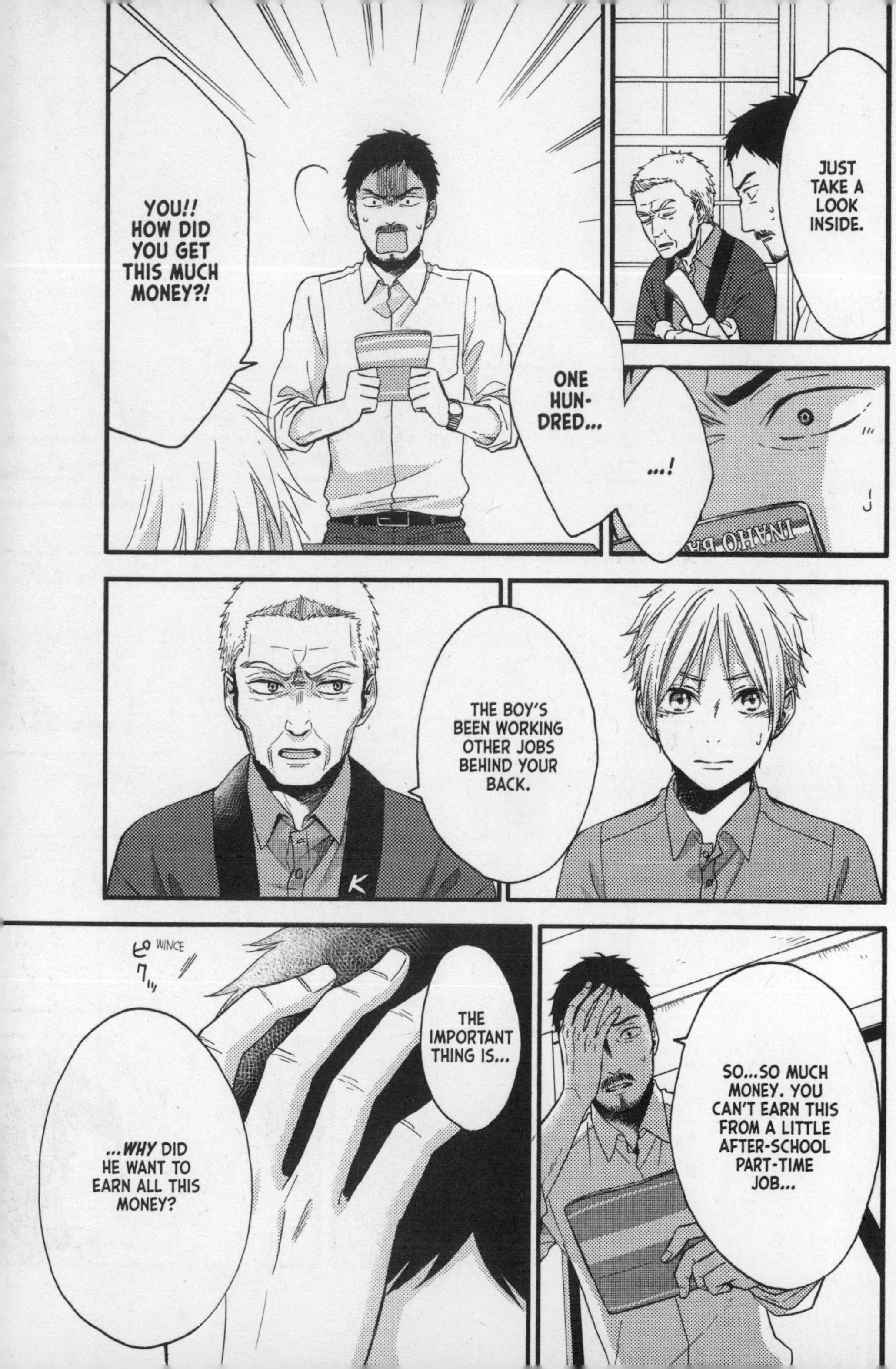
JUST TAKE A LOOK INSIDE.
ONE HUN-DRED...
...!
YOU!! HOW DID YOU GET THIS MUCH MONEY?!
THE BOY'S BEEN WORKING OTHER JOBS BEHIND YOUR BACK.
SO...SO MUCH MONEY. YOU CAN'T EARN THIS FROM A LITTLE AFTER-SCHOOL PART-TIME JOB...
THE IMPORTANT THING IS...
ピクッ WINCE
...*WHY* DID HE WANT TO EARN ALL THIS MONEY?

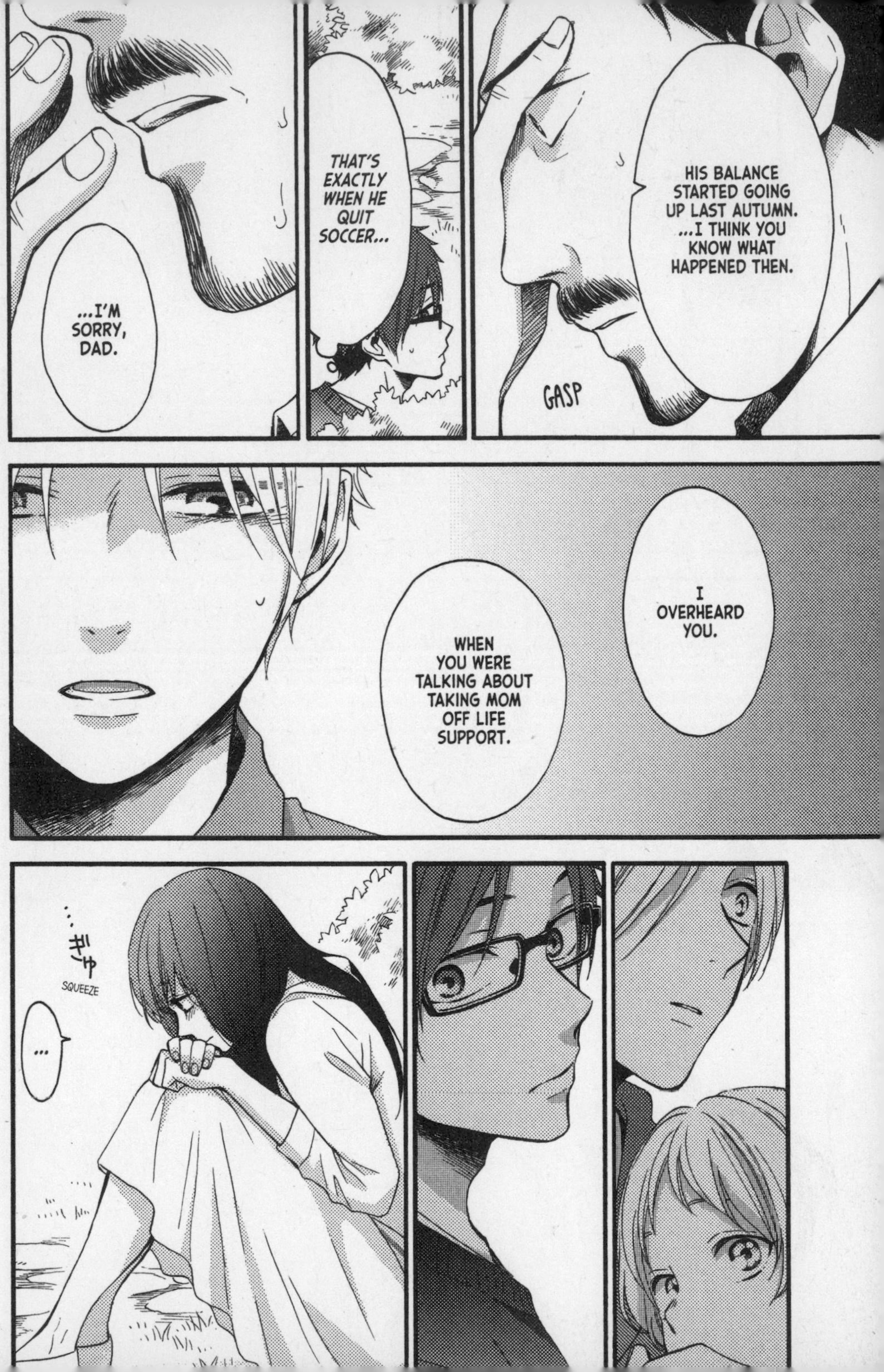
HIS BALANCE STARTED GOING UP LAST AUTUMN. ...I THINK YOU KNOW WHAT HAPPENED THEN.
GASP
THAT'S EXACTLY WHEN HE QUIT SOCCER...
...I'M SORRY, DAD.
I OVERHEARD YOU.
WHEN YOU WERE TALKING ABOUT TAKING MOM OFF LIFE SUPPORT.
…ぎゅ
SQUEEZE
...

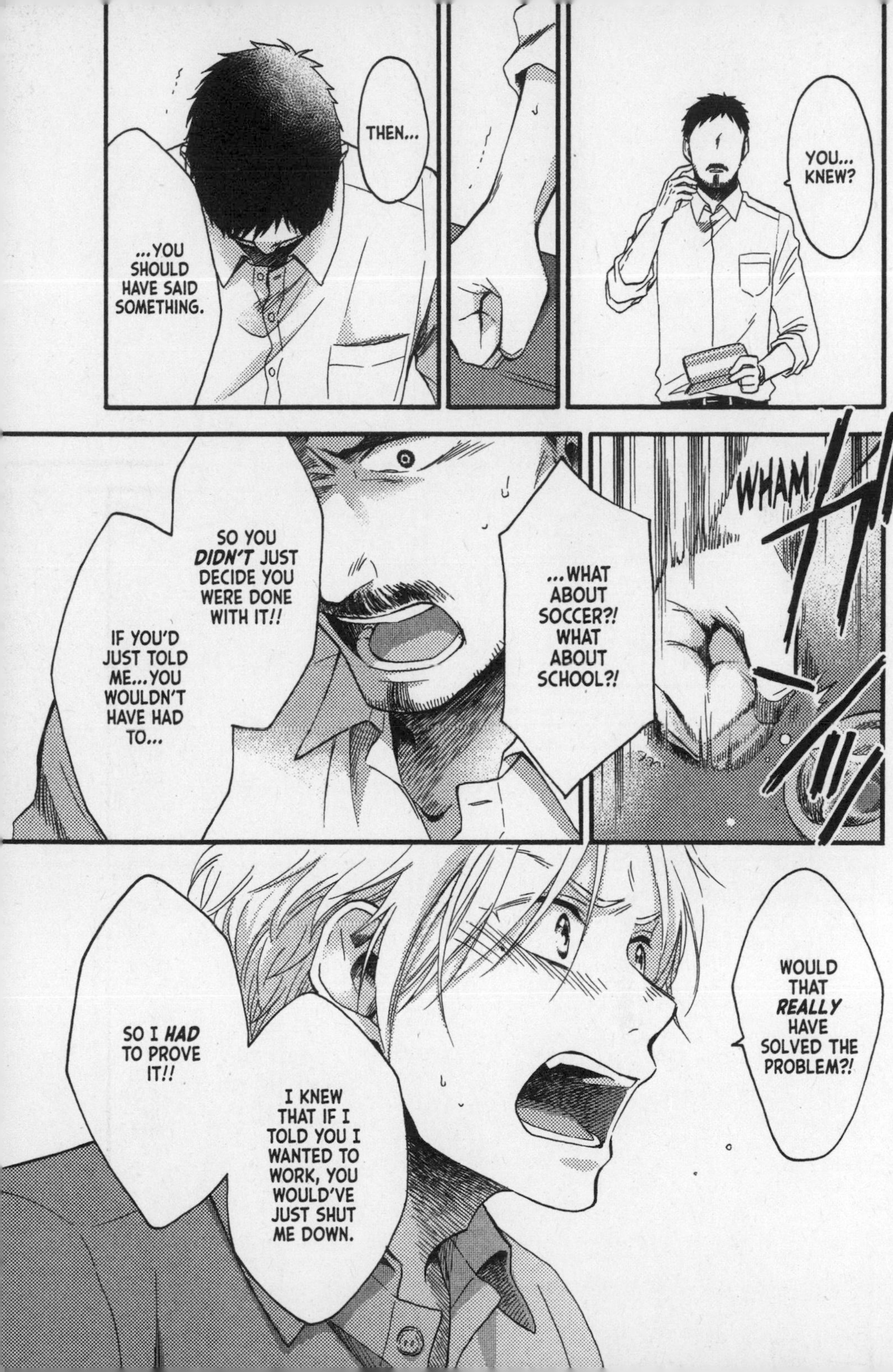
YOU... KNEW?
THEN...
...YOU SHOULD HAVE SAID SOMETHING.
WHAM
...WHAT ABOUT SOCCER?! WHAT ABOUT SCHOOL?!
SO YOU *DIDN'T* JUST DECIDE YOU WERE DONE WITH IT!!
IF YOU'D JUST TOLD ME...YOU WOULDN'T HAVE HAD TO...
WOULD THAT *REALLY* HAVE SOLVED THE PROBLEM?!
I KNEW THAT IF I TOLD YOU I WANTED TO WORK, YOU WOULD'VE JUST SHUT ME DOWN.
SO I *HAD* TO PROVE IT!!

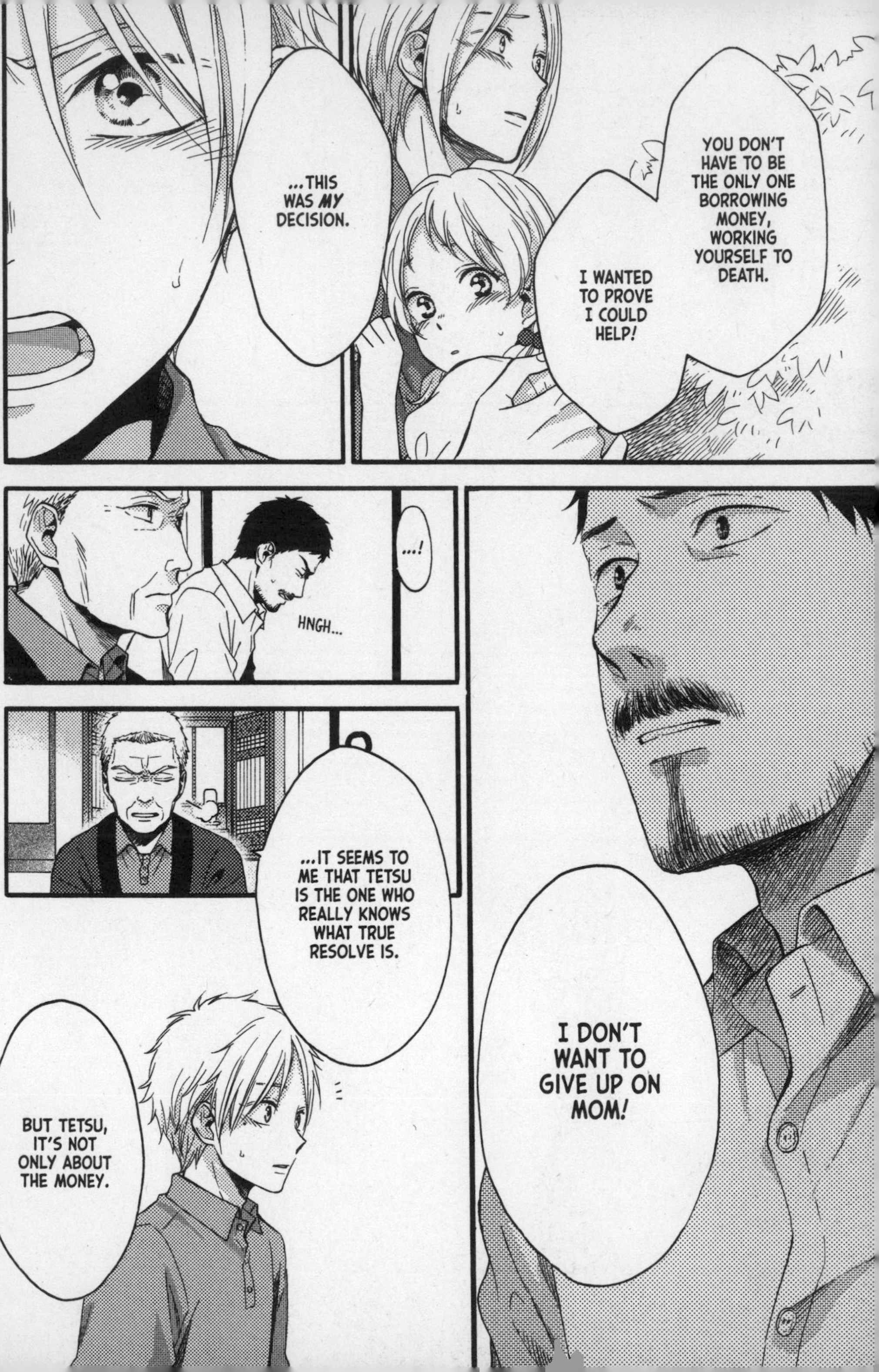
YOU DON'T HAVE TO BE THE ONLY ONE BORROWING MONEY, WORKING YOURSELF TO DEATH.
I WANTED TO PROVE I COULD HELP!
...THIS WAS *MY* DECISION.
I DON'T WANT TO GIVE UP ON MOM!
...!
HNGH...
...IT SEEMS TO ME THAT TETSU IS THE ONE WHO REALLY KNOWS WHAT TRUE RESOLVE IS.
BUT TETSU, IT'S NOT ONLY ABOUT THE MONEY.

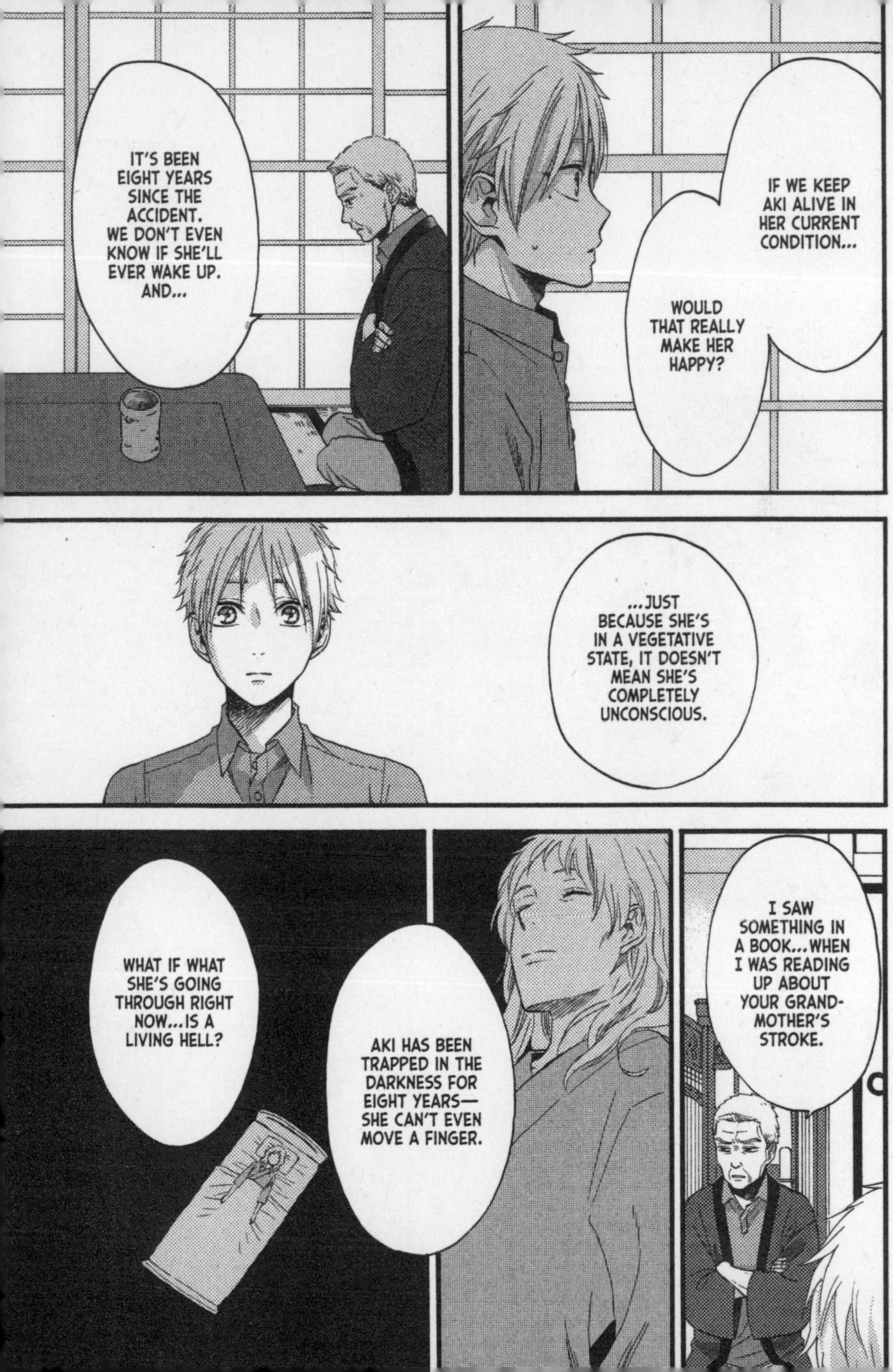
IF WE KEEP AKI ALIVE IN HER CURRENT CONDITION...
WOULD THAT REALLY MAKE HER HAPPY?
IT'S BEEN EIGHT YEARS SINCE THE ACCIDENT. WE DON'T EVEN KNOW IF SHE'LL EVER WAKE UP. AND...
...JUST BECAUSE SHE'S IN A VEGETATIVE STATE, IT DOESN'T MEAN SHE'S COMPLETELY UNCONSCIOUS.
I SAW SOMETHING IN A BOOK...WHEN I WAS READING UP ABOUT YOUR GRAND-MOTHER'S STROKE.
AKI HAS BEEN TRAPPED IN THE DARKNESS FOR EIGHT YEARS—SHE CAN'T EVEN MOVE A FINGER.
WHAT IF WHAT SHE'S GOING THROUGH RIGHT NOW...IS A LIVING HELL?

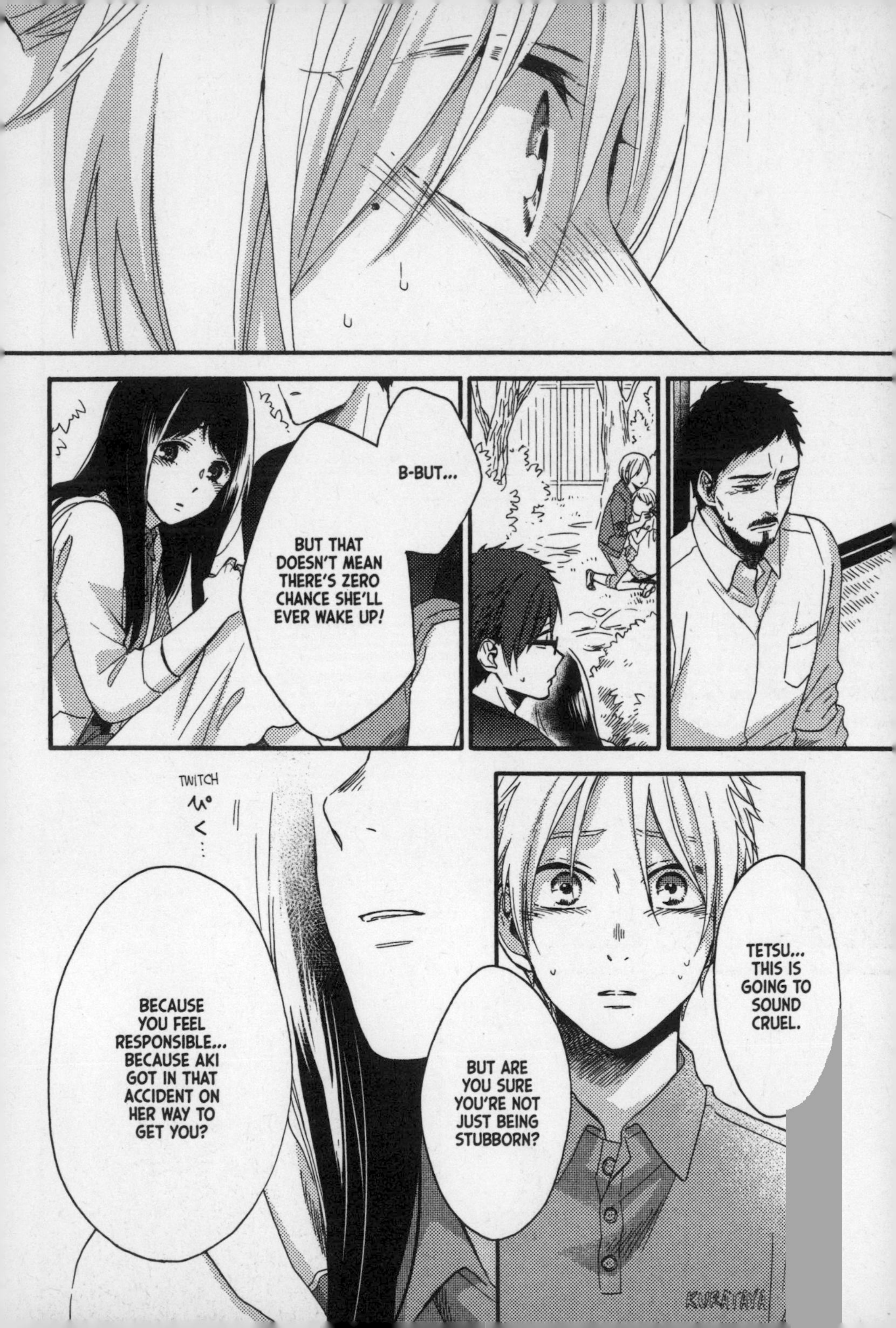
B-BUT...
BUT THAT DOESN'T MEAN THERE'S ZERO CHANCE SHE'LL EVER WAKE UP!
TETSU... THIS IS GOING TO SOUND CRUEL.
BUT ARE YOU SURE YOU'RE NOT JUST BEING STUBBORN?
TWITCH
ぴく…
BECAUSE YOU FEEL RESPONSIBLE... BECAUSE AKI GOT IN THAT ACCIDENT ON HER WAY TO GET YOU?
KURATAYA

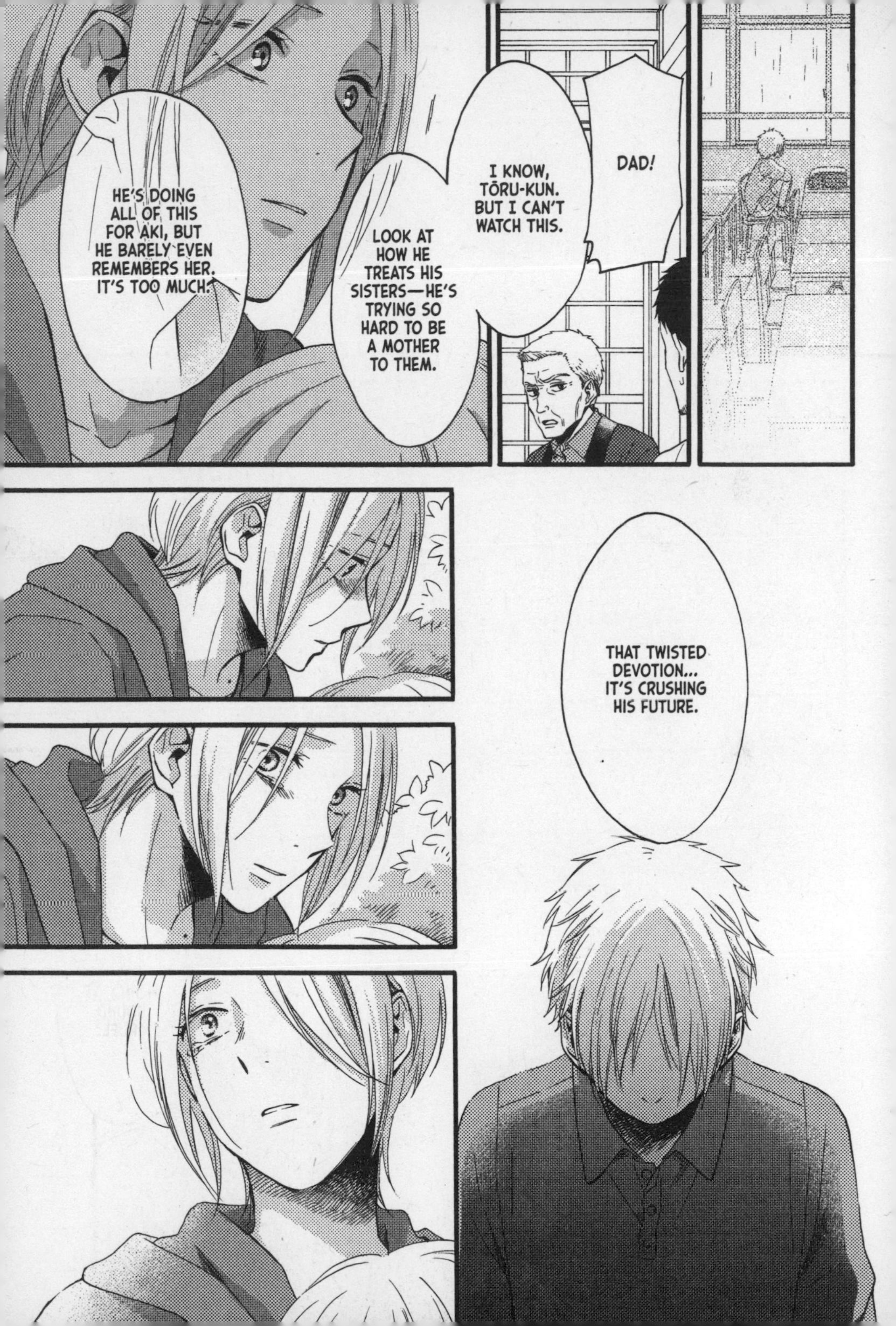
DAD!
I KNOW, TŌRU-KUN. BUT I CAN'T WATCH THIS.
LOOK AT HOW HE TREATS HIS SISTERS—HE'S TRYING SO HARD TO BE A MOTHER TO THEM.
HE'S DOING ALL OF THIS FOR AKI, BUT HE BARELY EVEN REMEMBERS HER. IT'S TOO MUCH.
THAT TWISTED DEVOTION... IT'S CRUSHING HIS FUTURE.

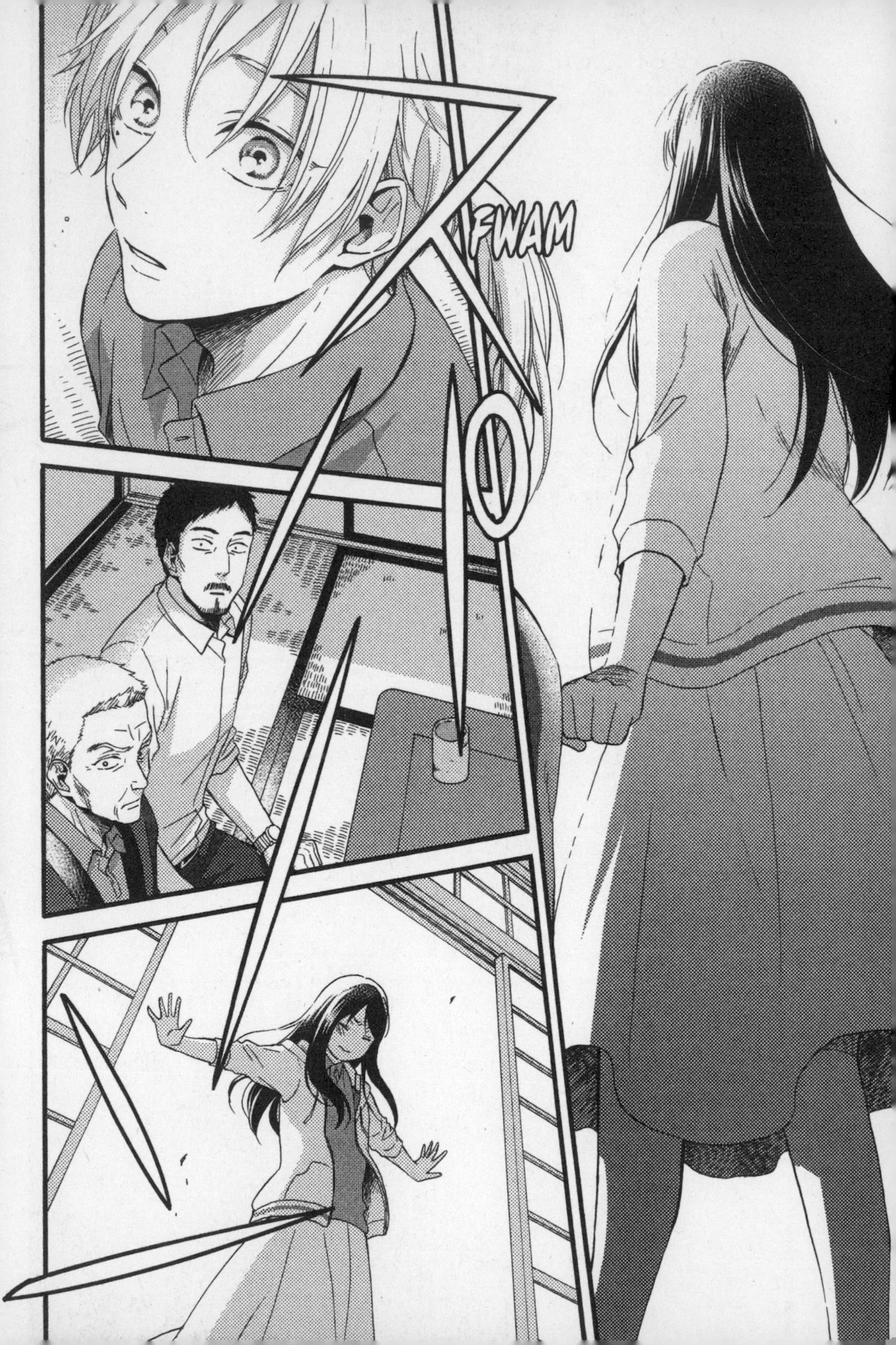
FWAM

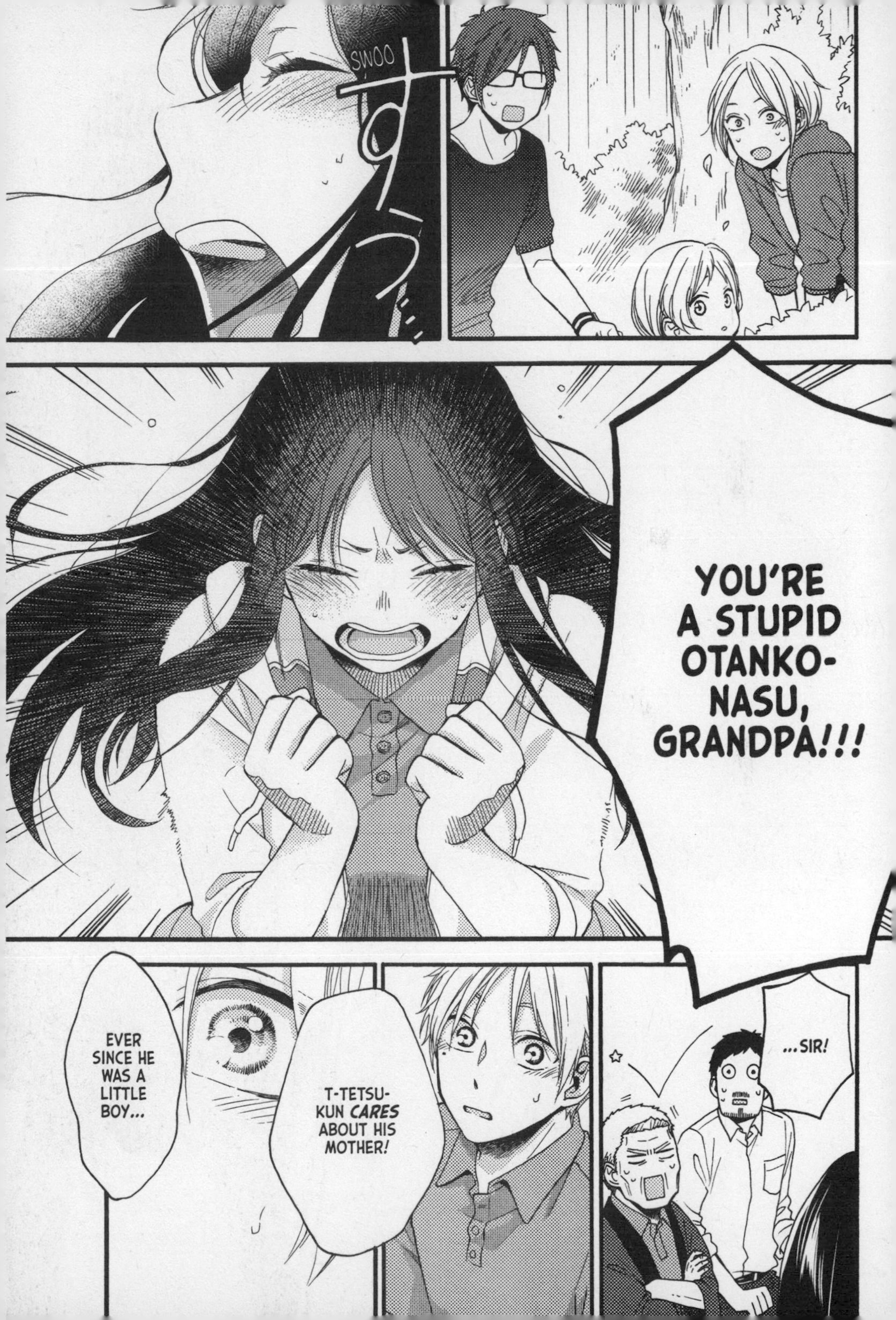
SWOO
YOU'RE A STUPID OTANKO-NASU, GRANDPA!!!
...SIR!
T-TETSU-KUN CARES ABOUT HIS MOTHER!
EVER SINCE HE WAS A LITTLE BOY...

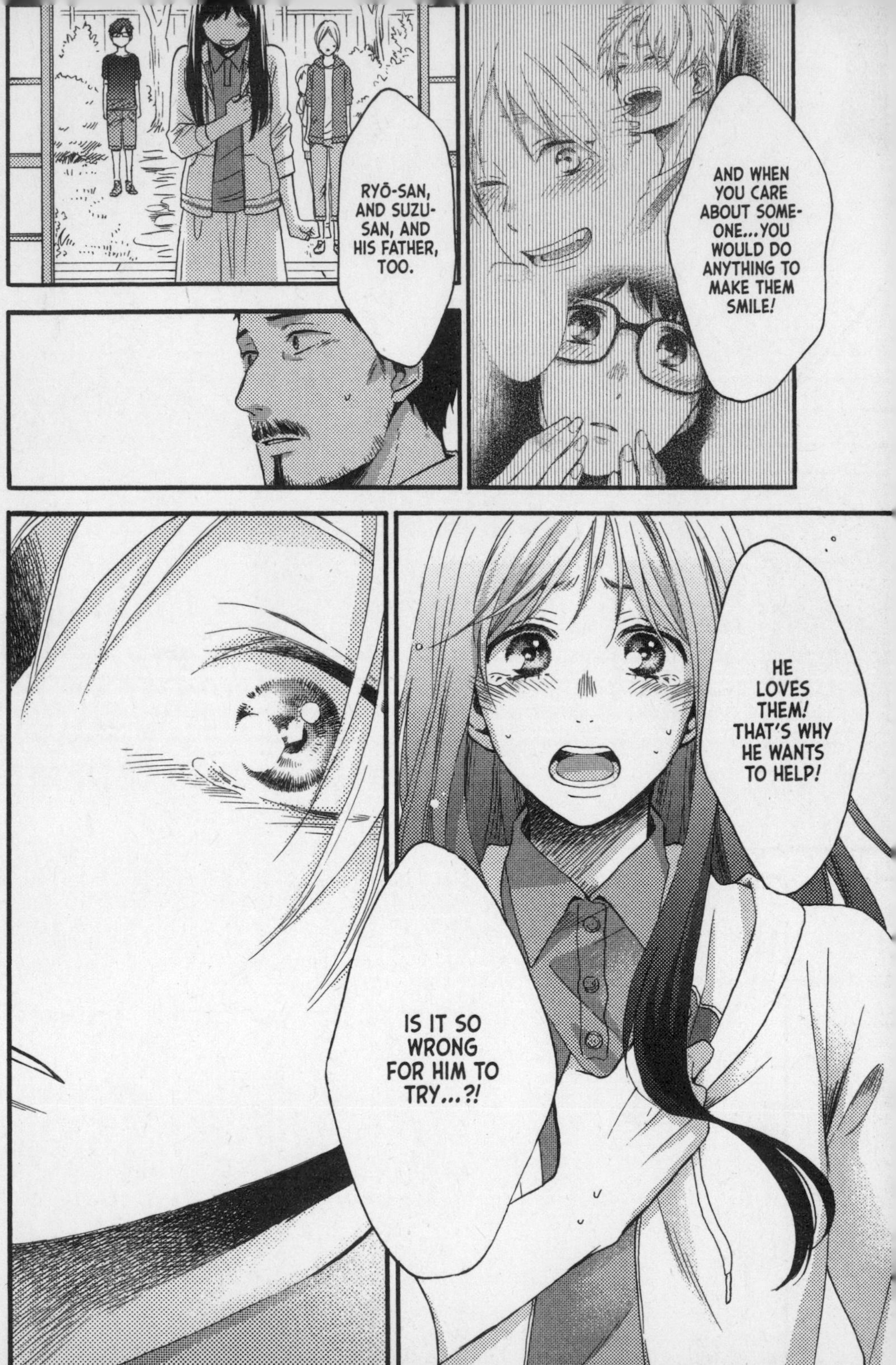
RYŌ-SAN, AND SUZU-SAN, AND HIS FATHER, TOO.
AND WHEN YOU CARE ABOUT SOME-ONE...YOU WOULD DO ANYTHING TO MAKE THEM SMILE!
HE LOVES THEM! THAT'S WHY HE WANTS TO HELP!
IS IT SO WRONG FOR HIM TO TRY...?!

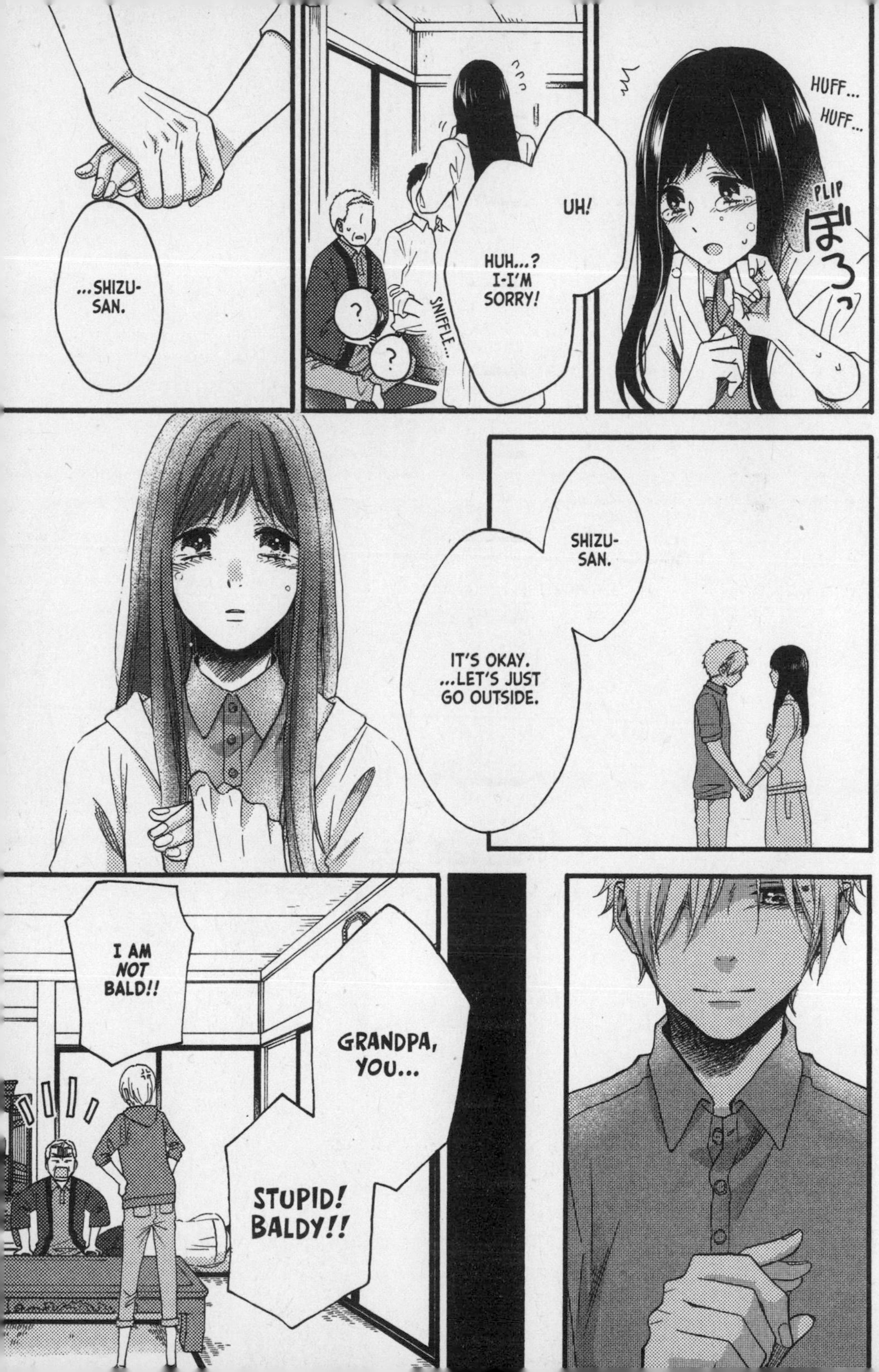
HUFF...
HUFF...
PLIP
ぼろっ
UH!
HUH...? I-I'M SORRY!
SNIFFLE...
?
?
...SHIZU-SAN.
SHIZU-SAN.
IT'S OKAY. ...LET'S JUST GO OUTSIDE.
GRANDPA, YOU...
STUPID! BALDY!!
I AM NOT BALD!!

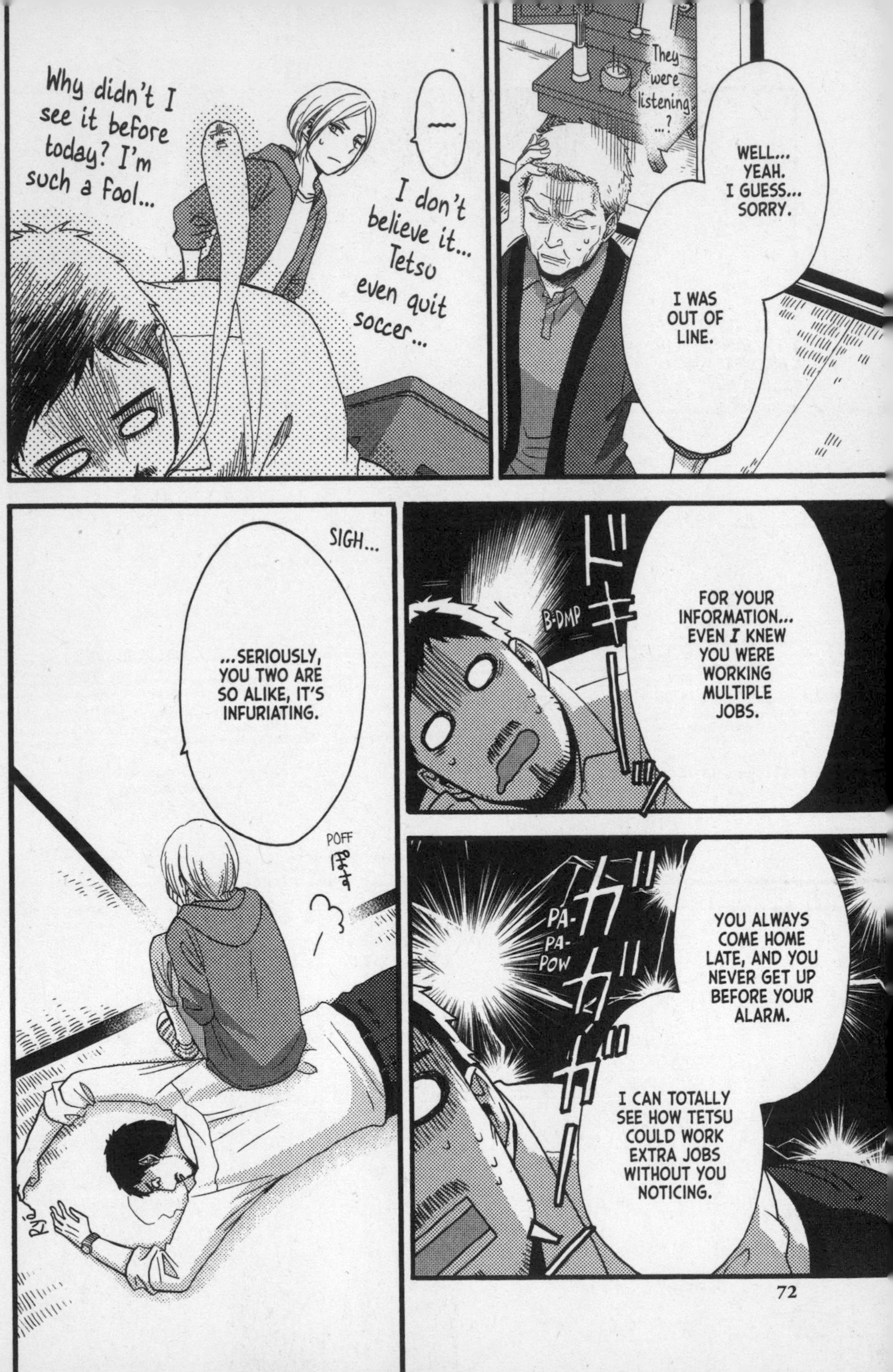
They were listening ...?
WELL... YEAH. I GUESS... SORRY.
I WAS OUT OF LINE.
I don't believe it... Tetsu even quit soccer...
Why didn't I see it before today? I'm such a fool...
B-DMP
FOR YOUR INFORMATION... EVEN I KNEW YOU WERE WORKING MULTIPLE JOBS.
PA-PA-POW
YOU ALWAYS COME HOME LATE, AND YOU NEVER GET UP BEFORE YOUR ALARM.
I CAN TOTALLY SEE HOW TETSU COULD WORK EXTRA JOBS WITHOUT YOU NOTICING.
SIGH...
...SERIOUSLY, YOU TWO ARE SO ALIKE, IT'S INFURIATING.
POFF

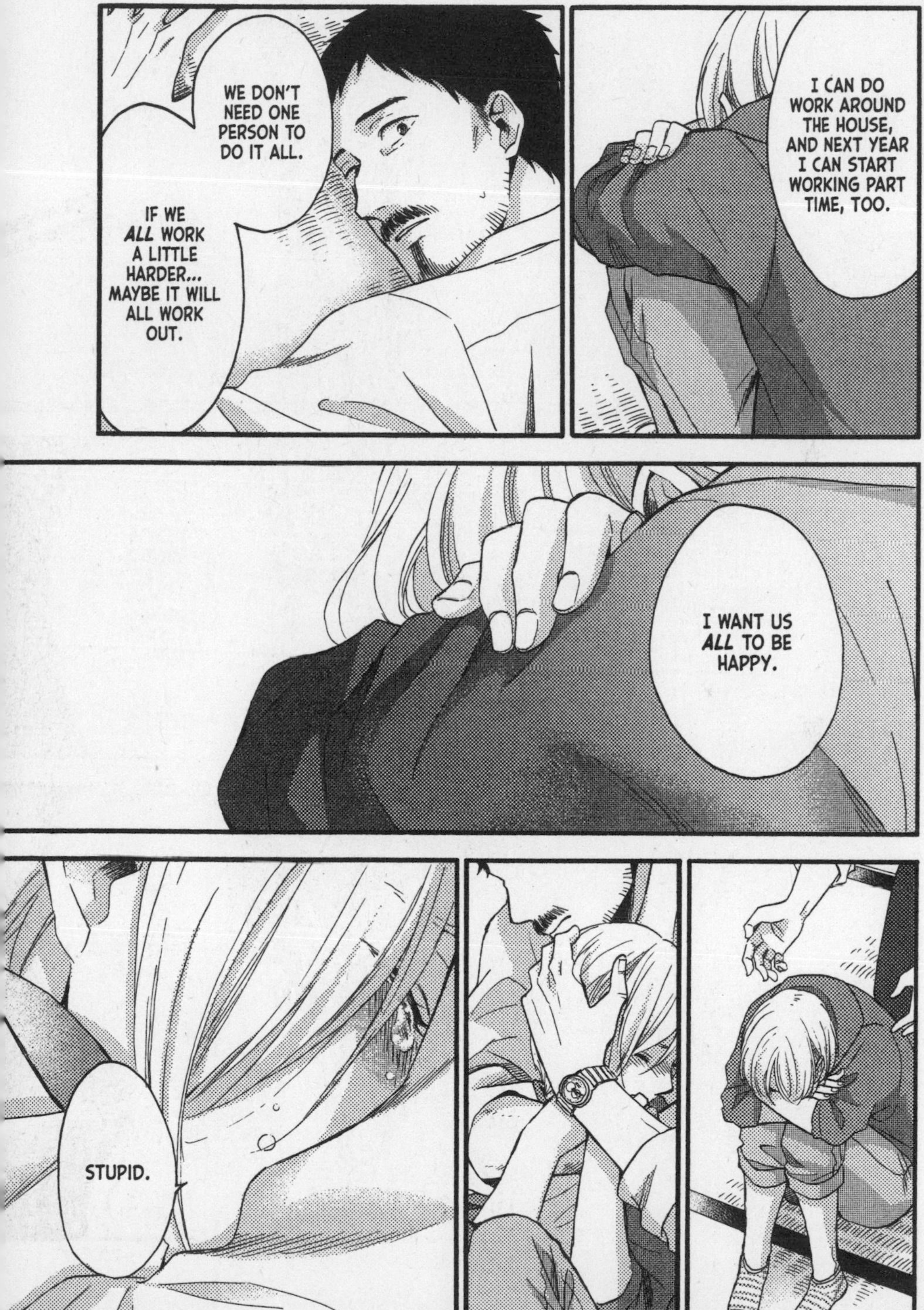
I CAN DO WORK AROUND THE HOUSE, AND NEXT YEAR I CAN START WORKING PART TIME, TOO.
WE DON'T NEED ONE PERSON TO DO IT ALL.
IF WE *ALL* WORK A LITTLE HARDER... MAYBE IT WILL ALL WORK OUT.
I WANT US *ALL* TO BE HAPPY.
STUPID.

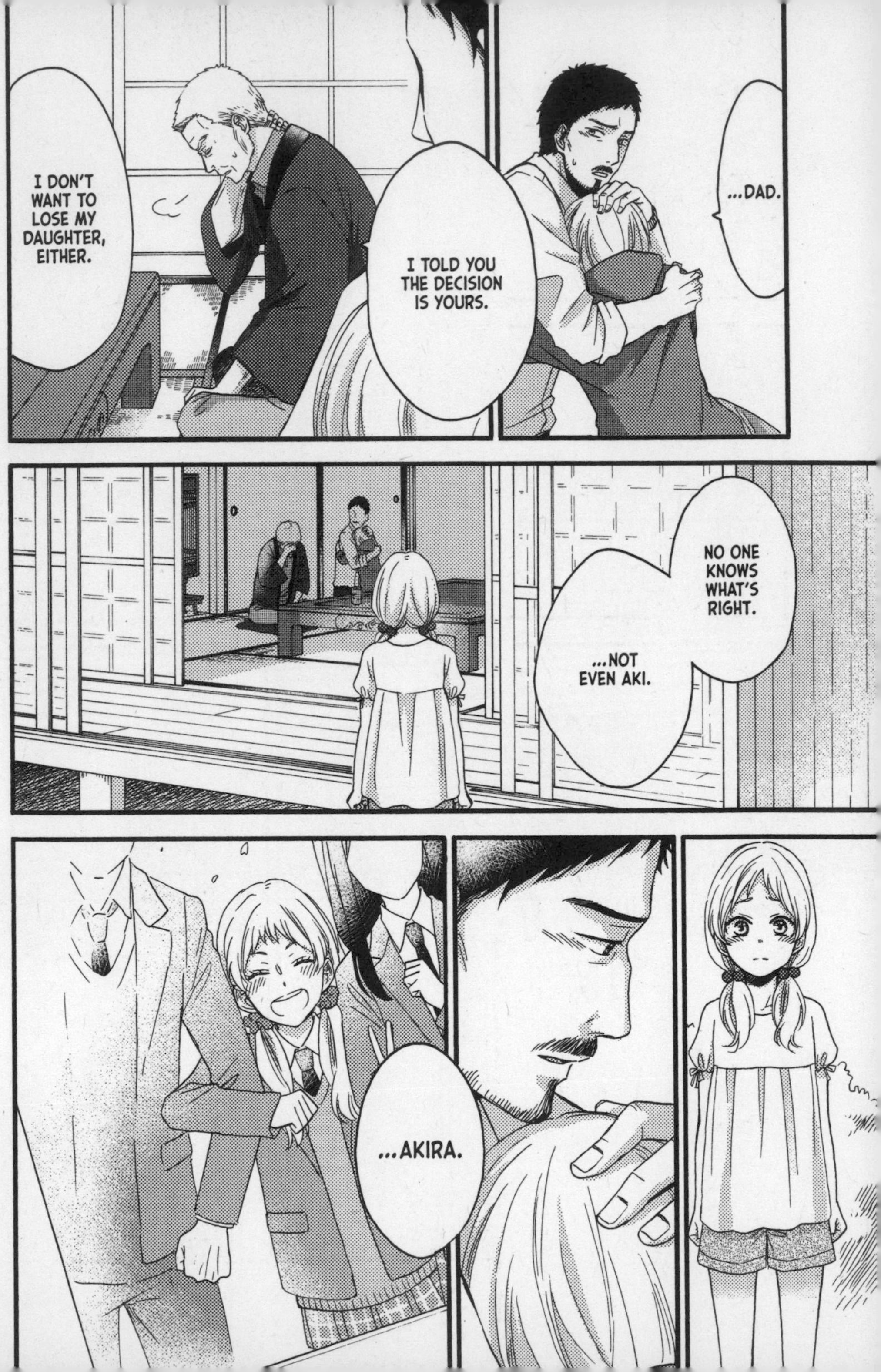
...DAD.
I TOLD YOU THE DECISION IS YOURS.
I DON'T WANT TO LOSE MY DAUGHTER, EITHER.
NO ONE KNOWS WHAT'S RIGHT.
...NOT EVEN AKI.
...AKIRA.

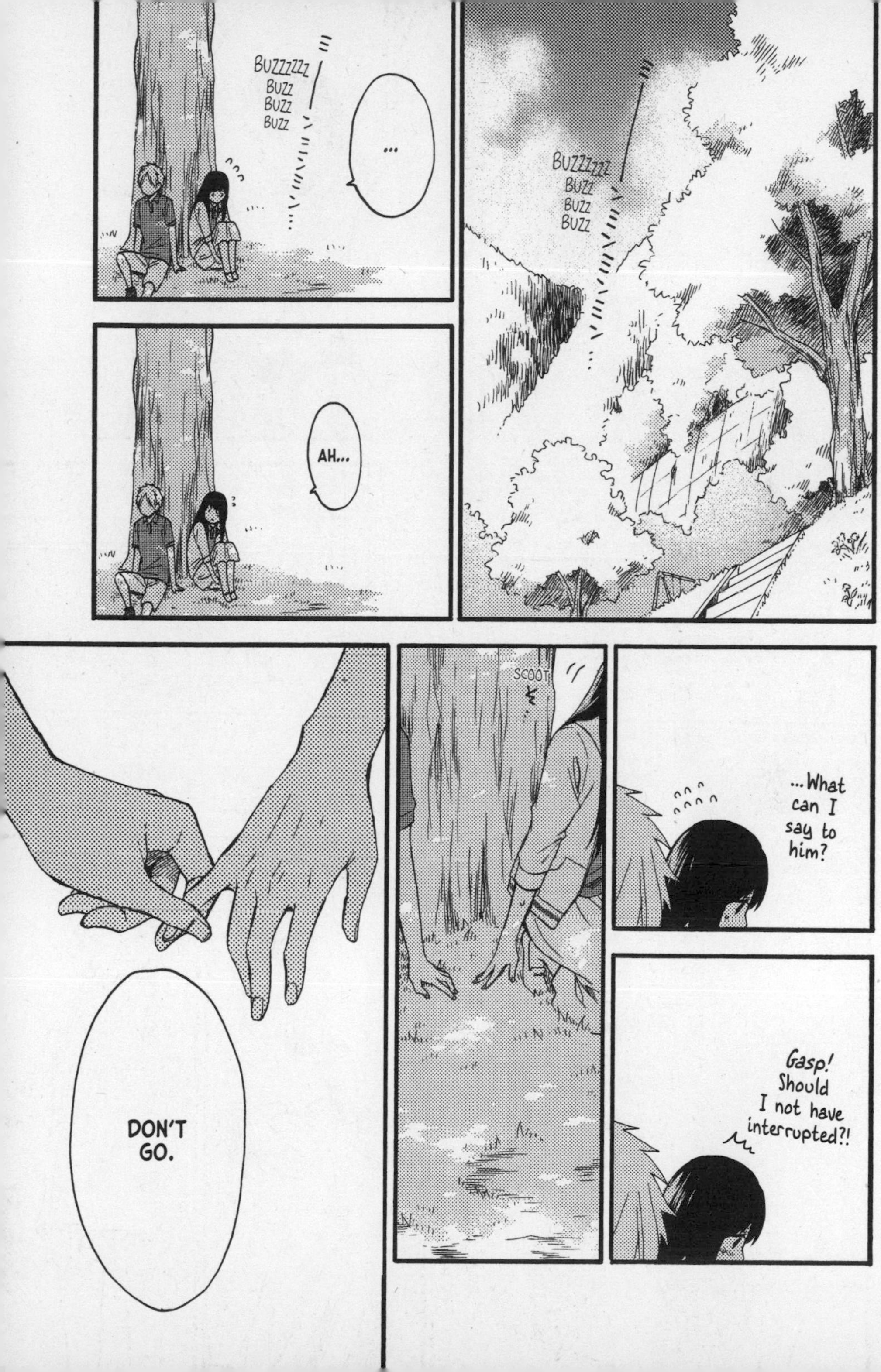
BUZZZZZZ BUZZ BUZZ BUZZ
BUZZZZZZ BUZZ BUZZ BUZZ
...
AH...
...What can I say to him?
Gasp! Should I not have interrupted?!
SCOOT
DON'T GO.

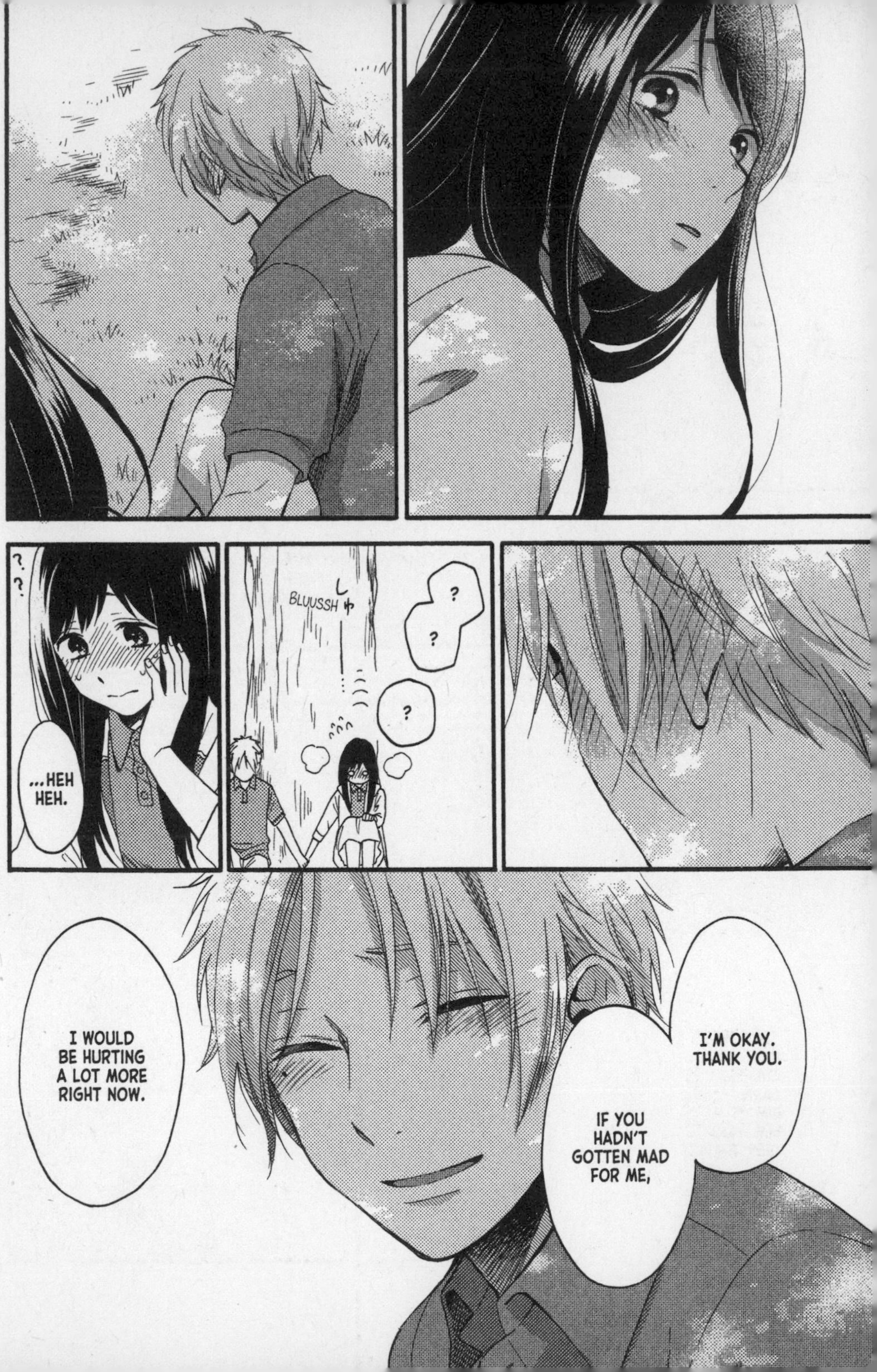
BLUUSSH
?
?
?
?
?
...HEH HEH.
I'M OKAY. THANK YOU.
IF YOU HADN'T GOTTEN MAD FOR ME,
I WOULD BE HURTING A LOT MORE RIGHT NOW.

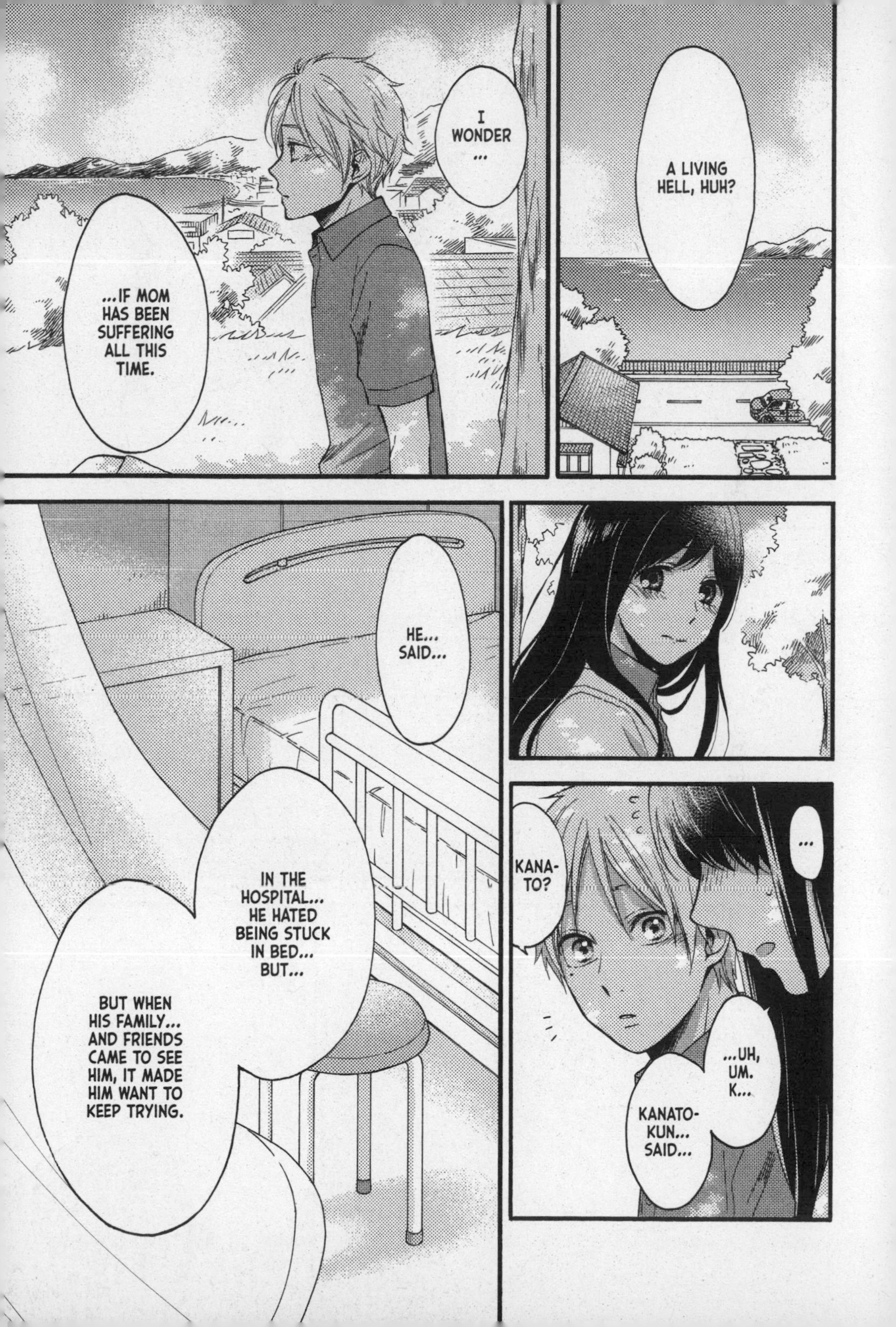
A LIVING HELL, HUH?
I WONDER ...
...IF MOM HAS BEEN SUFFERING ALL THIS TIME.
...
KANATO?
...UH, UM. K...
KANATO-KUN... SAID...
HE... SAID...
IN THE HOSPITAL... HE HATED BEING STUCK IN BED... BUT...
BUT WHEN HIS FAMILY... AND FRIENDS CAME TO SEE HIM, IT MADE HIM WANT TO KEEP TRYING.

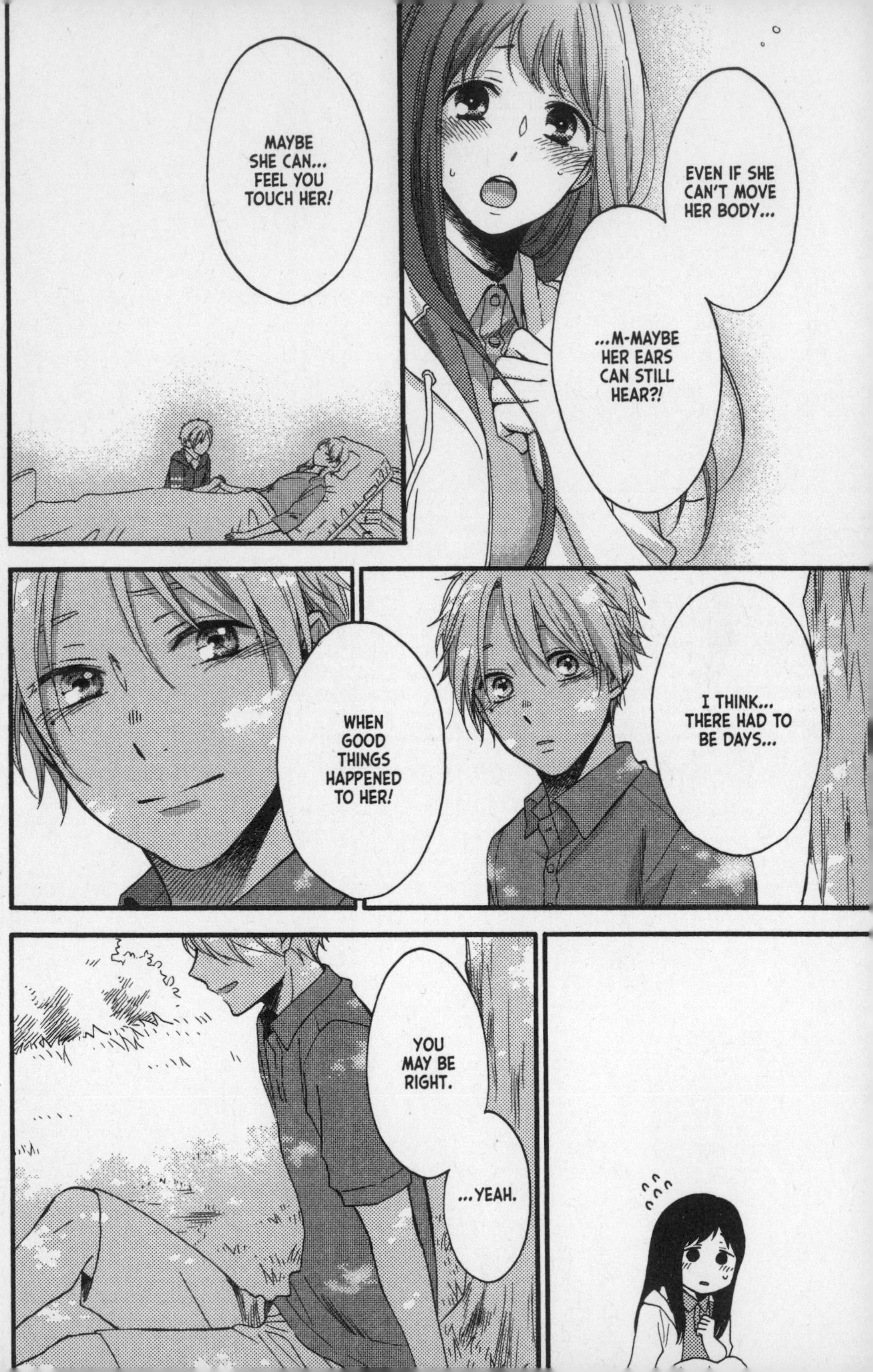
EVEN IF SHE CAN'T MOVE HER BODY...
...M-MAYBE HER EARS CAN STILL HEAR?!
MAYBE SHE CAN... FEEL YOU TOUCH HER!
I THINK... THERE HAD TO BE DAYS...
WHEN GOOD THINGS HAPPENED TO HER!
YOU MAY BE RIGHT.
...YEAH.

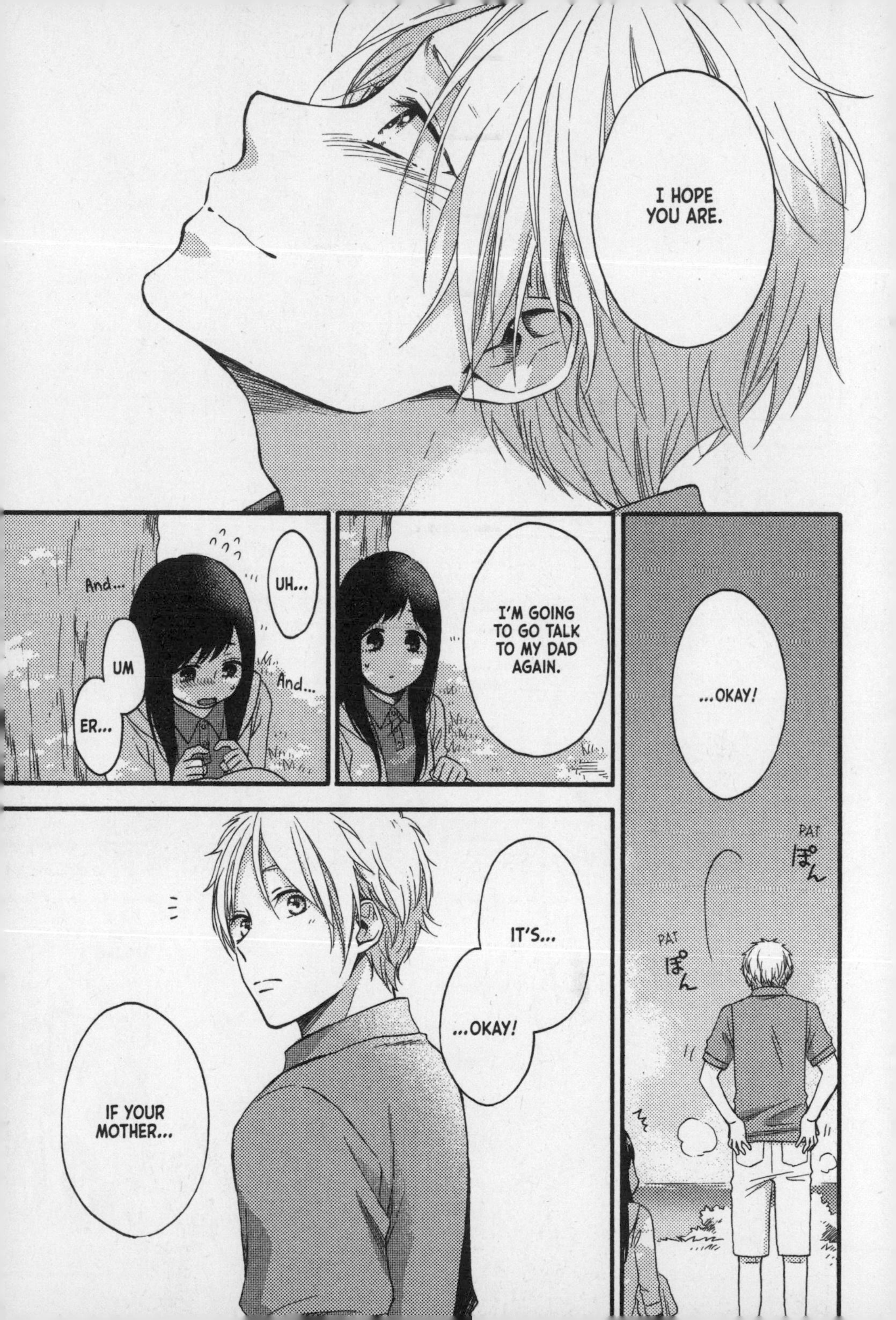
I HOPE YOU ARE.
I'M GOING TO GO TALK TO MY DAD AGAIN.
UH...
And...
UM
And...
ER...
IT'S...
...OKAY!
IF YOUR MOTHER...
...OKAY!
PAT
ぽん
PAT
ぽん

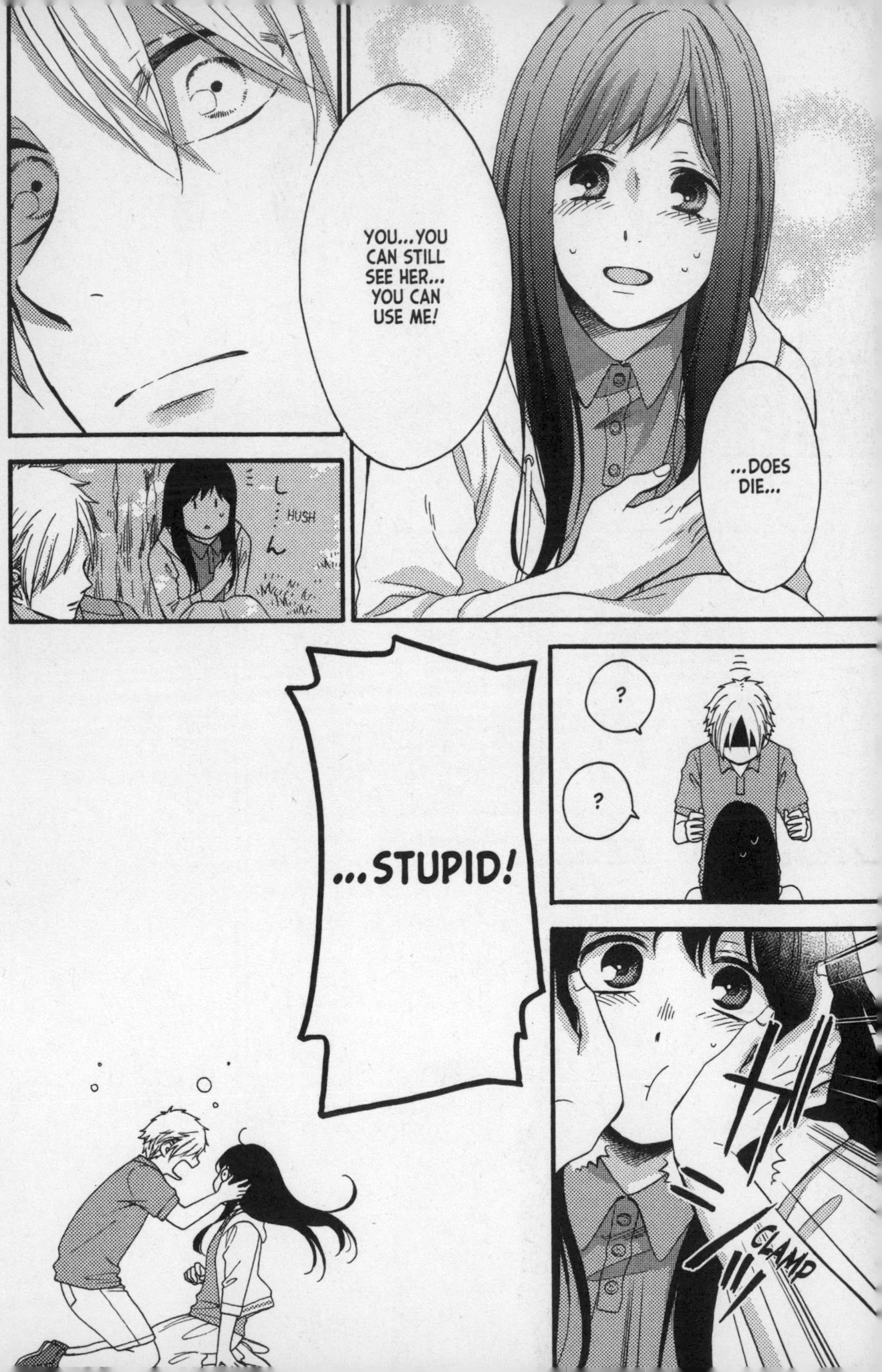
...DOES DIE...
YOU...YOU CAN STILL SEE HER... YOU CAN USE ME!
HUSH
?
?
CLAMP
...STUPID!

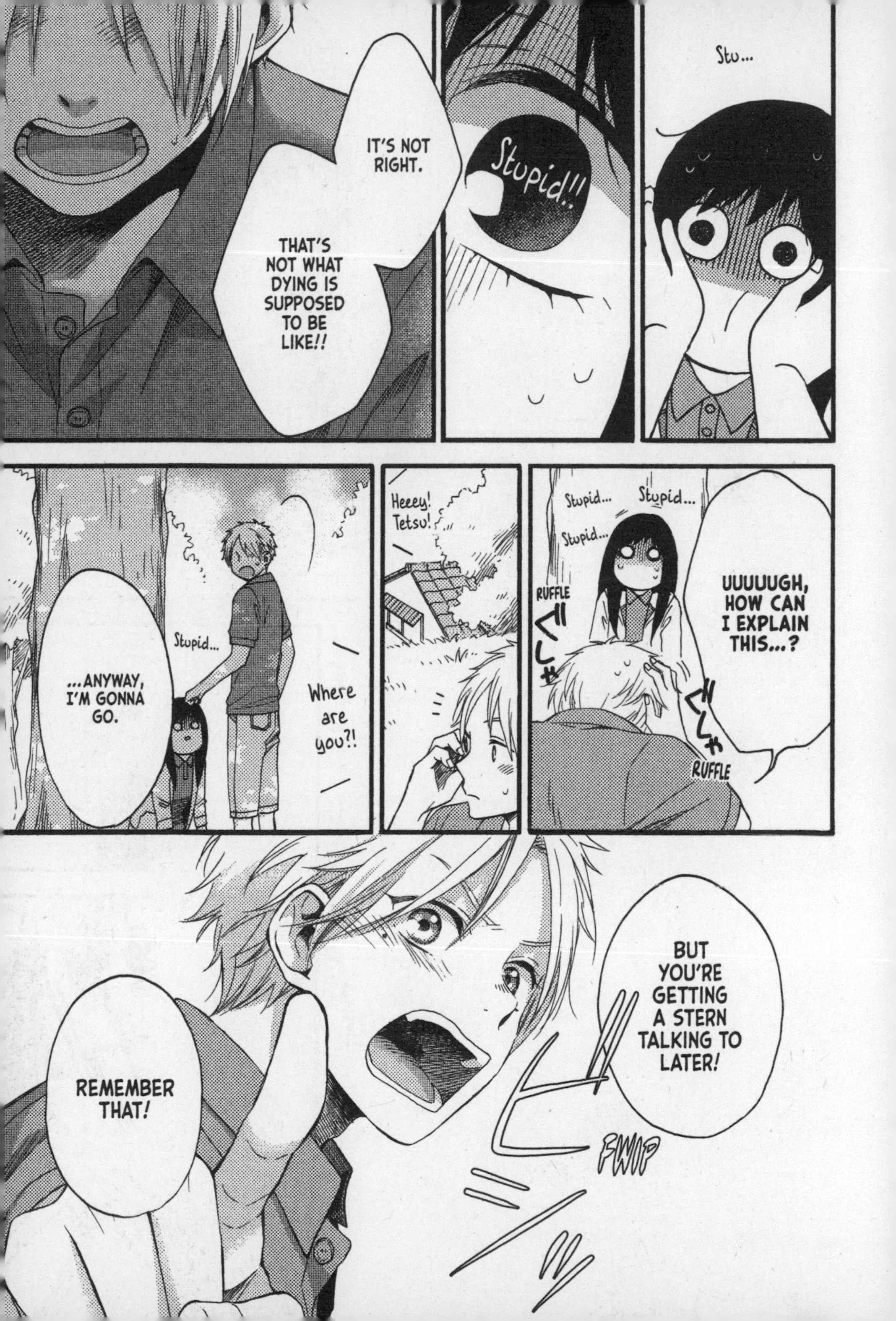
Stu...
Stupid!!
IT'S NOT RIGHT.
THAT'S NOT WHAT DYING IS SUPPOSED TO BE LIKE!!
UUUUUGH, HOW CAN I EXPLAIN THIS...?
Stupid...
Stupid...
Stupid...
RUFFLE
RUFFLE
Heeey! Tetsu!
Where are you?!
Stupid...
...ANYWAY, I'M GONNA GO.
BUT YOU'RE GETTING A STERN TALKING TO LATER!
FWIP
REMEMBER THAT!

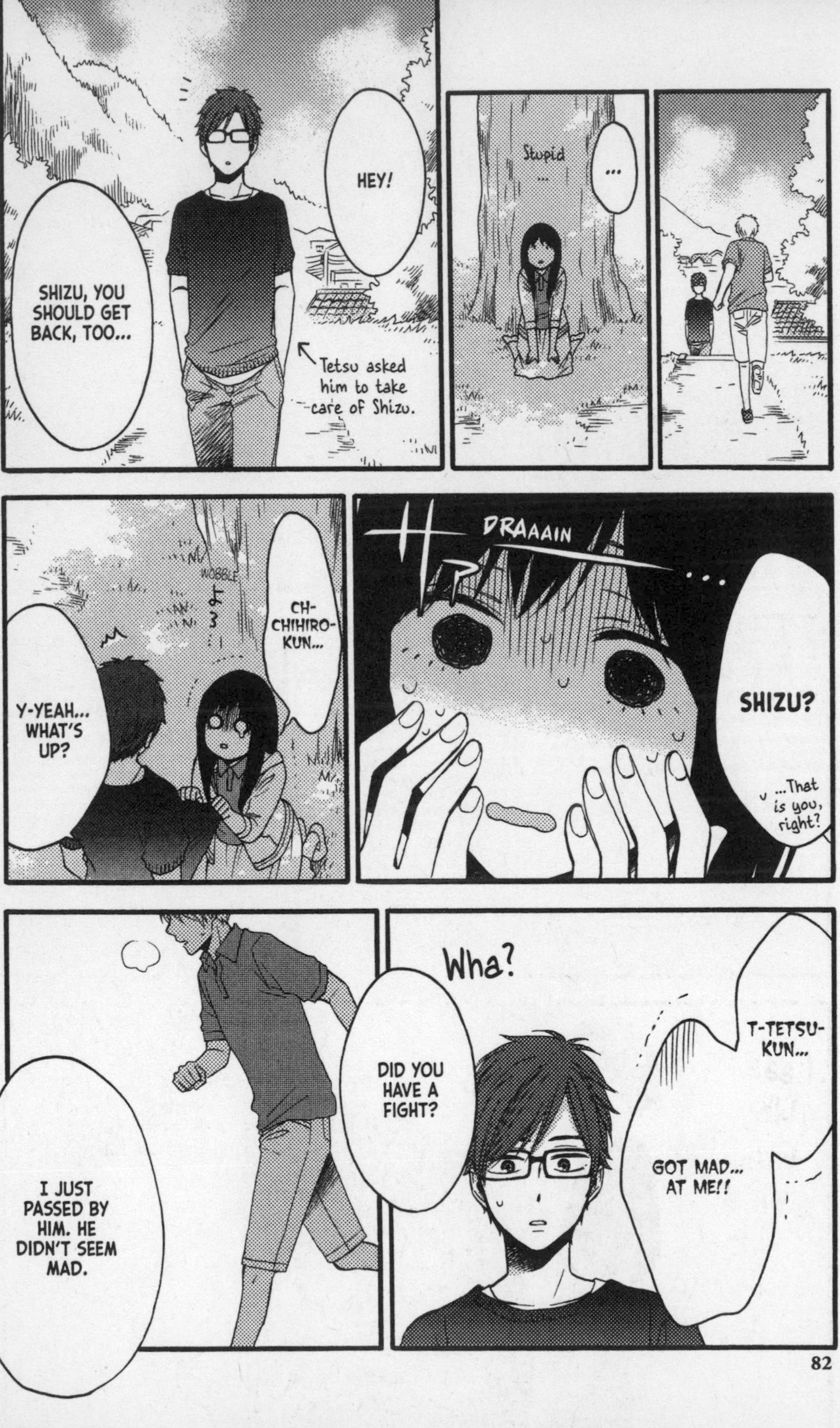
...
Stupid...
HEY!
SHIZU, YOU SHOULD GET BACK, TOO...
Tetsu asked him to take care of Shizu.
DRAAAIN
...
SHIZU?
...That is you, right?
CH-CHIHIRO-KUN...
WOBBLE
Y-YEAH... WHAT'S UP?
T-TETSU-KUN...
GOT MAD... AT ME!!
Wha?
DID YOU HAVE A FIGHT?
I JUST PASSED BY HIM. HE DIDN'T SEEM MAD.

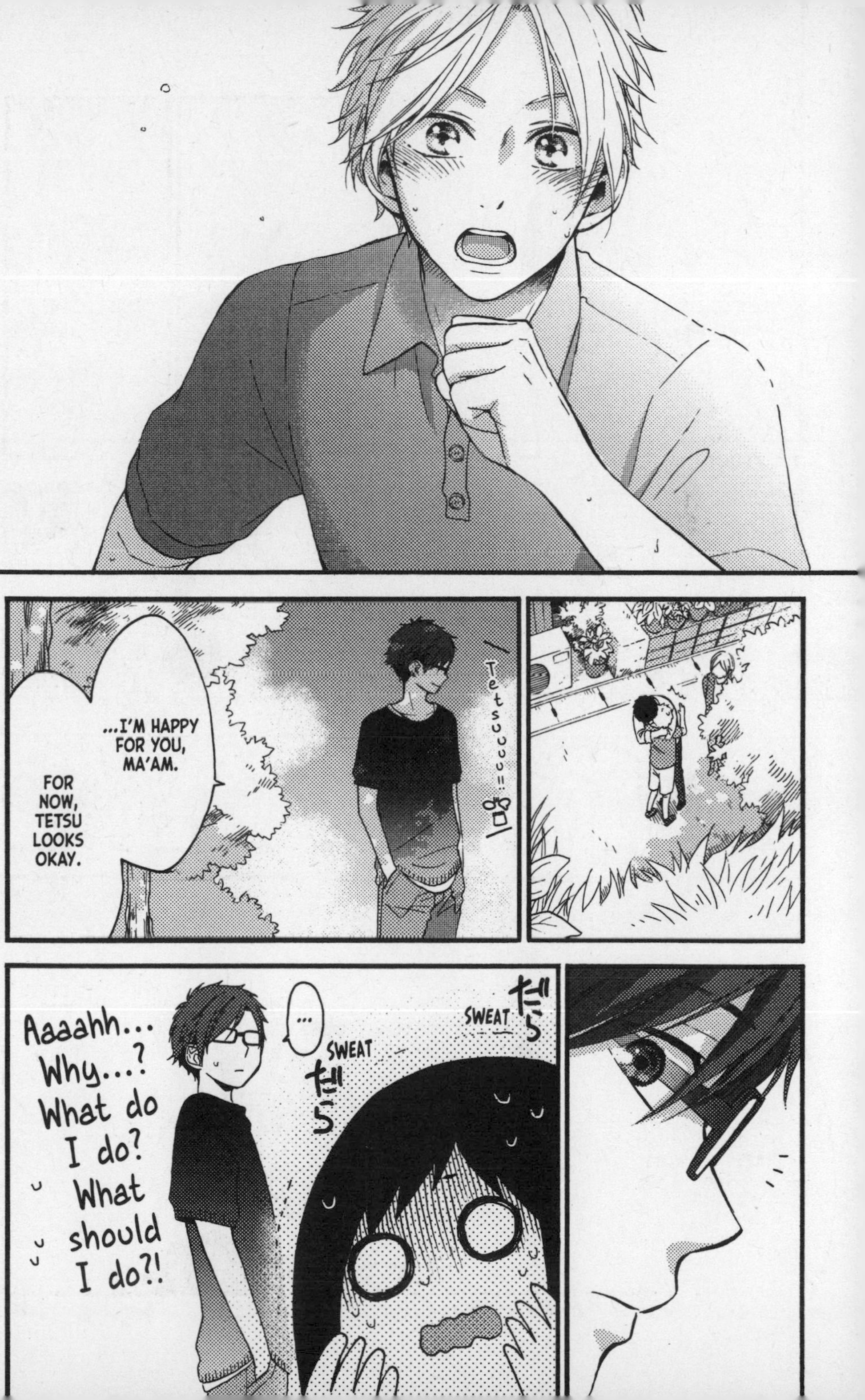

Tetsuuuu!!
...I'M HAPPY FOR YOU, MA'AM.
FOR NOW, TETSU LOOKS OKAY.
SWEAT
だら
SWEAT
だら
...
Aaaahh... Why...? What do I do? What should I do?!

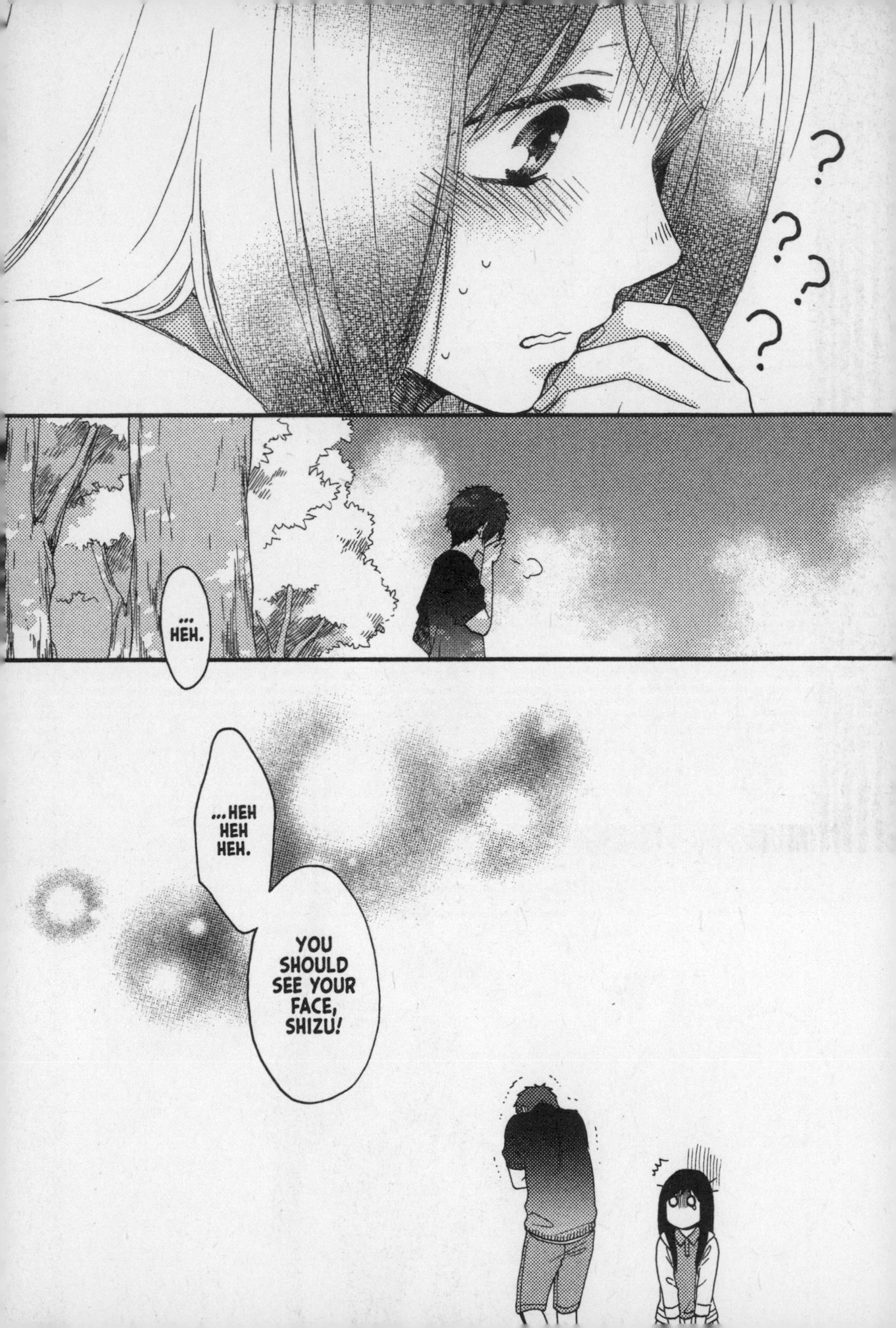
...HEH.
...HEH HEH HEH.
YOU SHOULD SEE YOUR FACE, SHIZU!

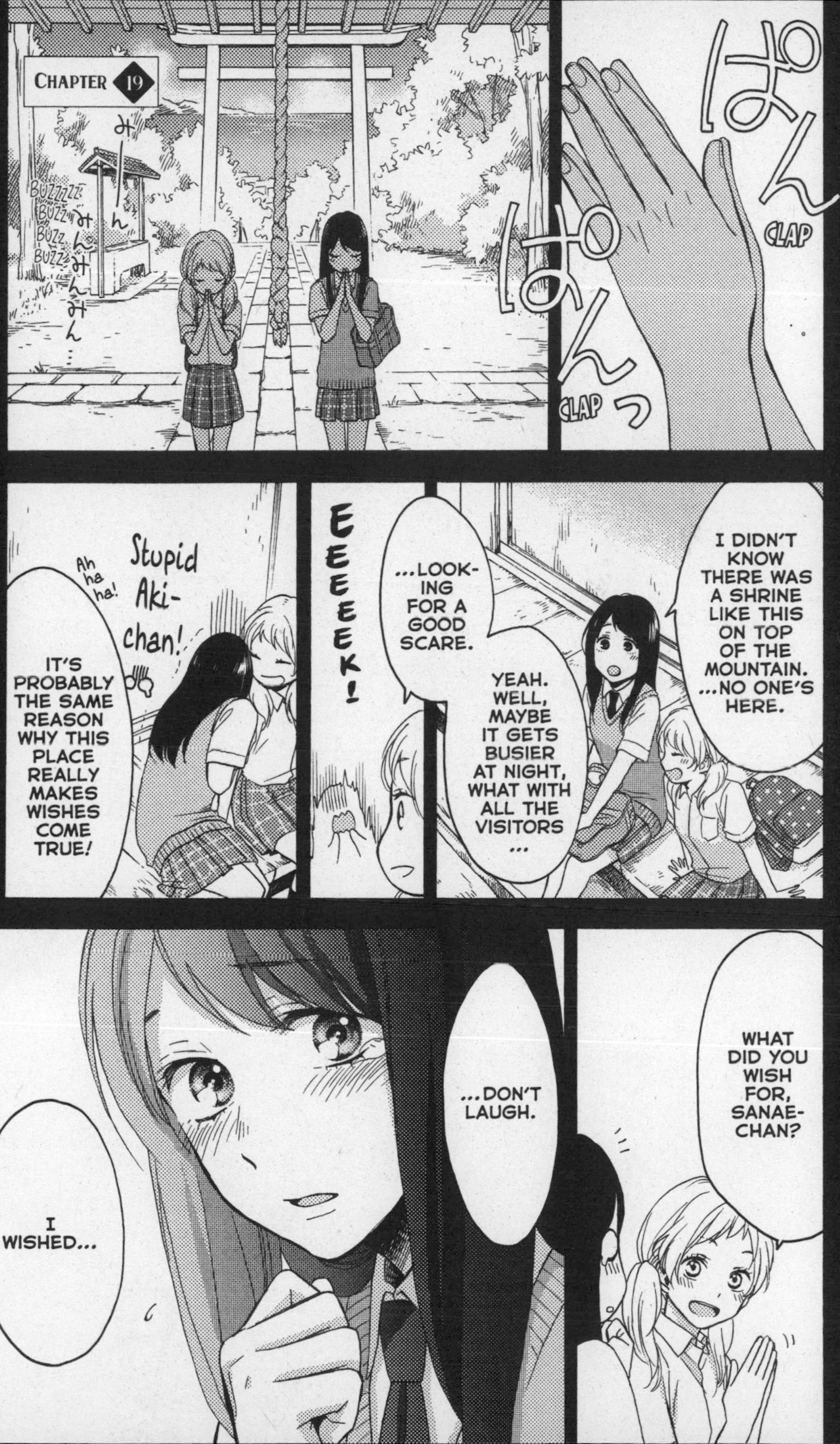
ぱん
CLAP
ぱんっ
CLAP
CHAPTER 19
みーんみんみんみん…
BUZZZZZ BUZZ BUZZ BUZZ
I DIDN'T KNOW THERE WAS A SHRINE LIKE THIS ON TOP OF THE MOUNTAIN. ...NO ONE'S HERE.
YEAH. WELL, MAYBE IT GETS BUSIER AT NIGHT, WHAT WITH ALL THE VISITORS ...
...LOOKING FOR A GOOD SCARE.
EEEEEK!
Stupid Aki-chan!
Ah ha ha!
IT'S PROBABLY THE SAME REASON WHY THIS PLACE REALLY MAKES WISHES COME TRUE!
WHAT DID YOU WISH FOR, SANAE-CHAN?
...DON'T LAUGH.
I WISHED...

Chapter 19

Two Mothers

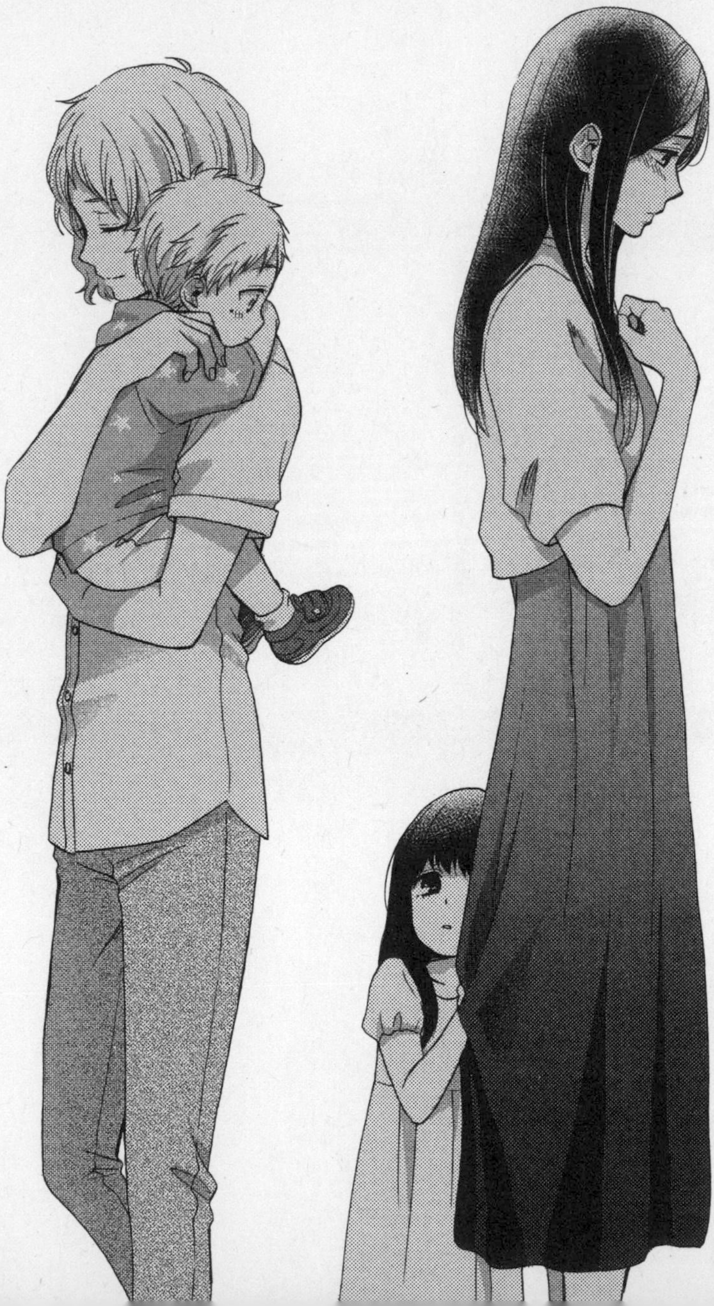

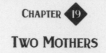

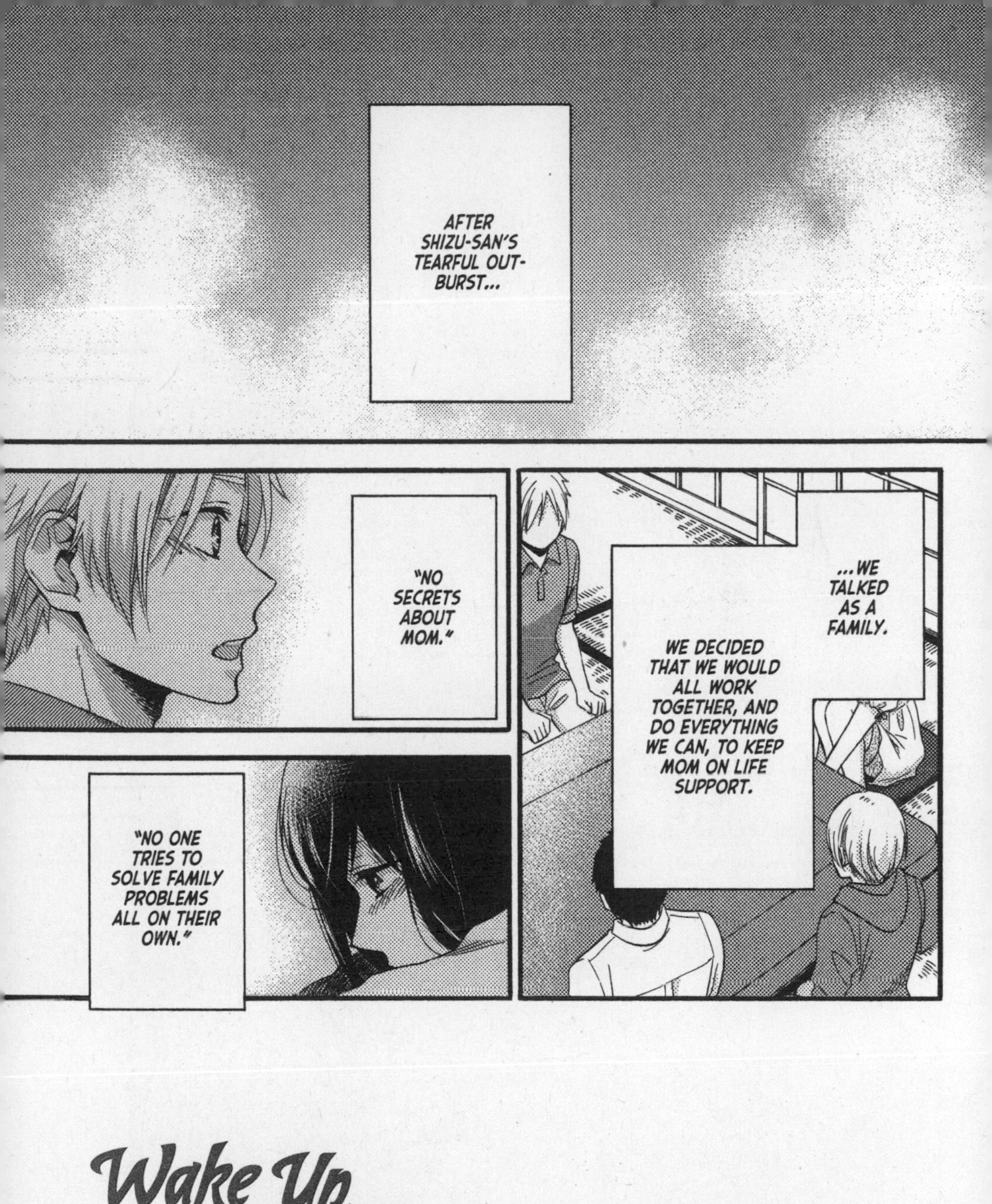
AFTER SHIZU-SAN'S TEARFUL OUT-BURST...
...WE TALKED AS A FAMILY.
WE DECIDED THAT WE WOULD ALL WORK TOGETHER, AND DO EVERYTHING WE CAN, TO KEEP MOM ON LIFE SUPPORT.
"NO SECRETS ABOUT MOM."
"NO ONE TRIES TO SOLVE FAMILY PROBLEMS ALL ON THEIR OWN."

Wake Up, Sleeping Beauty

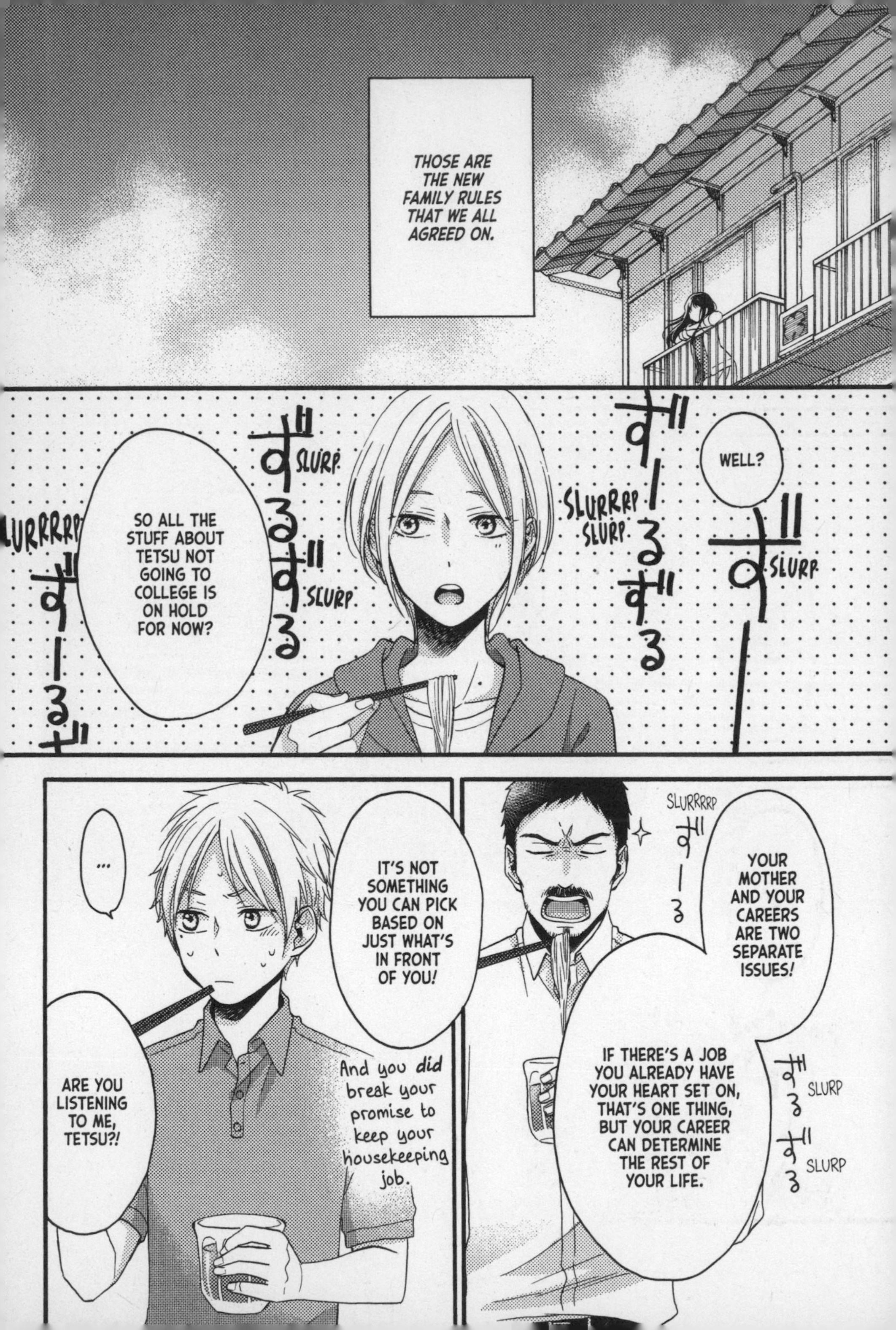

THOSE ARE THE NEW FAMILY RULES THAT WE ALL AGREED ON.
WELL?
SLURP
SLURRRP SLURP
SLURP
SLURP
SO ALL THE STUFF ABOUT TETSU NOT GOING TO COLLEGE IS ON HOLD FOR NOW?
SLURRRP
SLURRRP
YOUR MOTHER AND YOUR CAREERS ARE TWO SEPARATE ISSUES!
IF THERE'S A JOB YOU ALREADY HAVE YOUR HEART SET ON, THAT'S ONE THING, BUT YOUR CAREER CAN DETERMINE THE REST OF YOUR LIFE.
SLURP
SLURP
IT'S NOT SOMETHING YOU CAN PICK BASED ON JUST WHAT'S IN FRONT OF YOU!
...
And you did break your promise to keep your housekeeping job.
ARE YOU LISTENING TO ME, TETSU?!

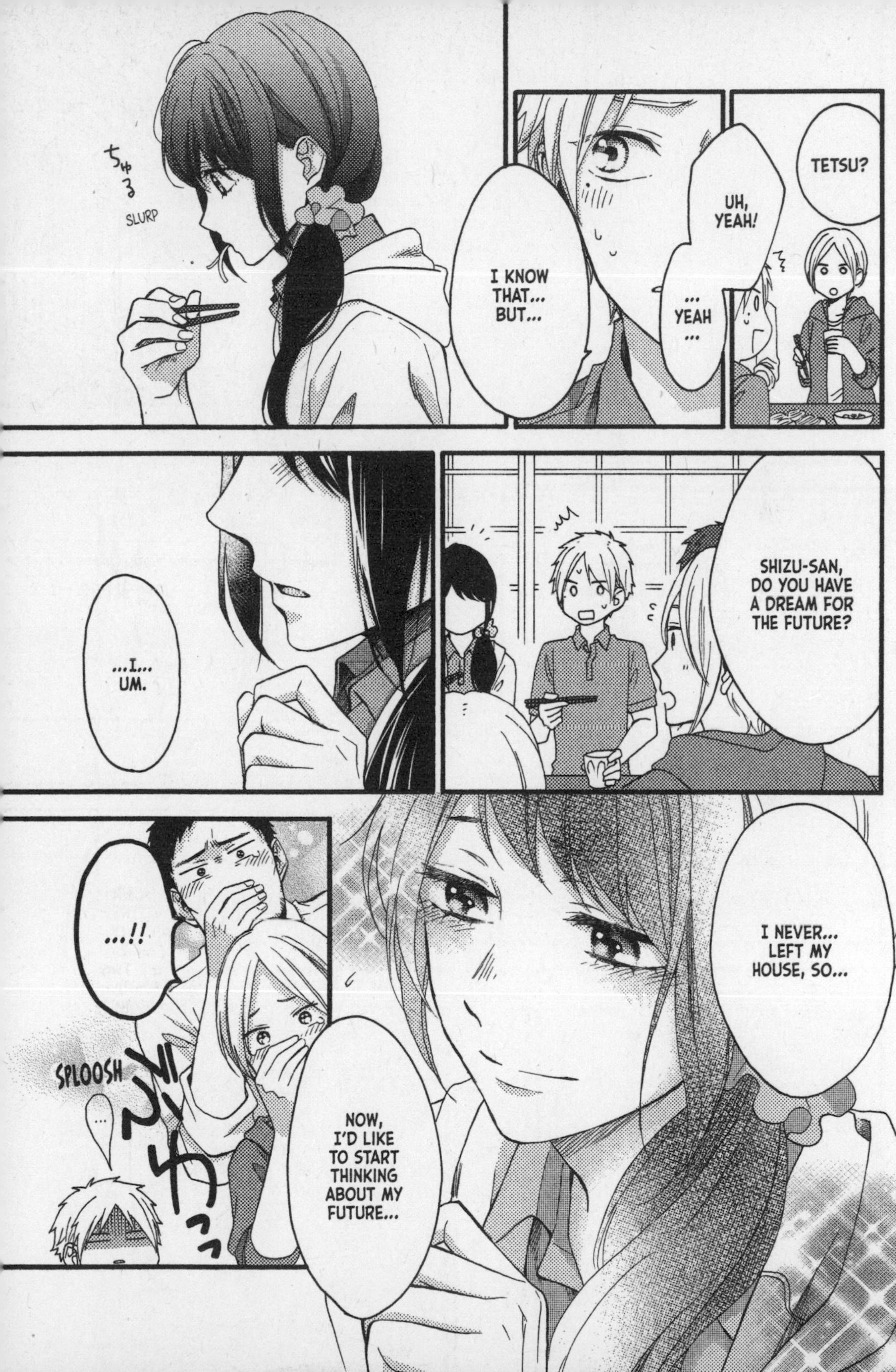
TETSU?
UH, YEAH!
... YEAH ...
I KNOW THAT... BUT...
ちゅる
SLURP
SHIZU-SAN, DO YOU HAVE A DREAM FOR THE FUTURE?
...I... UM.
I NEVER... LEFT MY HOUSE, SO...
NOW, I'D LIKE TO START THINKING ABOUT MY FUTURE...
...!!
SPLOOSH
...

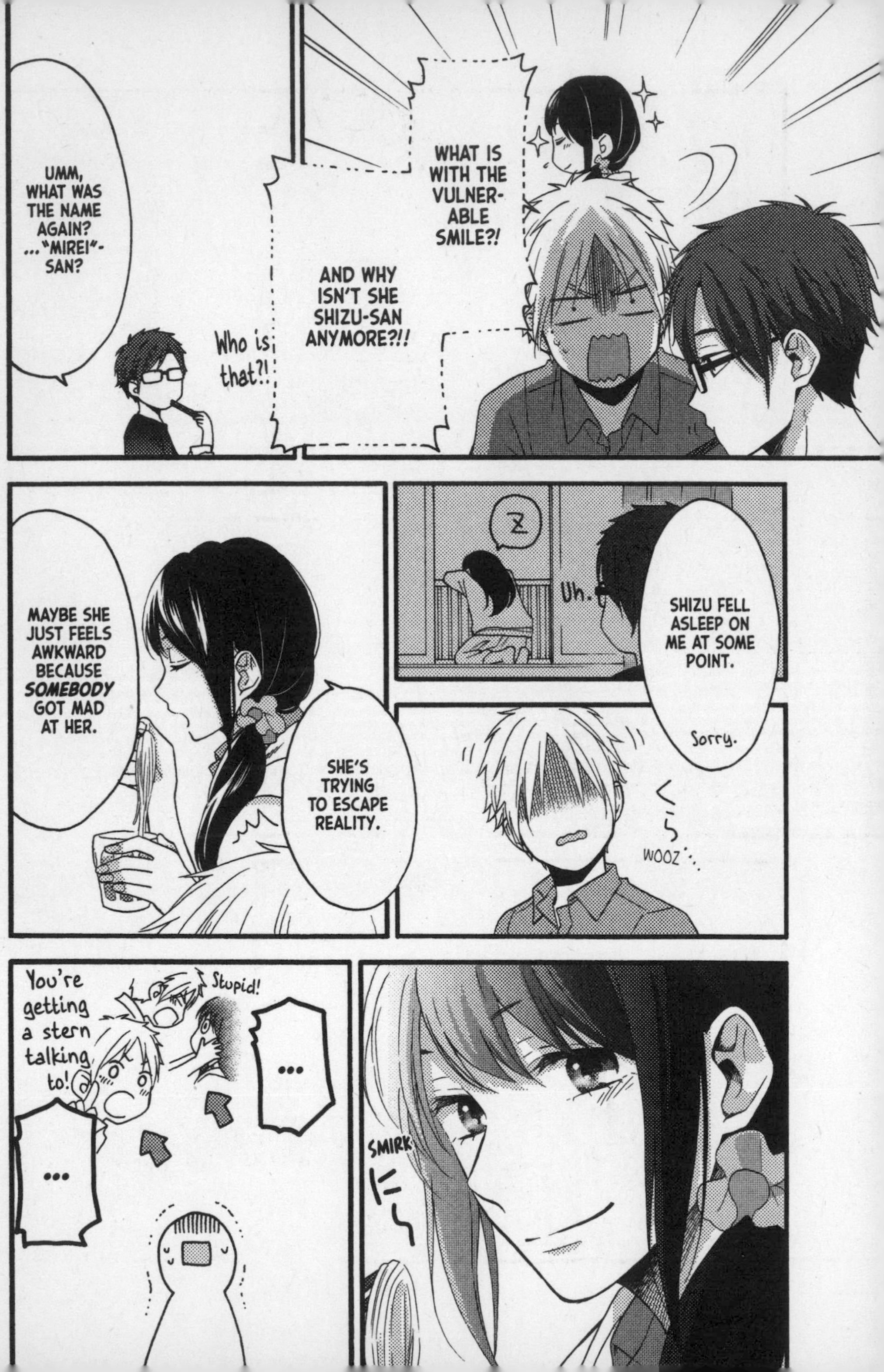
WHAT IS WITH THE VULNER-ABLE SMILE?!
AND WHY ISN'T SHE SHIZU-SAN ANYMORE?!!
UMM, WHAT WAS THE NAME AGAIN? ..."MIREI"-SAN?
Who is that?!
Uh.
SHIZU FELL ASLEEP ON ME AT SOME POINT.
Sorry.
WOOZ
SHE'S TRYING TO ESCAPE REALITY.
MAYBE SHE JUST FEELS AWKWARD BECAUSE SOMEBODY GOT MAD AT HER.
SMIRK
...
Stupid!
You're getting a stern talking to!
...

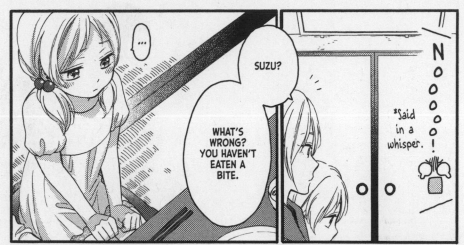

NOOOOO!
O O
*Said in a whisper.
SUZU?
WHAT'S WRONG? YOU HAVEN'T EATEN A BITE.
...
Are you feeling okay?
GOING TO THE BEACH TO PICK UP GUYS IS OUT OF THE QUESTION!
YOU BETTER NOT DO ANYTHING UNCALLED-FOR! I MEAN IT!
Yes, mommy.

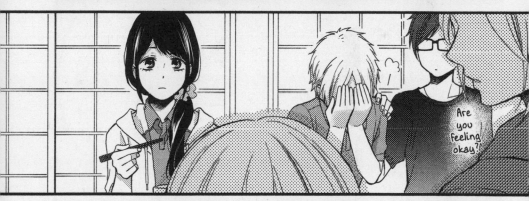

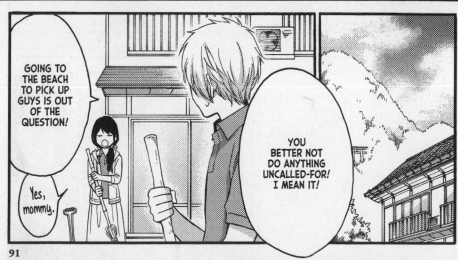

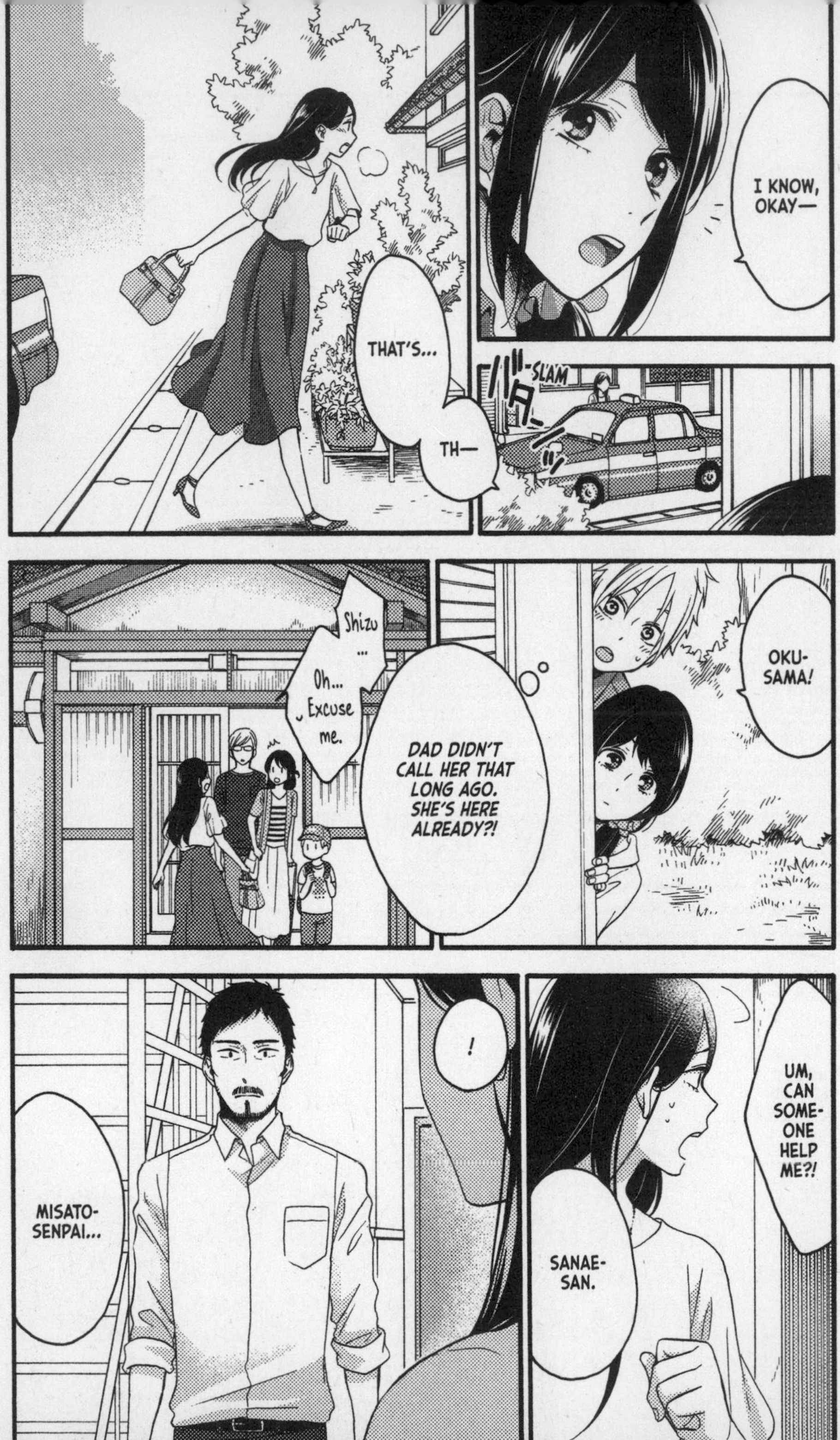
I KNOW, OKAY—
SLAM
THAT'S...
TH—
OKU-SAMA!
DAD DIDN'T CALL HER THAT LONG AGO. SHE'S HERE ALREADY?!
Shizu...
Oh... Excuse me.
UM, CAN SOMEONE HELP ME?!
SANAE-SAN.
!
MISATO-SENPAI...

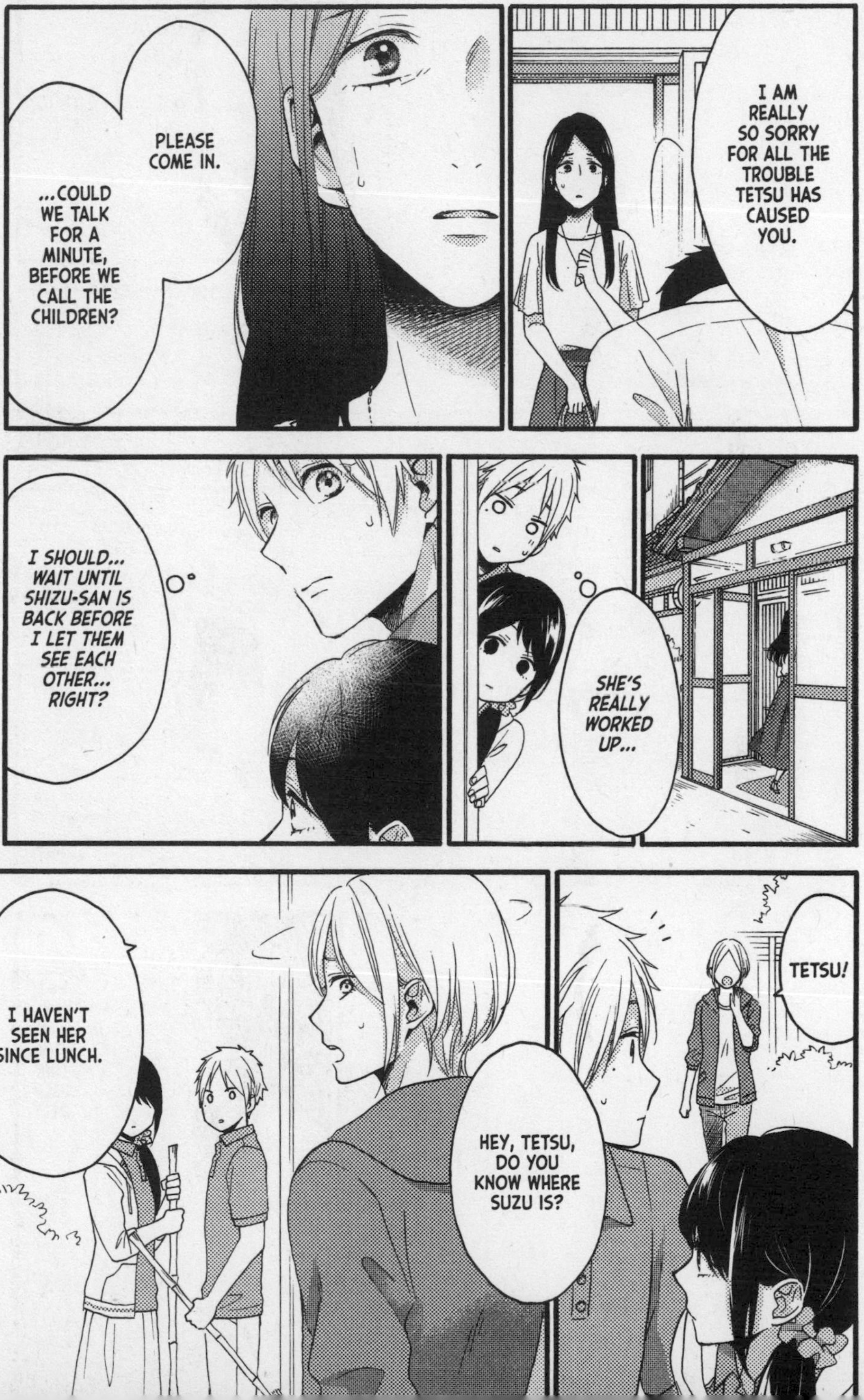
I AM REALLY SO SORRY FOR ALL THE TROUBLE TETSU HAS CAUSED YOU.
PLEASE COME IN.
...COULD WE TALK FOR A MINUTE, BEFORE WE CALL THE CHILDREN?
SHE'S REALLY WORKED UP...
I SHOULD... WAIT UNTIL SHIZU-SAN IS BACK BEFORE I LET THEM SEE EACH OTHER... RIGHT?
TETSU!
HEY, TETSU, DO YOU KNOW WHERE SUZU IS?
I HAVEN'T SEEN HER SINCE LUNCH.

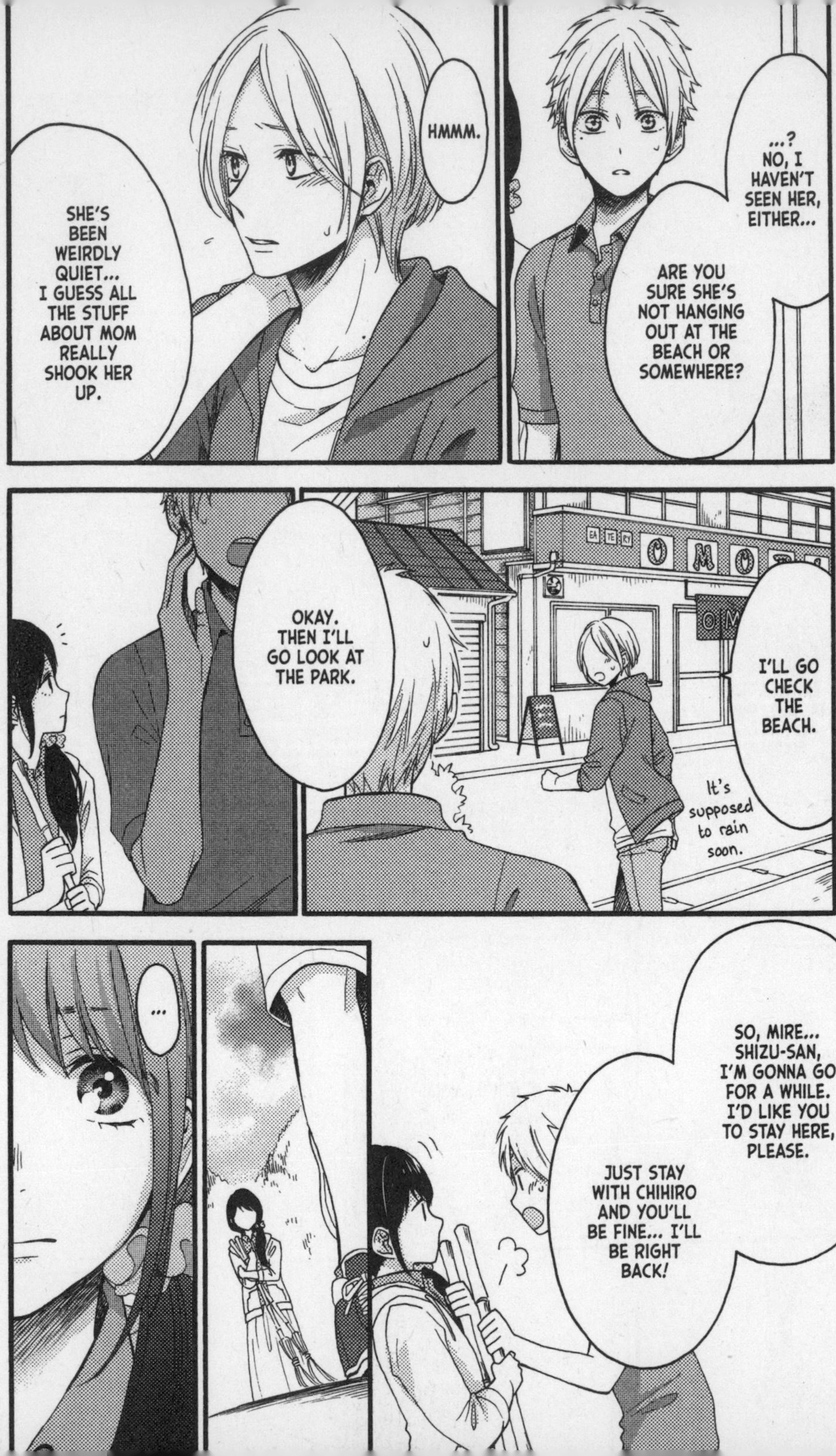
...? NO, I HAVEN'T SEEN HER, EITHER...
ARE YOU SURE SHE'S NOT HANGING OUT AT THE BEACH OR SOMEWHERE?
HMMM.
SHE'S BEEN WEIRDLY QUIET... I GUESS ALL THE STUFF ABOUT MOM REALLY SHOOK HER UP.
EATERY
I'LL GO CHECK THE BEACH.
It's supposed to rain soon.
OKAY. THEN I'LL GO LOOK AT THE PARK.
SO, MIRE... SHIZU-SAN, I'M GONNA GO FOR A WHILE. I'D LIKE YOU TO STAY HERE, PLEASE.
JUST STAY WITH CHIHIRO AND YOU'LL BE FINE... I'LL BE RIGHT BACK!
...

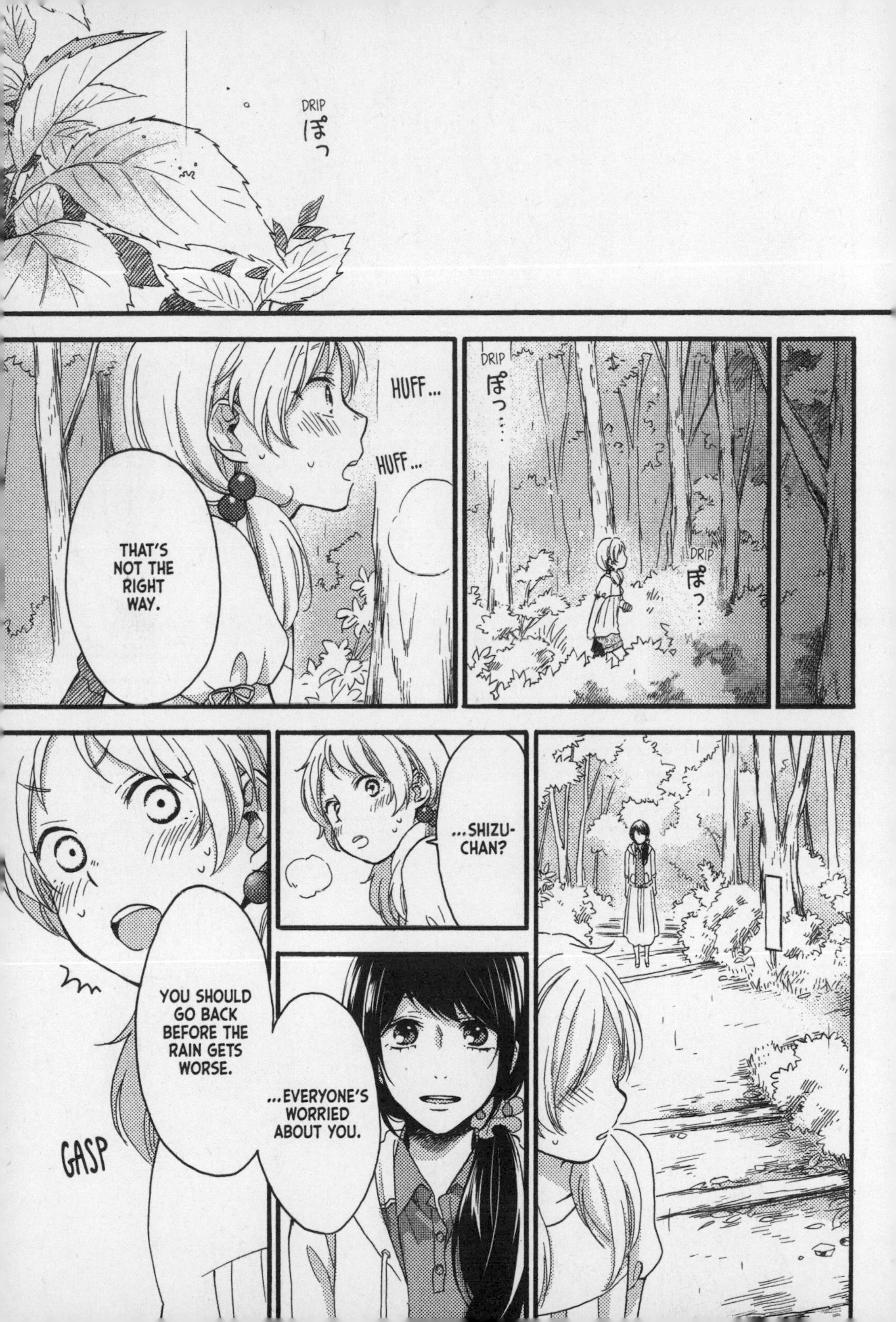
DRIP
ぽっ
DRIP
ぽっ…
DRIP
ぽっ…
HUFF...
HUFF...
THAT'S NOT THE RIGHT WAY.
...SHIZU-CHAN?
YOU SHOULD GO BACK BEFORE THE RAIN GETS WORSE.
...EVERYONE'S WORRIED ABOUT YOU.
GASP

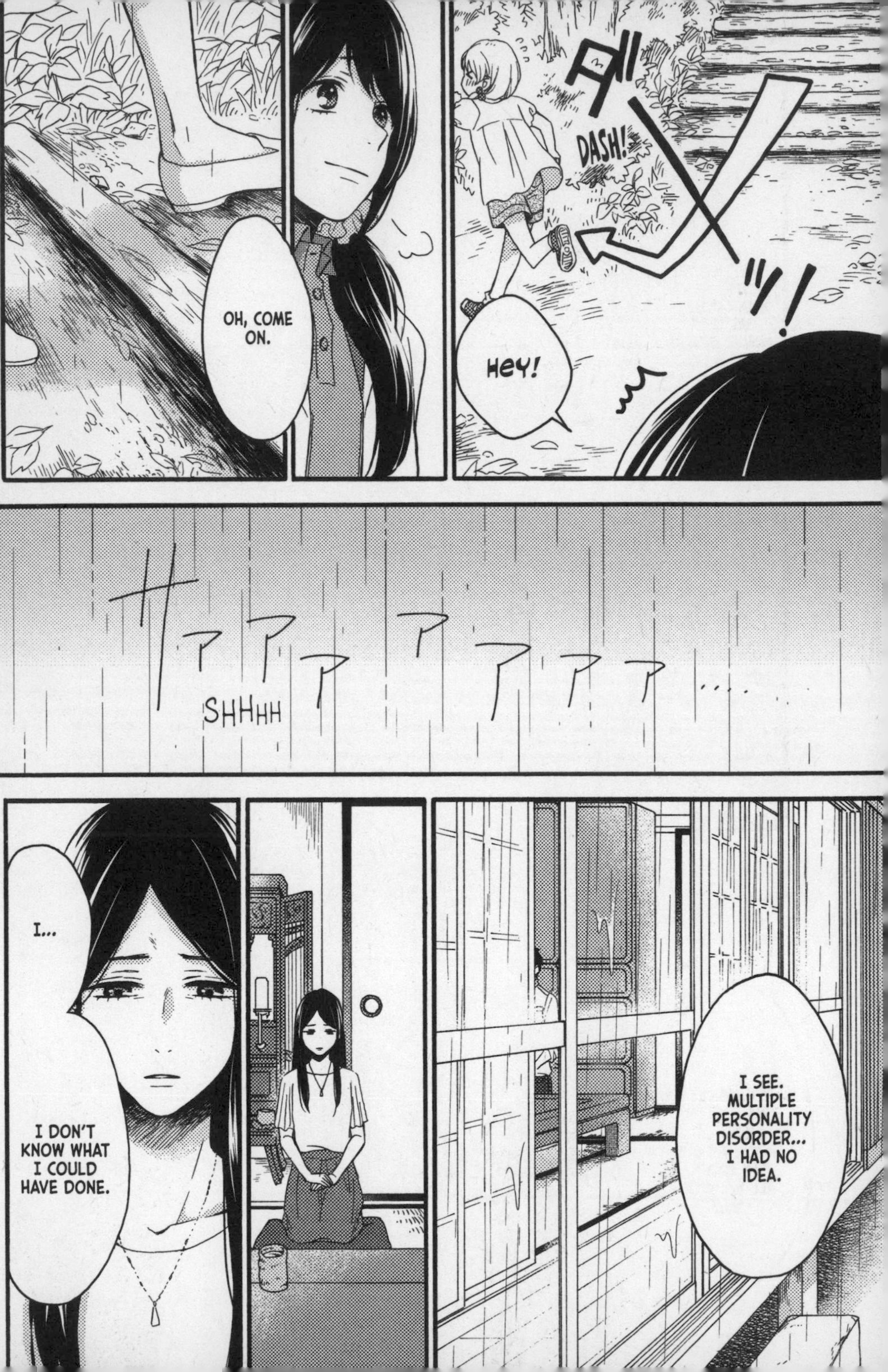
DASH!
HEY!
OH, COME ON.
SHHHH
I SEE. MULTIPLE PERSONALITY DISORDER... I HAD NO IDEA.
I...
I DON'T KNOW WHAT I COULD HAVE DONE.

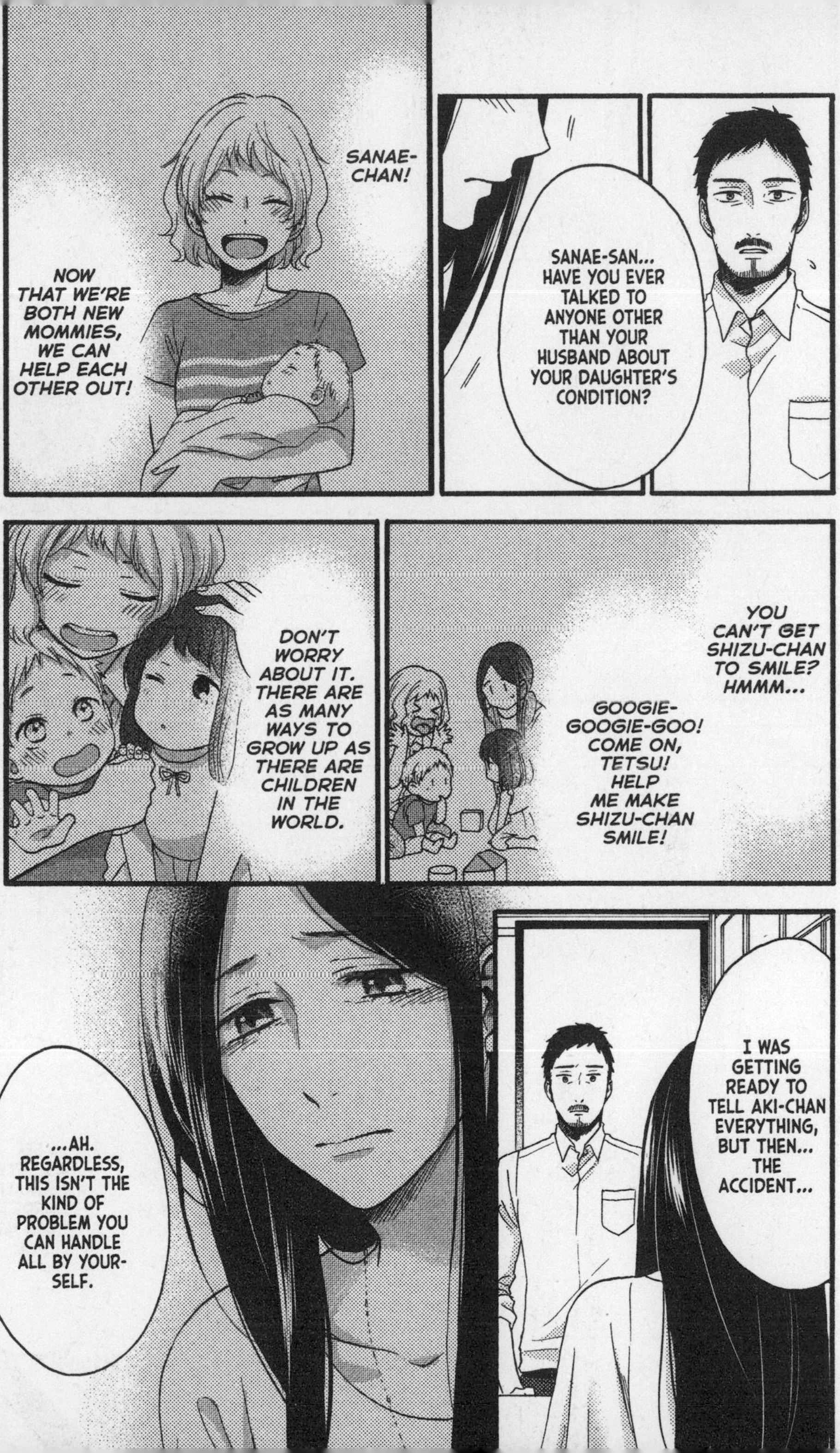
SANAE-SAN... HAVE YOU EVER TALKED TO ANYONE OTHER THAN YOUR HUSBAND ABOUT YOUR DAUGHTER'S CONDITION?
SANAE-CHAN!
NOW THAT WE'RE BOTH NEW MOMMIES, WE CAN HELP EACH OTHER OUT!
YOU CAN'T GET SHIZU-CHAN TO SMILE? HMMM...
GOOGIE-GOOGIE-GOO! COME ON, TETSU! HELP ME MAKE SHIZU-CHAN SMILE!
DON'T WORRY ABOUT IT. THERE ARE AS MANY WAYS TO GROW UP AS THERE ARE CHILDREN IN THE WORLD.
I WAS GETTING READY TO TELL AKI-CHAN EVERYTHING, BUT THEN... THE ACCIDENT...
...AH. REGARDLESS, THIS ISN'T THE KIND OF PROBLEM YOU CAN HANDLE ALL BY YOUR-SELF.

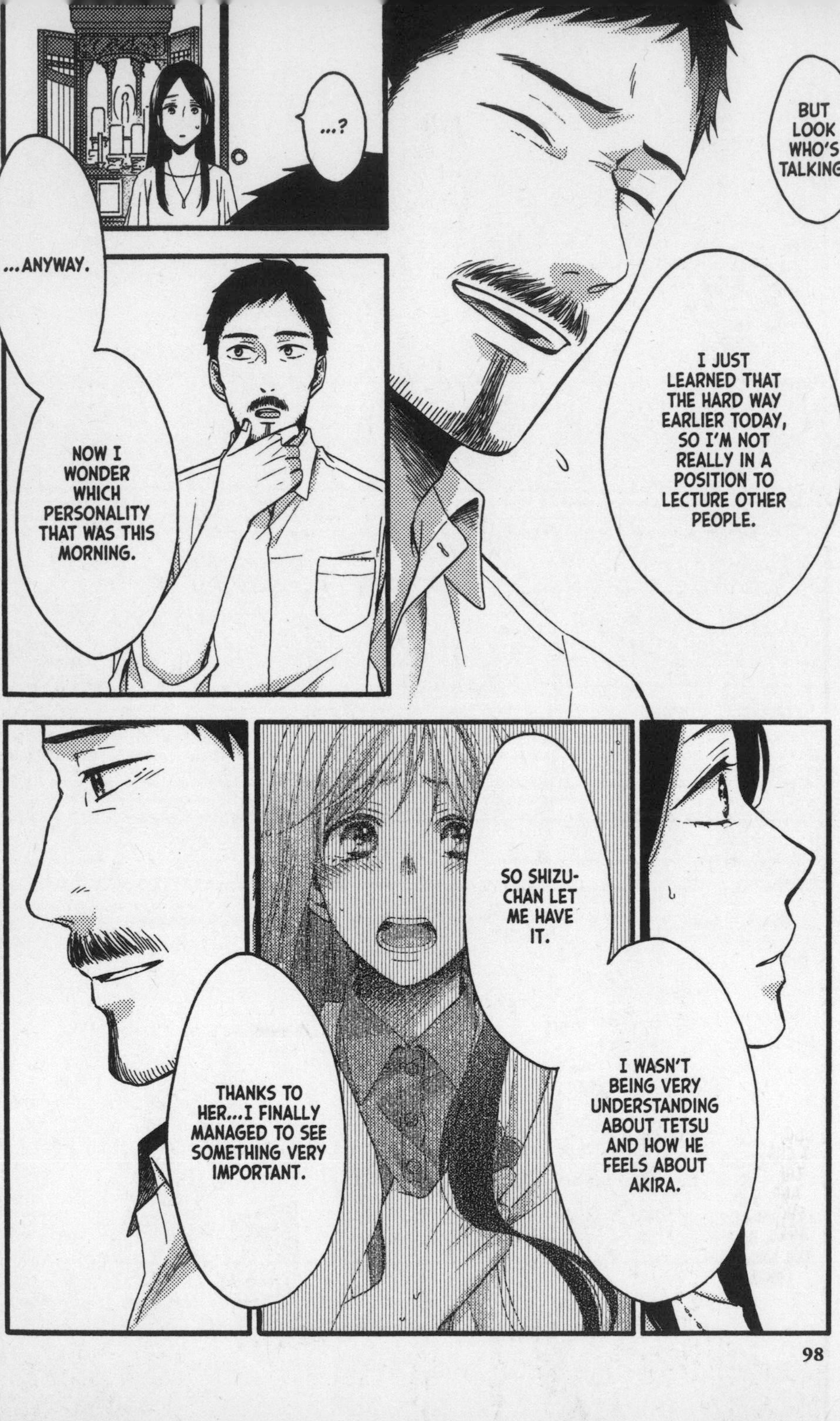
BUT LOOK WHO'S TALKING.
I JUST LEARNED THAT THE HARD WAY EARLIER TODAY, SO I'M NOT REALLY IN A POSITION TO LECTURE OTHER PEOPLE.
...?
...ANYWAY.
NOW I WONDER WHICH PERSONALITY THAT WAS THIS MORNING.
I WASN'T BEING VERY UNDERSTANDING ABOUT TETSU AND HOW HE FEELS ABOUT AKIRA.
SO SHIZU-CHAN LET ME HAVE IT.
THANKS TO HER...I FINALLY MANAGED TO SEE SOMETHING VERY IMPORTANT.

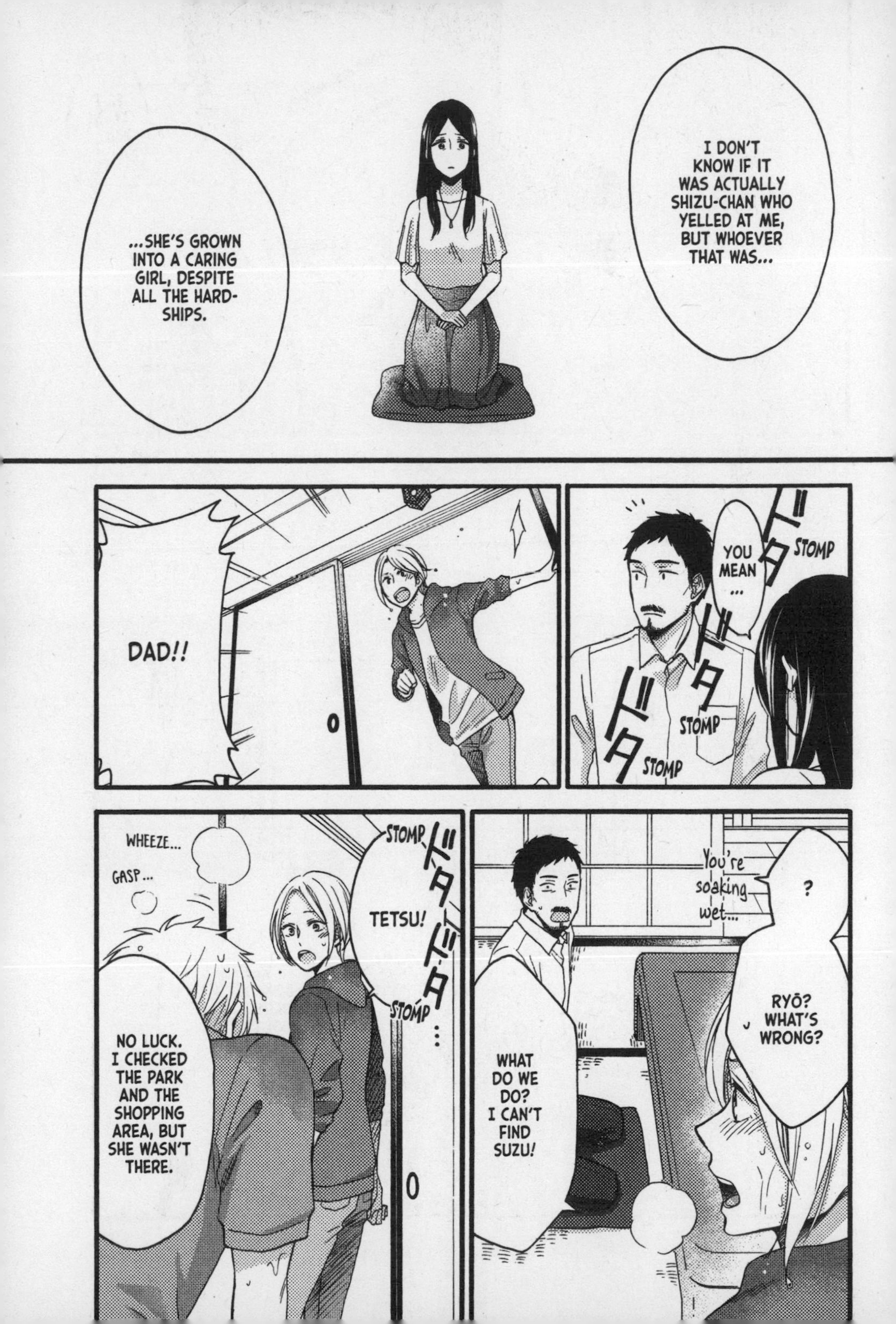
I DON'T KNOW IF IT WAS ACTUALLY SHIZU-CHAN WHO YELLED AT ME, BUT WHOEVER THAT WAS...
...SHE'S GROWN INTO A CARING GIRL, DESPITE ALL THE HARD-SHIPS.
ドタ
STOMP
YOU MEAN ...
ドタ
STOMP
ドタ
STOMP
DAD!!
You're soaking wet...
?
RYŌ? WHAT'S WRONG?
WHAT DO WE DO? I CAN'T FIND SUZU!
STOMP
ドタ
TETSU!
ドタ
STOMP
...
WHEEZE...
GASP...
NO LUCK. I CHECKED THE PARK AND THE SHOPPING AREA, BUT SHE WASN'T THERE.

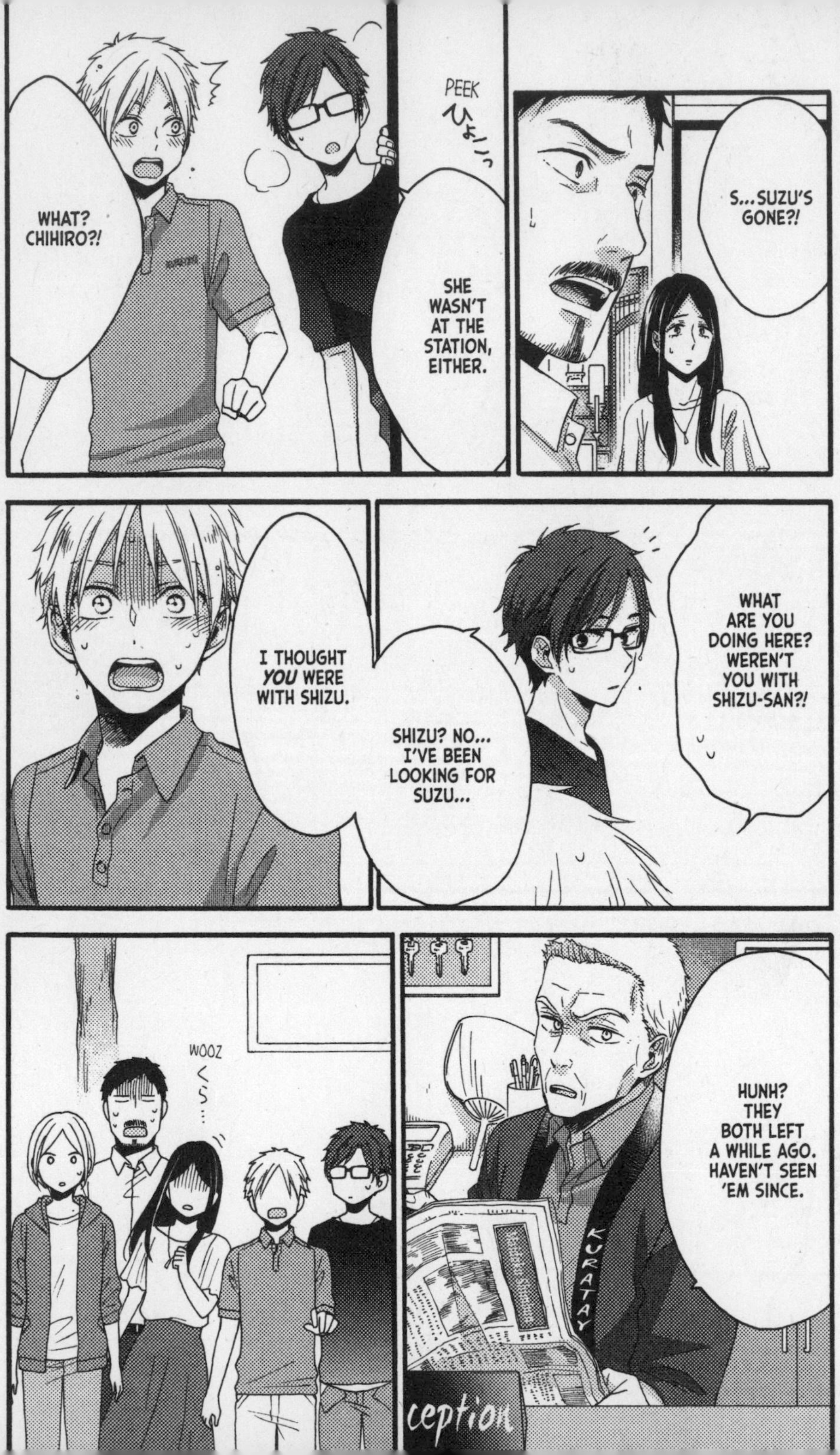
S...SUZU'S GONE?!
PEEK
ひょこっ
SHE WASN'T AT THE STATION, EITHER.
WHAT? CHIHIRO?!
WHAT ARE YOU DOING HERE? WEREN'T YOU WITH SHIZU-SAN?!
SHIZU? NO... I'VE BEEN LOOKING FOR SUZU...
I THOUGHT *YOU* WERE WITH SHIZU.
HUNH? THEY BOTH LEFT A WHILE AGO. HAVEN'T SEEN 'EM SINCE.
KURATAY
ception
WOOZ
くら…

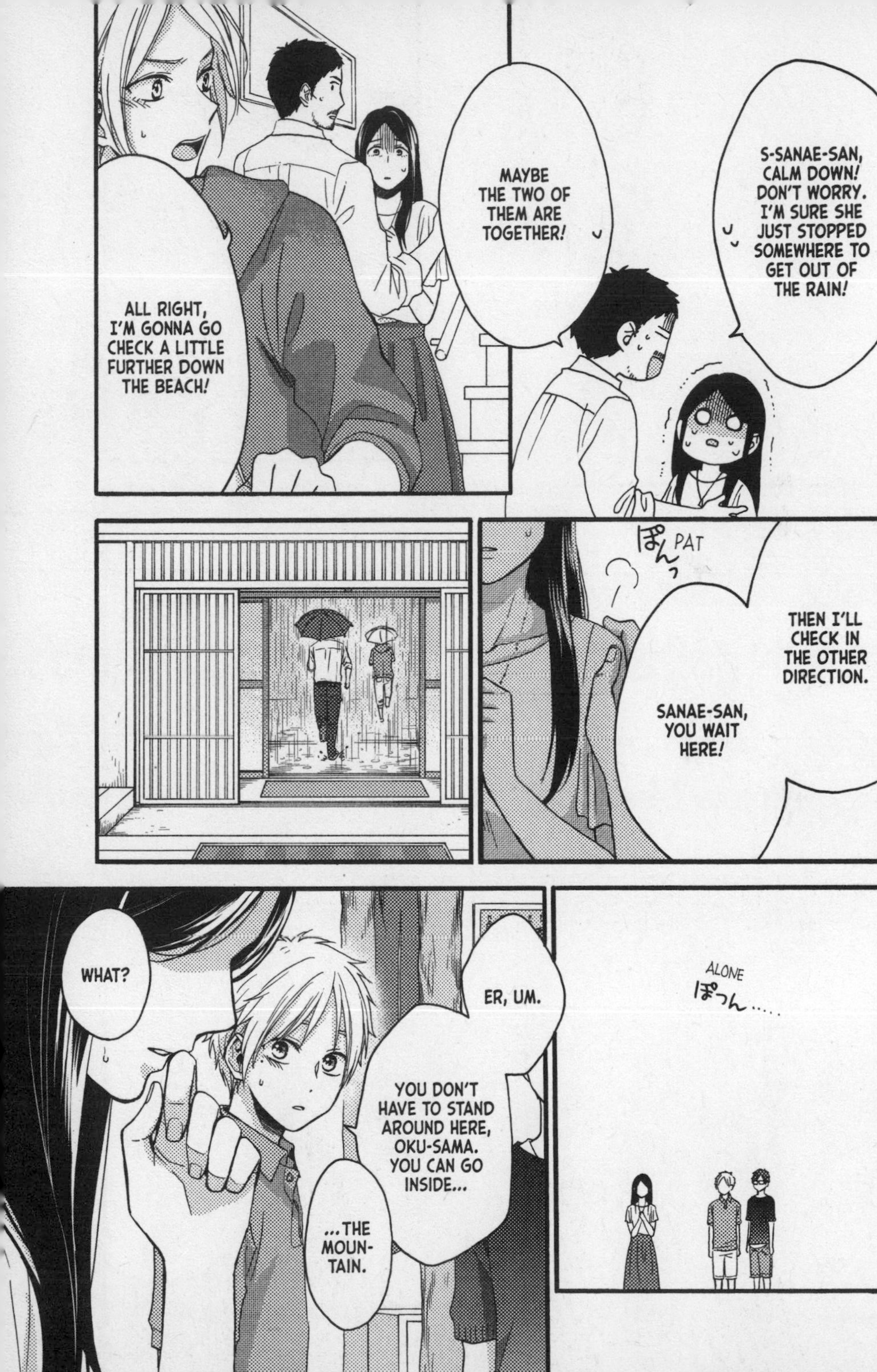
S-SANAE-SAN, CALM DOWN! DON'T WORRY. I'M SURE SHE JUST STOPPED SOMEWHERE TO GET OUT OF THE RAIN!
MAYBE THE TWO OF THEM ARE TOGETHER!
ALL RIGHT, I'M GONNA GO CHECK A LITTLE FURTHER DOWN THE BEACH!
ぽんっ PAT
THEN I'LL CHECK IN THE OTHER DIRECTION.
SANAE-SAN, YOU WAIT HERE!
ALONE
ぽつん.....
ER, UM.
WHAT?
YOU DON'T HAVE TO STAND AROUND HERE, OKU-SAMA. YOU CAN GO INSIDE...
...THE MOUN-TAIN.

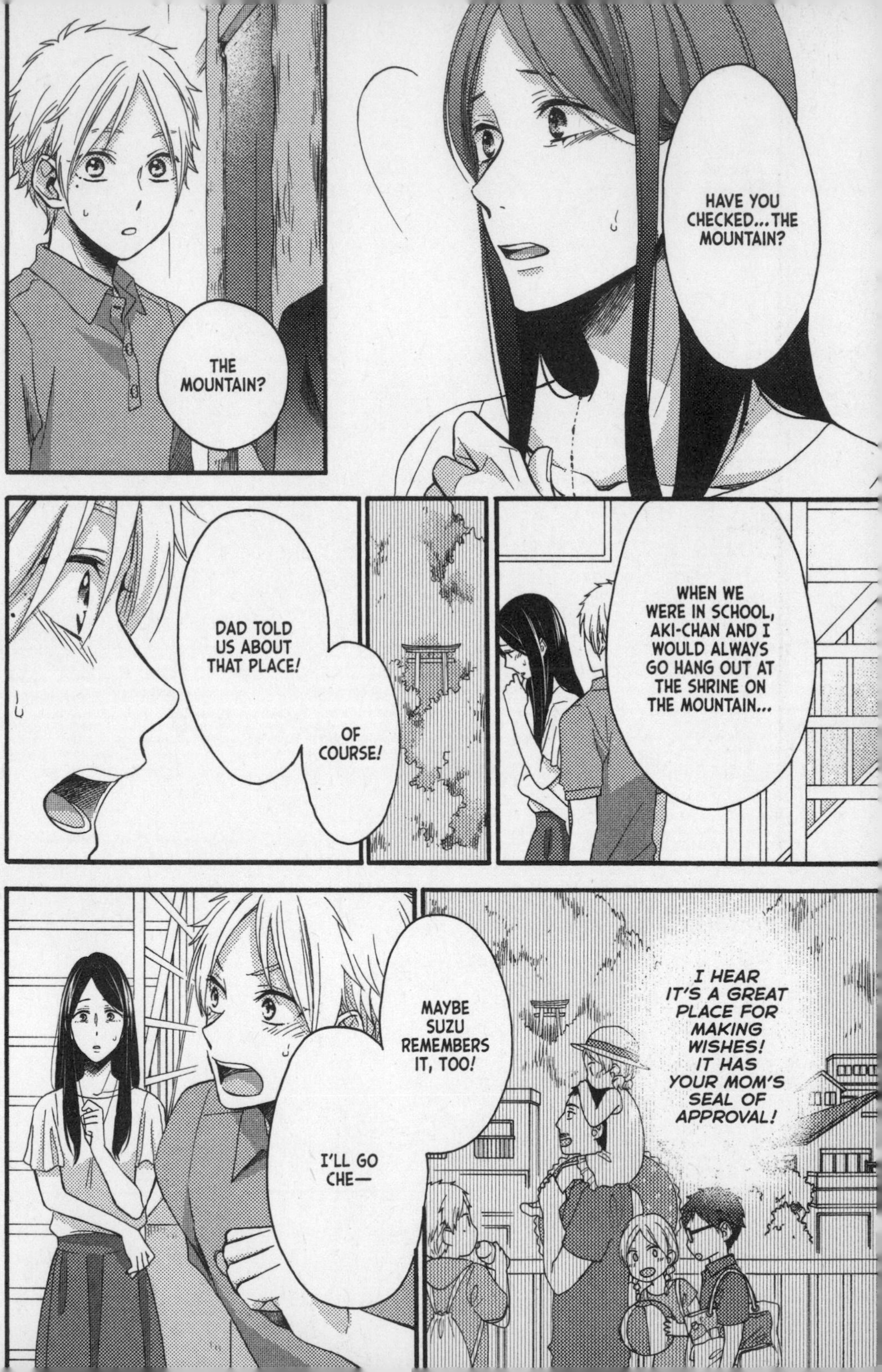
HAVE YOU CHECKED...THE MOUNTAIN?
THE MOUNTAIN?
WHEN WE WERE IN SCHOOL, AKI-CHAN AND I WOULD ALWAYS GO HANG OUT AT THE SHRINE ON THE MOUNTAIN...
OF COURSE!
DAD TOLD US ABOUT THAT PLACE!
I HEAR IT'S A GREAT PLACE FOR MAKING WISHES! IT HAS YOUR MOM'S SEAL OF APPROVAL!
MAYBE SUZU REMEMBERS IT, TOO!
I'LL GO CHE—

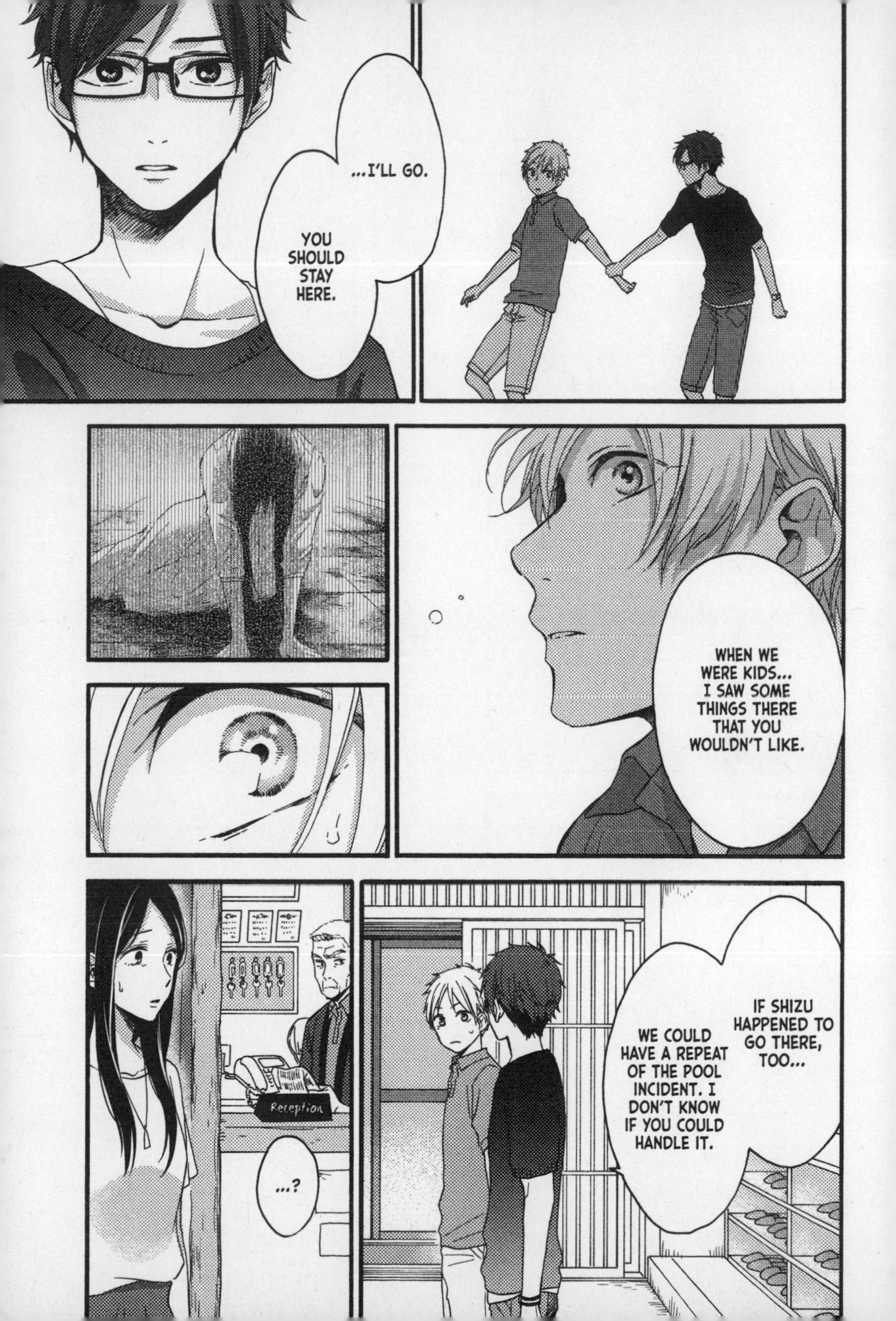
...I'LL GO.
YOU SHOULD STAY HERE.
WHEN WE WERE KIDS... I SAW SOME THINGS THERE THAT YOU WOULDN'T LIKE.
IF SHIZU HAPPENED TO GO THERE, TOO...
WE COULD HAVE A REPEAT OF THE POOL INCIDENT. I DON'T KNOW IF YOU COULD HANDLE IT.
Reception
...?

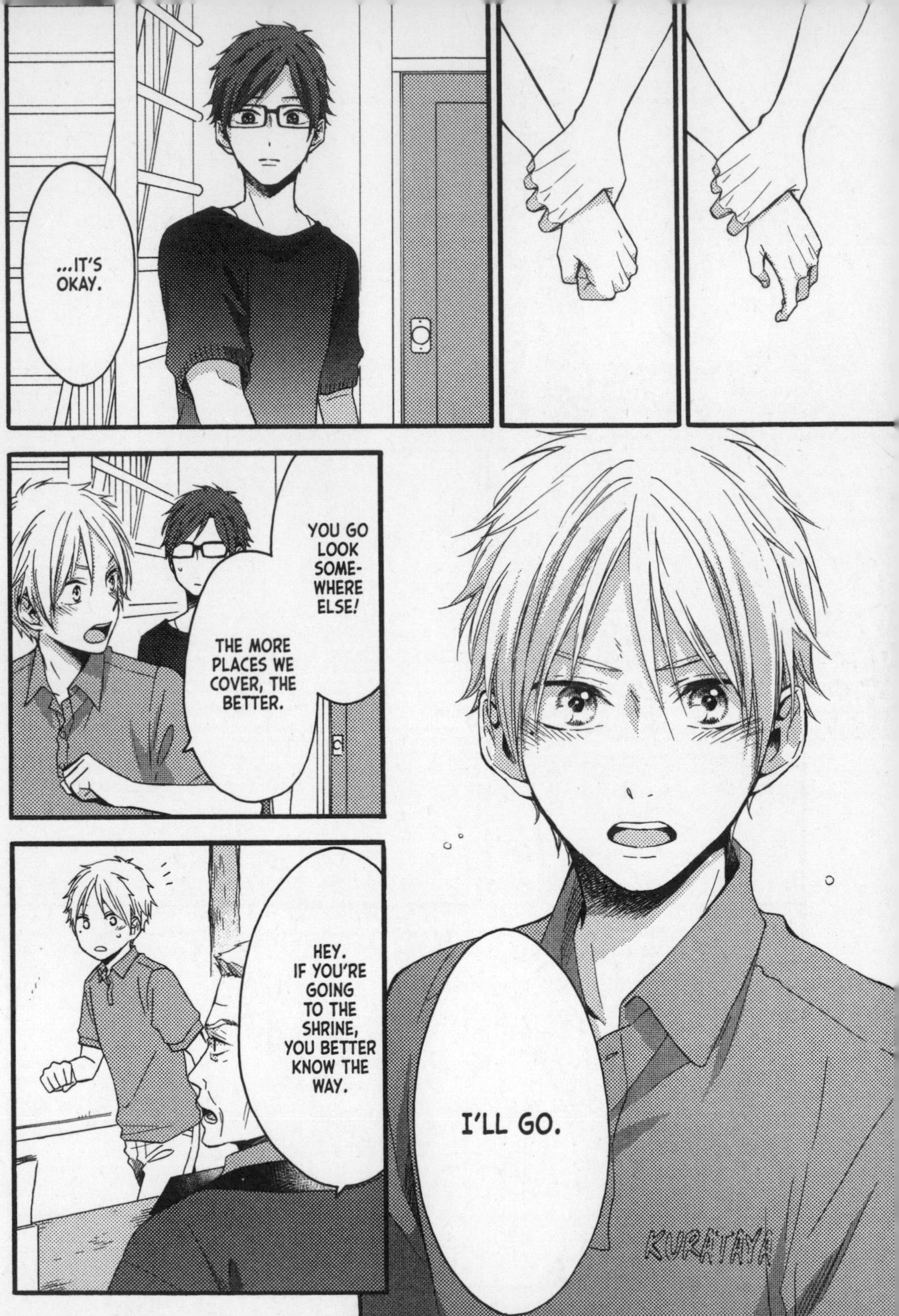
...IT'S OKAY.
I'LL GO.
KURATAYA
YOU GO LOOK SOME-WHERE ELSE!
THE MORE PLACES WE COVER, THE BETTER.
HEY. IF YOU'RE GOING TO THE SHRINE, YOU BETTER KNOW THE WAY.

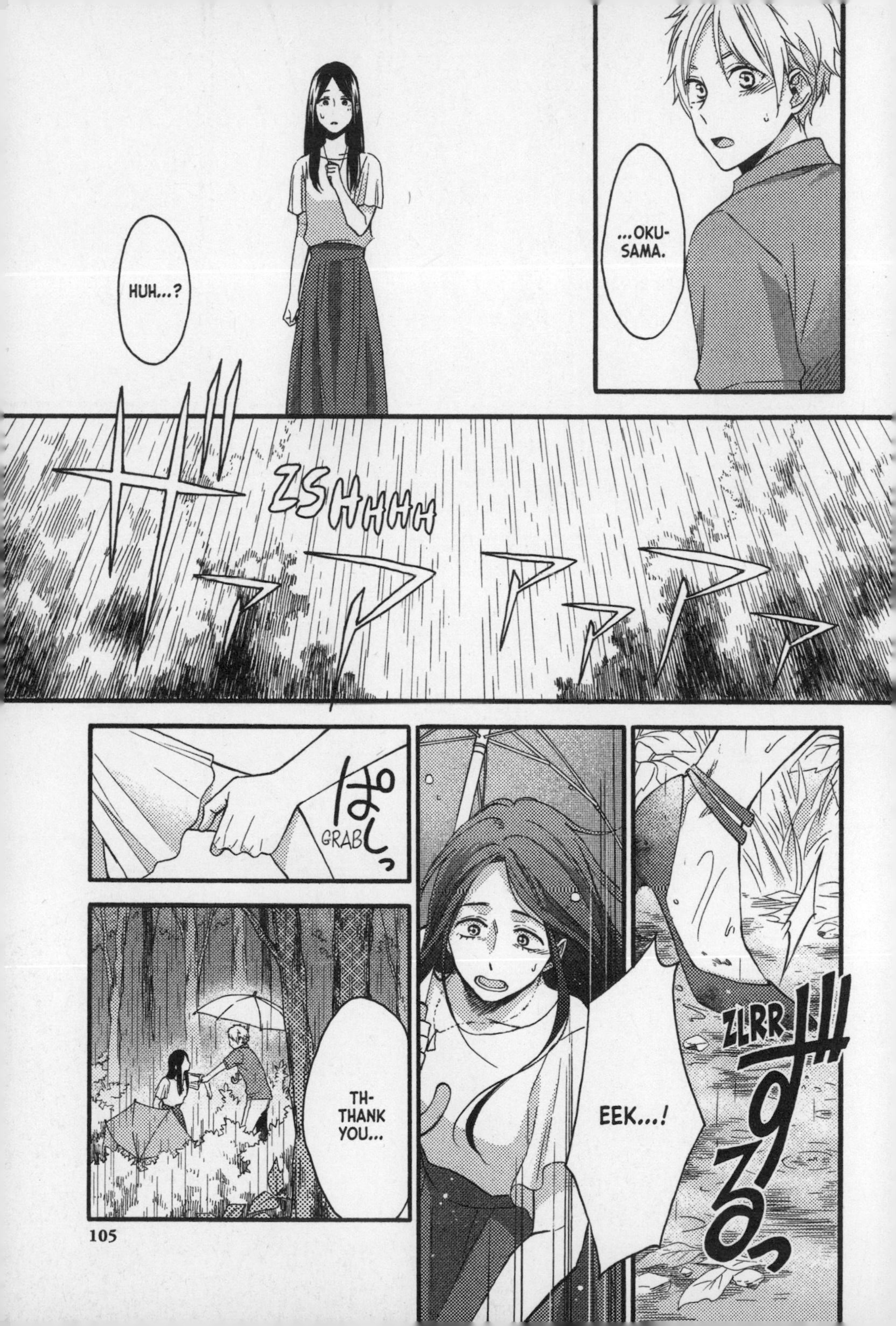
...OKU-SAMA.
HUH...?
ZSHHHH
ザァァァァ
ZLRR
ずるっ
EEK...!
GRAB
ぱしっ
TH-THANK YOU...

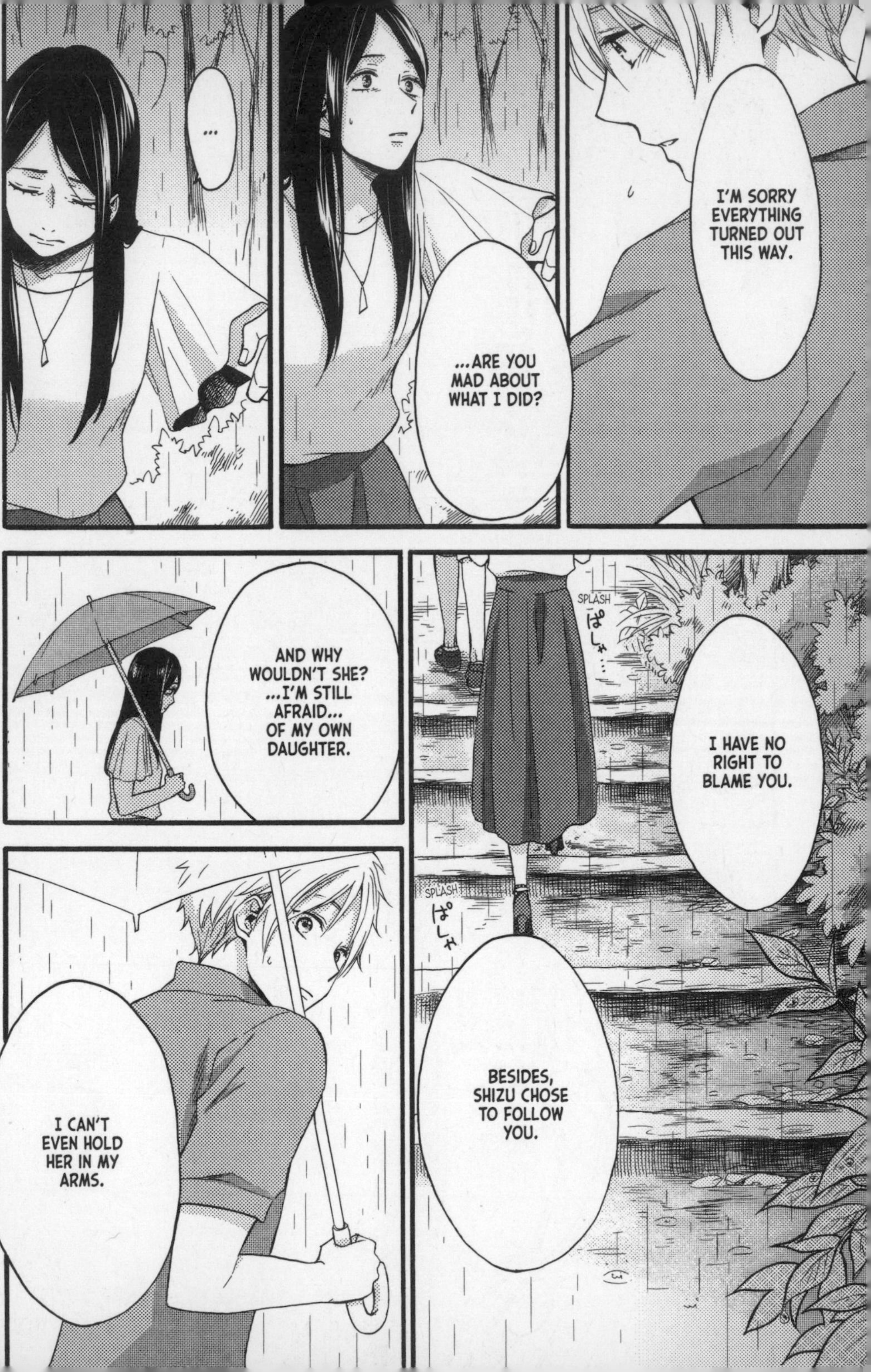
I'M SORRY EVERYTHING TURNED OUT THIS WAY.
...ARE YOU MAD ABOUT WHAT I DID?
...
SPLASH ぱしゃ…
I HAVE NO RIGHT TO BLAME YOU.
SPLASH ぱしゃ
BESIDES, SHIZU CHOSE TO FOLLOW YOU.
AND WHY WOULDN'T SHE? ...I'M STILL AFRAID... OF MY OWN DAUGHTER.
I CAN'T EVEN HOLD HER IN MY ARMS.

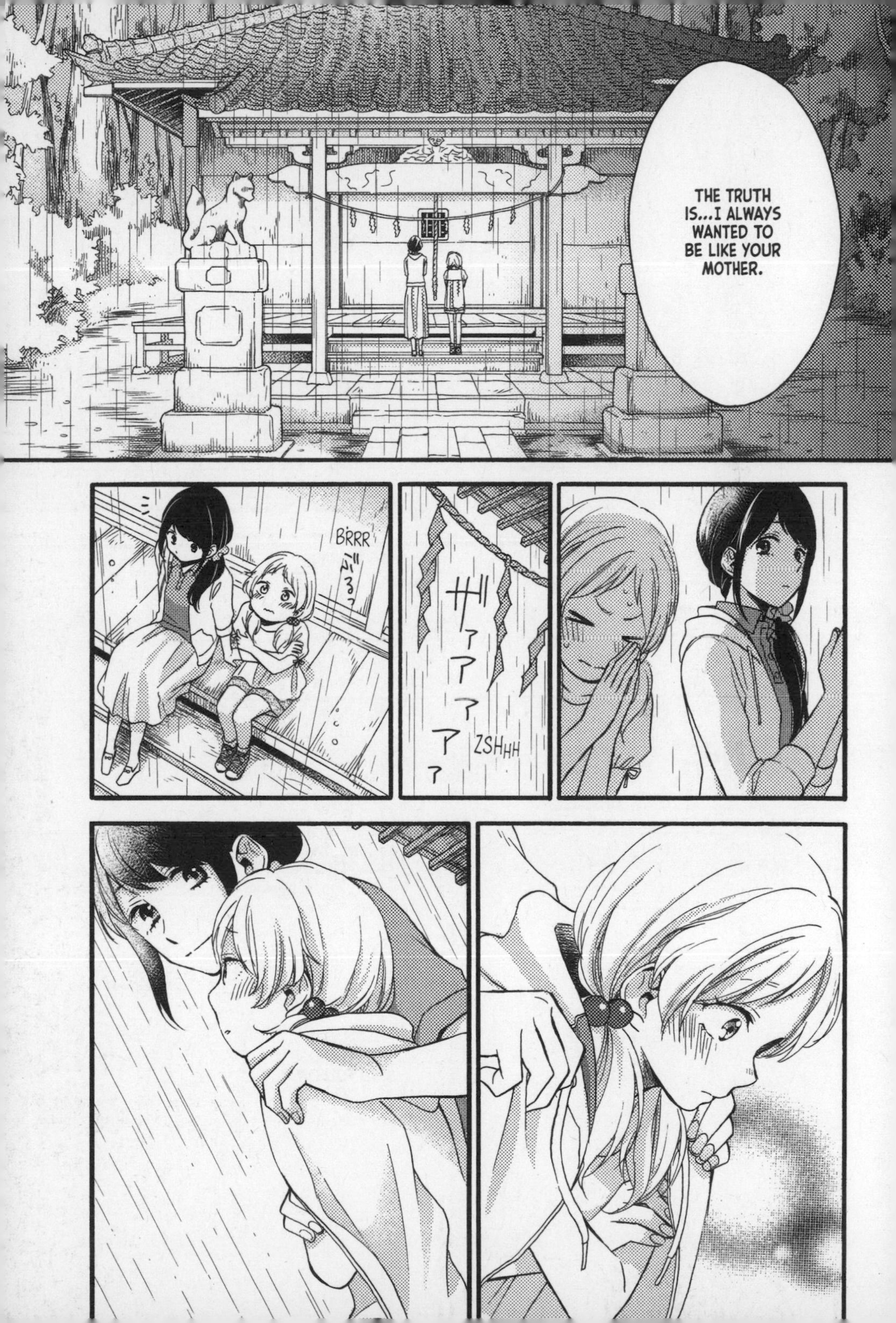
THE TRUTH IS...I ALWAYS WANTED TO BE LIKE YOUR MOTHER.
ザァアアア
ZSHHH
BRRR
ぶるっ

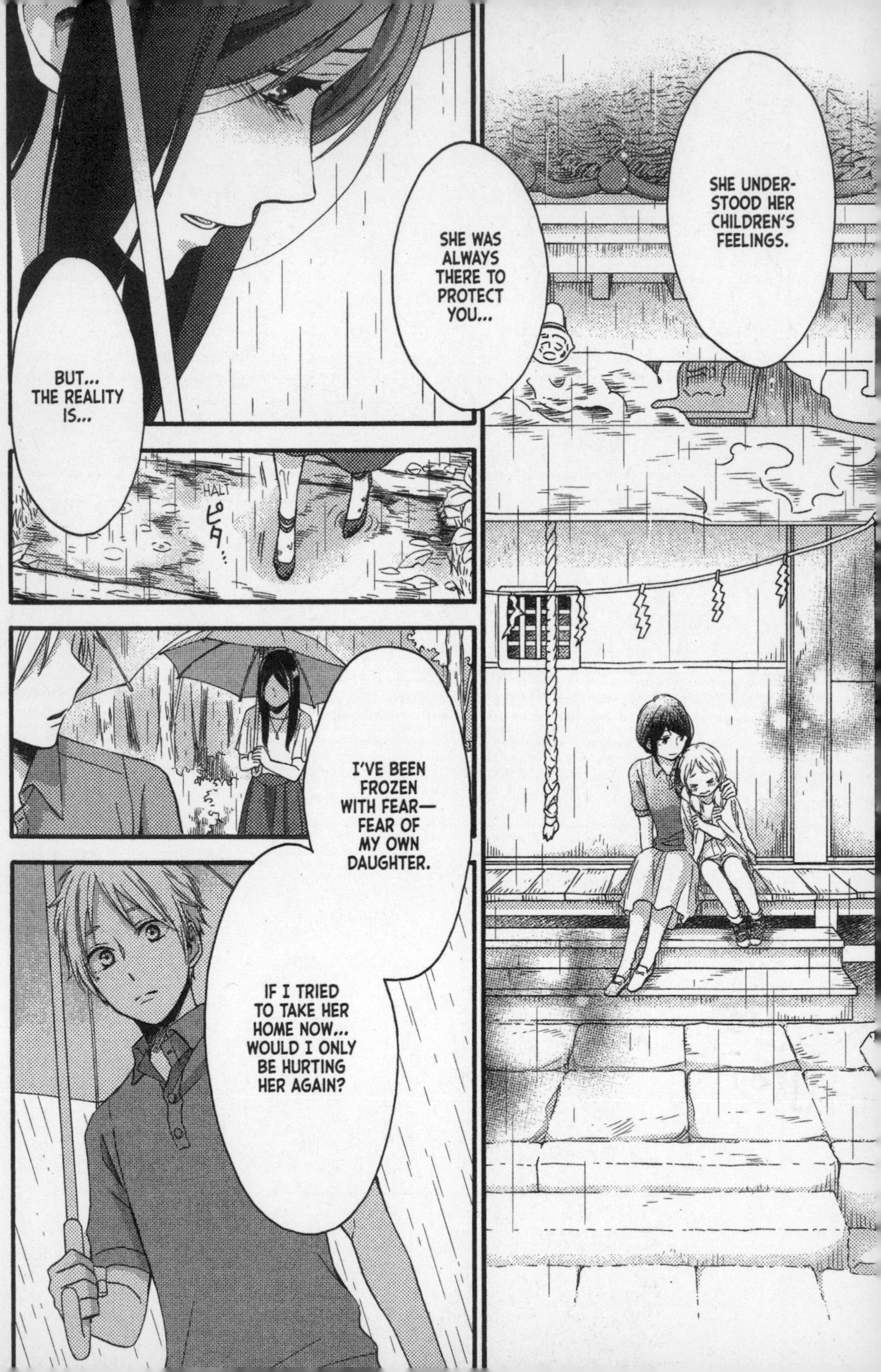
SHE UNDER-STOOD HER CHILDREN'S FEELINGS.
SHE WAS ALWAYS THERE TO PROTECT YOU...
BUT... THE REALITY IS...
HALT
ピタ…
I'VE BEEN FROZEN WITH FEAR—FEAR OF MY OWN DAUGHTER.
IF I TRIED TO TAKE HER HOME NOW... WOULD I ONLY BE HURTING HER AGAIN?

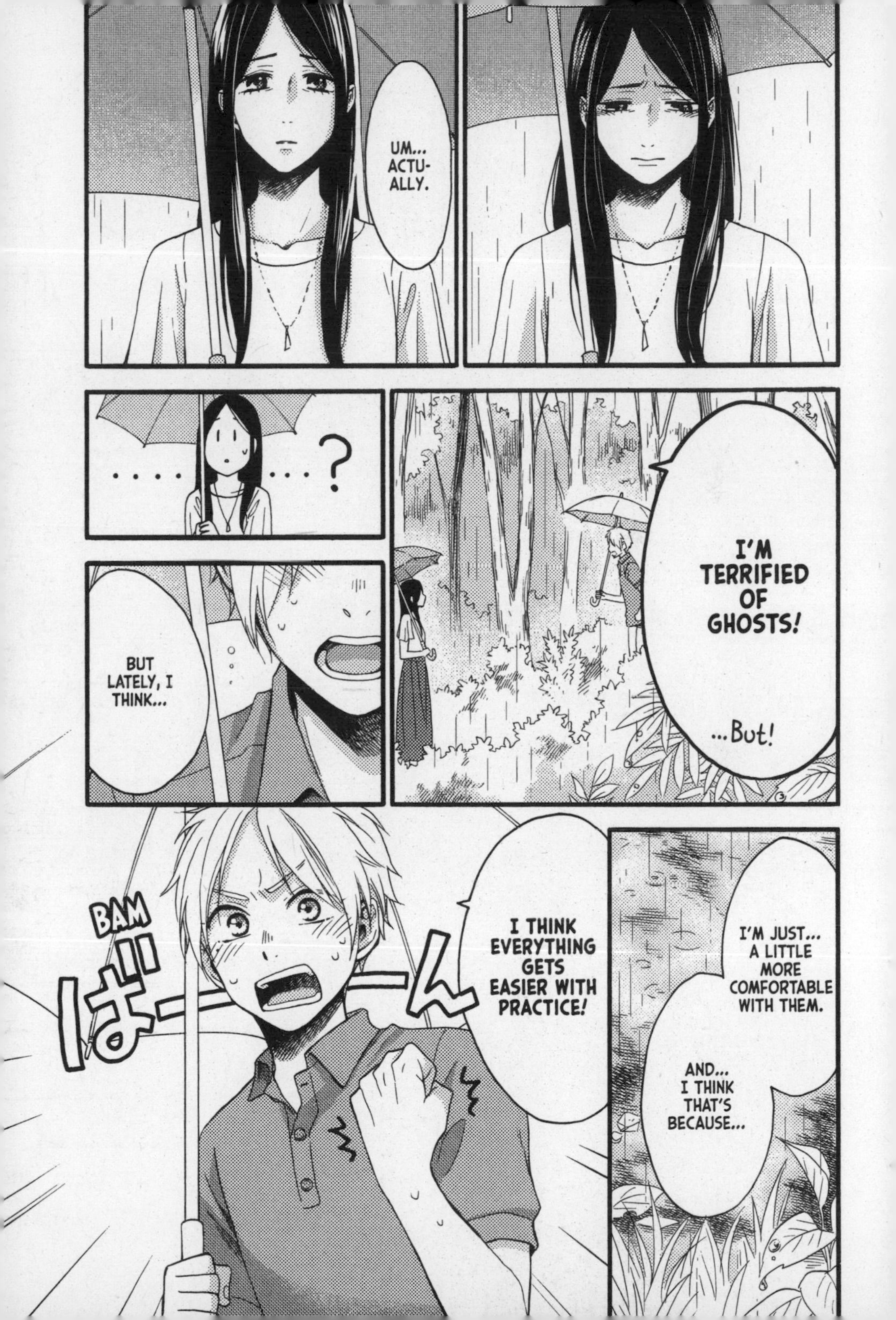
UM... ACTU-ALLY.
I'M TERRIFIED OF GHOSTS!
...But!
....?
BUT LATELY, I THINK...
I'M JUST... A LITTLE MORE COMFORTABLE WITH THEM.
AND... I THINK THAT'S BECAUSE...
I THINK EVERYTHING GETS EASIER WITH PRACTICE!
BAM
ばーーん

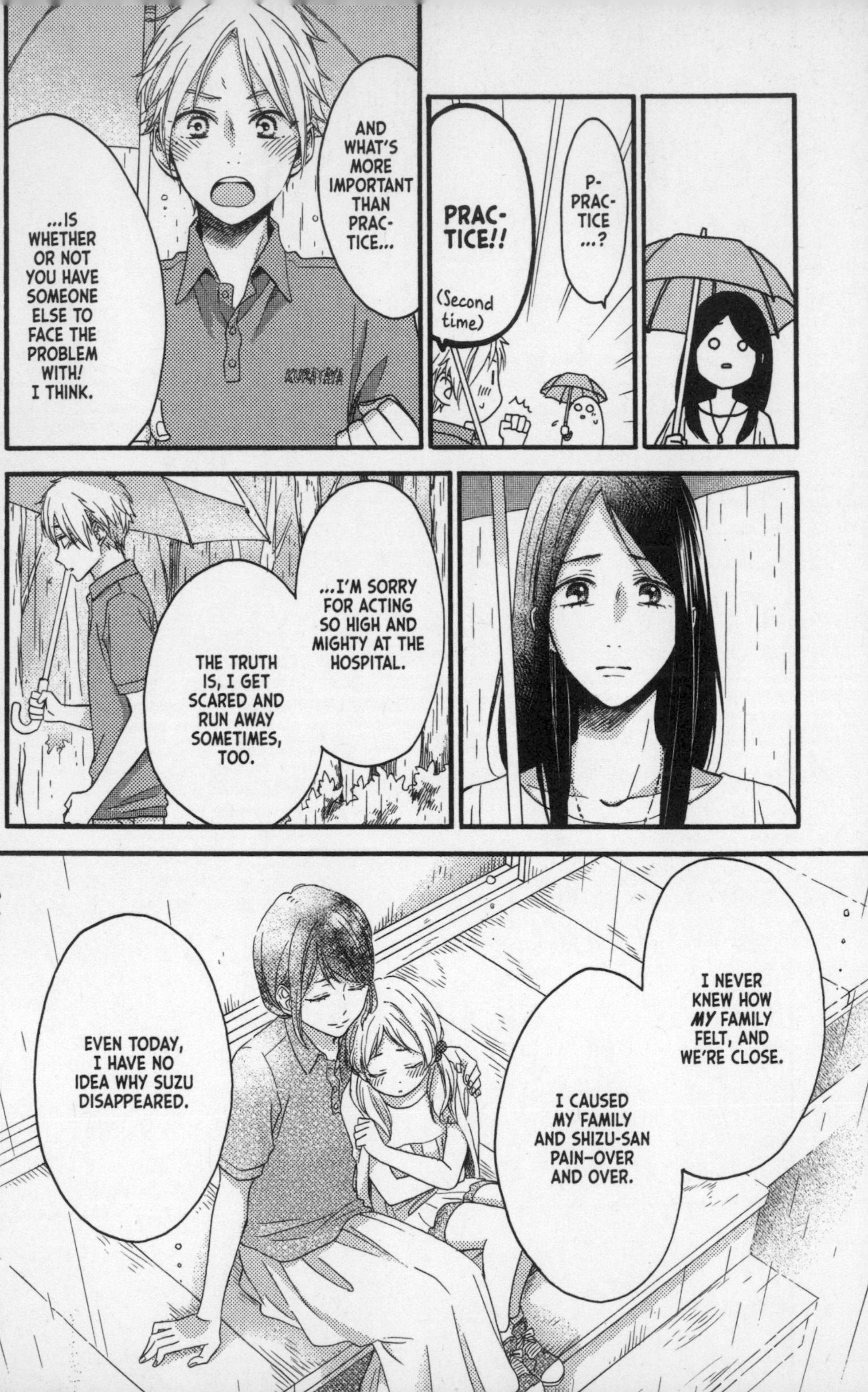
P-PRACTICE...?
PRACTICE!!
(Second time)
AND WHAT'S MORE IMPORTANT THAN PRACTICE...
...IS WHETHER OR NOT YOU HAVE SOMEONE ELSE TO FACE THE PROBLEM WITH! I THINK.
...I'M SORRY FOR ACTING SO HIGH AND MIGHTY AT THE HOSPITAL.
THE TRUTH IS, I GET SCARED AND RUN AWAY SOMETIMES, TOO.
I NEVER KNEW HOW *MY* FAMILY FELT, AND WE'RE CLOSE.
I CAUSED MY FAMILY AND SHIZU-SAN PAIN—OVER AND OVER.
EVEN TODAY, I HAVE NO IDEA WHY SUZU DISAPPEARED.

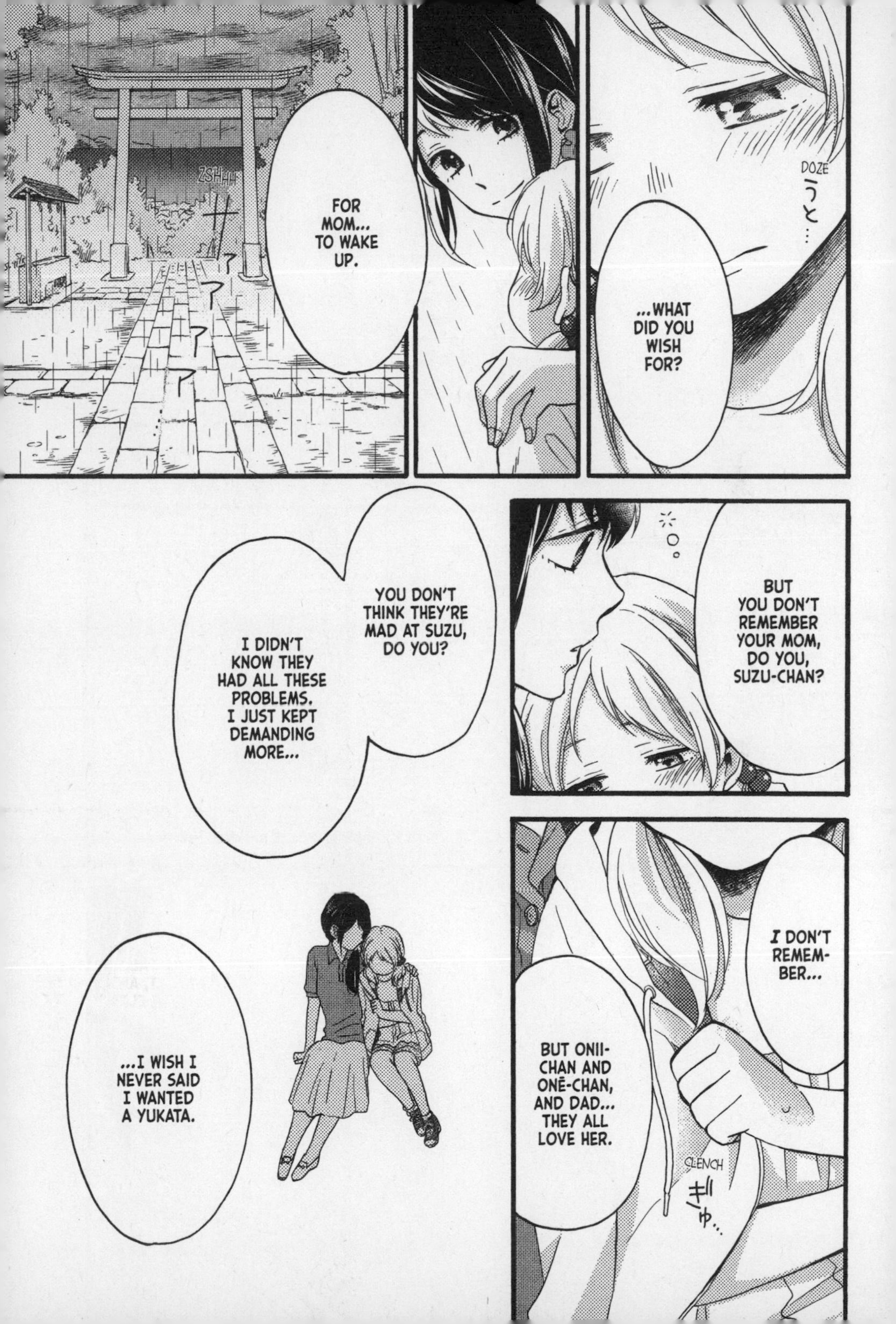

DOZE
うと…
...WHAT DID YOU WISH FOR?
FOR MOM... TO WAKE UP.
ZSHHH
BUT YOU DON'T REMEMBER YOUR MOM, DO YOU, SUZU-CHAN?
YOU DON'T THINK THEY'RE MAD AT SUZU, DO YOU?
I DIDN'T KNOW THEY HAD ALL THESE PROBLEMS. I JUST KEPT DEMANDING MORE...
I DON'T REMEMBER...
BUT ONII-CHAN AND ONĒ-CHAN, AND DAD... THEY ALL LOVE HER.
CLENCH
ぎゅ…
...I WISH I NEVER SAID I WANTED A YUKATA.

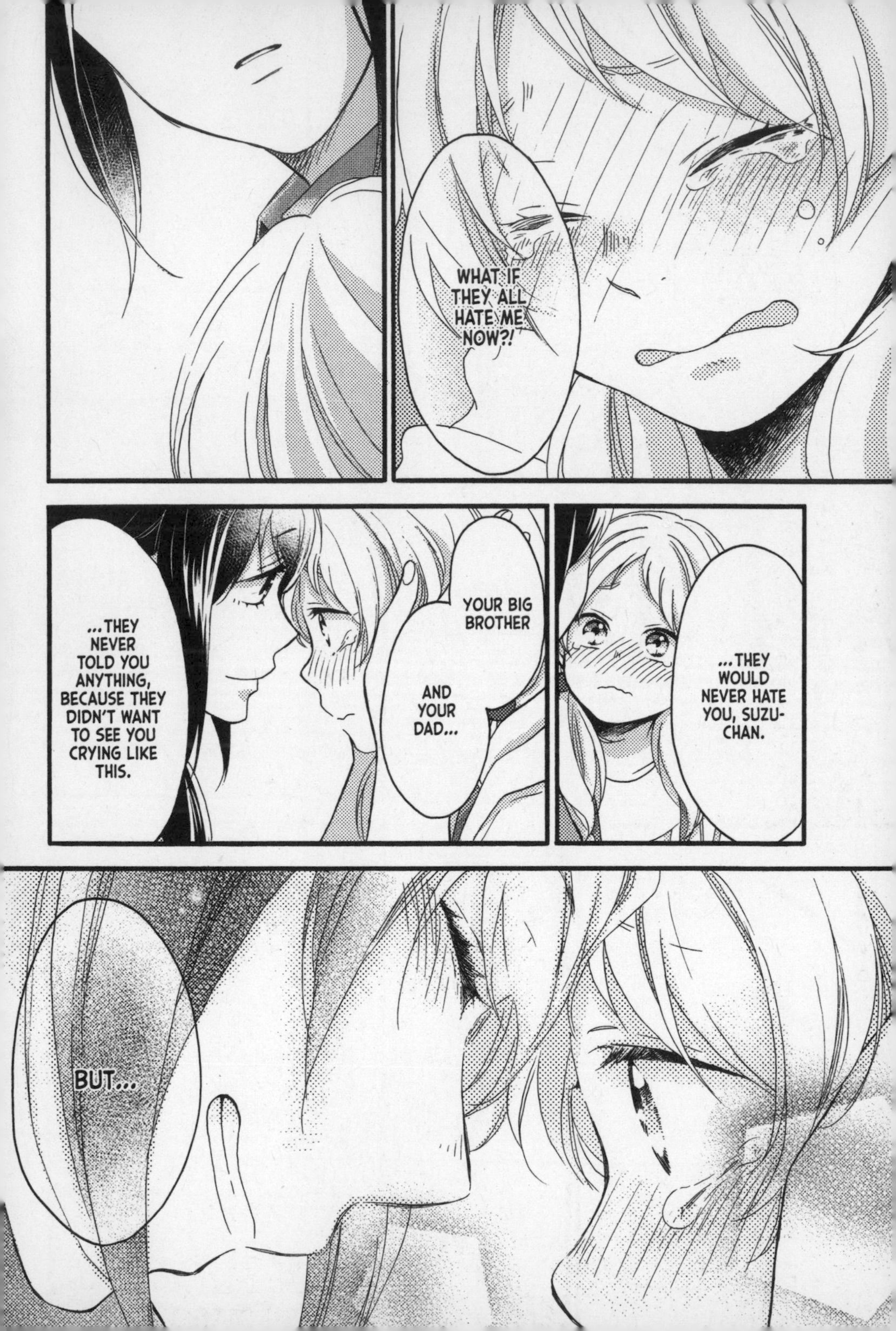
WHAT IF THEY ALL HATE ME NOW?!
...THEY WOULD NEVER HATE YOU, SUZU-CHAN.
YOUR BIG BROTHER
AND YOUR DAD...
...THEY NEVER TOLD YOU ANYTHING, BECAUSE THEY DIDN'T WANT TO SEE YOU CRYING LIKE THIS.
BUT...

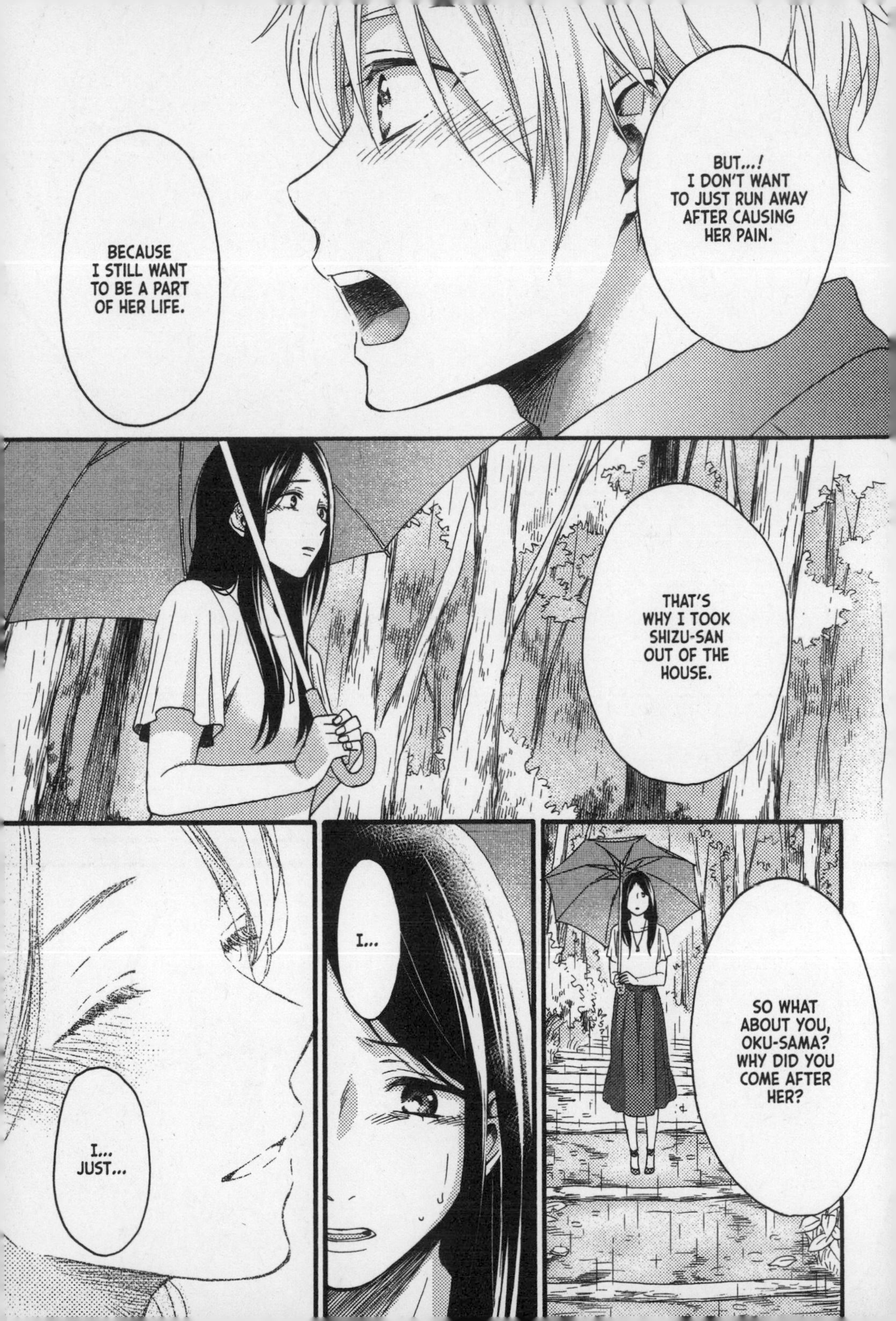
BUT...! I DON'T WANT TO JUST RUN AWAY AFTER CAUSING HER PAIN.
BECAUSE I STILL WANT TO BE A PART OF HER LIFE.
THAT'S WHY I TOOK SHIZU-SAN OUT OF THE HOUSE.
SO WHAT ABOUT YOU, OKU-SAMA? WHY DID YOU COME AFTER HER?
I...
I... JUST...

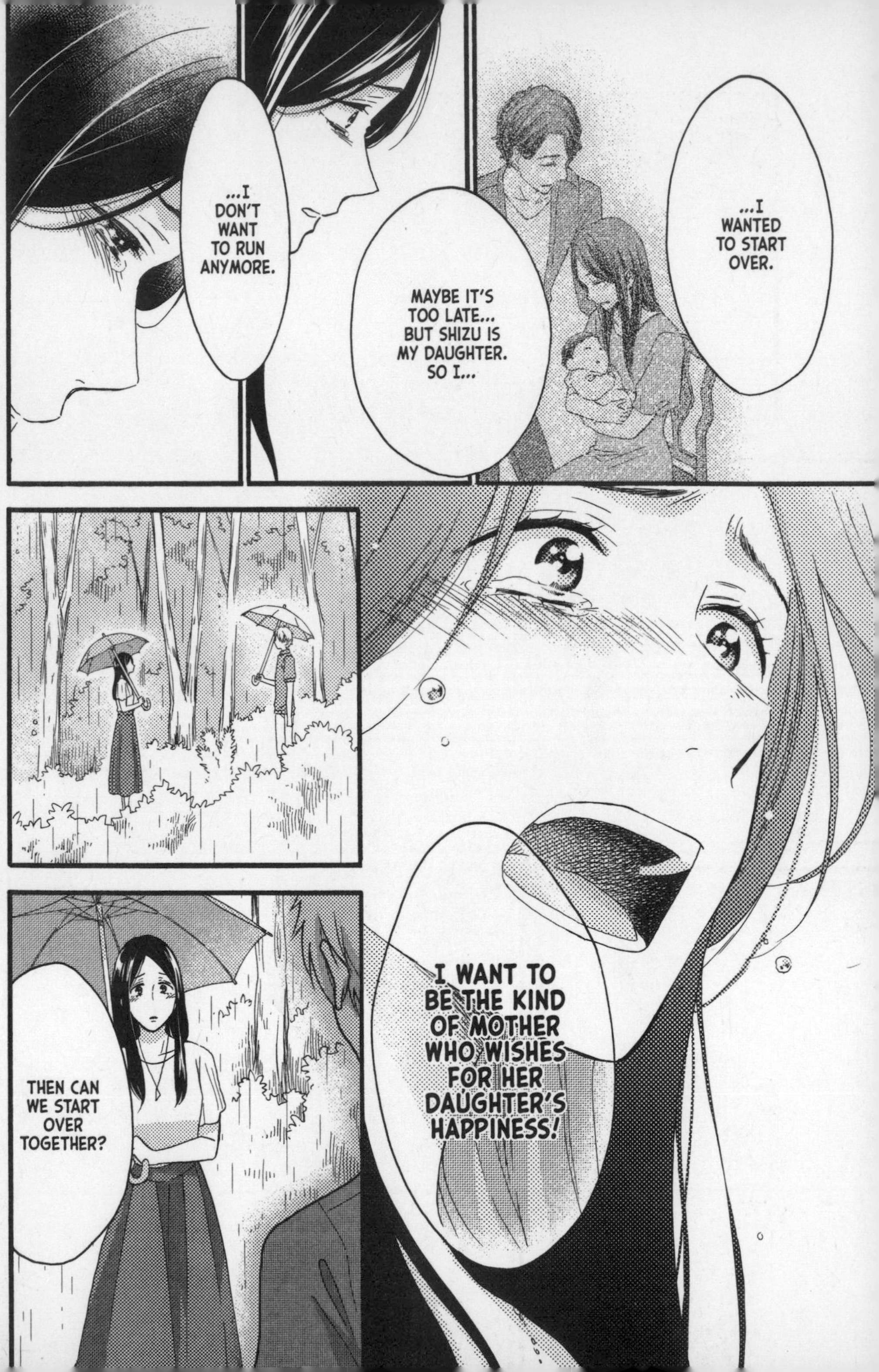
...I WANTED TO START OVER.
MAYBE IT'S TOO LATE... BUT SHIZU IS MY DAUGHTER. SO I...
...I DON'T WANT TO RUN ANYMORE.
I WANT TO BE THE KIND OF MOTHER WHO WISHES FOR HER DAUGHTER'S HAPPINESS!
THEN CAN WE START OVER TOGETHER?

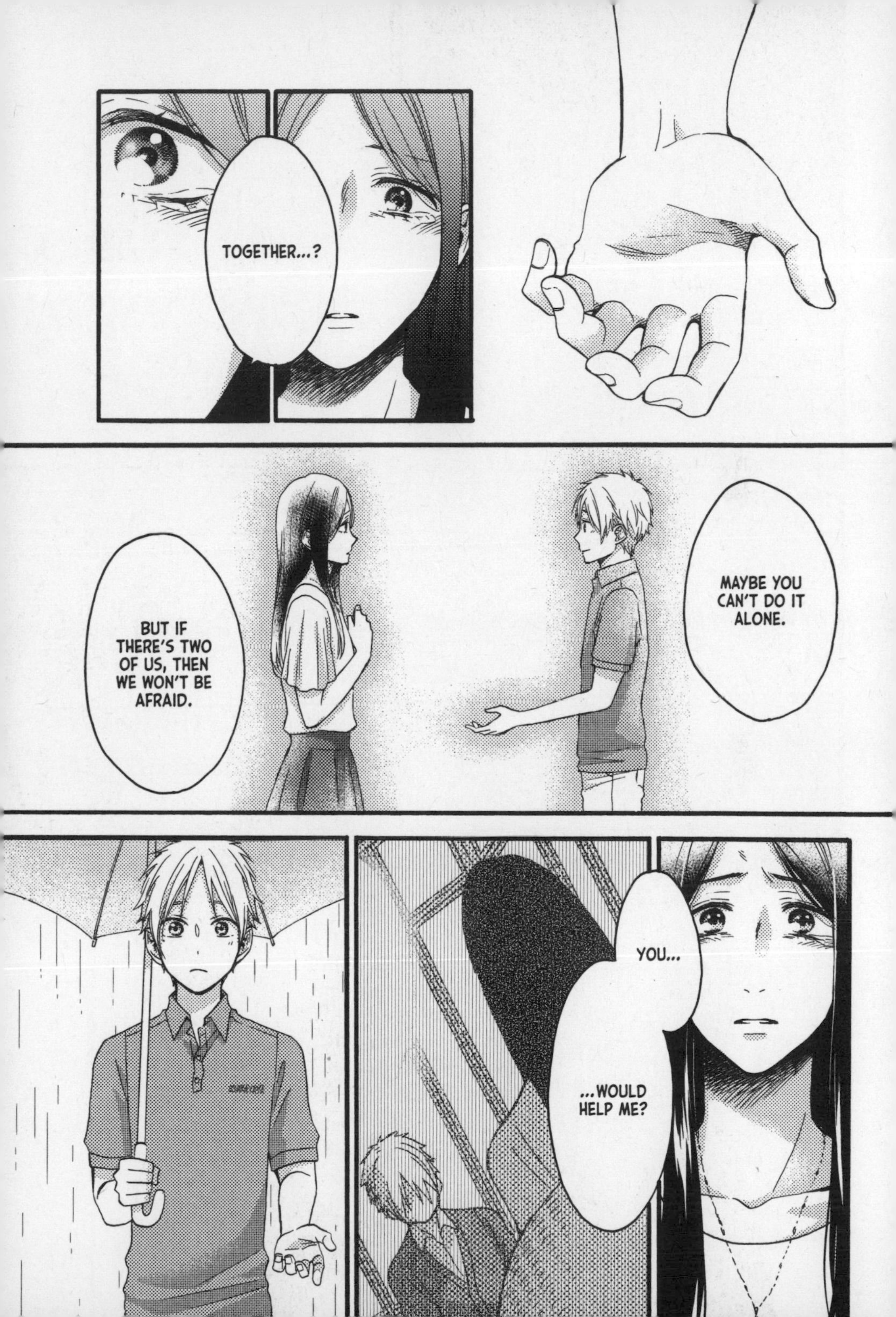
TOGETHER...?
MAYBE YOU CAN'T DO IT ALONE.
BUT IF THERE'S TWO OF US, THEN WE WON'T BE AFRAID.
YOU...
...WOULD HELP ME?

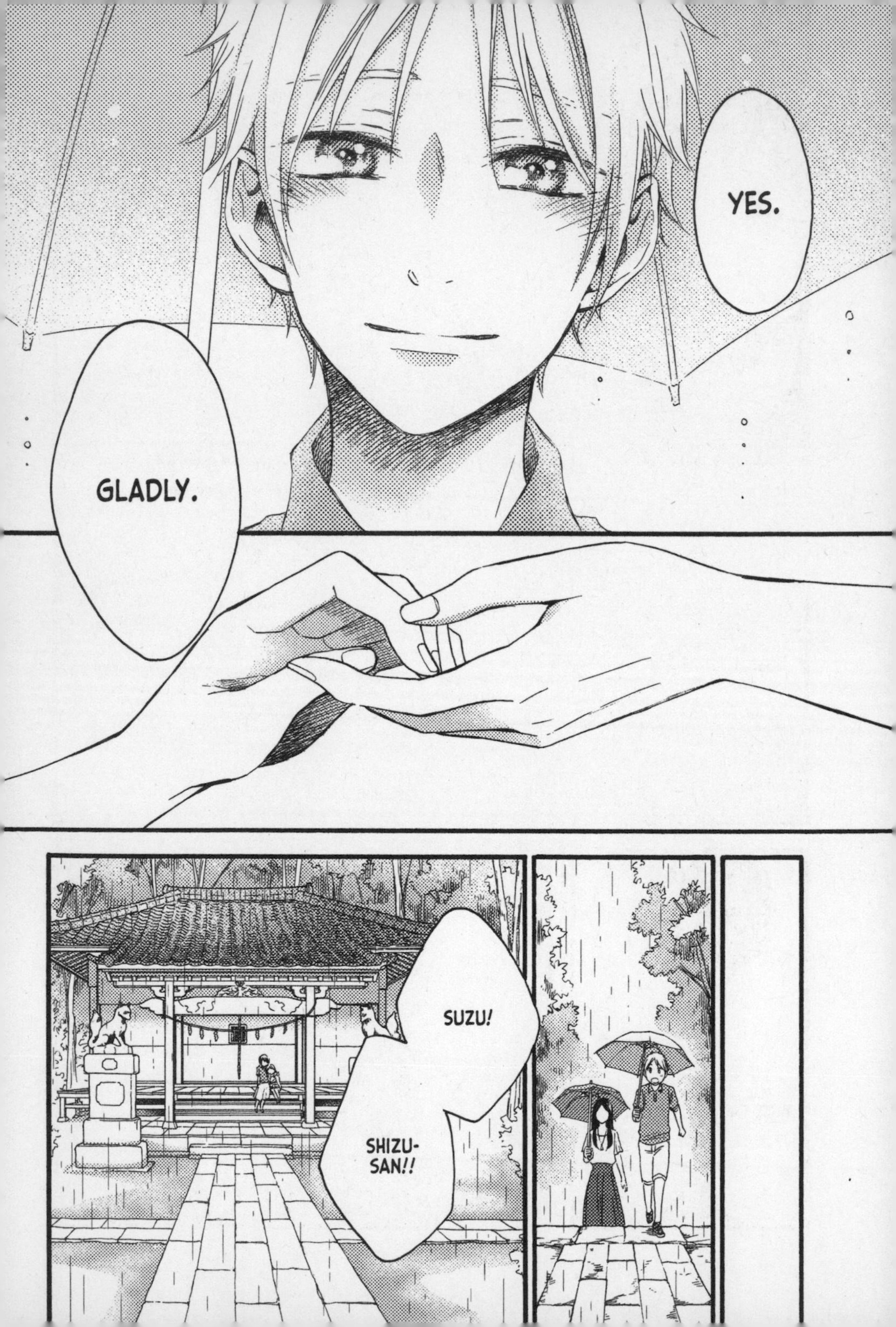
YES.
GLADLY.
SUZU!
SHIZU-SAN!!

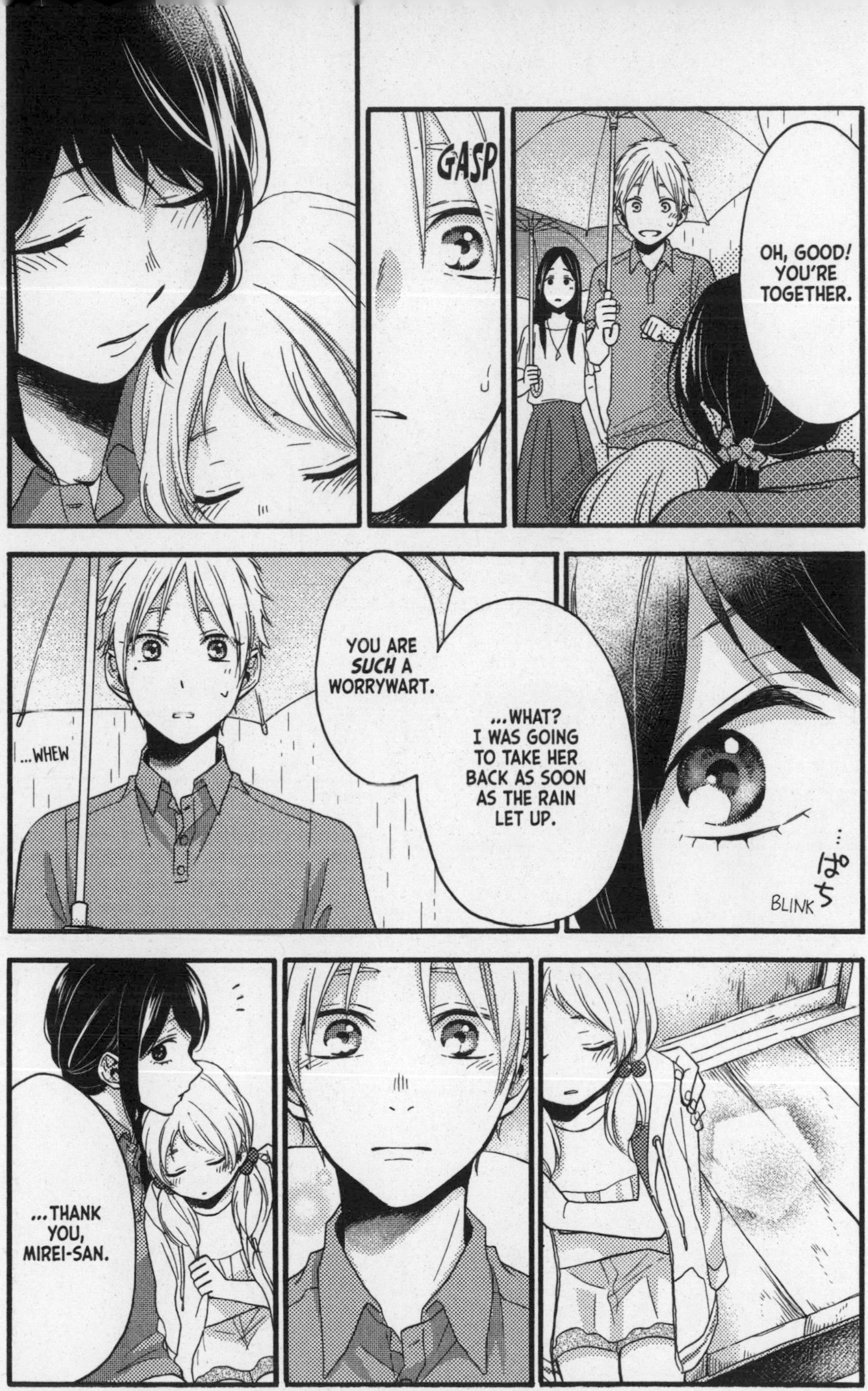
OH, GOOD! YOU'RE TOGETHER.
GASP
ぱち
BLINK
YOU ARE SUCH A WORRYWART.
...WHAT? I WAS GOING TO TAKE HER BACK AS SOON AS THE RAIN LET UP.
...WHEW
...THANK YOU, MIREI-SAN.

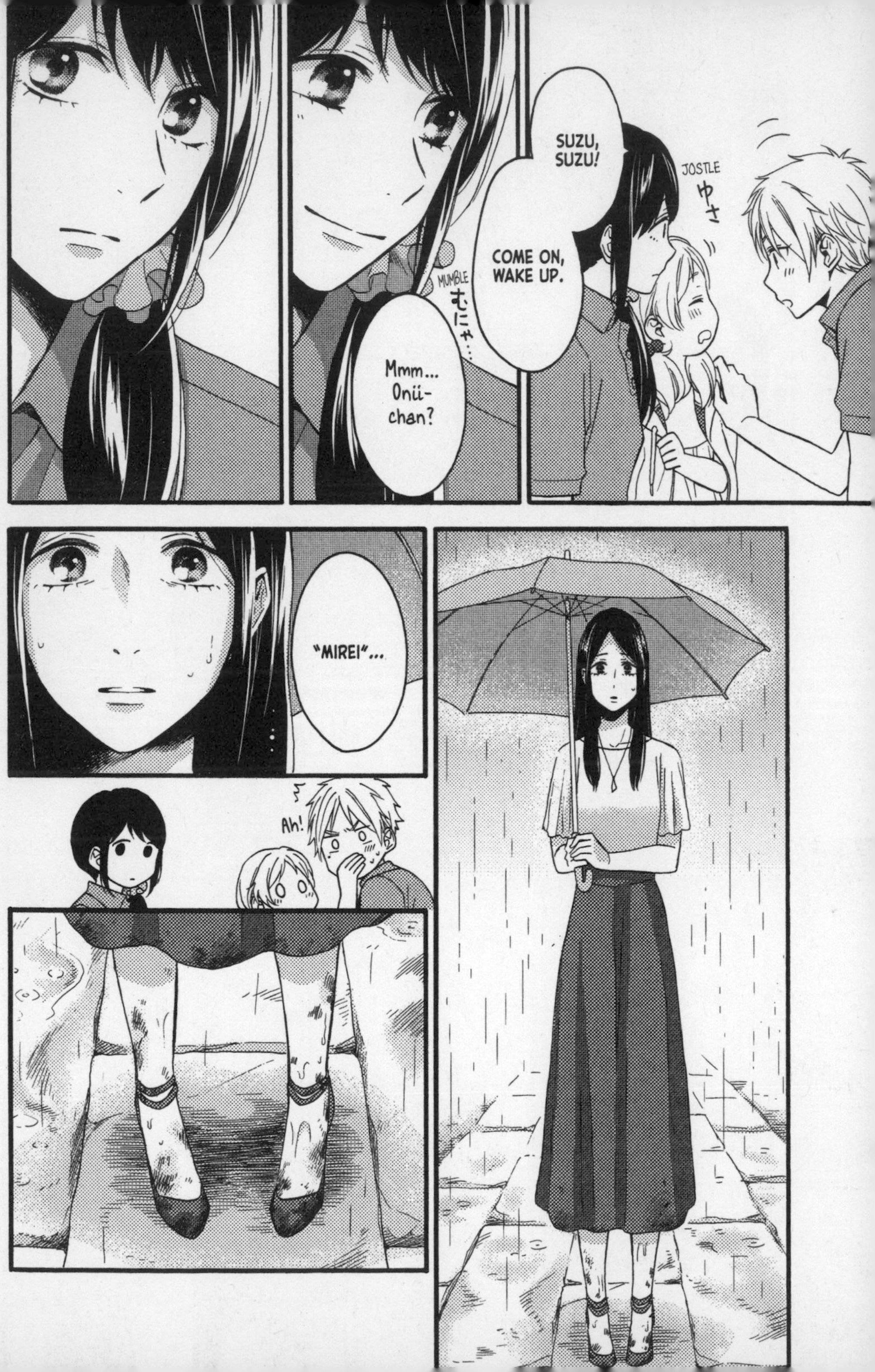
SUZU, SUZU!
JOSTLE
ゆさ
COME ON, WAKE UP.
MUMBLE
むにゃ…
Mmm... Onii-chan?
"MIREI"...
Ah!

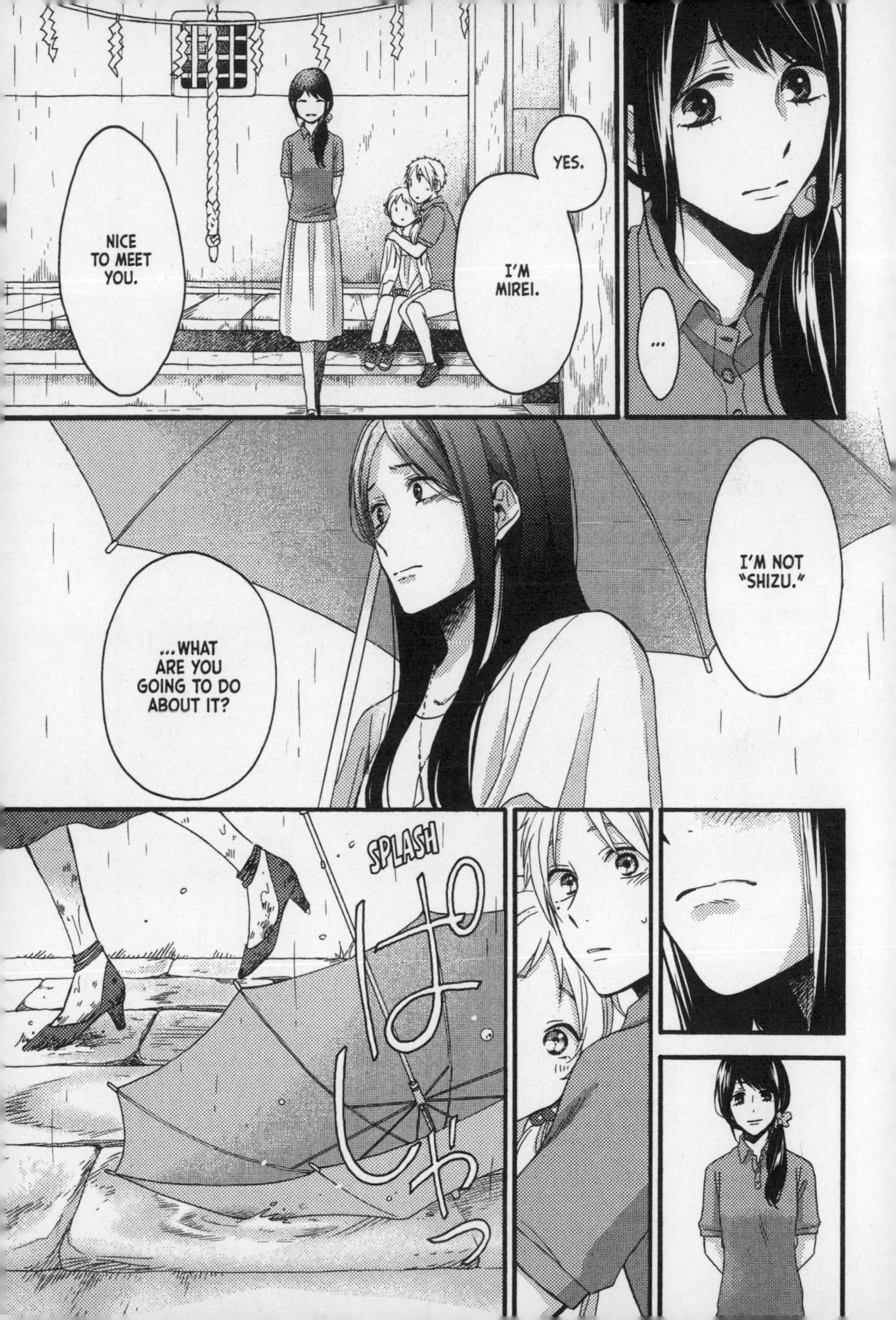
...
YES.
I'M MIREI.
NICE TO MEET YOU.
I'M NOT "SHIZU."
...WHAT ARE YOU GOING TO DO ABOUT IT?
SPLASH

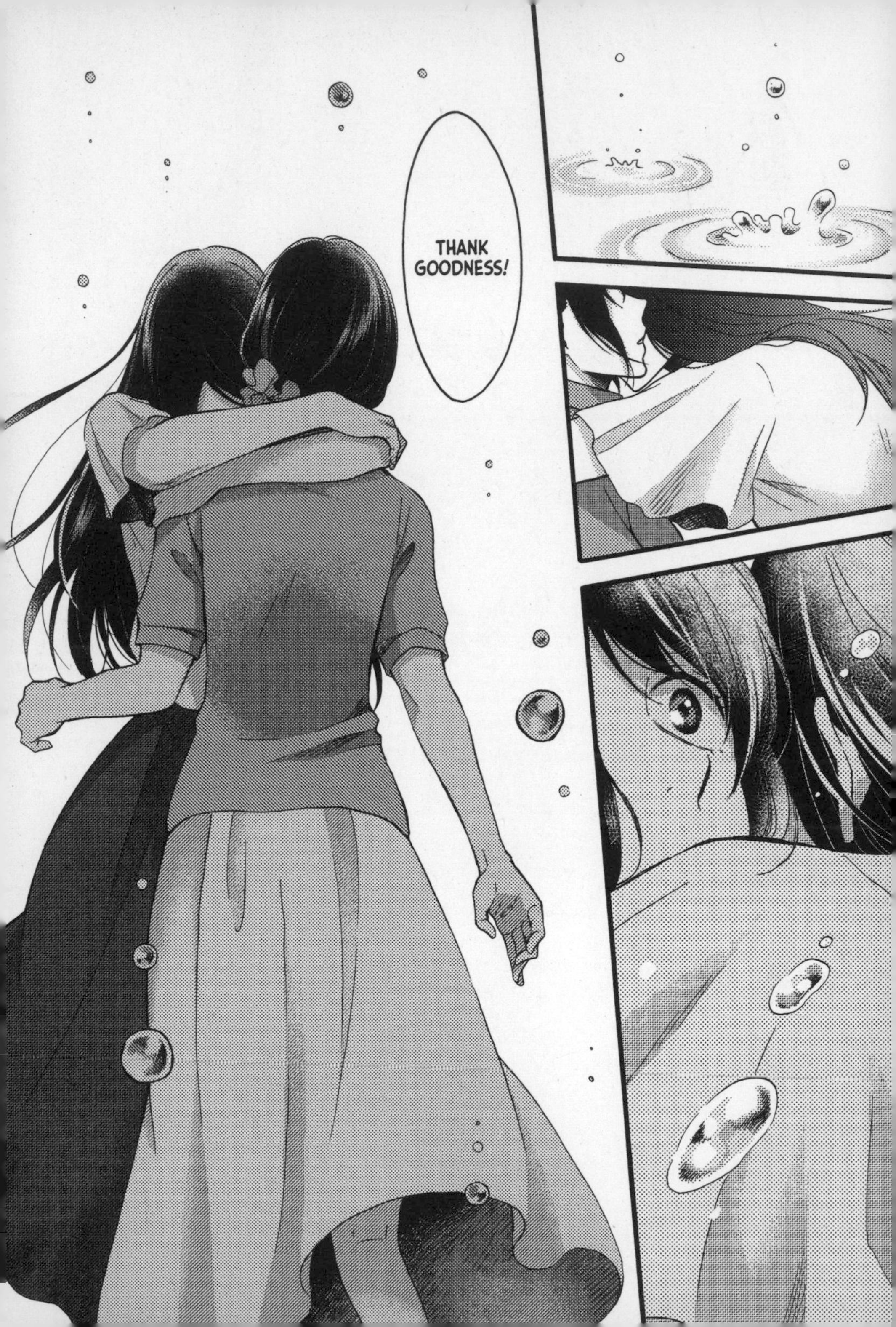
THANK GOODNESS!

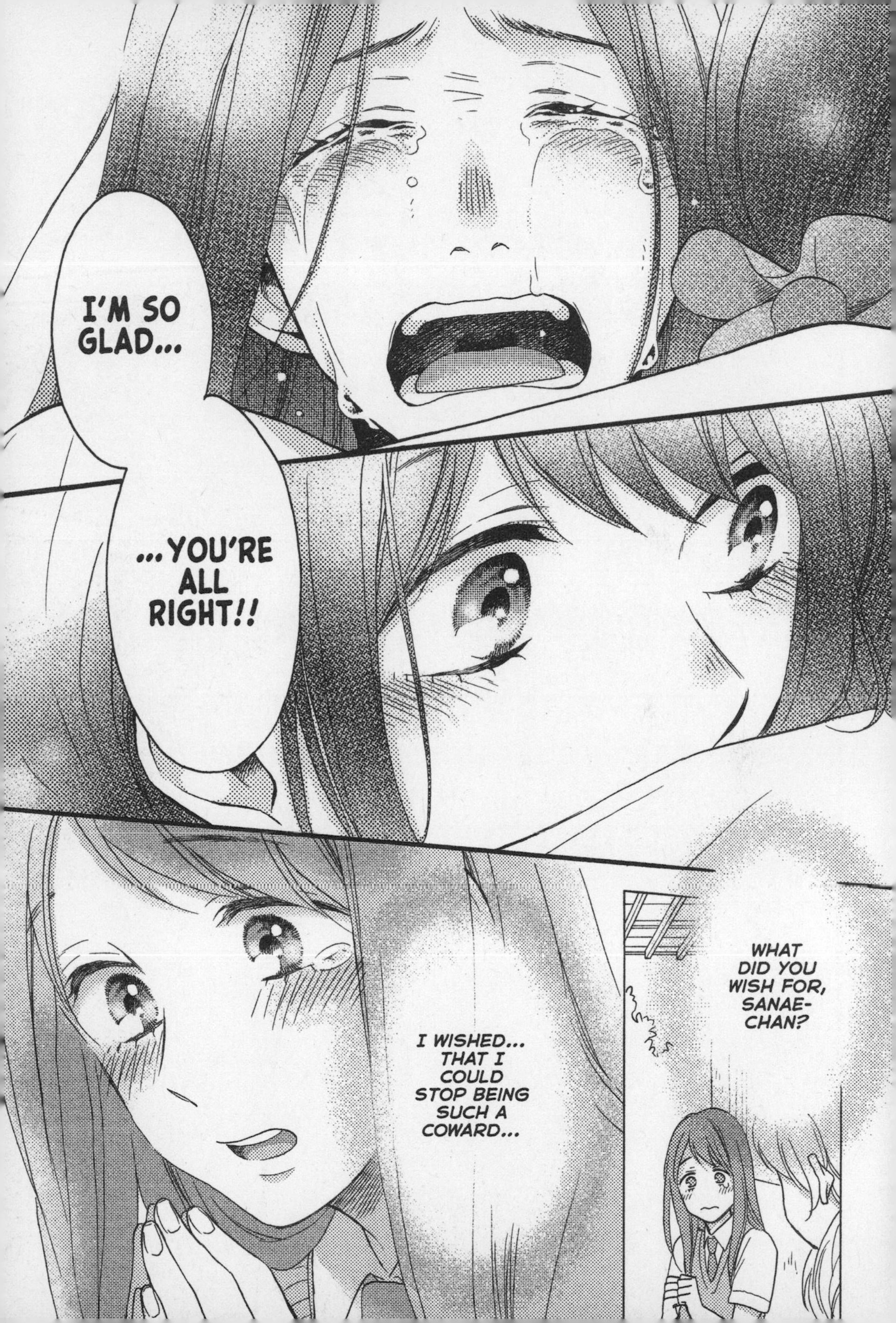
I'M SO GLAD...
...YOU'RE ALL RIGHT!!
WHAT DID YOU WISH FOR, SANAE-CHAN?
I WISHED... THAT I COULD STOP BEING SUCH A COWARD...

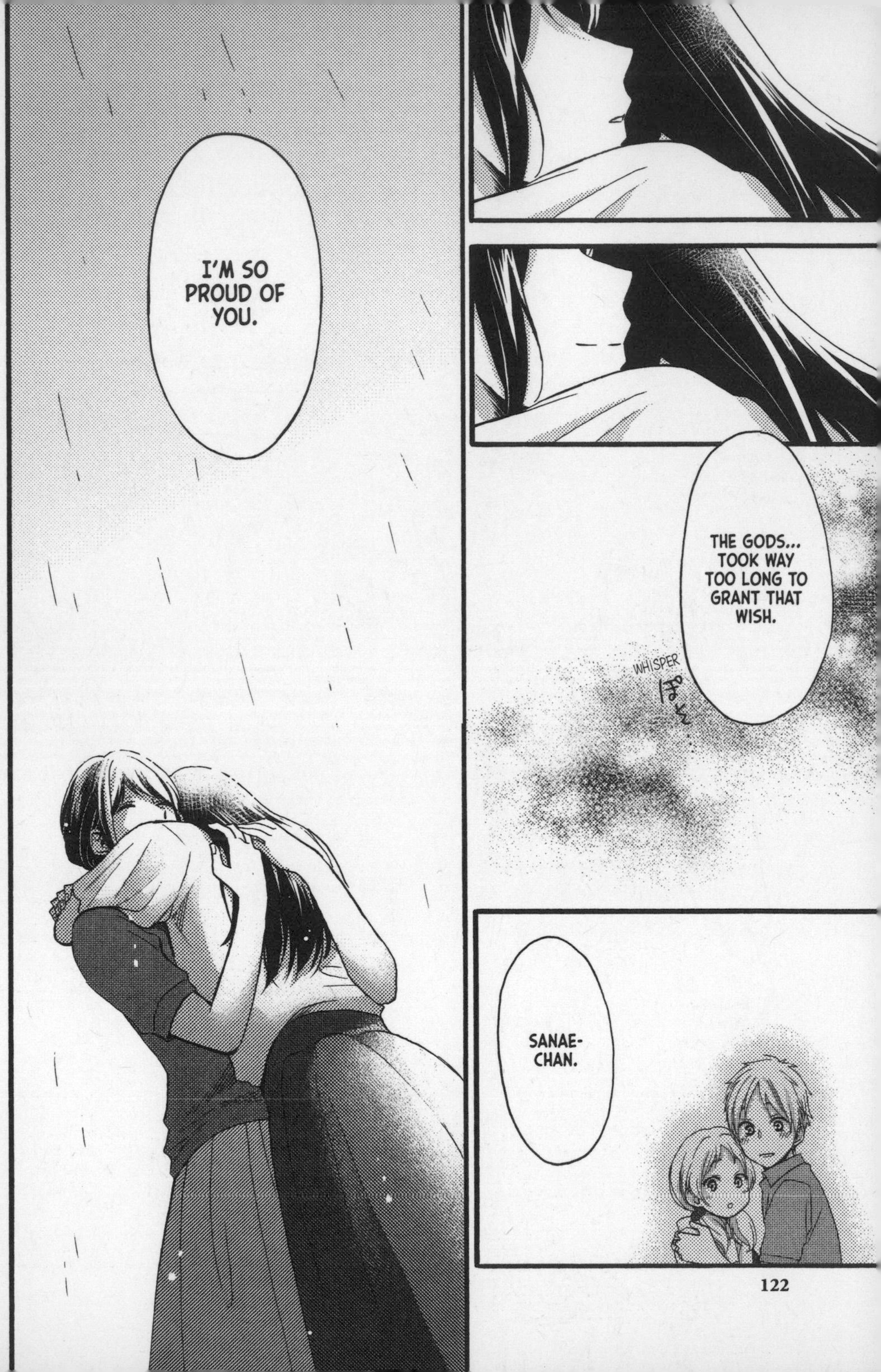
THE GODS... TOOK WAY TOO LONG TO GRANT THAT WISH.
WHISPER
SANAE-CHAN.
I'M SO PROUD OF YOU.

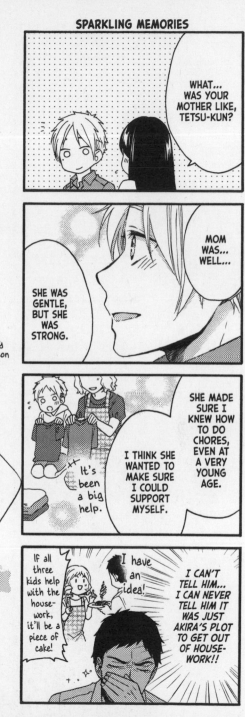

SPARKLING MEMORIES

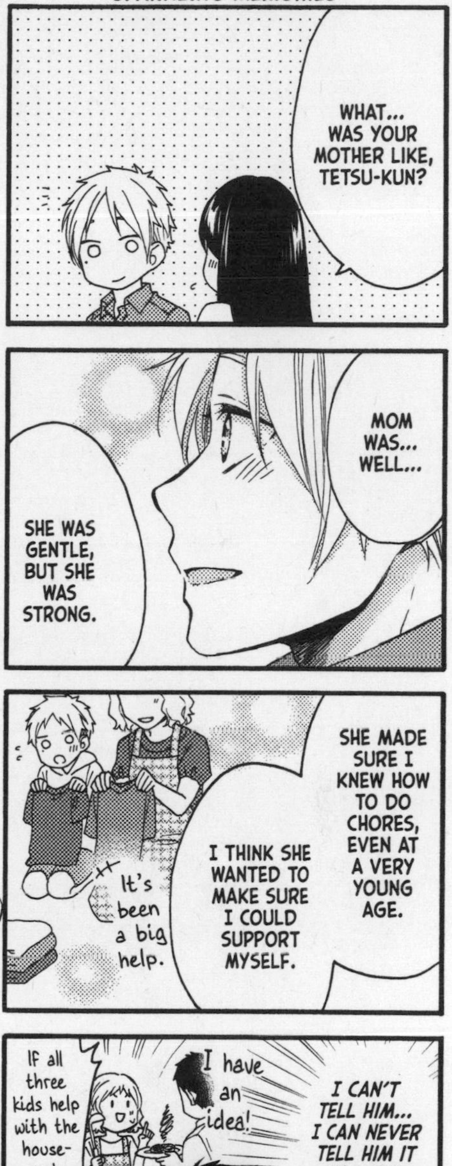
WHAT... WAS YOUR MOTHER LIKE, TETSU-KUN?
MOM WAS... WELL...
SHE WAS GENTLE, BUT SHE WAS STRONG.
SHE MADE SURE I KNEW HOW TO DO CHORES, EVEN AT A VERY YOUNG AGE.
I THINK SHE WANTED TO MAKE SURE I COULD SUPPORT MYSELF.
It's been a big help.
I CAN'T TELL HIM... I CAN NEVER TELL HIM IT WAS JUST AKIRA'S PLOT TO GET OUT OF HOUSE-WORK!!
I have an idea!
If all three kids help with the house-work, it'll be a piece of cake!

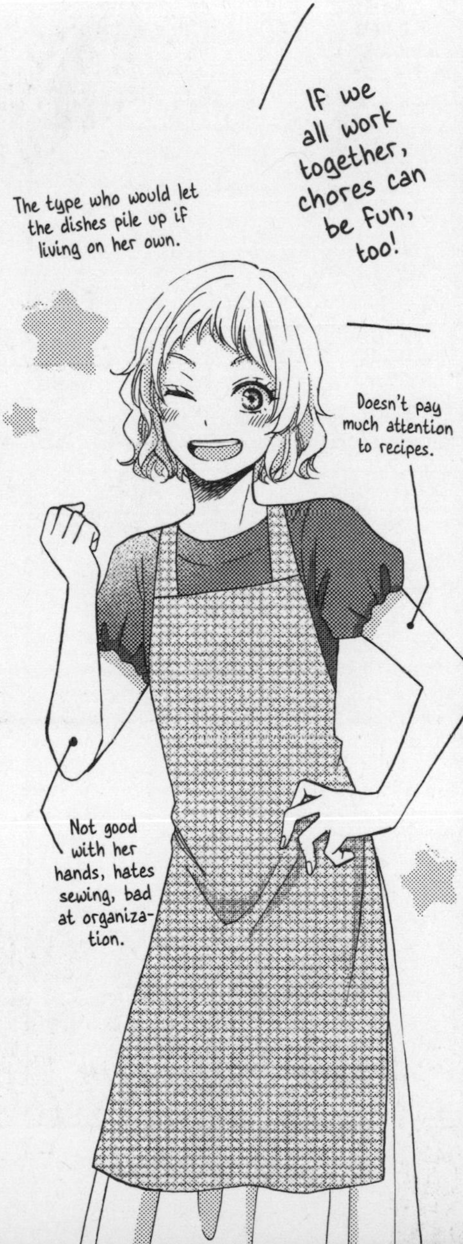
If we all work together, chores can be fun, too!
The type who would let the dishes pile up if living on her own.
Doesn't pay much attention to recipes.
Not good with her hands, hates sewing, bad at organiza-tion.

SHINING MEMORIES

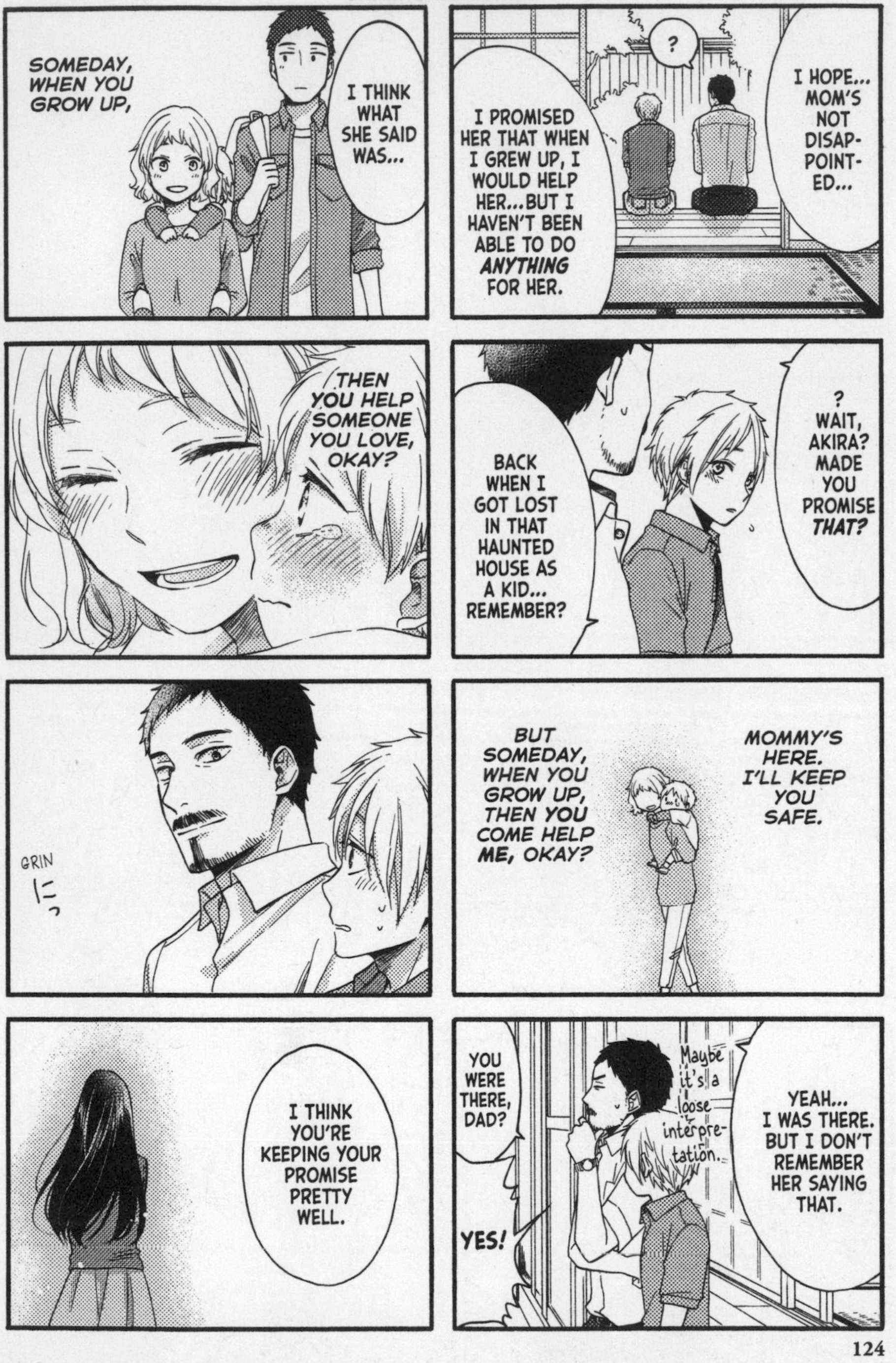
I HOPE... MOM'S NOT DISAPPOINTED...
?
I PROMISED HER THAT WHEN I GREW UP, I WOULD HELP HER...BUT I HAVEN'T BEEN ABLE TO DO *ANYTHING* FOR HER.
? WAIT, AKIRA? MADE YOU PROMISE *THAT?*
BACK WHEN I GOT LOST IN THAT HAUNTED HOUSE AS A KID... REMEMBER?
MOMMY'S HERE. I'LL KEEP YOU SAFE.
BUT SOMEDAY, WHEN YOU GROW UP, THEN YOU COME HELP ME, OKAY?
YEAH... I WAS THERE. BUT I DON'T REMEMBER HER SAYING THAT.
Maybe it's a loose interpretation.
YOU WERE THERE, DAD?
YES!
I THINK WHAT SHE SAID WAS...
SOMEDAY, WHEN YOU GROW UP,
THEN YOU HELP SOMEONE YOU LOVE, OKAY?
GRIN
にっ
I THINK YOU'RE KEEPING YOUR PROMISE PRETTY WELL.

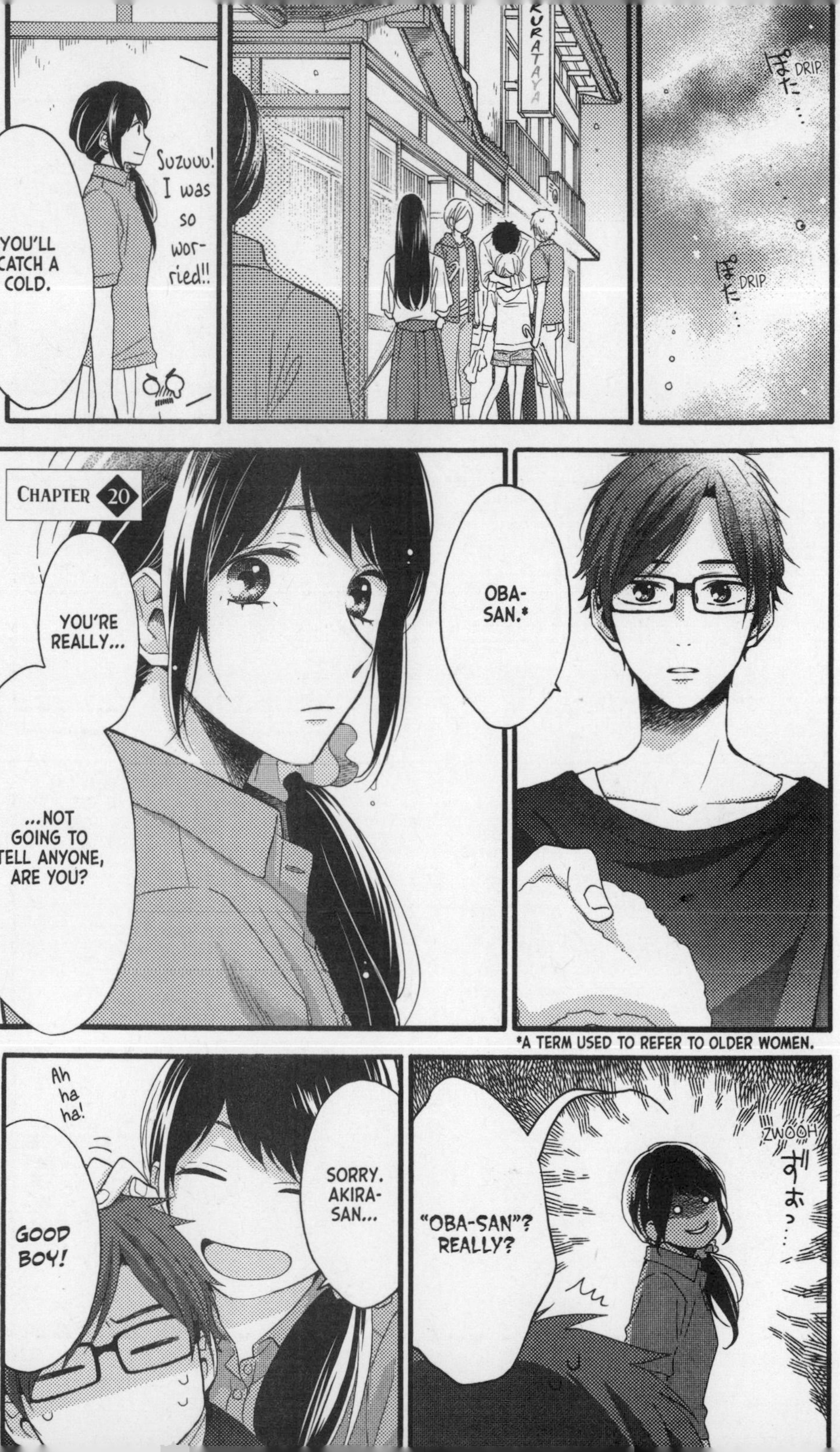
ぽた…
DRIP
ぽた…
DRIP
KURATAYA
Suzuuu! I was so wor-ried!!
YOU'LL CATCH A COLD.
OBA-SAN.*
CHAPTER 20
YOU'RE REALLY...
...NOT GOING TO TELL ANYONE, ARE YOU?
*A TERM USED TO REFER TO OLDER WOMEN.
ZWOOH
ずおっ…
"OBA-SAN"? REALLY?
SORRY. AKIRA-SAN...
Ah ha ha!
GOOD BOY!

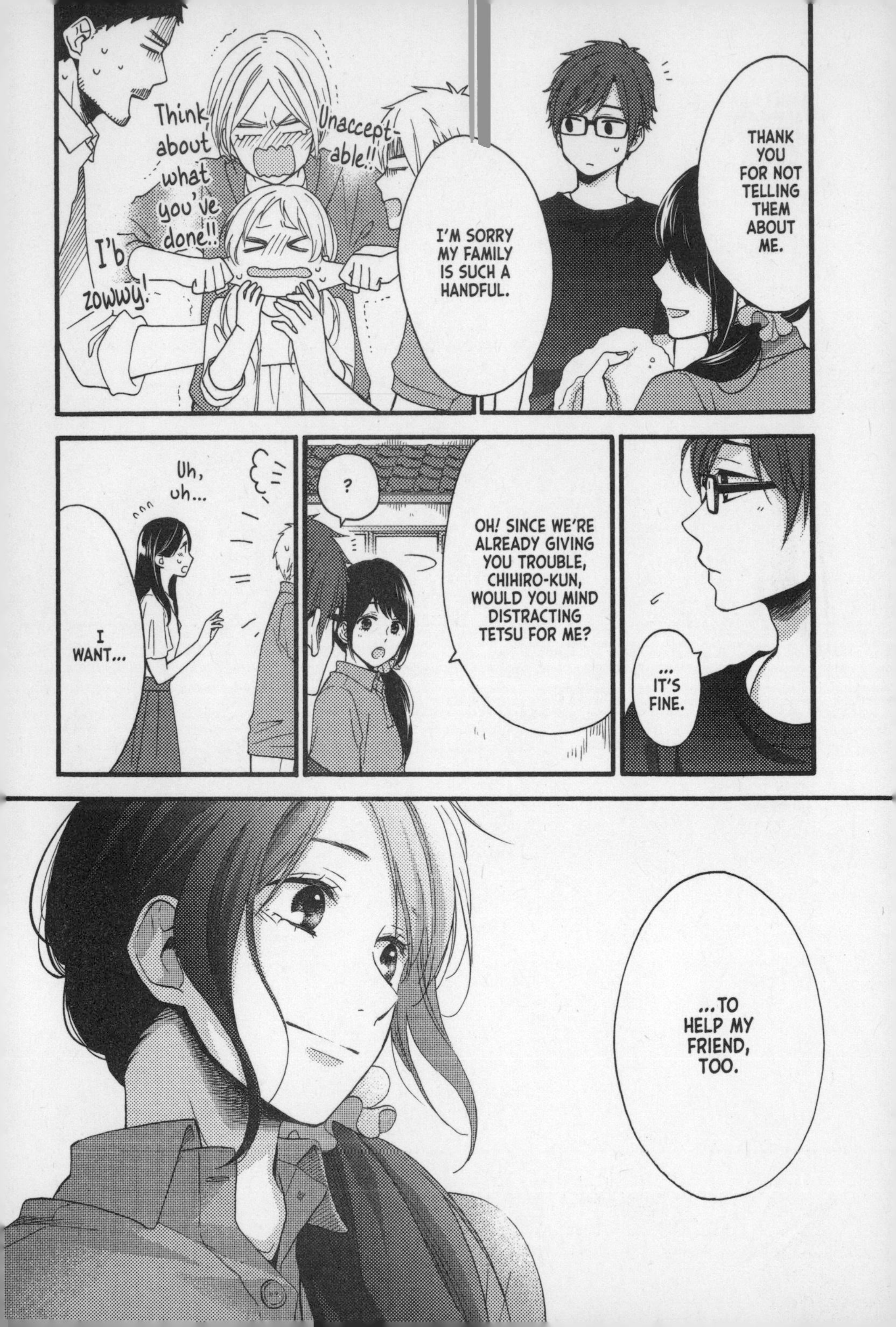
THANK YOU FOR NOT TELLING THEM ABOUT ME.
I'M SORRY MY FAMILY IS SUCH A HANDFUL.
Unaccept-able!!
Think about what you've done!!
I'b zowwy!
...IT'S FINE.
OH! SINCE WE'RE ALREADY GIVING YOU TROUBLE, CHIHIRO-KUN, WOULD YOU MIND DISTRACTING TETSU FOR ME?
?
Uh, uh...
I WANT...
...TO HELP MY FRIEND, TOO.

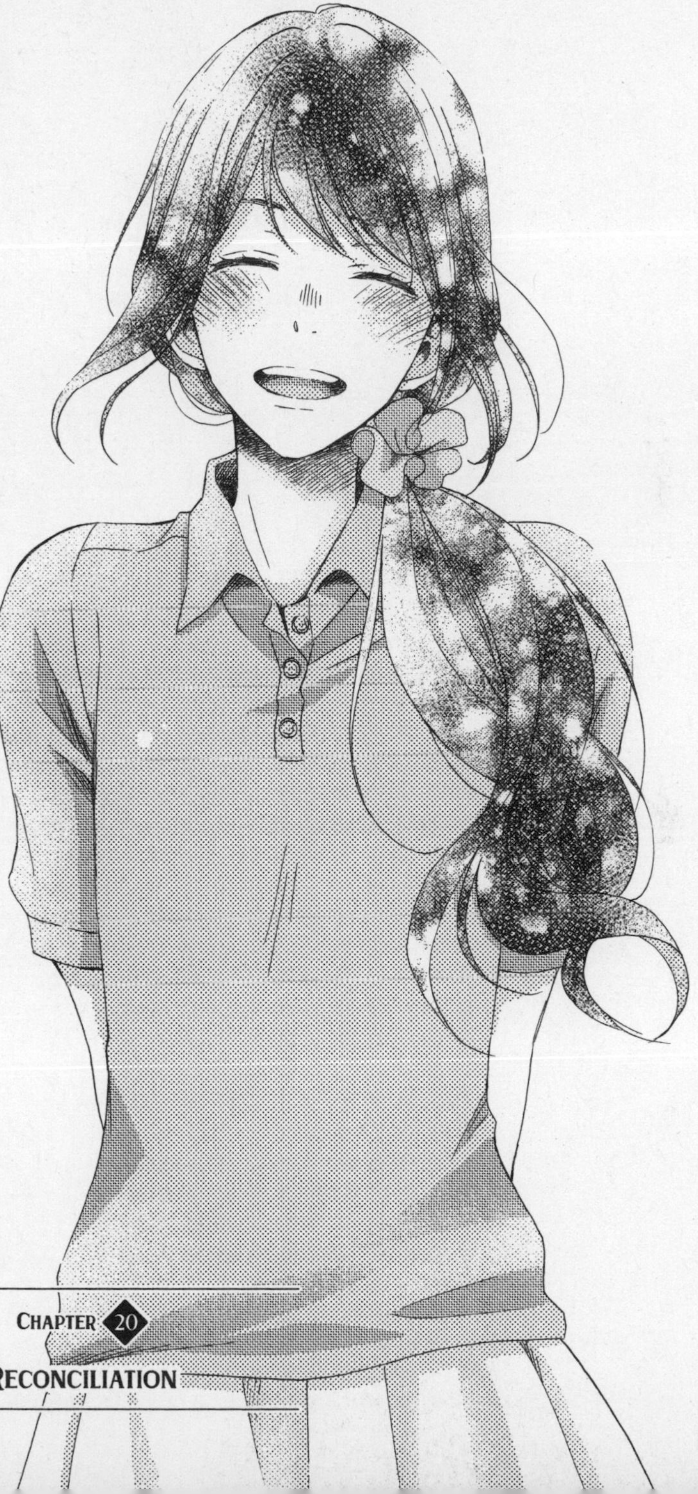

Chapter 20
Reconciliation

SANAE-
SAN.

DO YOU
REMEMBER
WHEN I TOLD
YOU THAT I
WANTED YOU

TO FORM A
CIRCLE OF
HAPPINESS
WITH
TAKASHI?

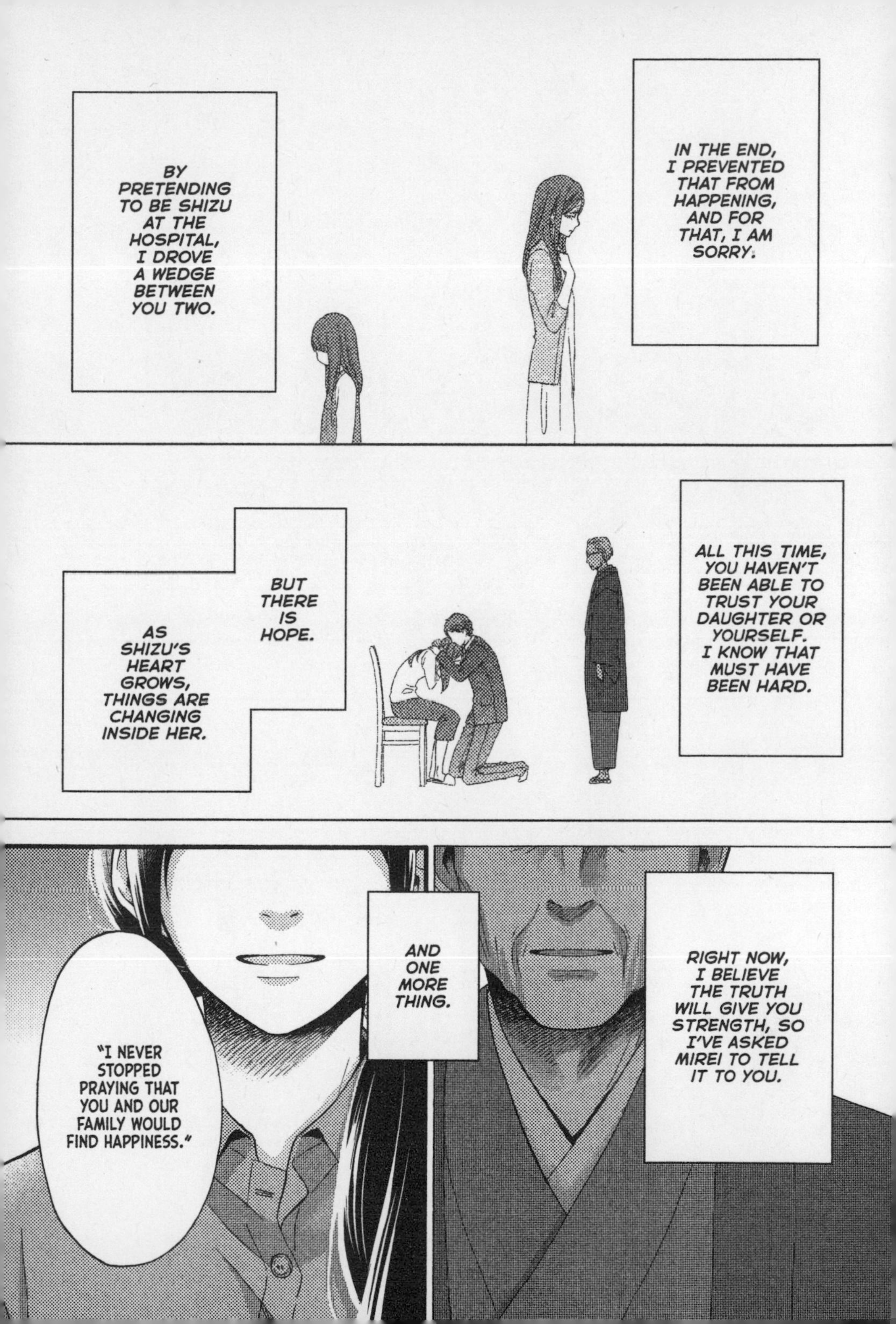
IN THE END, I PREVENTED THAT FROM HAPPENING, AND FOR THAT, I AM SORRY.
BY PRETENDING TO BE SHIZU AT THE HOSPITAL, I DROVE A WEDGE BETWEEN YOU TWO.
ALL THIS TIME, YOU HAVEN'T BEEN ABLE TO TRUST YOUR DAUGHTER OR YOURSELF. I KNOW THAT MUST HAVE BEEN HARD.
BUT THERE IS HOPE.
AS SHIZU'S HEART GROWS, THINGS ARE CHANGING INSIDE HER.
RIGHT NOW, I BELIEVE THE TRUTH WILL GIVE YOU STRENGTH, SO I'VE ASKED MIREI TO TELL IT TO YOU.
AND ONE MORE THING.
"I NEVER STOPPED PRAYING THAT YOU AND OUR FAMILY WOULD FIND HAPPINESS."

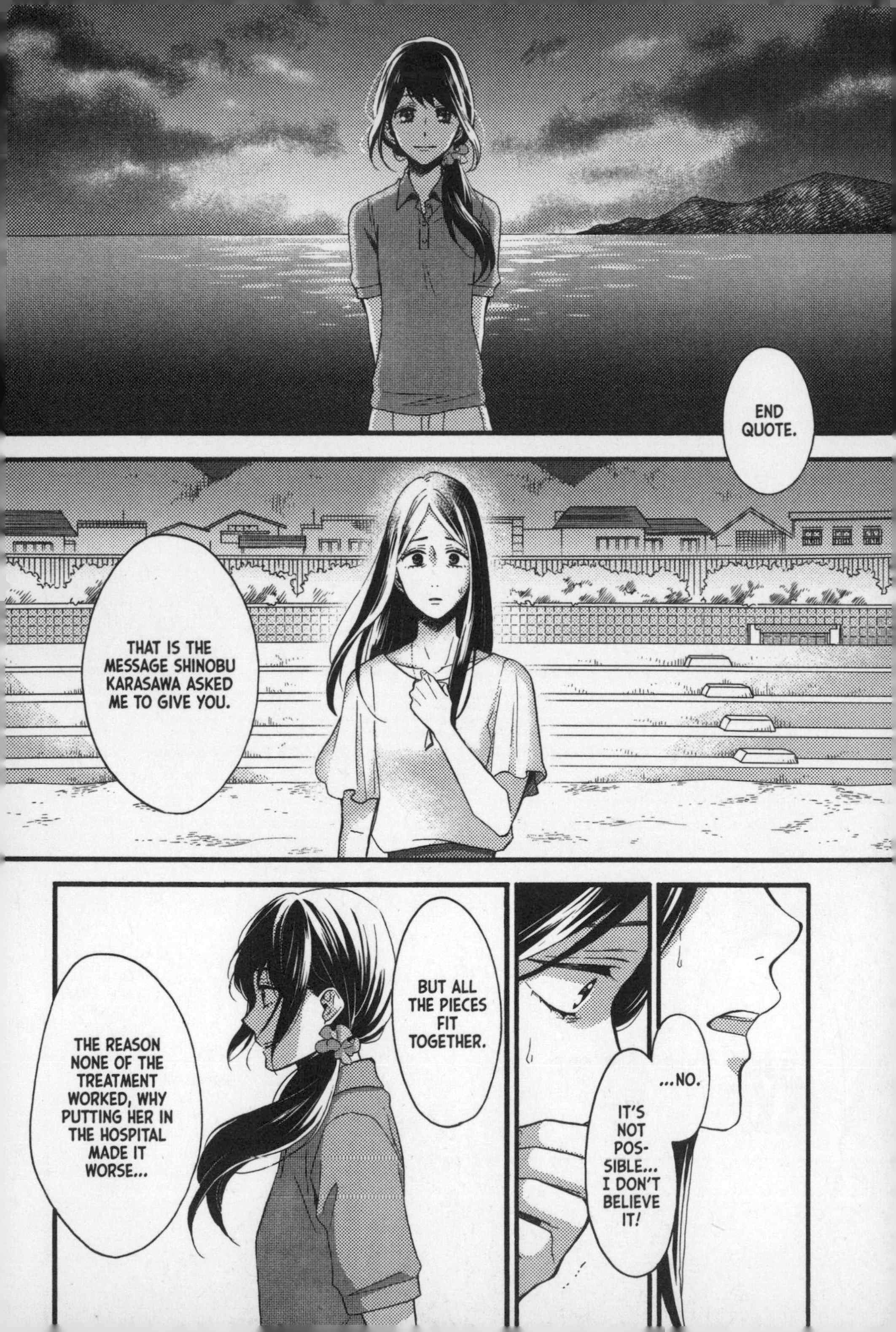

END QUOTE.
THAT IS THE MESSAGE SHINOBU KARASAWA ASKED ME TO GIVE YOU.
...NO.
IT'S NOT POS-SIBLE... I DON'T BELIEVE IT!
BUT ALL THE PIECES FIT TOGETHER.
THE REASON NONE OF THE TREATMENT WORKED, WHY PUTTING HER IN THE HOSPITAL MADE IT WORSE...

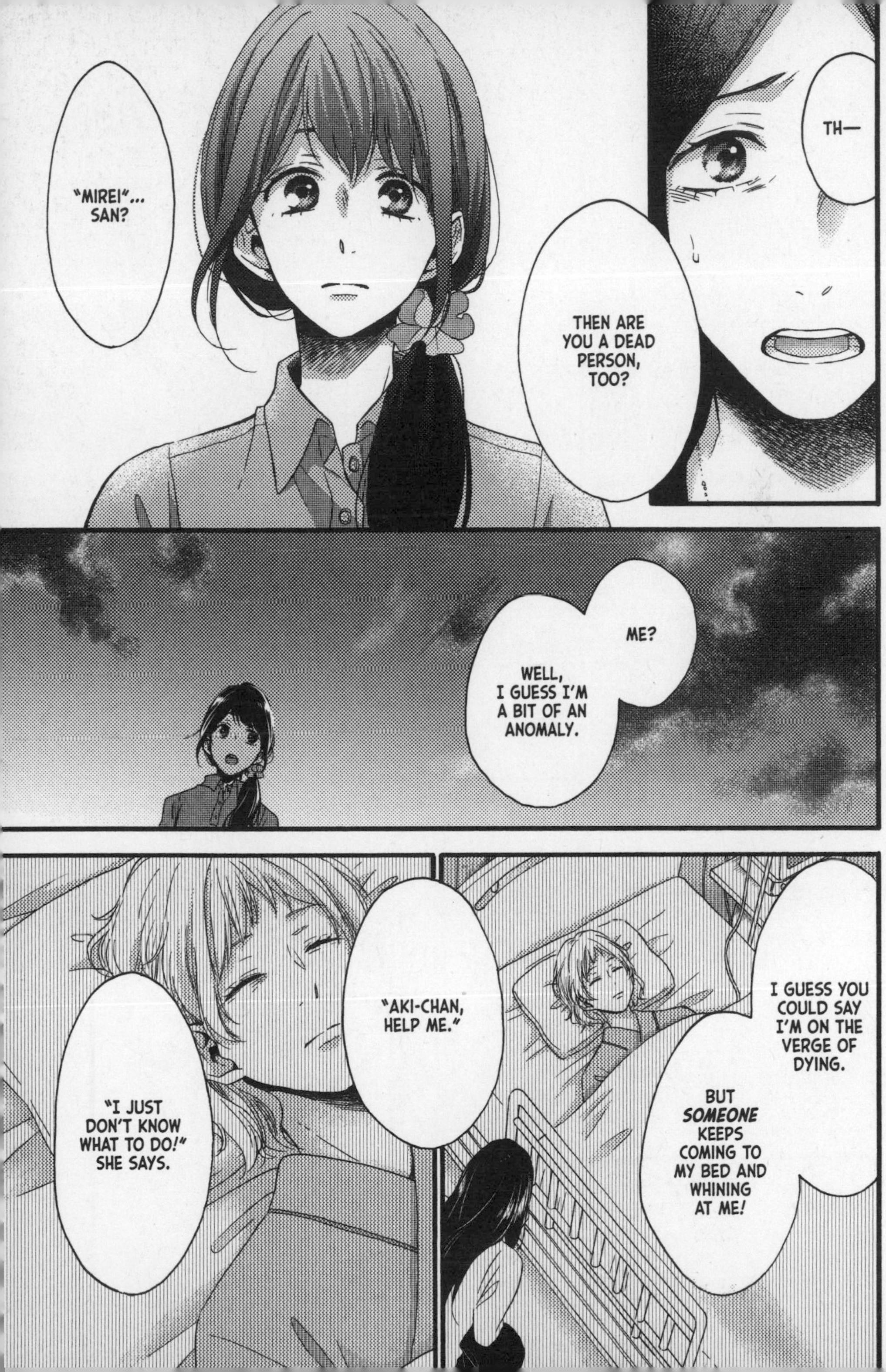
TH—
THEN ARE YOU A DEAD PERSON, TOO?
"MIREI"... SAN?
ME?
WELL, I GUESS I'M A BIT OF AN ANOMALY.
I GUESS YOU COULD SAY I'M ON THE VERGE OF DYING.
BUT *SOMEONE* KEEPS COMING TO MY BED AND WHINING AT ME!
"AKI-CHAN, HELP ME."
"I JUST DON'T KNOW WHAT TO DO!" SHE SAYS.

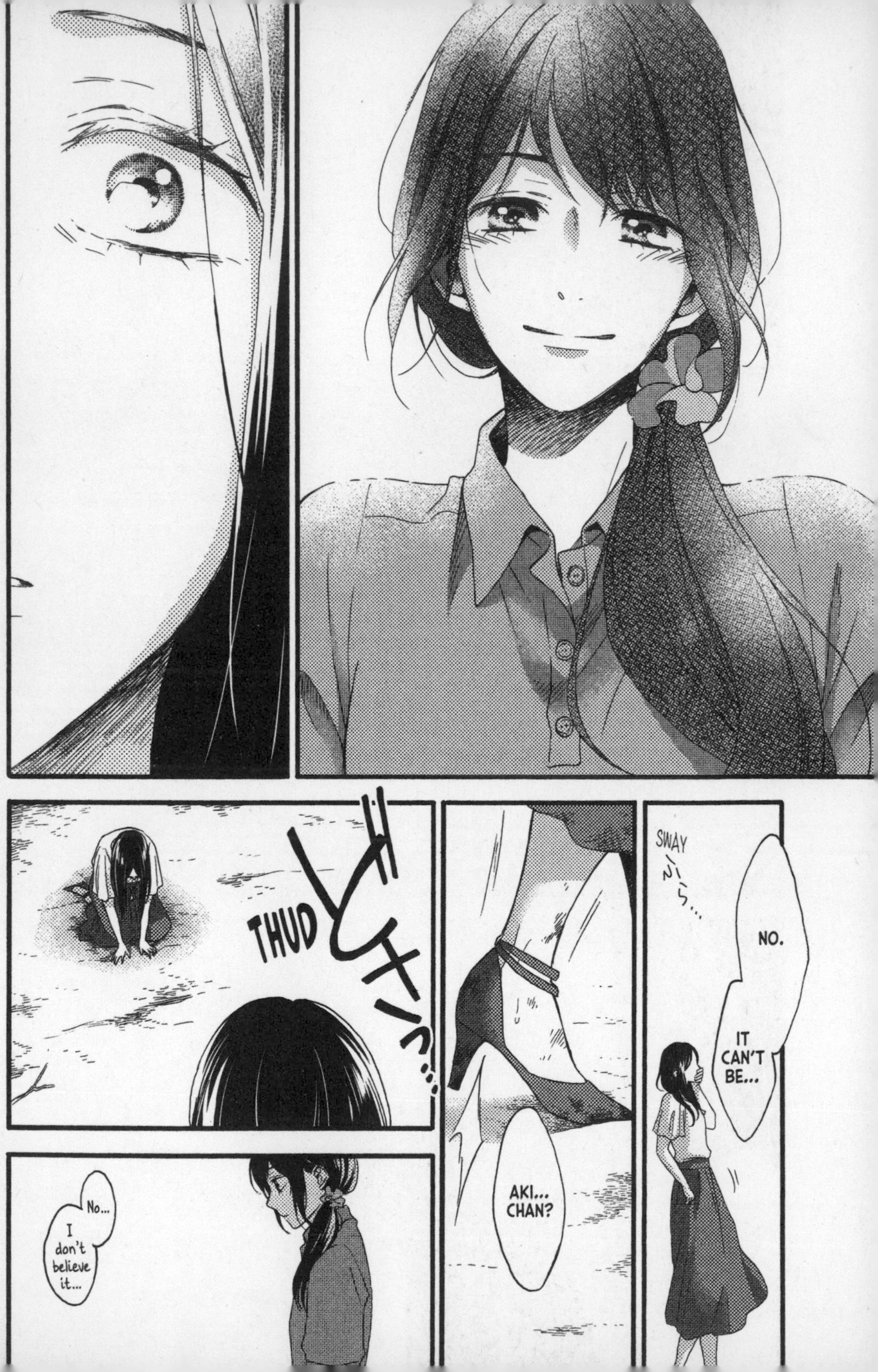
SWAY
NO.
IT CAN'T BE...
AKI... CHAN?
THUD
No... I don't believe it...

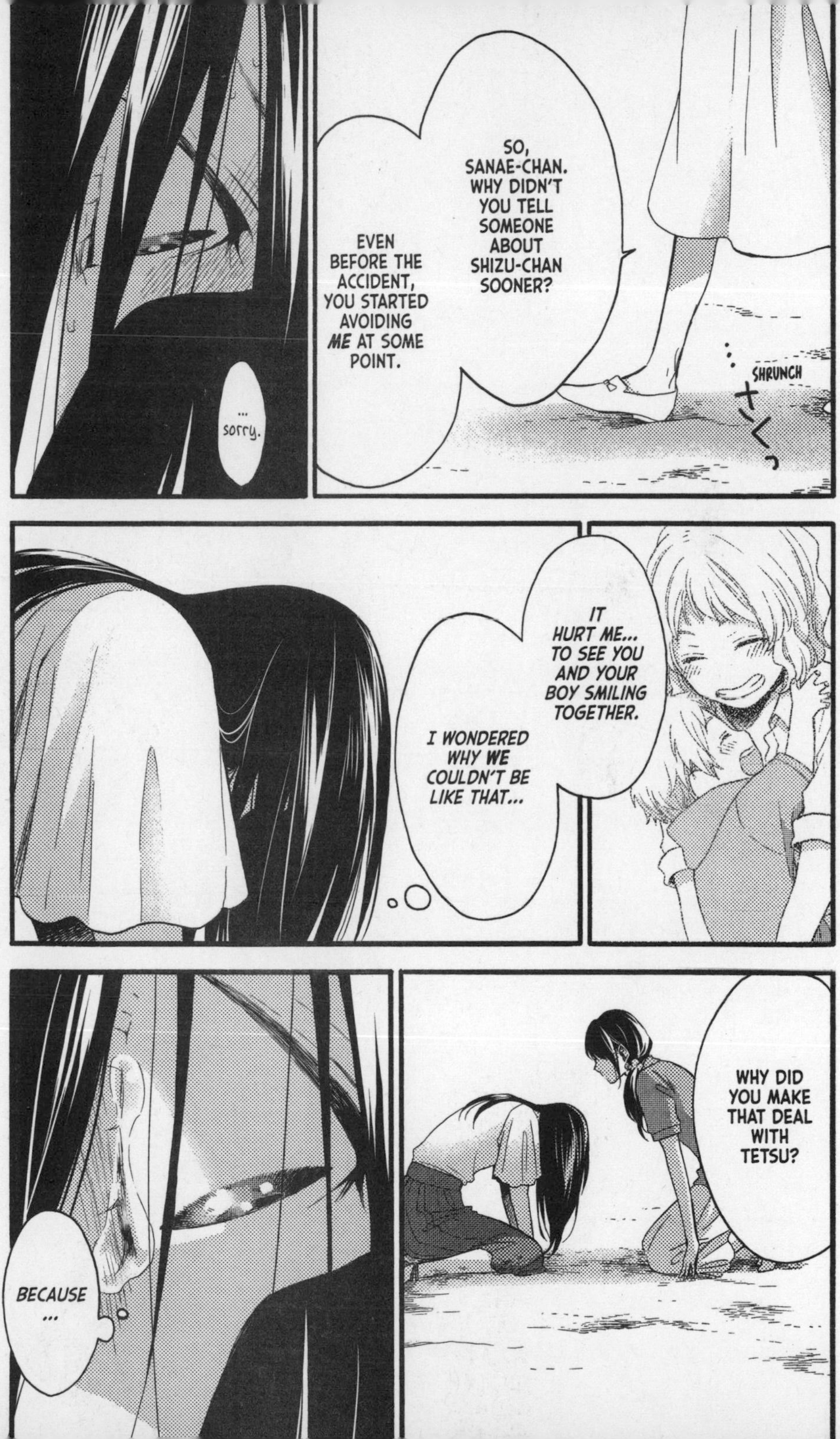
SHRUNCH
SO, SANAE-CHAN. WHY DIDN'T YOU TELL SOMEONE ABOUT SHIZU-CHAN SOONER?
EVEN BEFORE THE ACCIDENT, YOU STARTED AVOIDING *ME* AT SOME POINT.
... sorry.
IT HURT ME... TO SEE YOU AND YOUR BOY SMILING TOGETHER.
I WONDERED WHY *WE* COULDN'T BE LIKE THAT...
WHY DID YOU MAKE THAT DEAL WITH TETSU?
BECAUSE ...

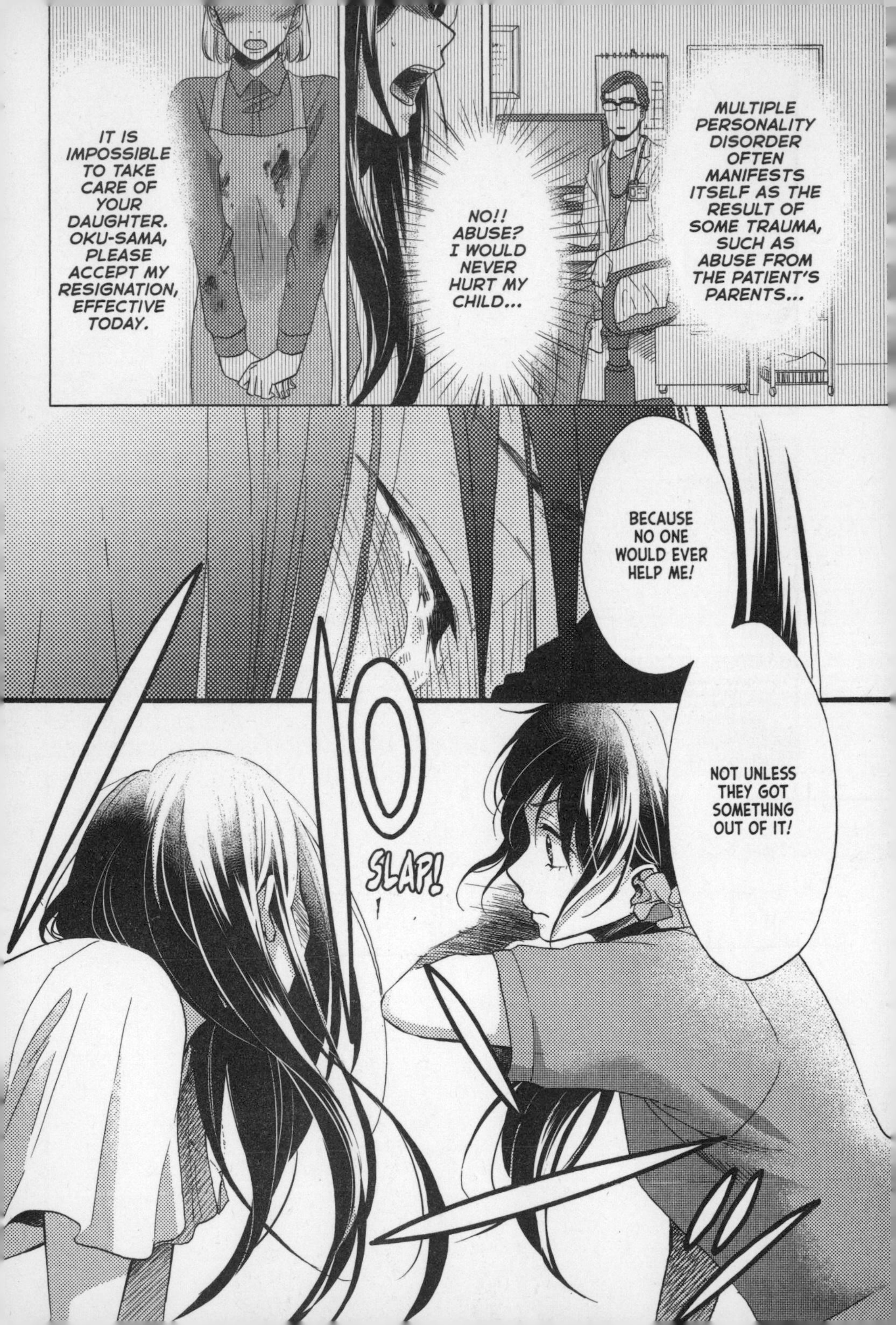
MULTIPLE PERSONALITY DISORDER OFTEN MANIFESTS ITSELF AS THE RESULT OF SOME TRAUMA, SUCH AS ABUSE FROM THE PATIENT'S PARENTS...
NO!! ABUSE? I WOULD NEVER HURT MY CHILD...
IT IS IMPOSSIBLE TO TAKE CARE OF YOUR DAUGHTER. OKU-SAMA, PLEASE ACCEPT MY RESIGNATION, EFFECTIVE TODAY.
BECAUSE NO ONE WOULD EVER HELP ME!
NOT UNLESS THEY GOT SOMETHING OUT OF IT!
SLAP!

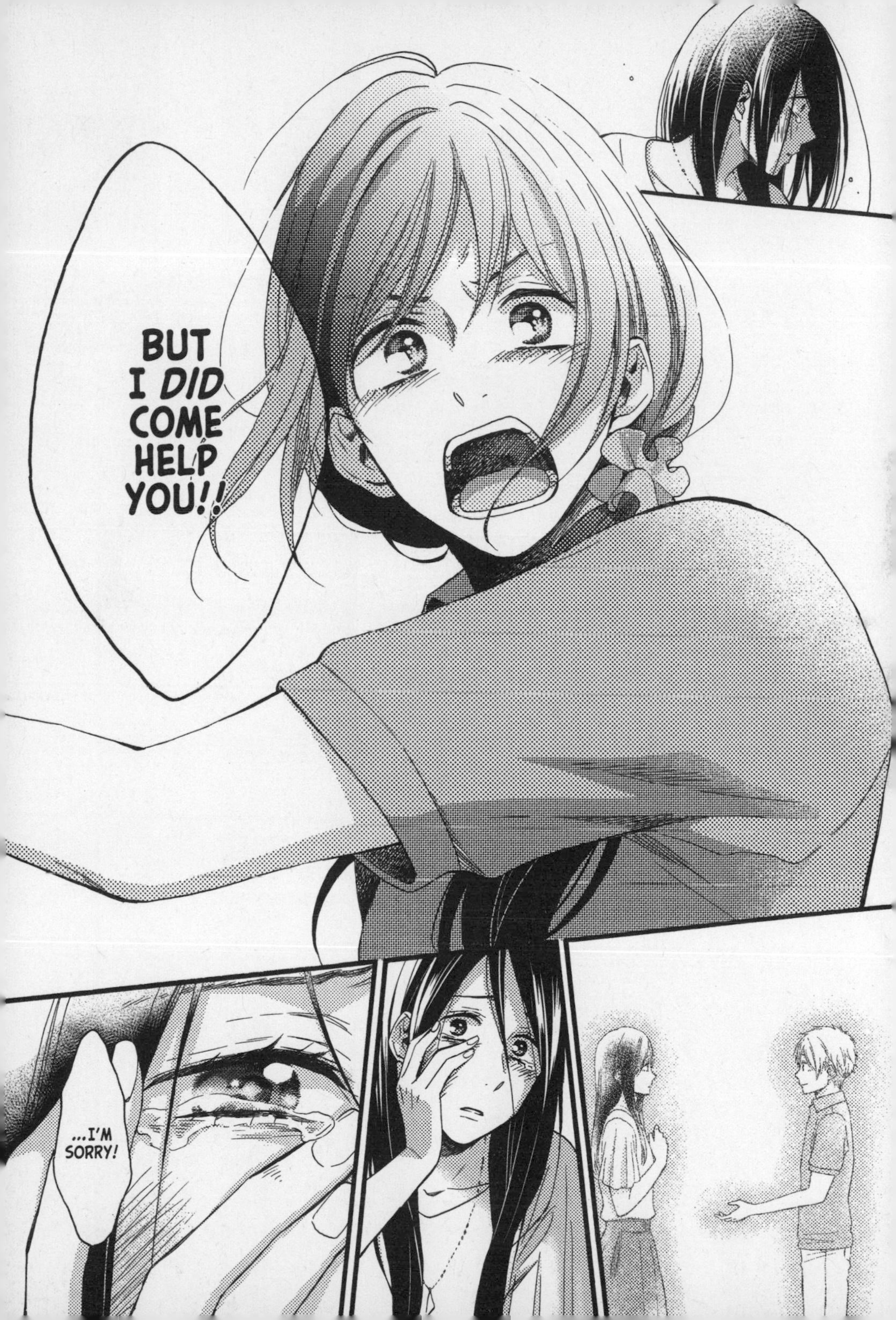
BUT I DID COME HELP YOU!!
...I'M SORRY!

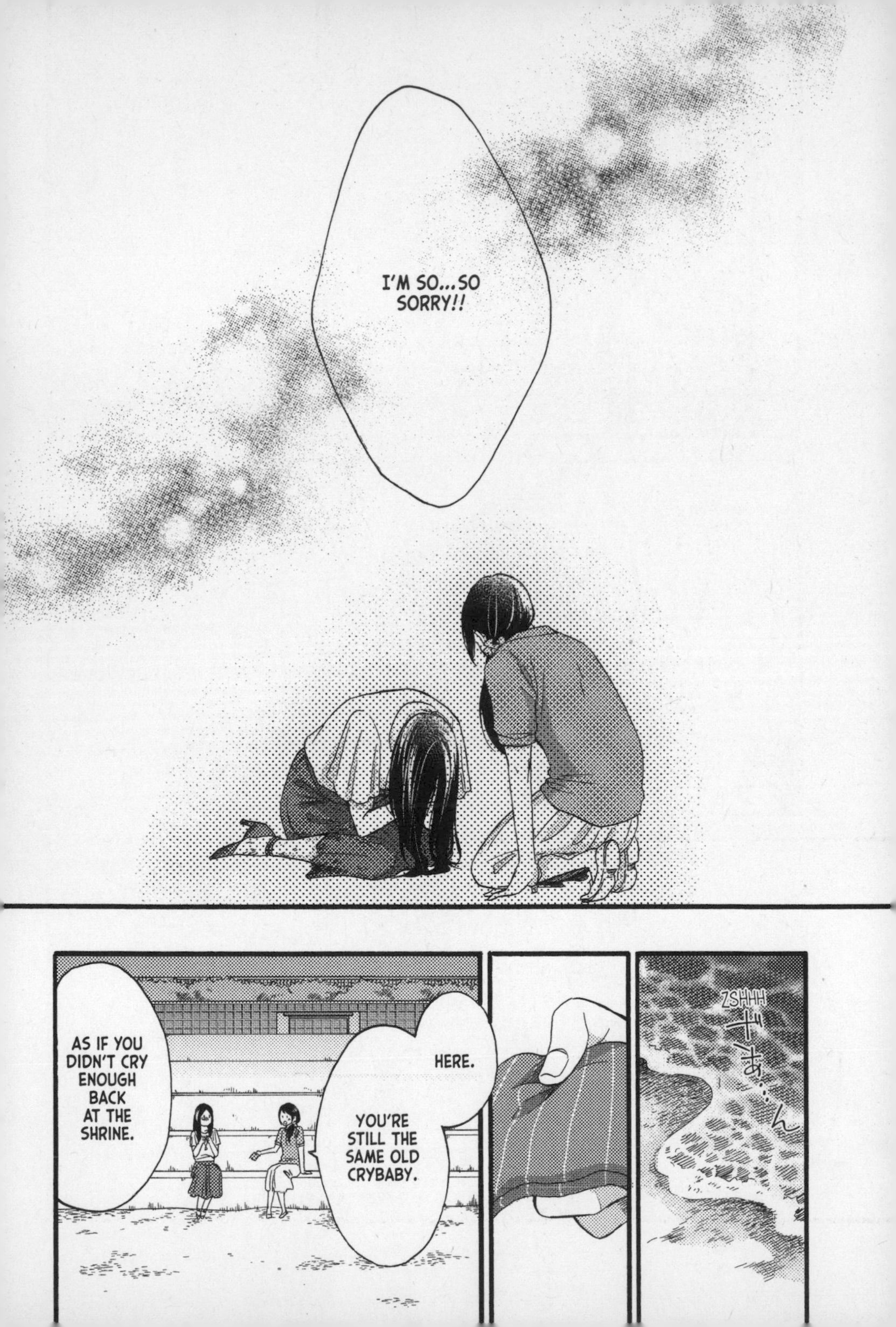
I'M SO...SO SORRY!!
ZSHHH
ザぁ…ん
HERE.
YOU'RE STILL THE SAME OLD CRYBABY.
AS IF YOU DIDN'T CRY ENOUGH BACK AT THE SHRINE.

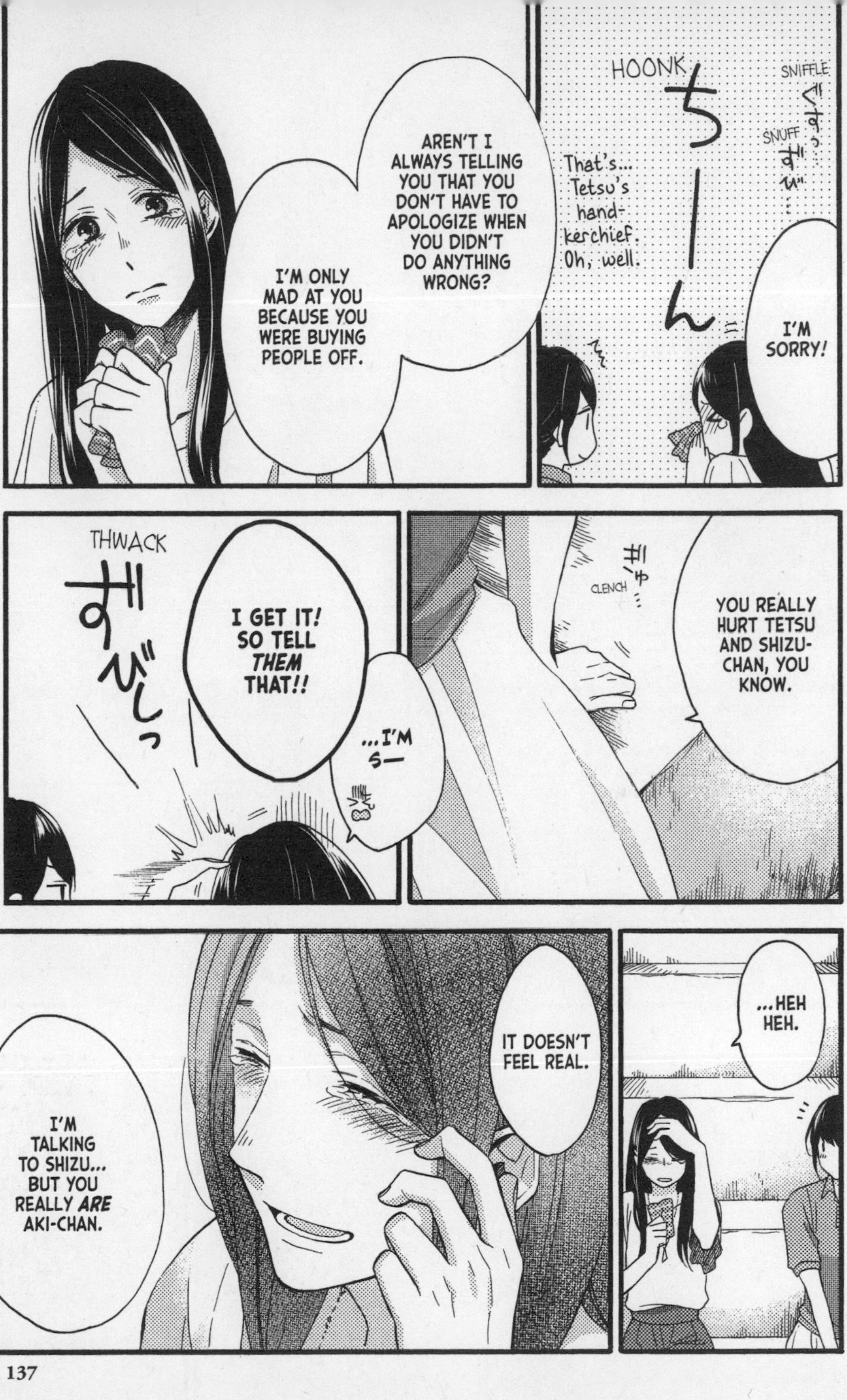
SNIFFLE
SNUFF
HOONK
I'M SORRY!
That's... Tetsu's hand-kerchief. Oh, well.
AREN'T I ALWAYS TELLING YOU THAT YOU DON'T HAVE TO APOLOGIZE WHEN YOU DIDN'T DO ANYTHING WRONG?
I'M ONLY MAD AT YOU BECAUSE YOU WERE BUYING PEOPLE OFF.
CLENCH
YOU REALLY HURT TETSU AND SHIZU-CHAN, YOU KNOW.
THWACK
I GET IT! SO TELL *THEM* THAT!!
...I'M S—
...HEH HEH.
IT DOESN'T FEEL REAL.
I'M TALKING TO SHIZU... BUT YOU REALLY *ARE* AKI-CHAN.

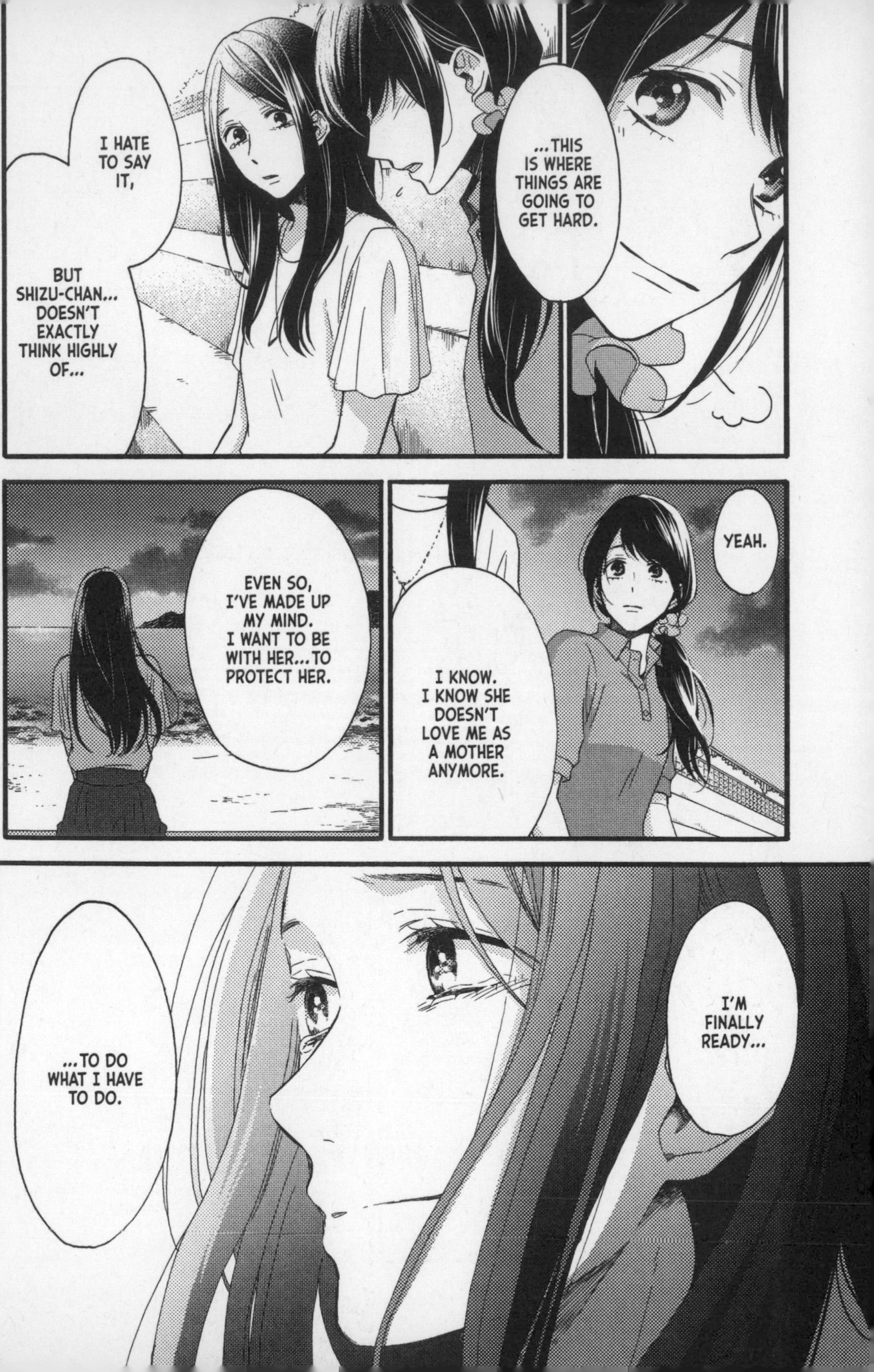
...THIS IS WHERE THINGS ARE GOING TO GET HARD.
I HATE TO SAY IT,
BUT SHIZU-CHAN... DOESN'T EXACTLY THINK HIGHLY OF...
YEAH.
I KNOW. I KNOW SHE DOESN'T LOVE ME AS A MOTHER ANYMORE.
EVEN SO, I'VE MADE UP MY MIND. I WANT TO BE WITH HER...TO PROTECT HER.
I'M FINALLY READY...
...TO DO WHAT I HAVE TO DO.

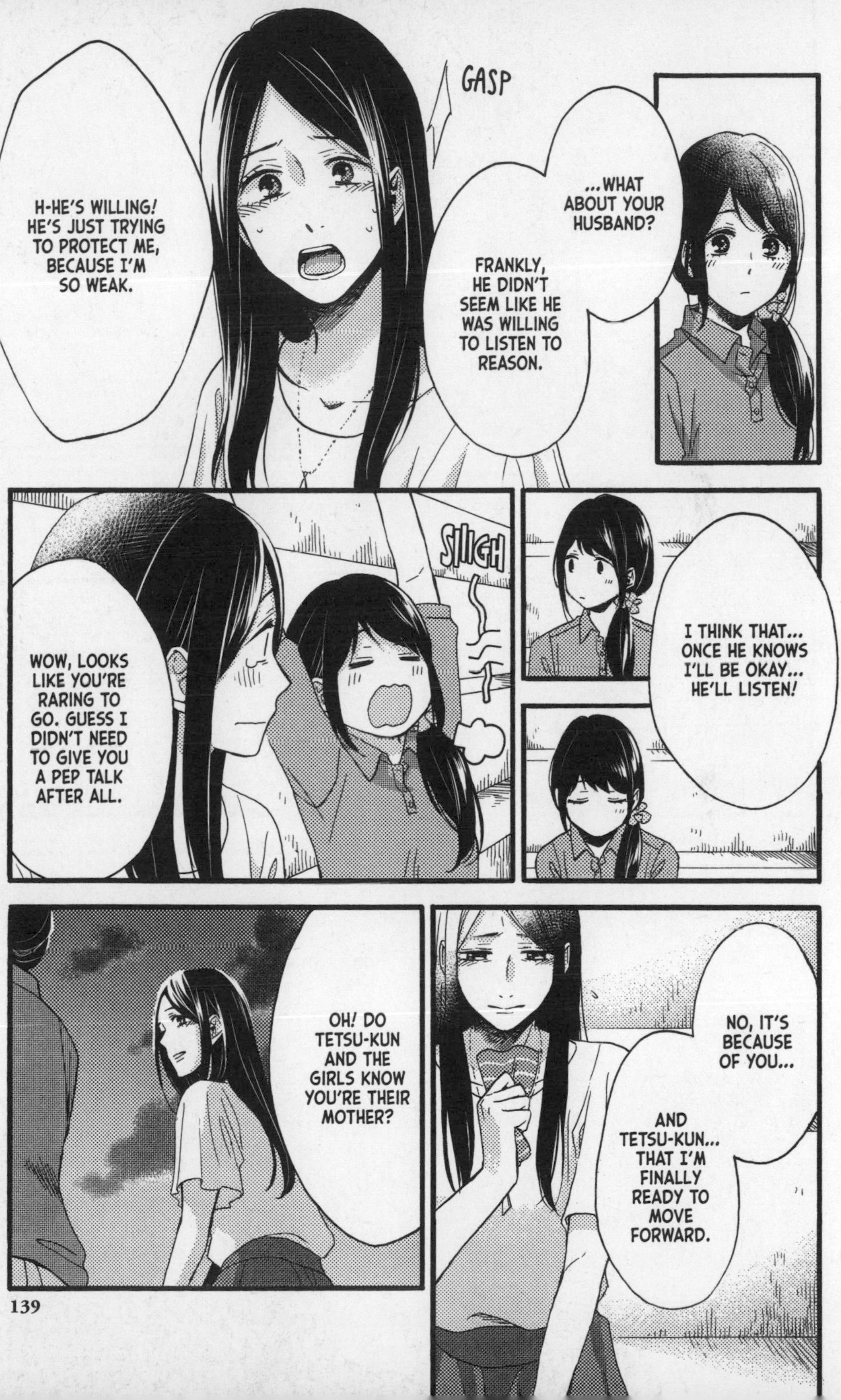
...WHAT ABOUT YOUR HUSBAND?
FRANKLY, HE DIDN'T SEEM LIKE HE WAS WILLING TO LISTEN TO REASON.
GASP
H-HE'S WILLING! HE'S JUST TRYING TO PROTECT ME, BECAUSE I'M SO WEAK.
I THINK THAT... ONCE HE KNOWS I'LL BE OKAY... HE'LL LISTEN!
SIIGH
WOW, LOOKS LIKE YOU'RE RARING TO GO. GUESS I DIDN'T NEED TO GIVE YOU A PEP TALK AFTER ALL.
NO, IT'S BECAUSE OF YOU...
AND TETSU-KUN... THAT I'M FINALLY READY TO MOVE FORWARD.
OH! DO TETSU-KUN AND THE GIRLS KNOW YOU'RE THEIR MOTHER?

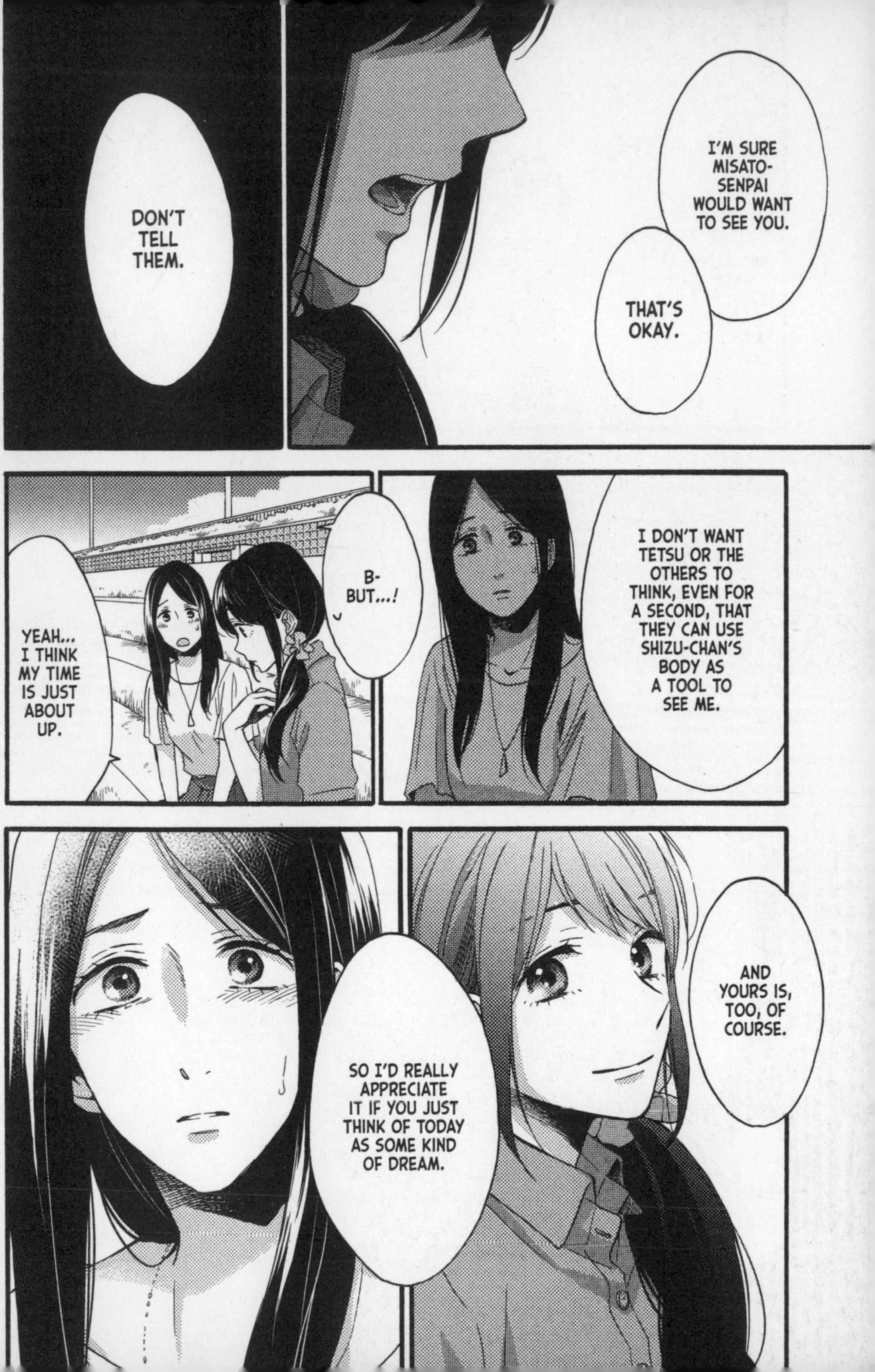
I'M SURE MISATO-SENPAI WOULD WANT TO SEE YOU.
THAT'S OKAY.
DON'T TELL THEM.
I DON'T WANT TETSU OR THE OTHERS TO THINK, EVEN FOR A SECOND, THAT THEY CAN USE SHIZU-CHAN'S BODY AS A TOOL TO SEE ME.
B-BUT...!
YEAH... I THINK MY TIME IS JUST ABOUT UP.
AND YOURS IS, TOO, OF COURSE.
SO I'D REALLY APPRECIATE IT IF YOU JUST THINK OF TODAY AS SOME KIND OF DREAM.

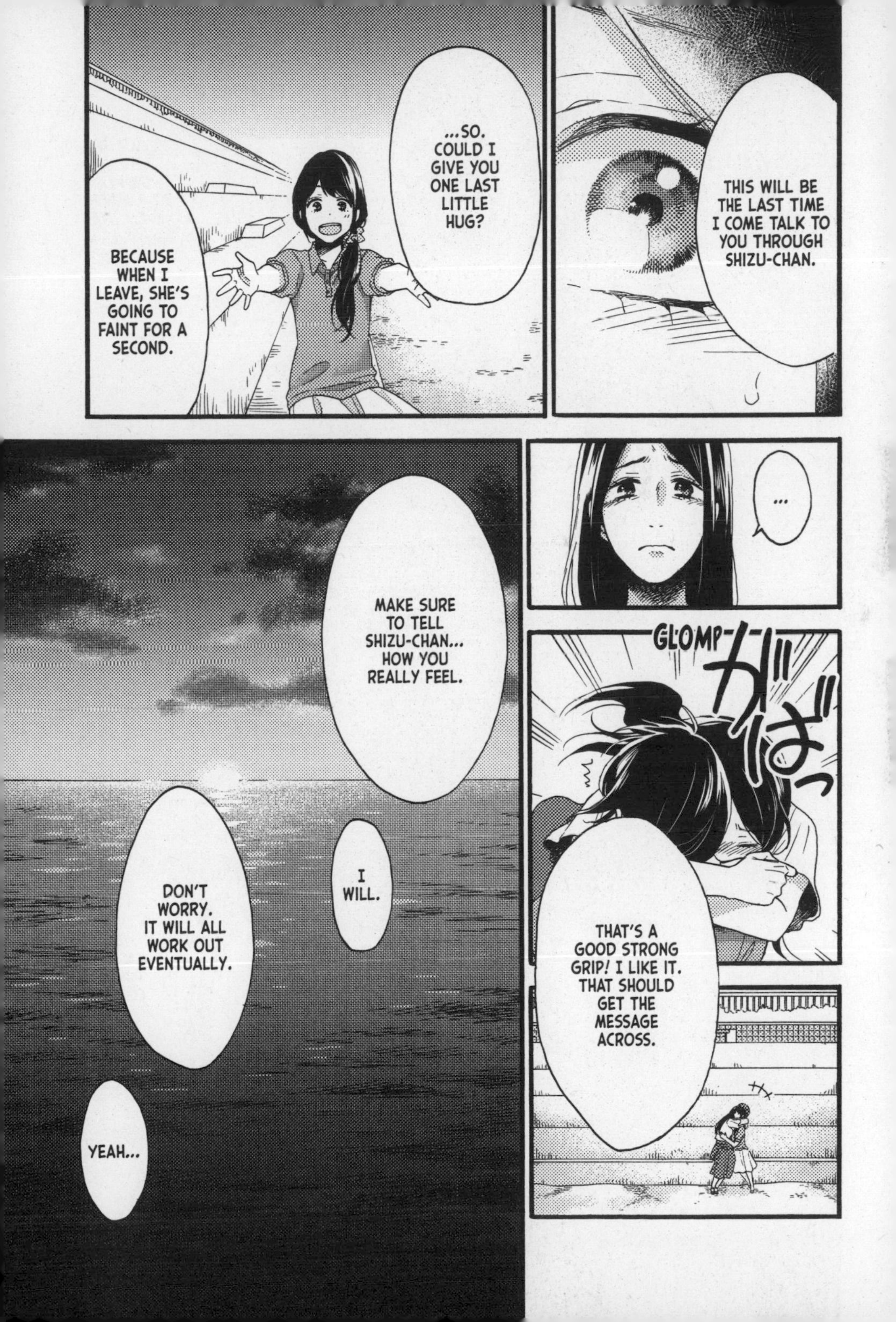
THIS WILL BE THE LAST TIME I COME TALK TO YOU THROUGH SHIZU-CHAN.
...SO. COULD I GIVE YOU ONE LAST LITTLE HUG?
BECAUSE WHEN I LEAVE, SHE'S GOING TO FAINT FOR A SECOND.
...
GLOMP
がばっ
THAT'S A GOOD STRONG GRIP! I LIKE IT. THAT SHOULD GET THE MESSAGE ACROSS.
MAKE SURE TO TELL SHIZU-CHAN... HOW YOU REALLY FEEL.
I WILL.
DON'T WORRY. IT WILL ALL WORK OUT EVENTUALLY.
YEAH...

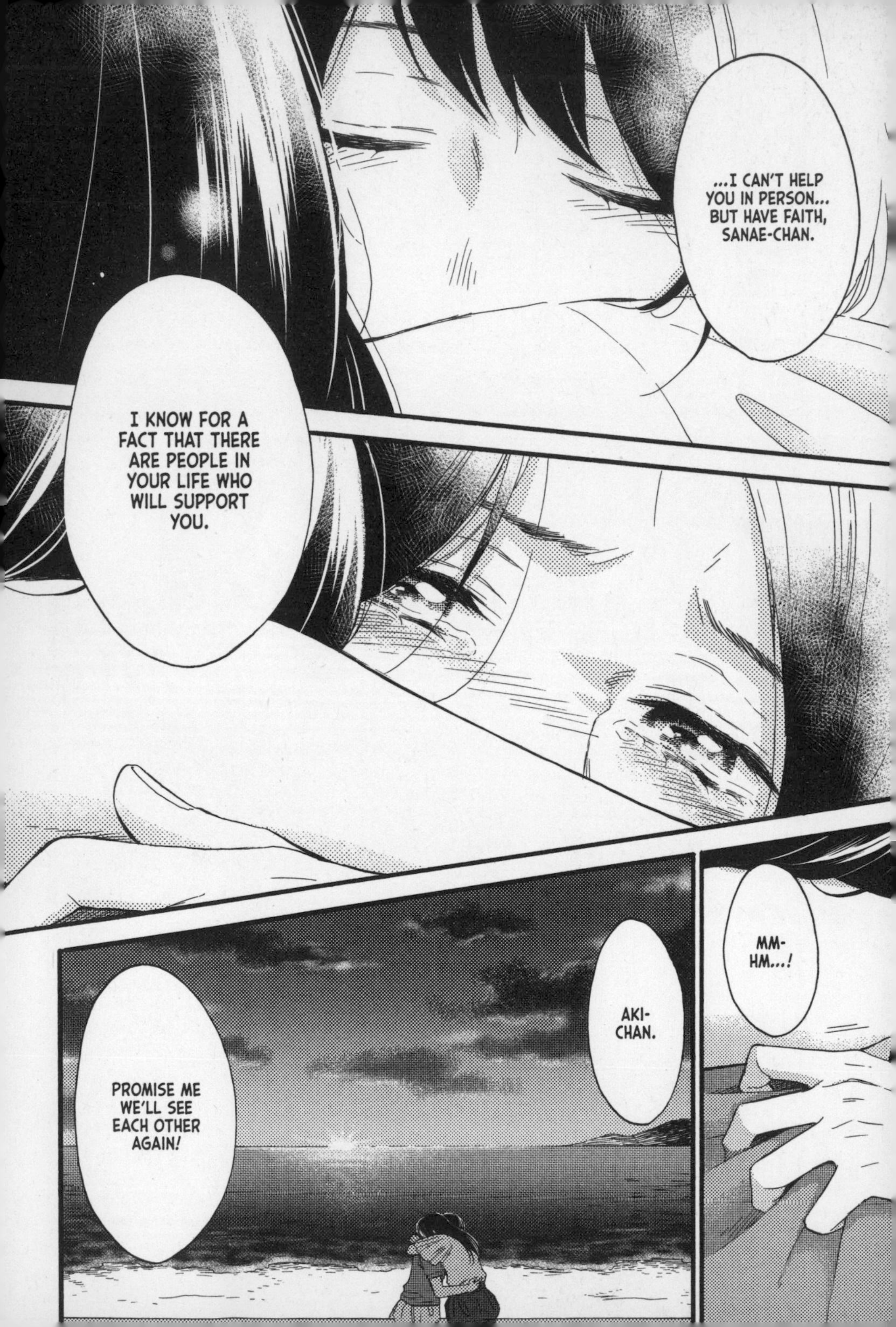
...I CAN'T HELP YOU IN PERSON... BUT HAVE FAITH, SANAE-CHAN.
I KNOW FOR A FACT THAT THERE ARE PEOPLE IN YOUR LIFE WHO WILL SUPPORT YOU.
MM-HM...!
AKI-CHAN.
PROMISE ME WE'LL SEE EACH OTHER AGAIN!

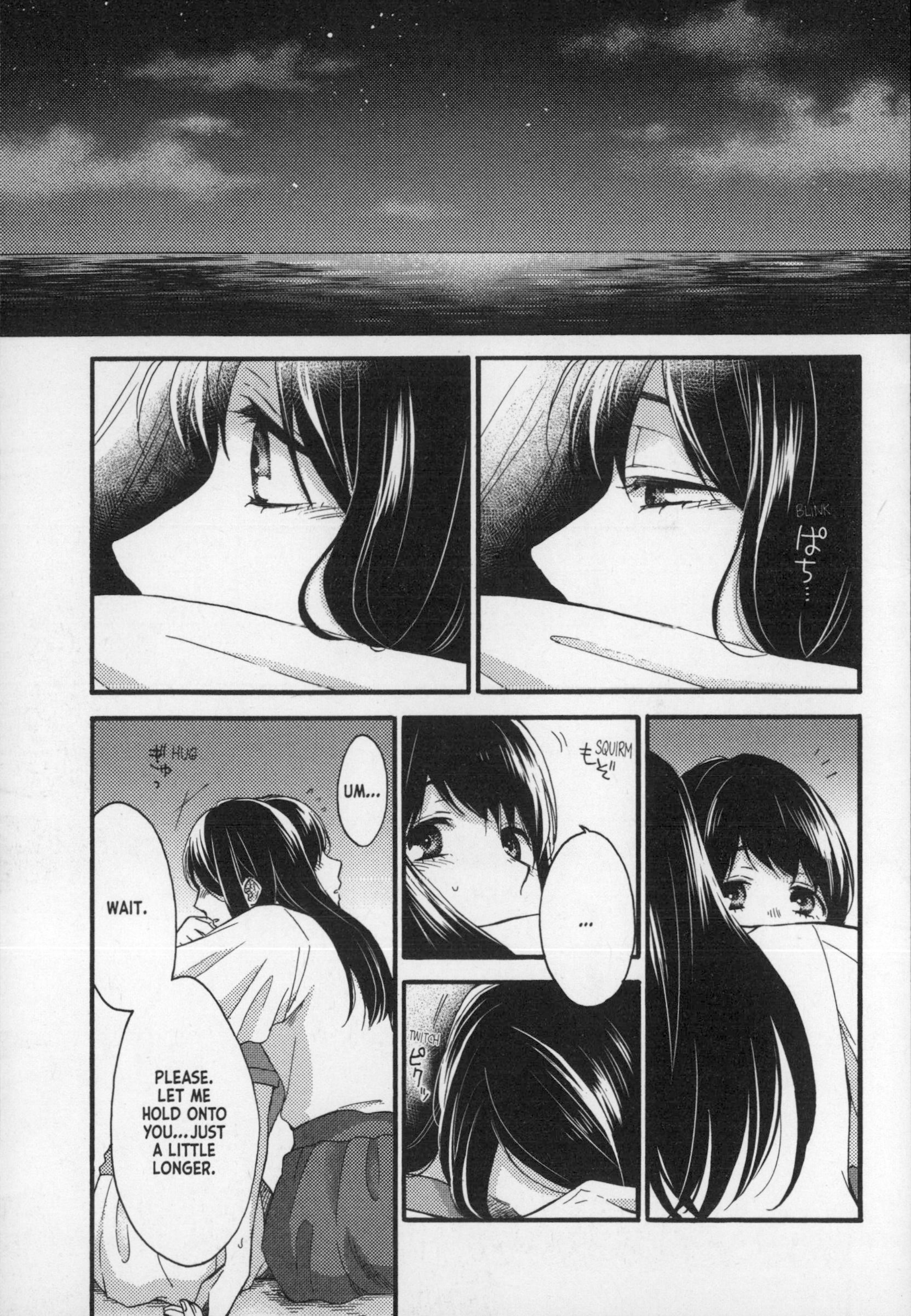
BLINK
ぱち…
SQUIRM
もぞ
...
TWITCH
ピクッ
UM...
HUG
ぎゅ
WAIT.
PLEASE. LET ME HOLD ONTO YOU...JUST A LITTLE LONGER.

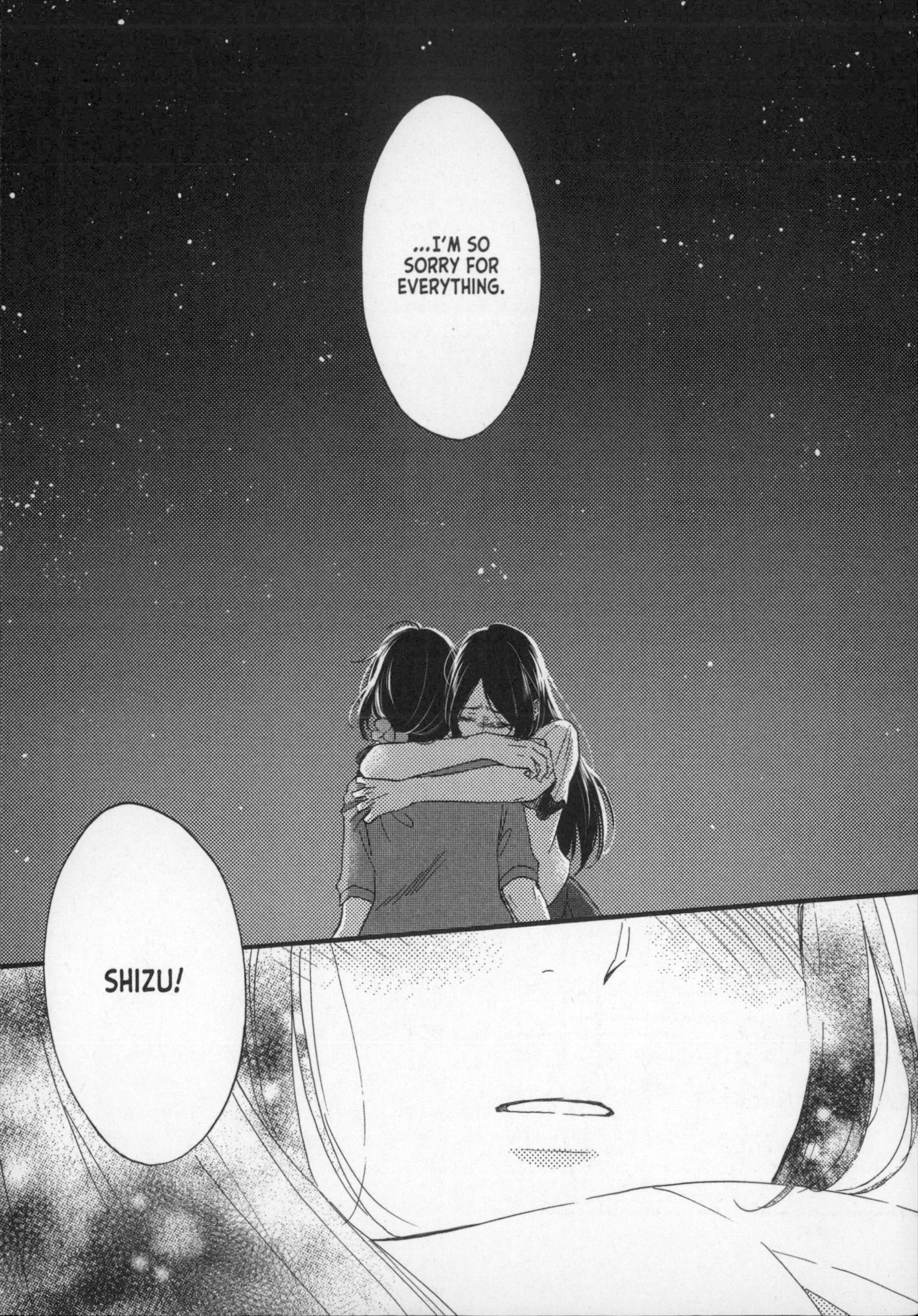
...I'M SO SORRY FOR EVERYTHING.
SHIZU!

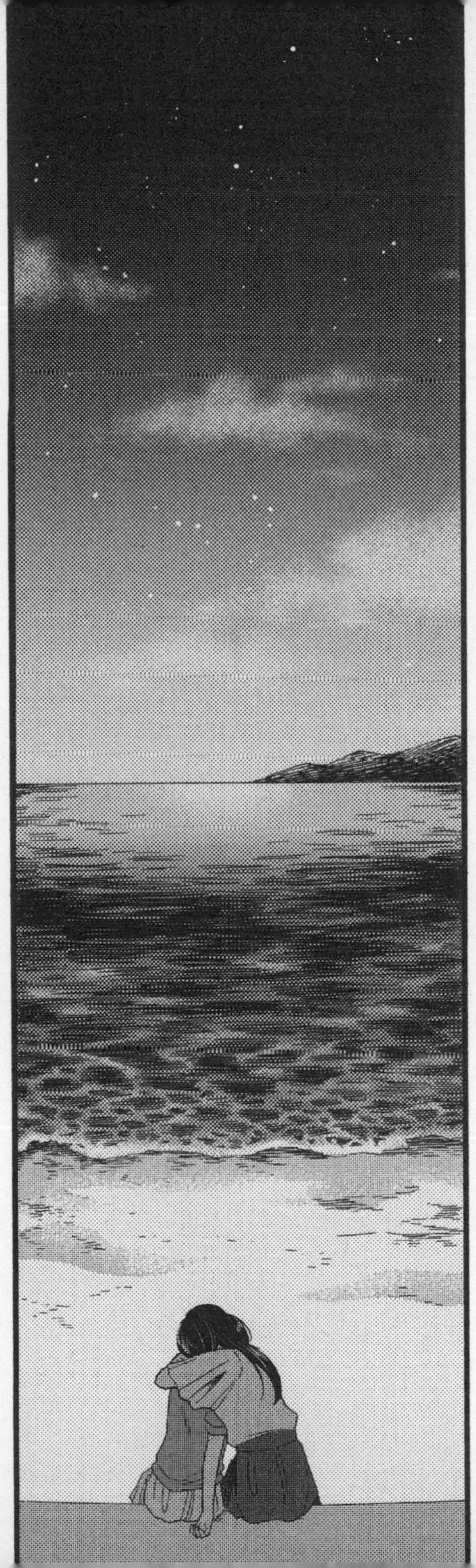

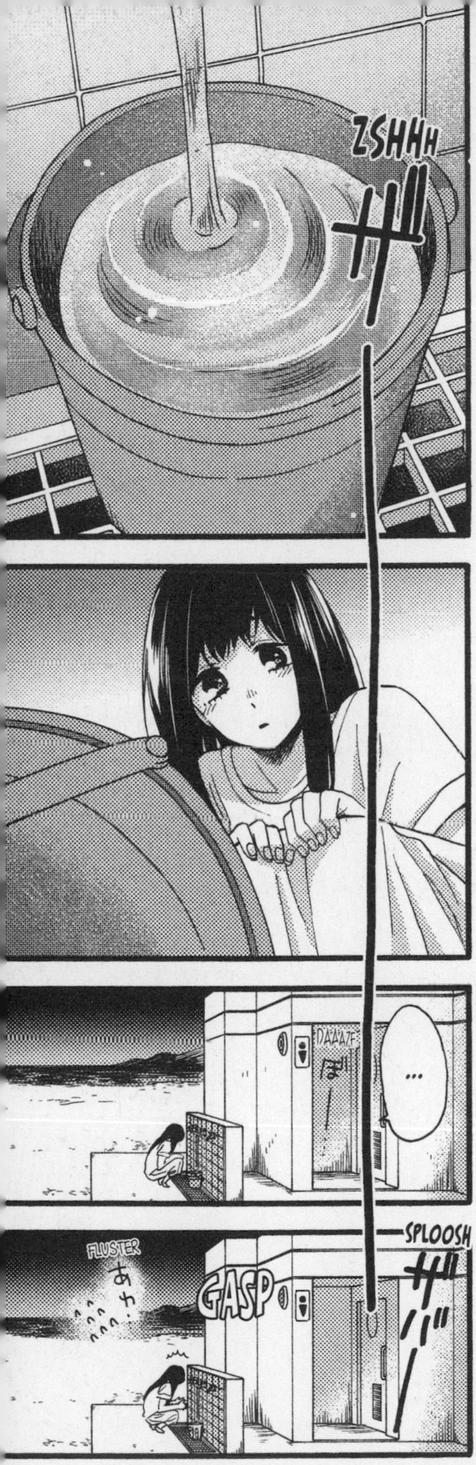
ZSHHH
...
DAAAZE
ぼー
SPLOOSH
GASP
FLUSTER

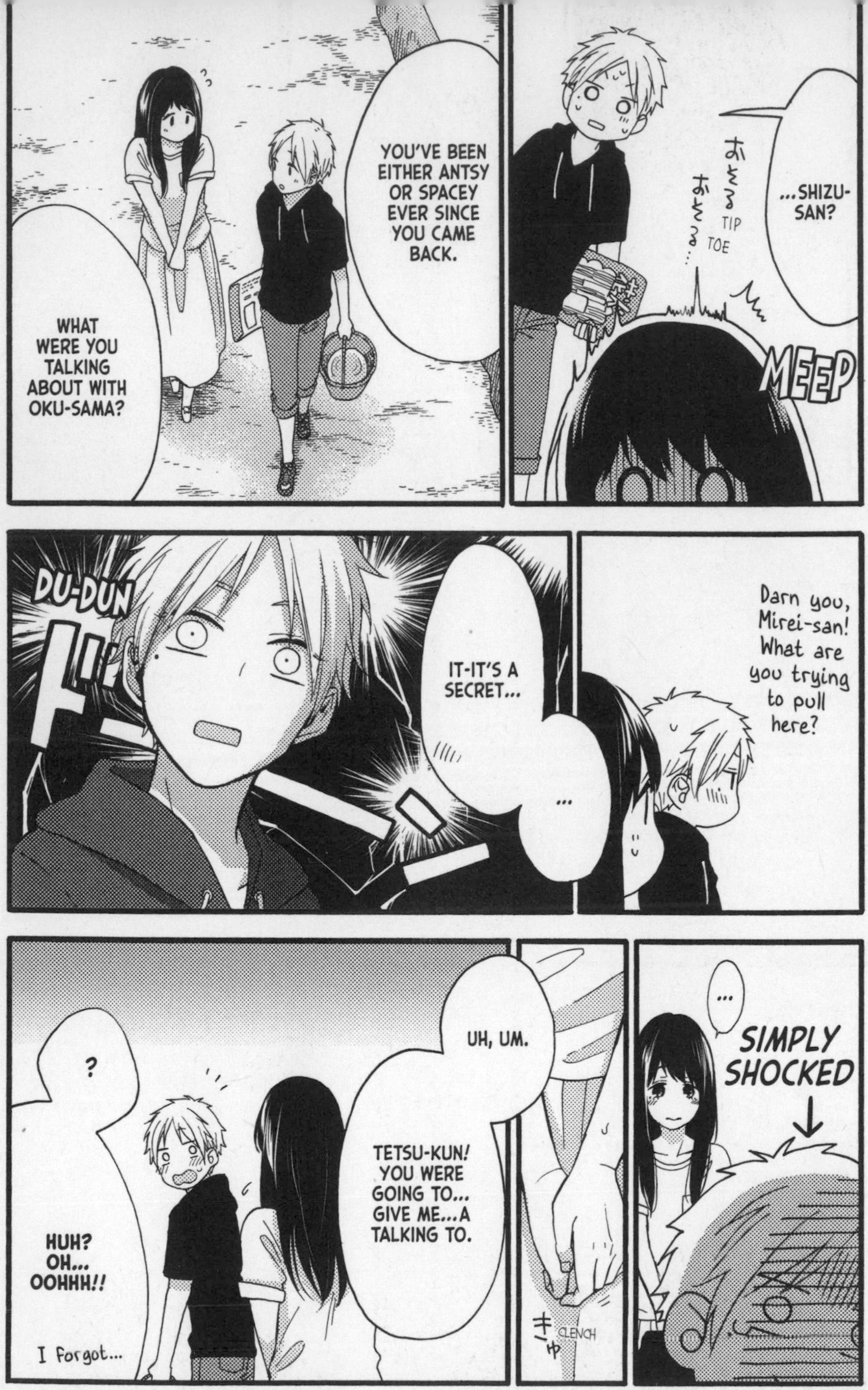
...SHIZU-SAN?
TIP TOE
MEEP
YOU'VE BEEN EITHER ANTSY OR SPACEY EVER SINCE YOU CAME BACK.
WHAT WERE YOU TALKING ABOUT WITH OKU-SAMA?
Darn you, Mirei-san! What are you trying to pull here?
...
IT-IT'S A SECRET...
DU-DUN
...
SIMPLY SHOCKED
CLENCH
UH, UM.
TETSU-KUN! YOU WERE GOING TO... GIVE ME...A TALKING TO.
?
HUH? OH... OOHHH!!
I forgot...

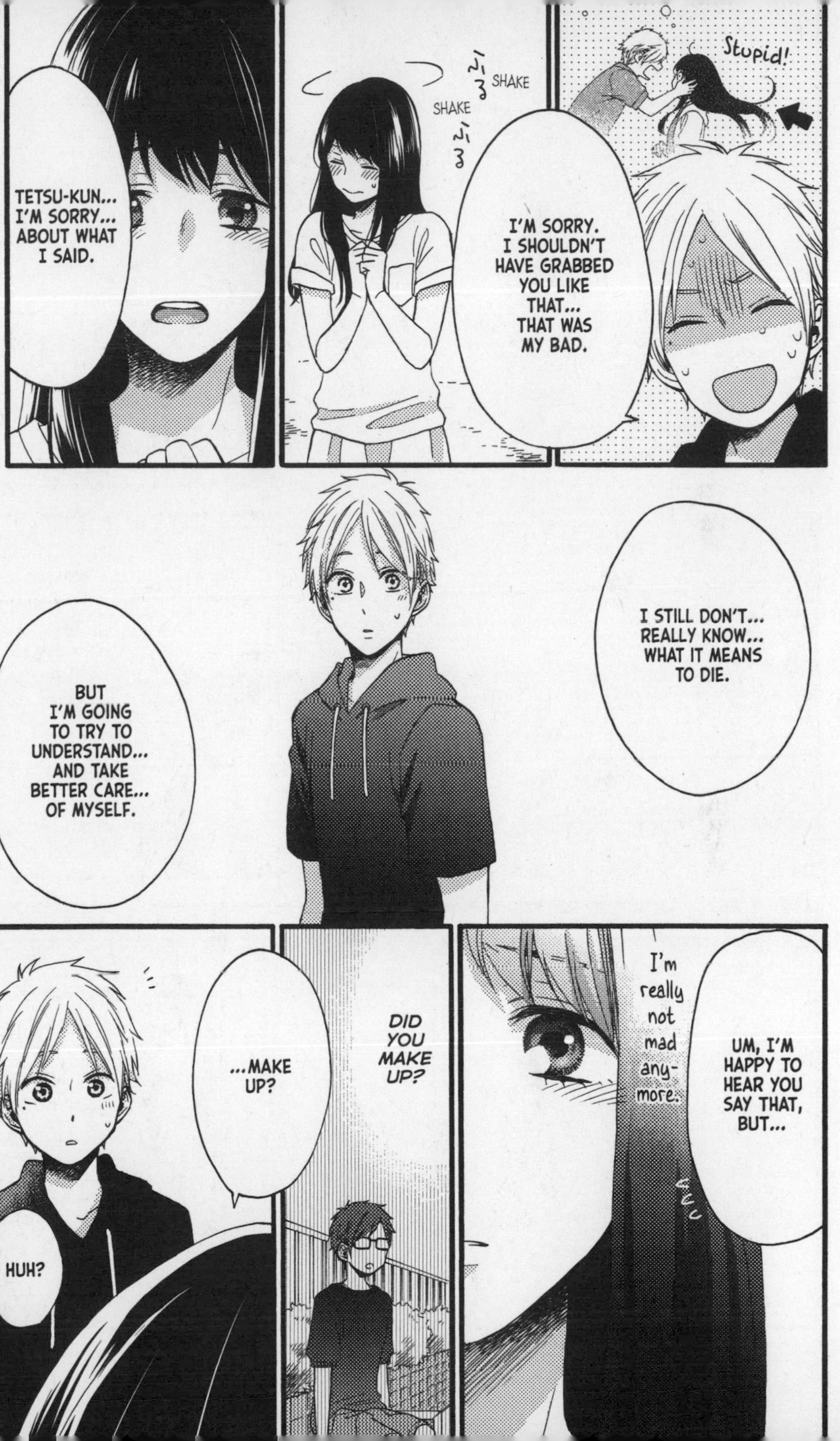
Stupid!
I'M SORRY. I SHOULDN'T HAVE GRABBED YOU LIKE THAT... THAT WAS MY BAD.
SHAKE
SHAKE
TETSU-KUN... I'M SORRY... ABOUT WHAT I SAID.
I STILL DON'T... REALLY KNOW... WHAT IT MEANS TO DIE.
BUT I'M GOING TO TRY TO UNDERSTAND... AND TAKE BETTER CARE... OF MYSELF.
UM, I'M HAPPY TO HEAR YOU SAY THAT, BUT...
I'm really not mad any-more.
DID YOU MAKE UP?
...MAKE UP?
HUH?

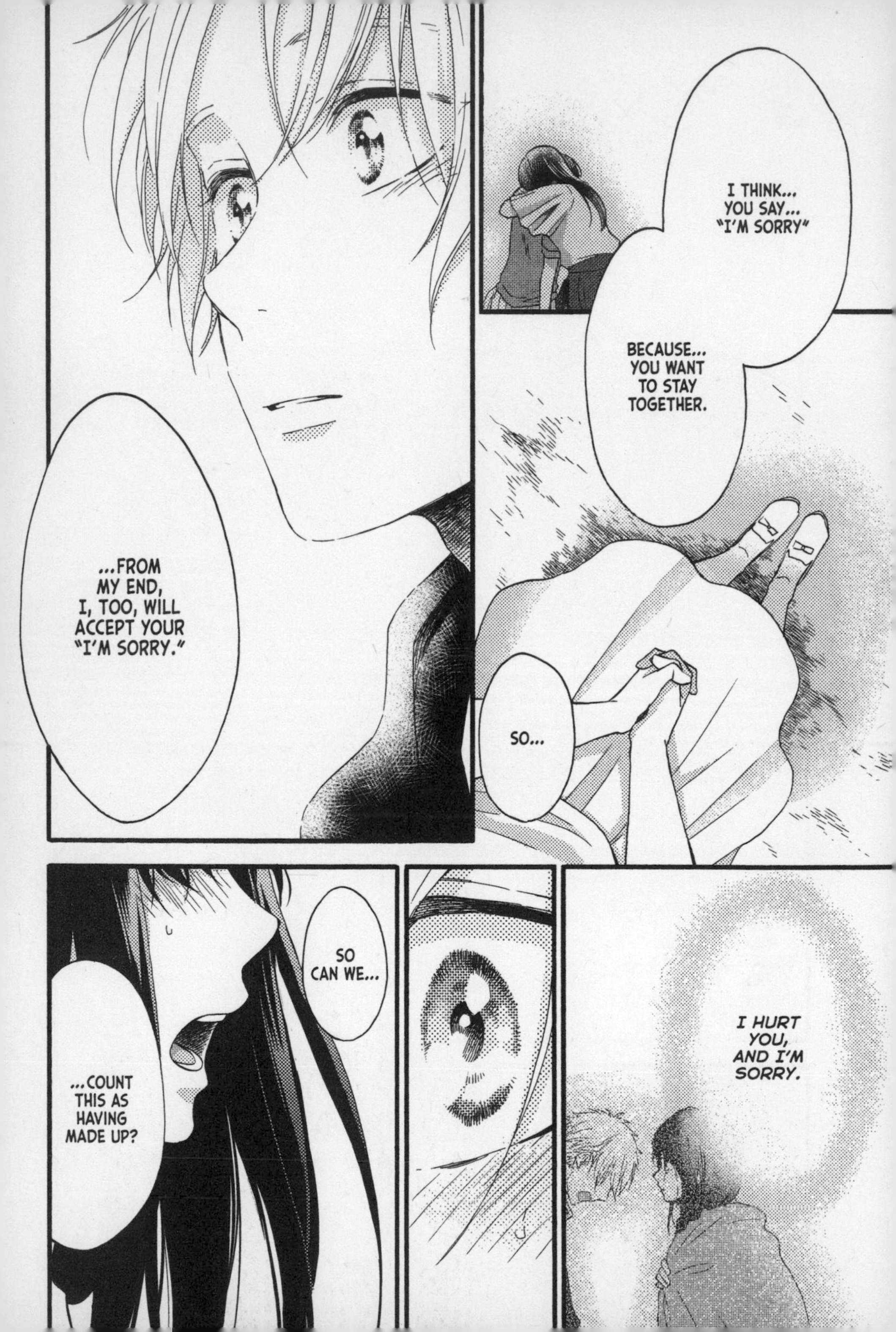
I THINK... YOU SAY... "I'M SORRY"
BECAUSE... YOU WANT TO STAY TOGETHER.
SO...
...FROM MY END, I, TOO, WILL ACCEPT YOUR "I'M SORRY."
I HURT YOU, AND I'M SORRY.
SO CAN WE...
...COUNT THIS AS HAVING MADE UP?

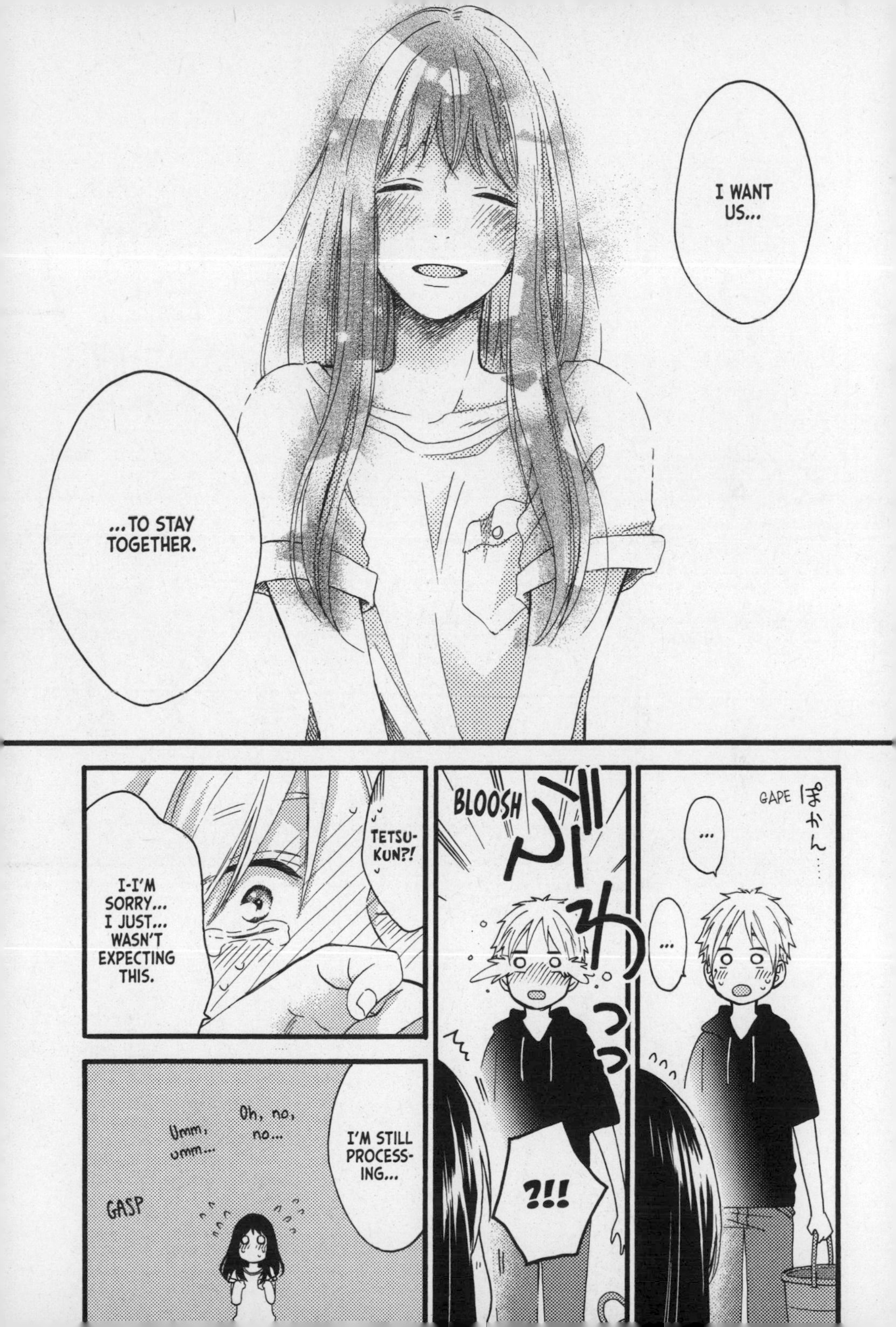
I WANT US...
...TO STAY TOGETHER.
GAPE ぽかん…
...
...
BLOOSH ざわっっ
?!!
TETSU-KUN?!
I-I'M SORRY... I JUST... WASN'T EXPECTING THIS.
I'M STILL PROCESSING...
Oh, no, no...
Umm, umm...
GASP

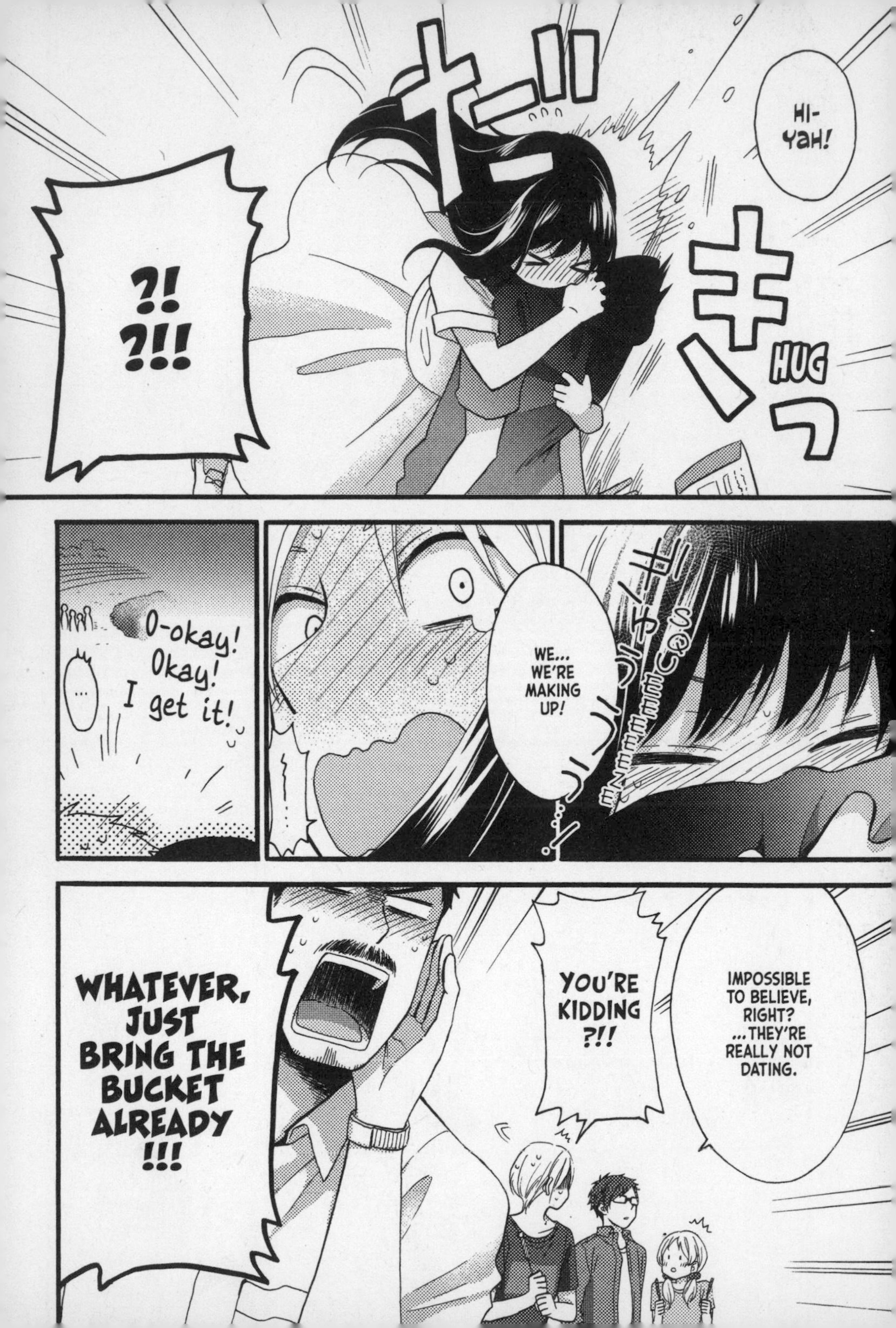
HI-YAH!
HUG
?! ?!!
SQUEEEEEZE
WE... WE'RE MAKING UP!
O-okay! Okay! I get it!
...
IMPOSSIBLE TO BELIEVE, RIGHT? ...THEY'RE REALLY NOT DATING.
YOU'RE KIDDING?!!
WHATEVER, JUST BRING THE BUCKET ALREADY!!!

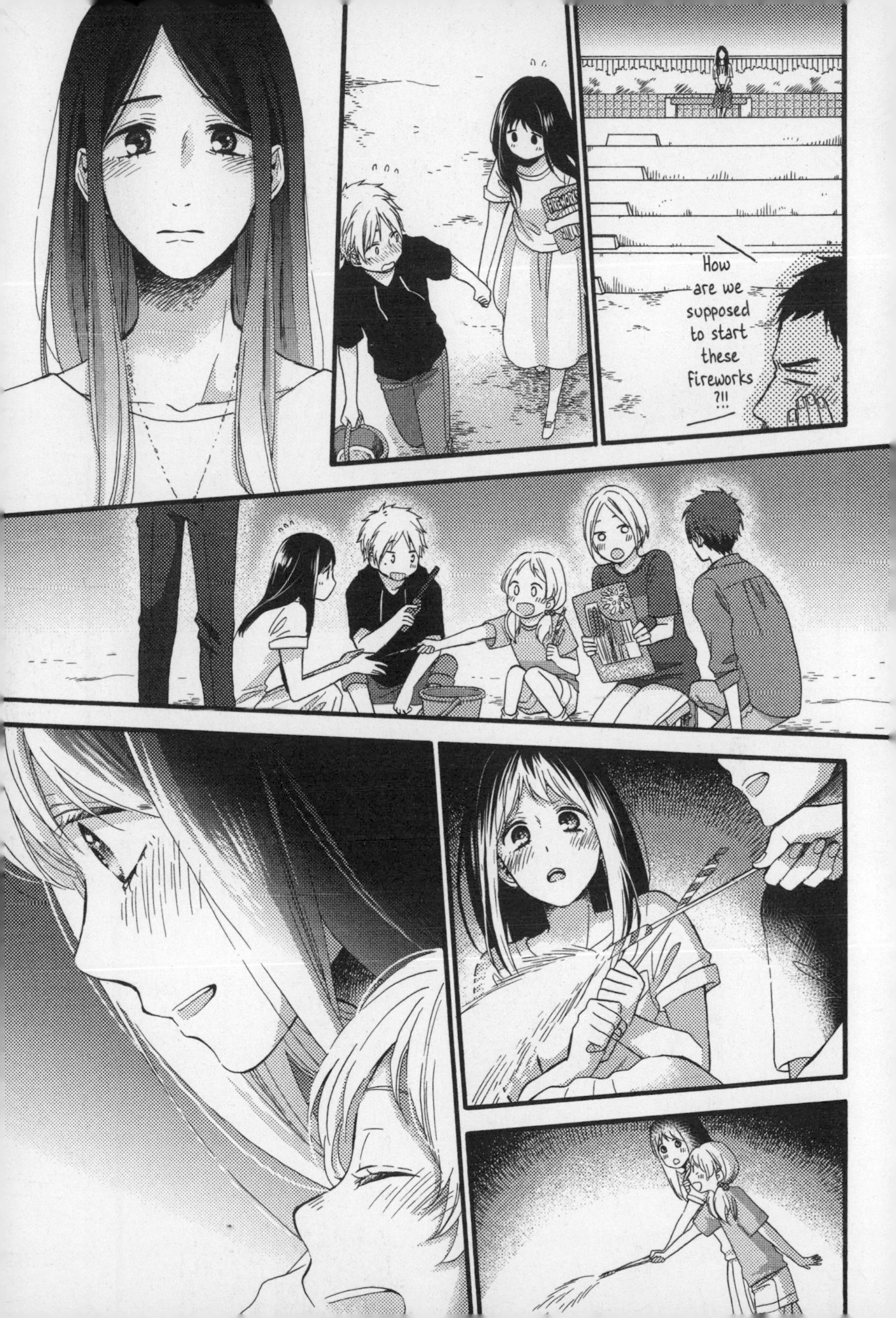
How are we supposed to start these fireworks?!!
FIREWORKS

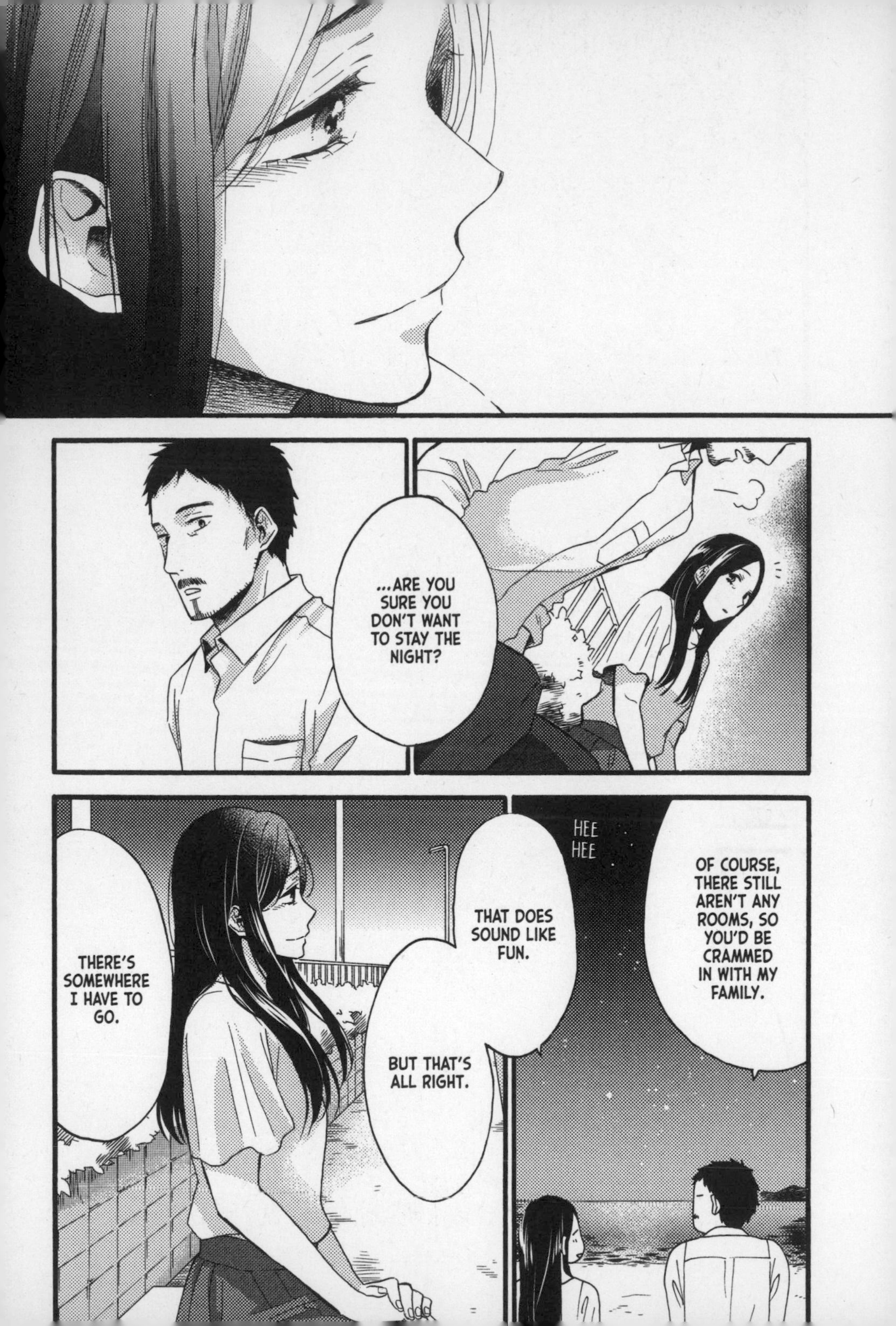
...ARE YOU SURE YOU DON'T WANT TO STAY THE NIGHT?
OF COURSE, THERE STILL AREN'T ANY ROOMS, SO YOU'D BE CRAMMED IN WITH MY FAMILY.
HEE HEE
THAT DOES SOUND LIKE FUN.
BUT THAT'S ALL RIGHT.
THERE'S SOMEWHERE I HAVE TO GO.

DON'T TELL THEM.

UM! AKI-CHAN IS...

...

I SEE.

...UM.

?

THANK YOU.

ABOUT AKI-CHAN... I MEAN.

IF THERE'S ANYTHING I CAN DO TO HELP...YOU CAN ALWAYS COME TO ME.

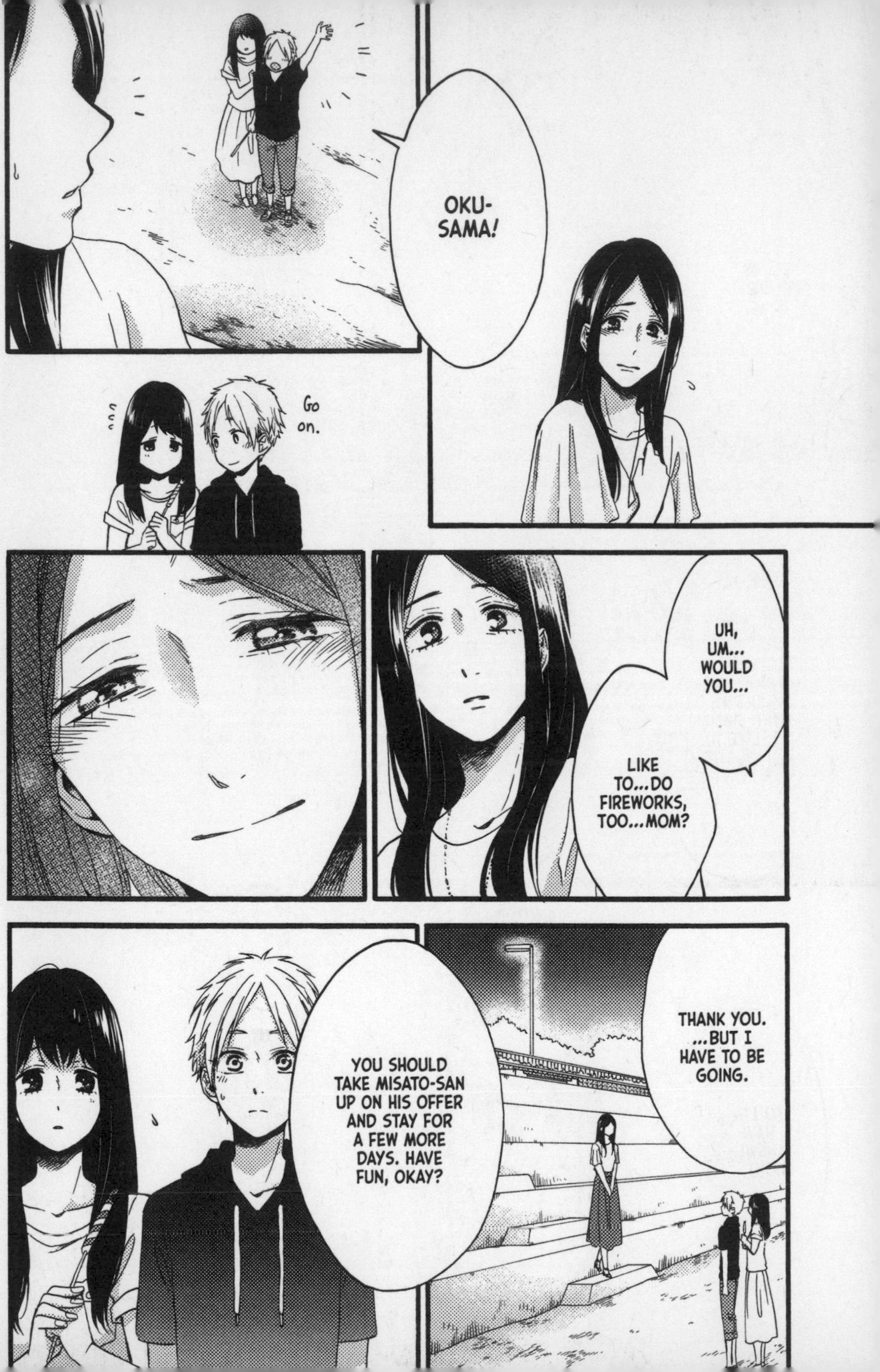
OKU-SAMA!
Go on.
UH, UM... WOULD YOU...
LIKE TO...DO FIREWORKS, TOO...MOM?
THANK YOU. ...BUT I HAVE TO BE GOING.
YOU SHOULD TAKE MISATO-SAN UP ON HIS OFFER AND STAY FOR A FEW MORE DAYS. HAVE FUN, OKAY?

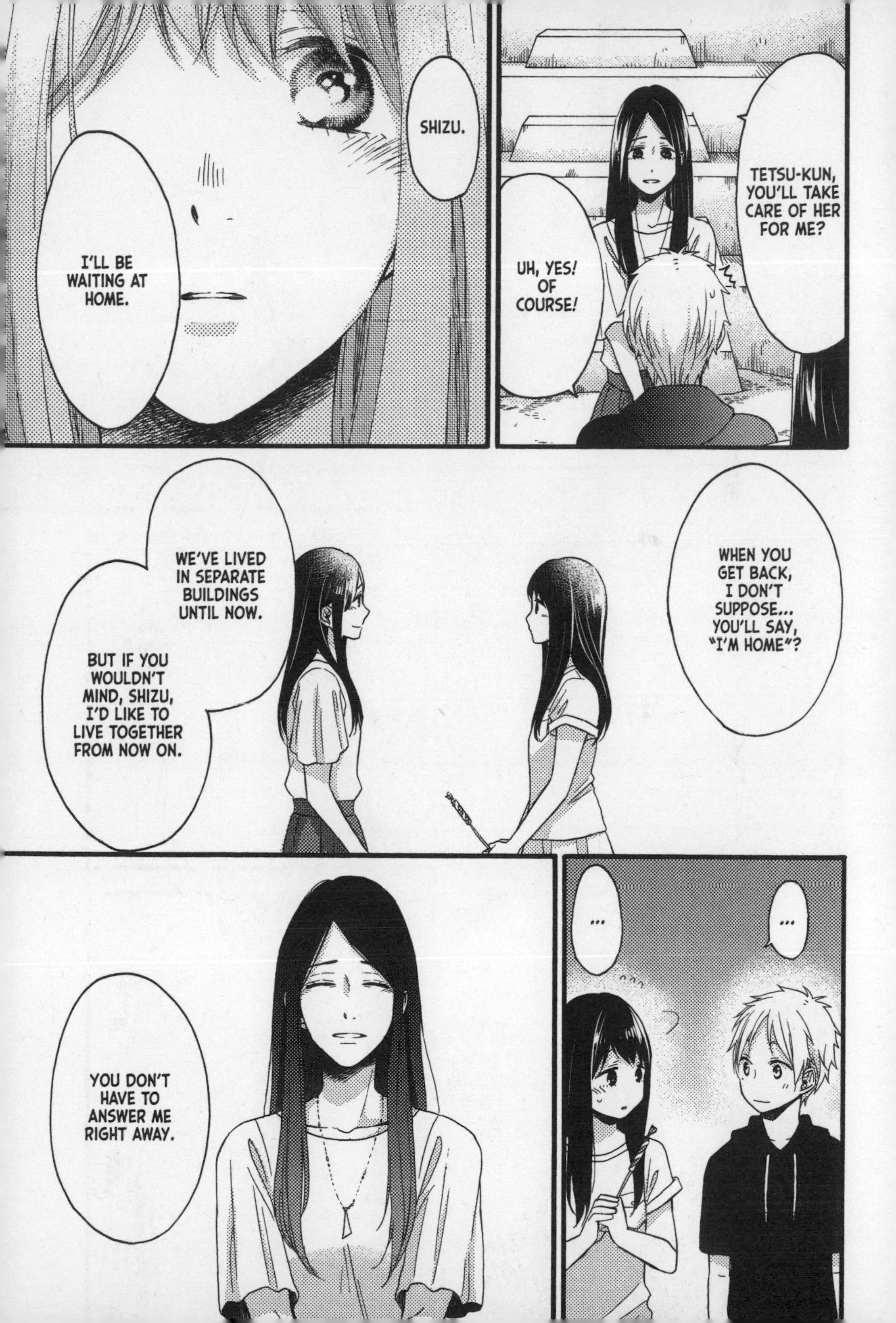
TETSU-KUN, YOU'LL TAKE CARE OF HER FOR ME?
UH, YES! OF COURSE!
SHIZU.
I'LL BE WAITING AT HOME.
WHEN YOU GET BACK, I DON'T SUPPOSE... YOU'LL SAY, "I'M HOME"?
WE'VE LIVED IN SEPARATE BUILDINGS UNTIL NOW.
BUT IF YOU WOULDN'T MIND, SHIZU, I'D LIKE TO LIVE TOGETHER FROM NOW ON.
...
...
YOU DON'T HAVE TO ANSWER ME RIGHT AWAY.

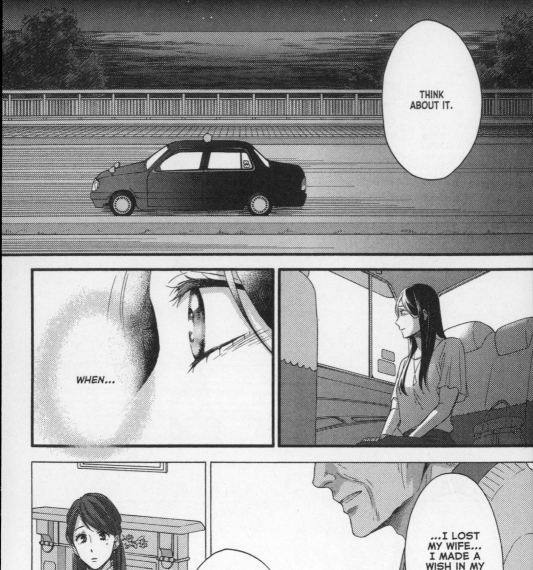

THINK ABOUT IT.

WHEN...

...I LOST MY WIFE... I MADE A WISH IN MY HEART.

I WISHED THAT MY SON, AND EVERYONE CONNECTED TO HIM, WOULD LIVE A HAPPY LIFE.

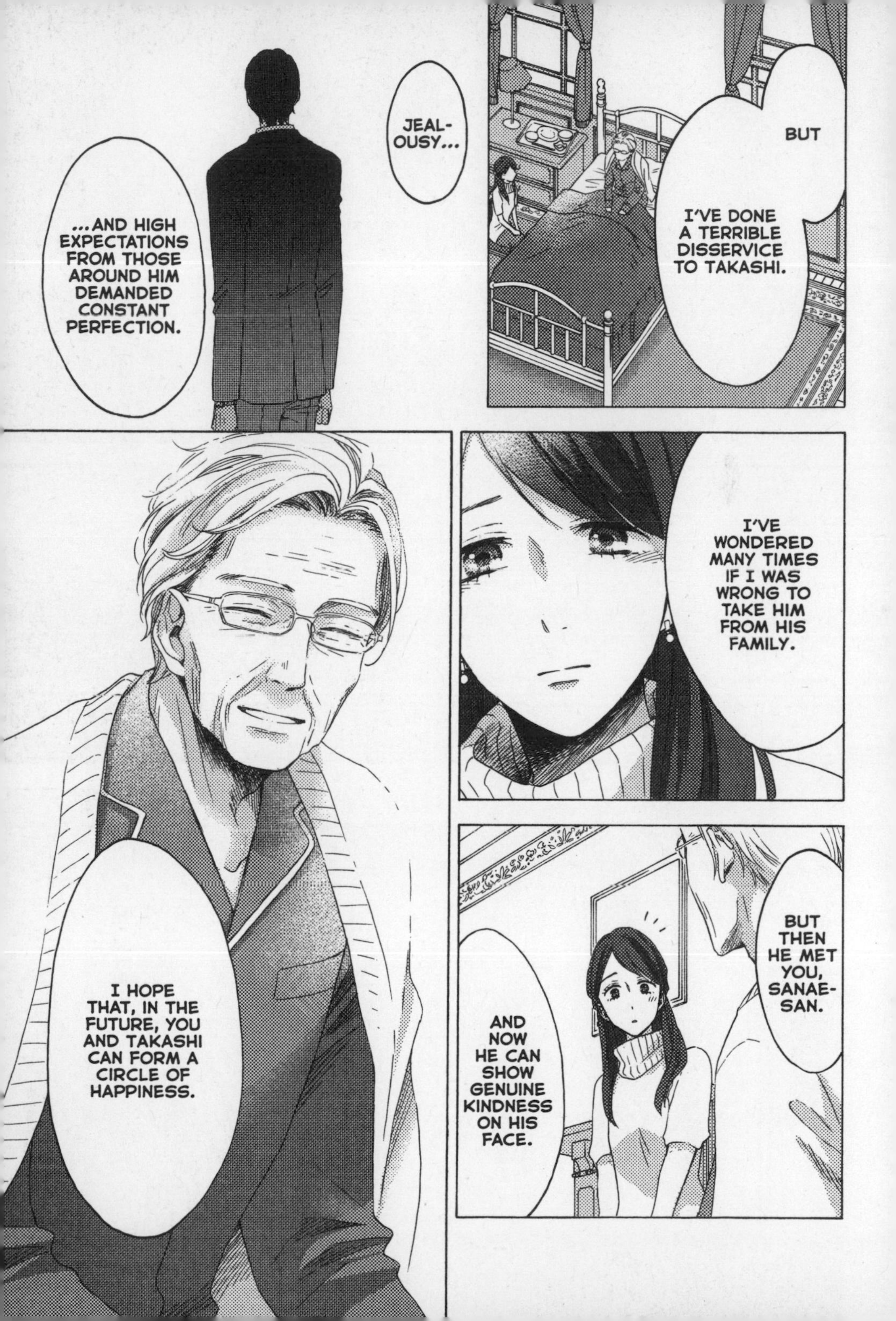
BUT
I'VE DONE A TERRIBLE DISSERVICE TO TAKASHI.
JEAL-OUSY...
...AND HIGH EXPECTATIONS FROM THOSE AROUND HIM DEMANDED CONSTANT PERFECTION.
I'VE WONDERED MANY TIMES IF I WAS WRONG TO TAKE HIM FROM HIS FAMILY.
BUT THEN HE MET YOU, SANAE-SAN.
AND NOW HE CAN SHOW GENUINE KINDNESS ON HIS FACE.
I HOPE THAT, IN THE FUTURE, YOU AND TAKASHI CAN FORM A CIRCLE OF HAPPINESS.

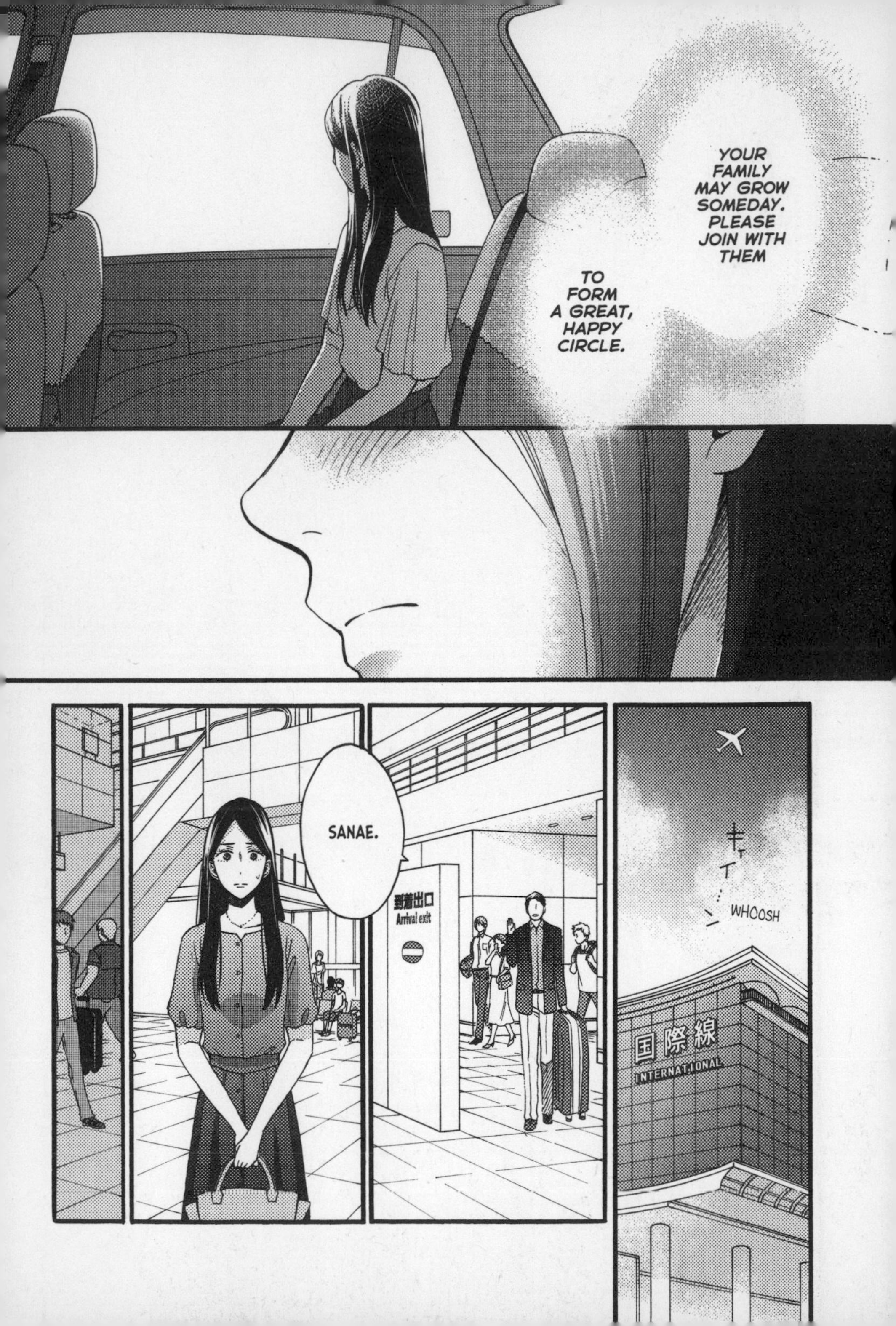
YOUR FAMILY MAY GROW SOMEDAY. PLEASE JOIN WITH THEM
TO FORM A GREAT, HAPPY CIRCLE.
WHOOSH
国際線
INTERNATIONAL
SANAE.
到着出口
Arrival exit

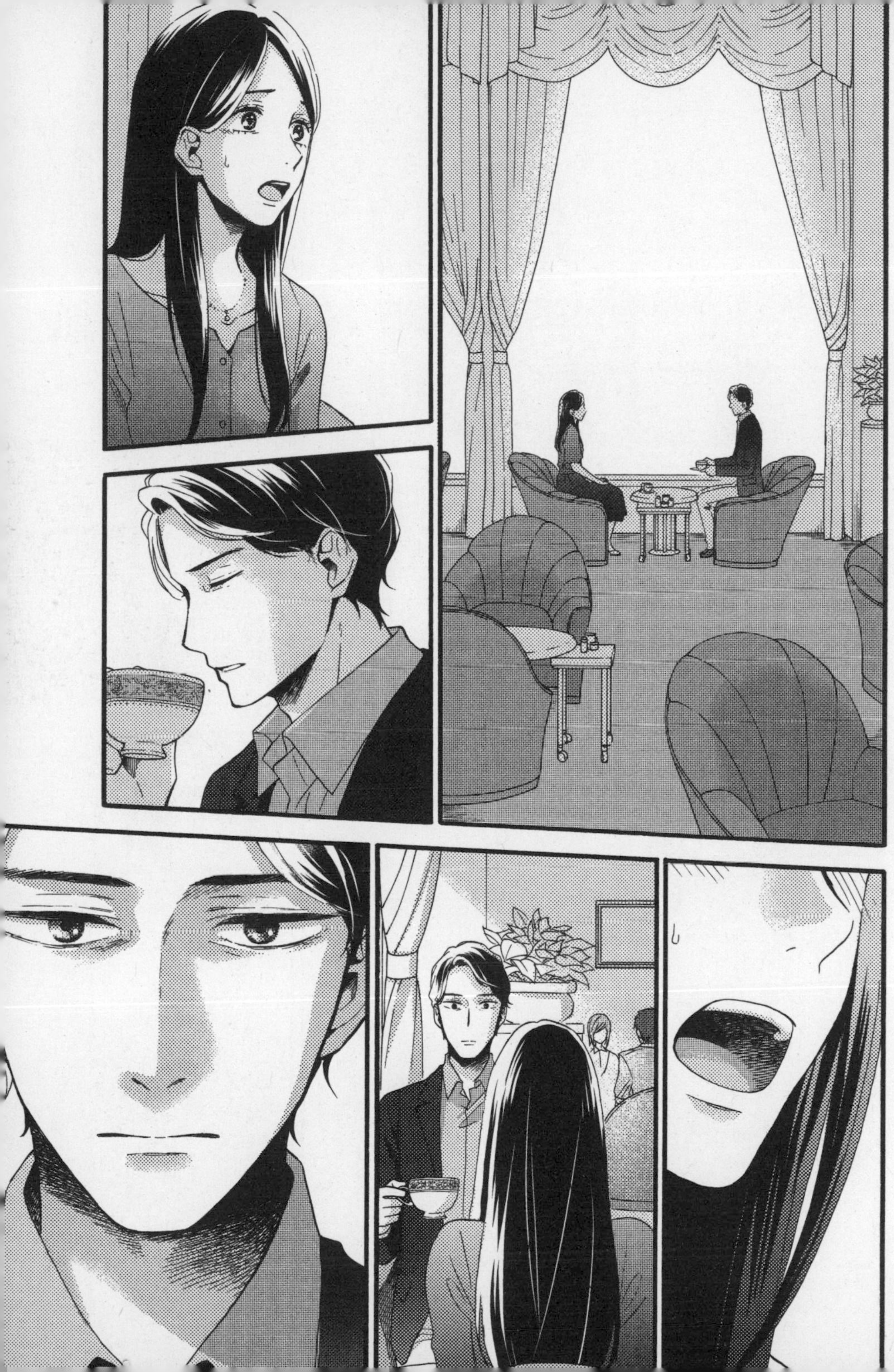

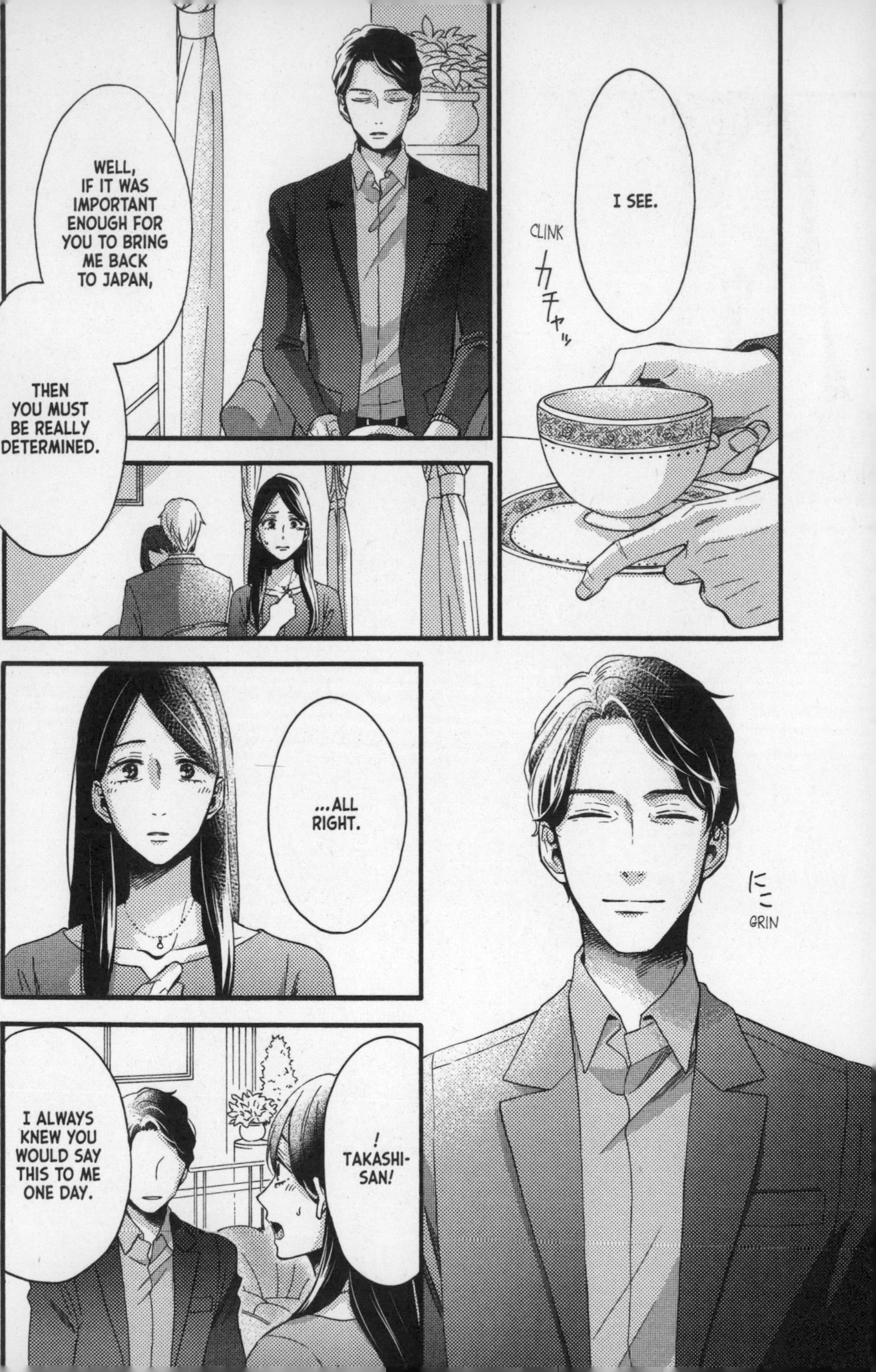
I SEE.
CLINK
カチャッ
WELL, IF IT WAS IMPORTANT ENOUGH FOR YOU TO BRING ME BACK TO JAPAN,
THEN YOU MUST BE REALLY DETERMINED.
にこ
GRIN
...ALL RIGHT.
! TAKASHI-SAN!
I ALWAYS KNEW YOU WOULD SAY THIS TO ME ONE DAY.

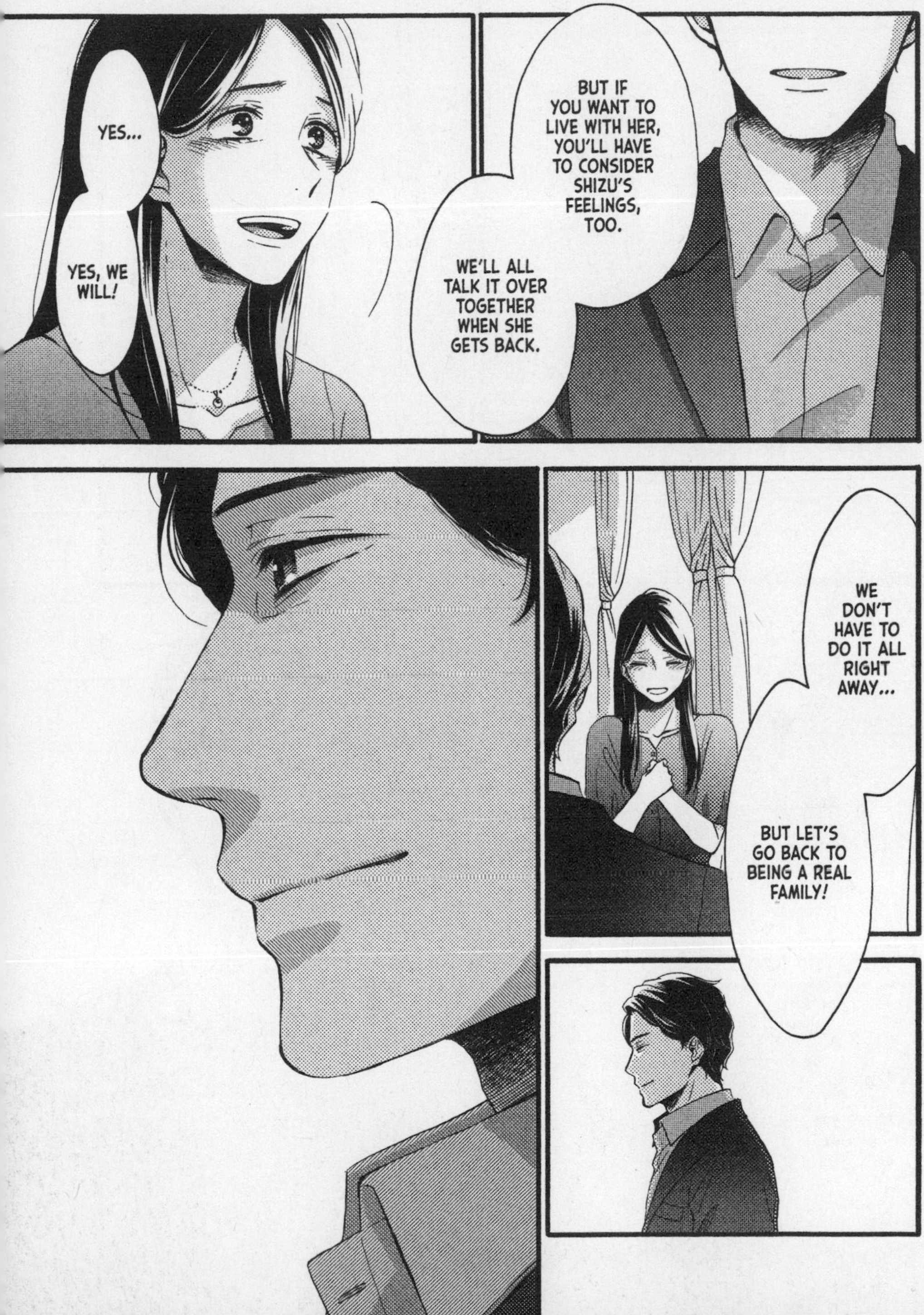
BUT IF YOU WANT TO LIVE WITH HER, YOU'LL HAVE TO CONSIDER SHIZU'S FEELINGS, TOO.
WE'LL ALL TALK IT OVER TOGETHER WHEN SHE GETS BACK.
YES...
YES, WE WILL!
WE DON'T HAVE TO DO IT ALL RIGHT AWAY...
BUT LET'S GO BACK TO BEING A REAL FAMILY!

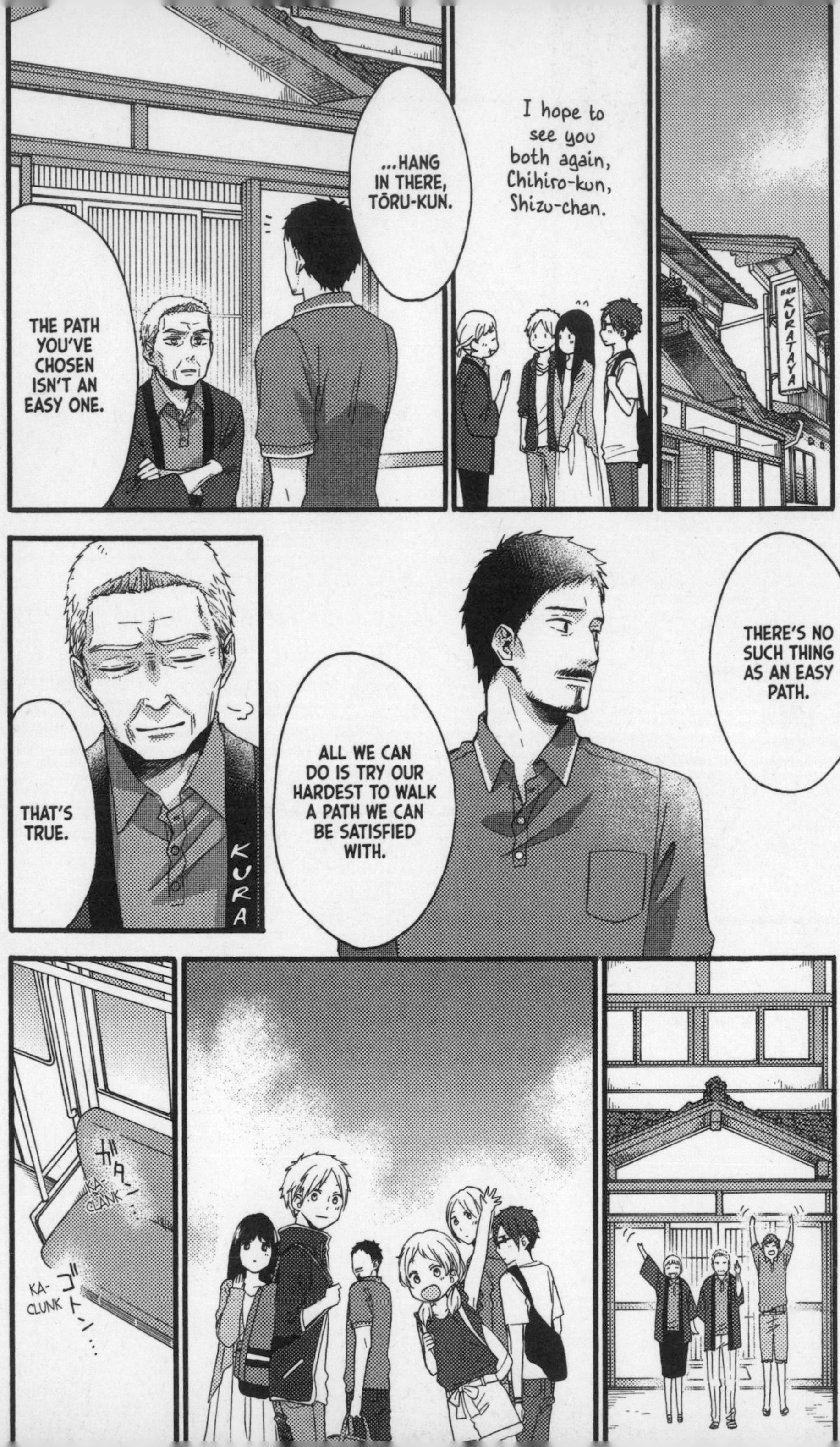
KURATAYA
I hope to see you both again, Chihiro-kun, Shizu-chan.
...HANG IN THERE, TŌRU-KUN.
THE PATH YOU'VE CHOSEN ISN'T AN EASY ONE.
THERE'S NO SUCH THING AS AN EASY PATH.
ALL WE CAN DO IS TRY OUR HARDEST TO WALK A PATH WE CAN BE SATISFIED WITH.
THAT'S TRUE.
KURA
KA-CLANK
KA-CLANK

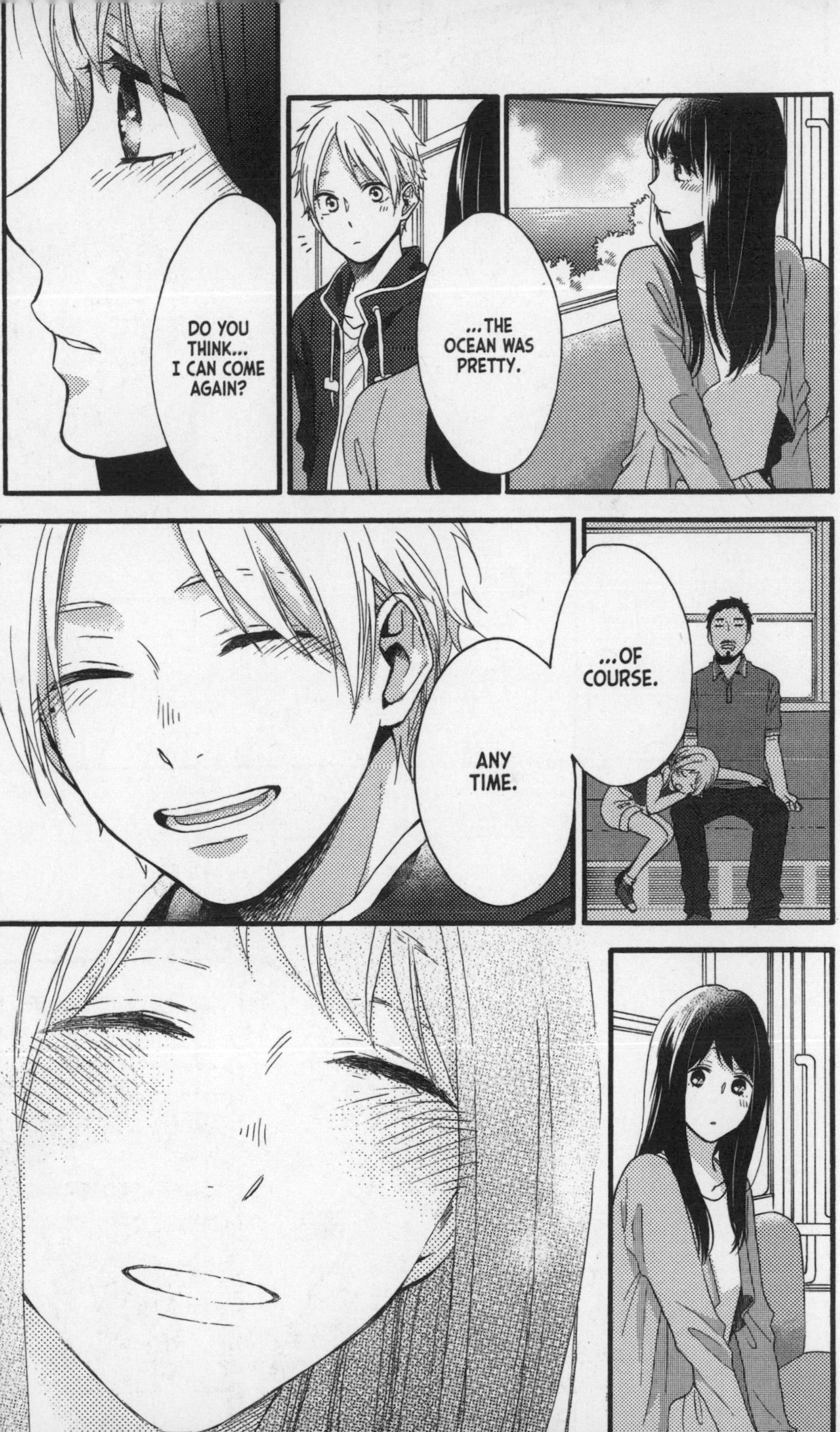
...THE OCEAN WAS PRETTY.
DO YOU THINK... I CAN COME AGAIN?
...OF COURSE.
ANY TIME.

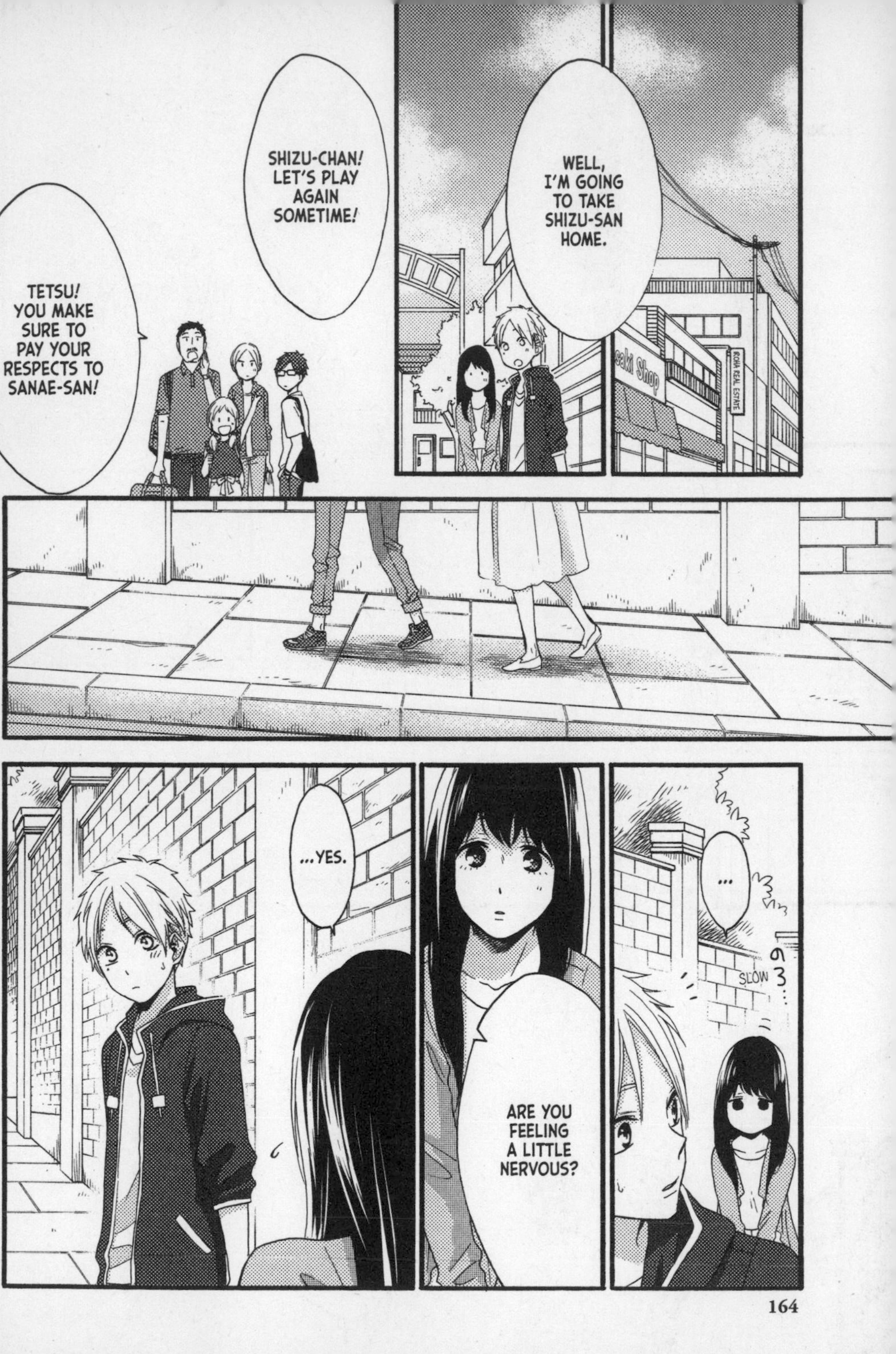
WELL, I'M GOING TO TAKE SHIZU-SAN HOME.
SHIZU-CHAN! LET'S PLAY AGAIN SOMETIME!
TETSU! YOU MAKE SURE TO PAY YOUR RESPECTS TO SANAE-SAN!
...
SLOW
ARE YOU FEELING A LITTLE NERVOUS?
...YES.

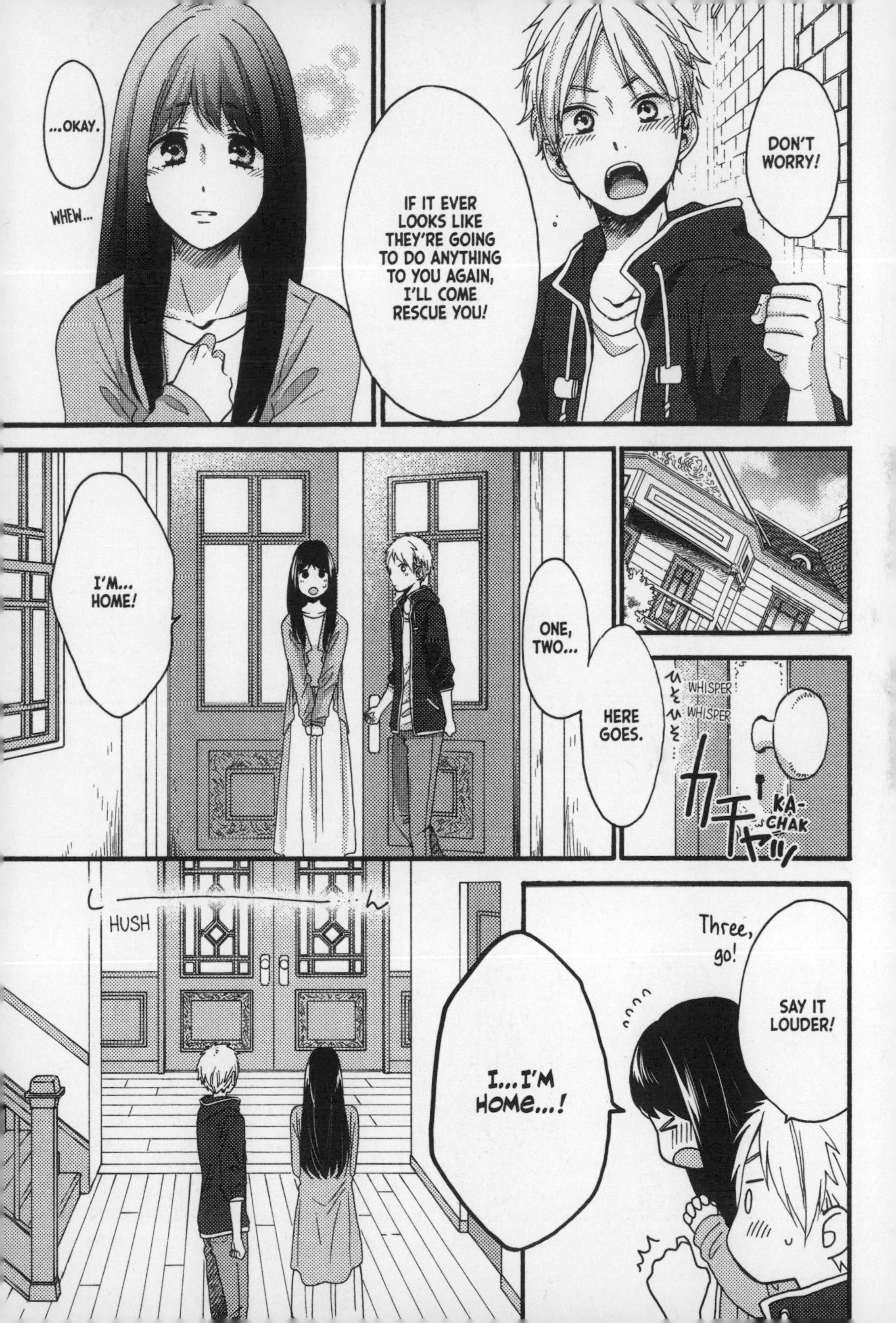
DON'T WORRY!
IF IT EVER LOOKS LIKE THEY'RE GOING TO DO ANYTHING TO YOU AGAIN, I'LL COME RESCUE YOU!
...OKAY.
WHEW...
WHISPER WHISPER
ONE, TWO...
HERE GOES.
KA-CHAK
I'M... HOME!
Three, go!
SAY IT LOUDER!
I...I'M HOME...!
HUSH

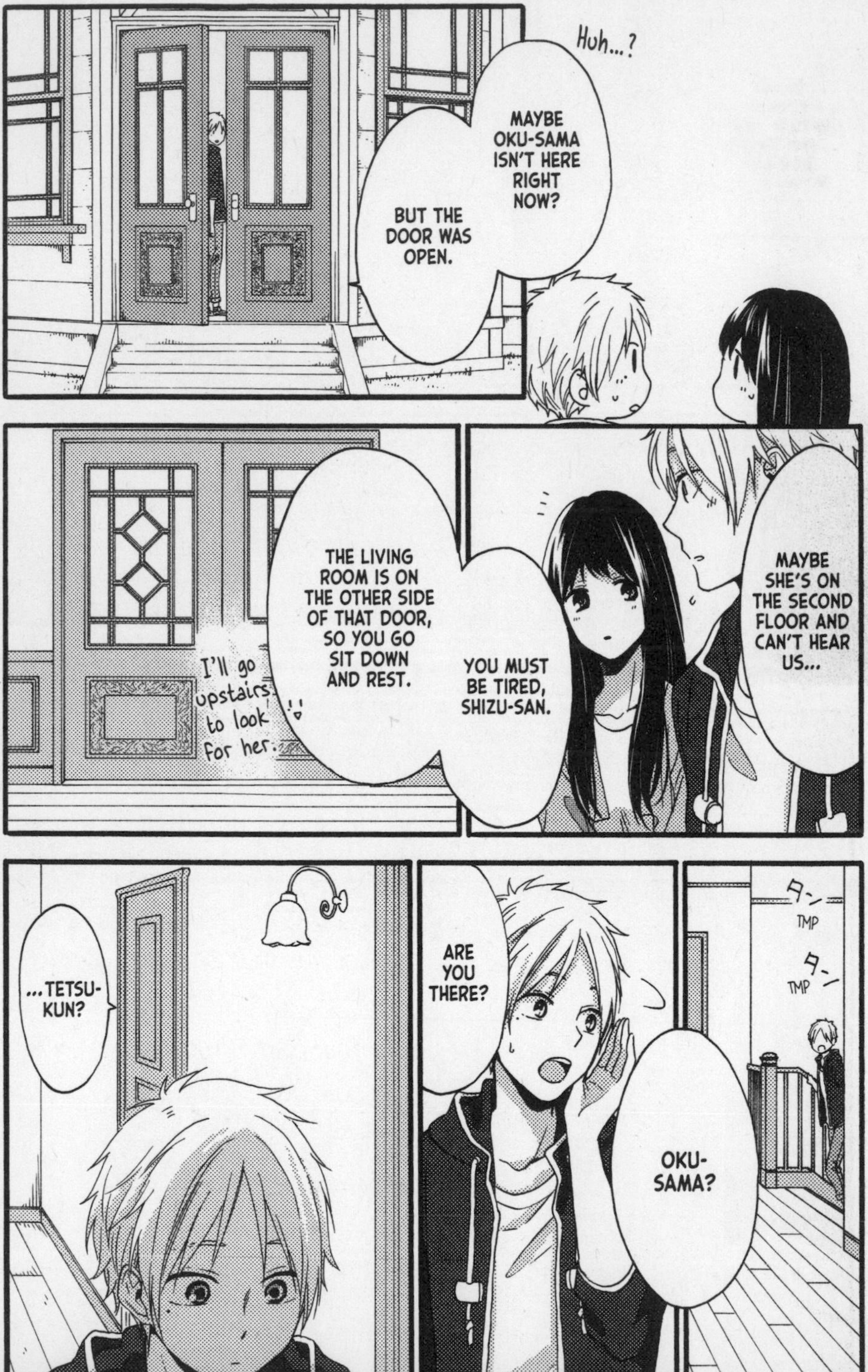
Huh...?
MAYBE OKU-SAMA ISN'T HERE RIGHT NOW?
BUT THE DOOR WAS OPEN.
MAYBE SHE'S ON THE SECOND FLOOR AND CAN'T HEAR US...
YOU MUST BE TIRED, SHIZU-SAN.
THE LIVING ROOM IS ON THE OTHER SIDE OF THAT DOOR, SO YOU GO SIT DOWN AND REST.
I'll go upstairs to look for her.
タン TMP
タン TMP
OKU-SAMA?
ARE YOU THERE?
...TETSU-KUN?

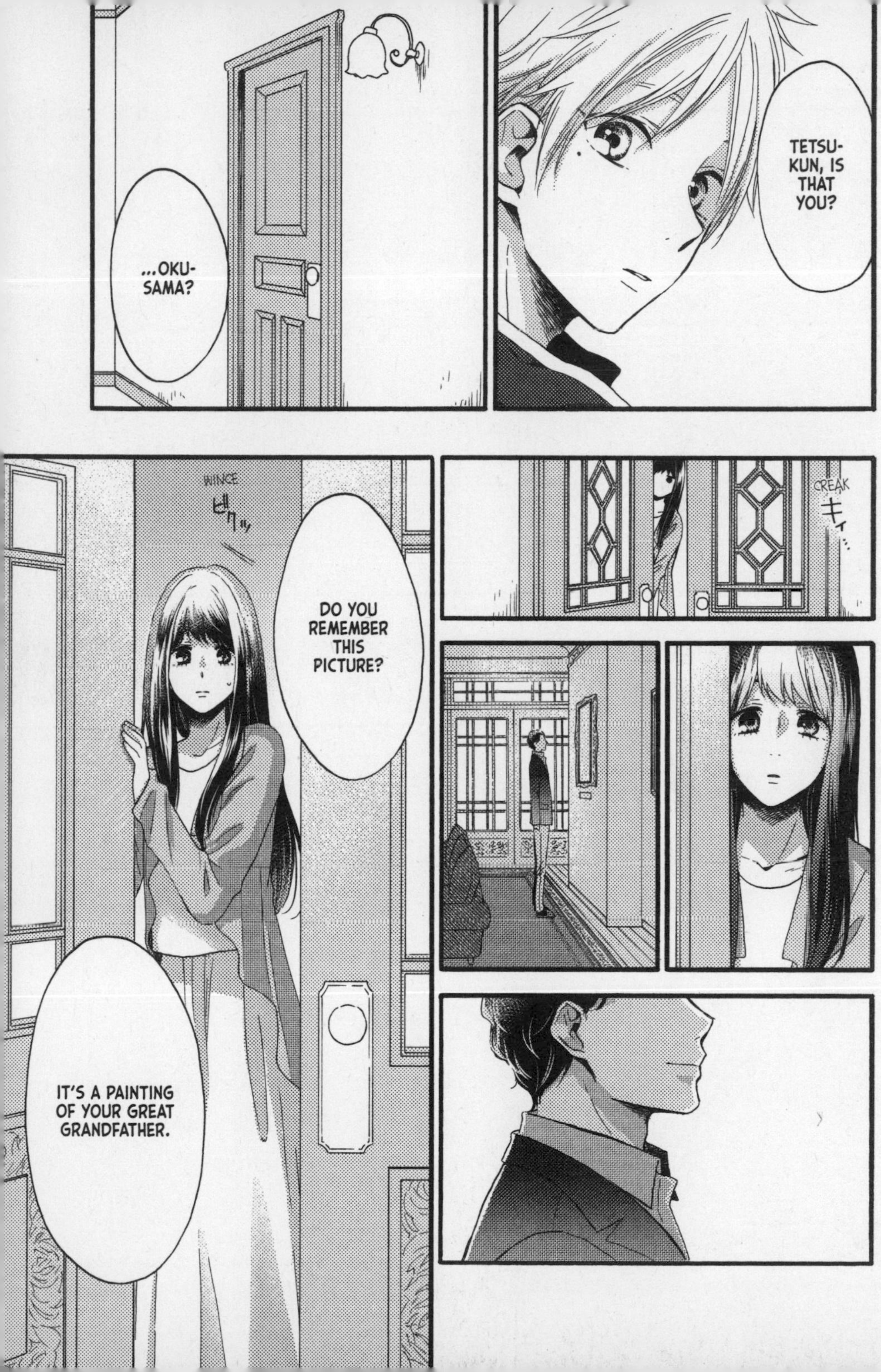
TETSU-KUN, IS THAT YOU?
...OKU-SAMA?
CREAK
キィ…
WINCE
ビクッ
DO YOU REMEMBER THIS PICTURE?
IT'S A PAINTING OF YOUR GREAT GRANDFATHER.

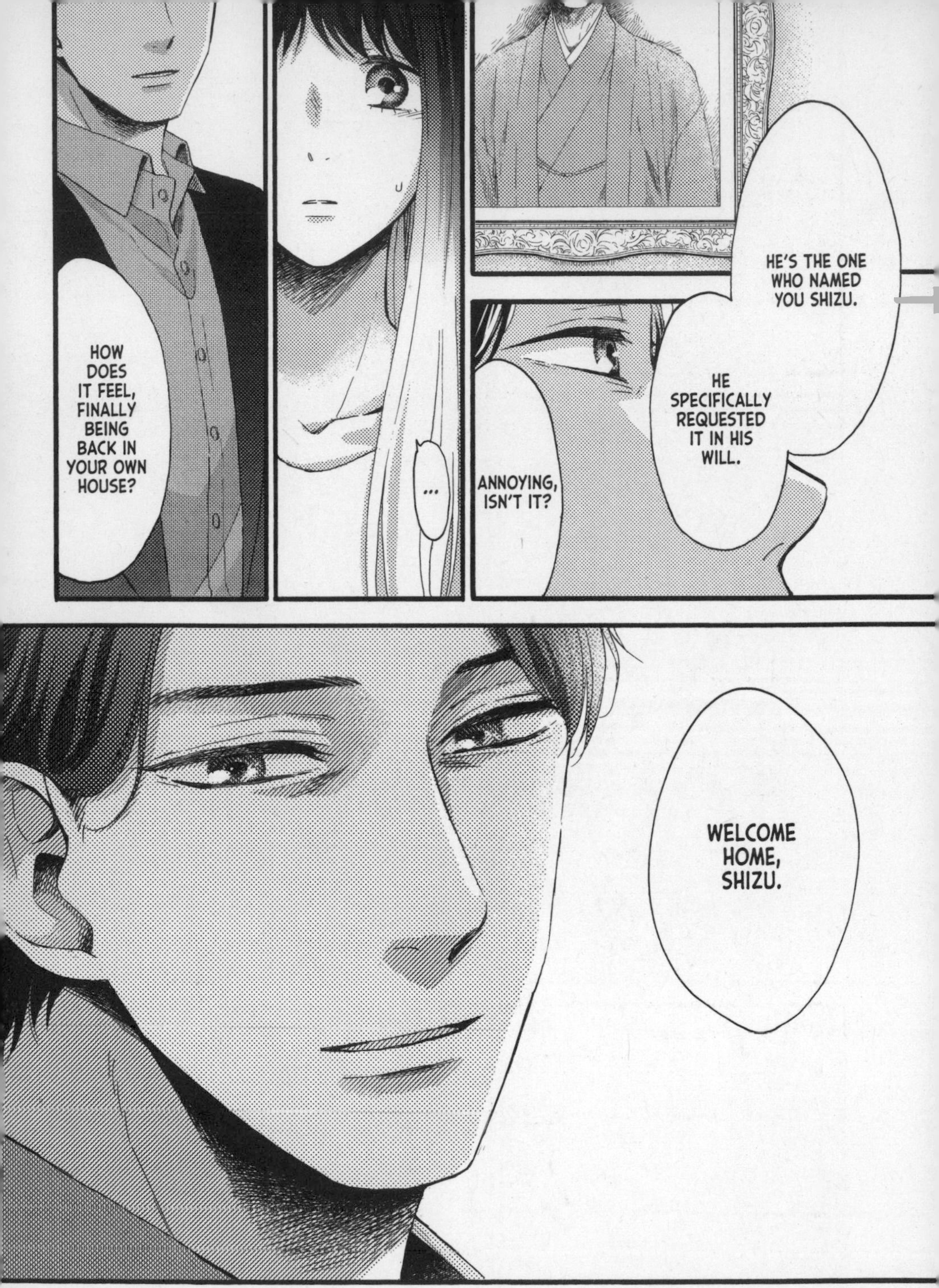
HE'S THE ONE WHO NAMED YOU SHIZU.
HE SPECIFICALLY REQUESTED IT IN HIS WILL.
ANNOYING, ISN'T IT?
...
HOW DOES IT FEEL, FINALLY BEING BACK IN YOUR OWN HOUSE?
WELCOME HOME, SHIZU.

ON THE TRAIN HOME PART 1

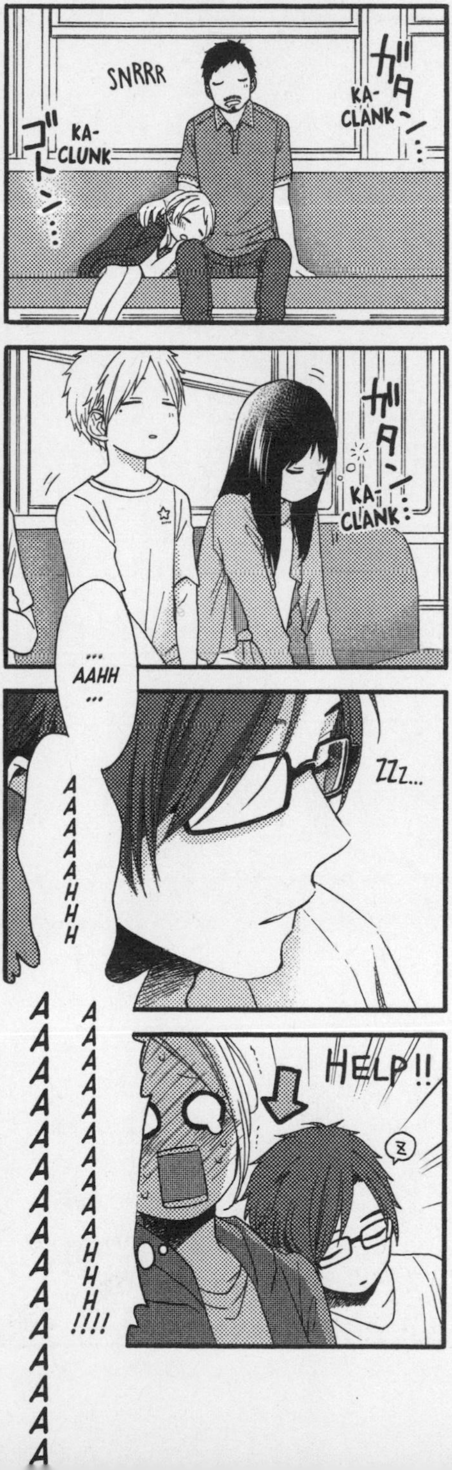
ガタン…
KA-CLANK
SNRRR
ゴトン…
KA-CLUNK
ガタン…
KA-CLANK
...AAHH...
ZZz...
AAAAAAAHHH
HELP!!
z
AAAAAAAAAAAAAAAAAAAAAA
AAAAAAAAAAAHHH!!!!

ON THE TRAIN HOME PART 2

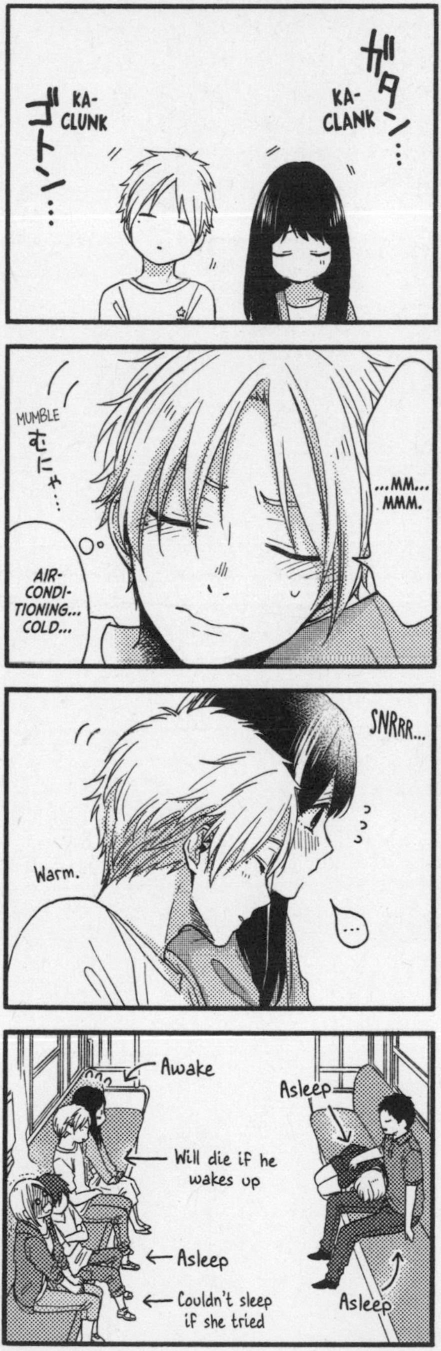
ガタン…
KA-CLANK
ゴトン…
KA-CLUNK
...MM... MMM.
MUMBLE
むにゃ…
AIR-CONDITIONING... COLD...
SNRRR...
Warm.
...
Awake
Will die if he wakes up
Asleep
Couldn't sleep if she tried
Asleep
Asleep

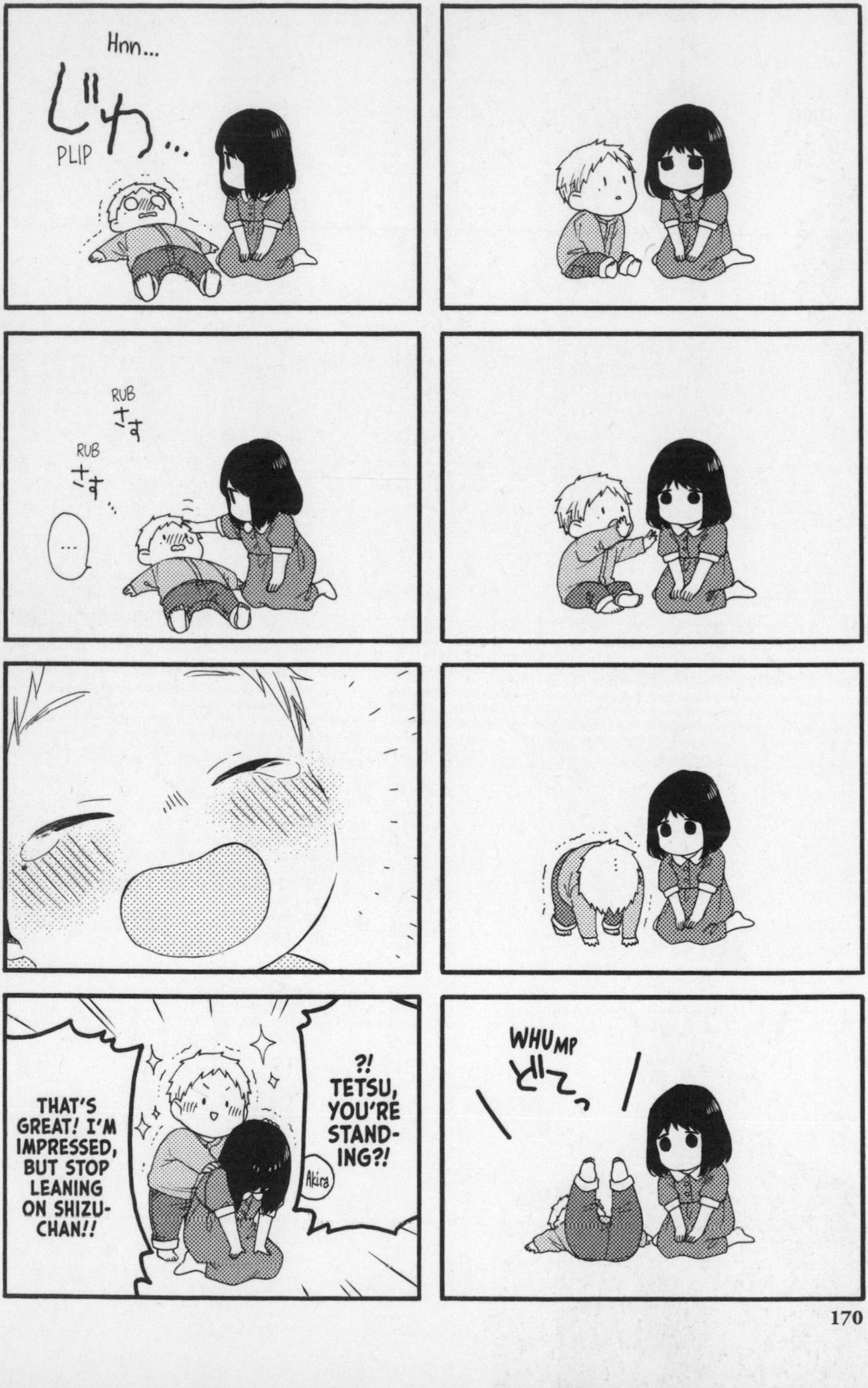
Hnn...
じわ...
PLIP
RUB
さす
RUB
さす...
...
...
WHUMP
どてっ
?! TETSU, YOU'RE STAND-ING?!
Akira
THAT'S GREAT! I'M IMPRESSED, BUT STOP LEANING ON SHIZU-CHAN!!

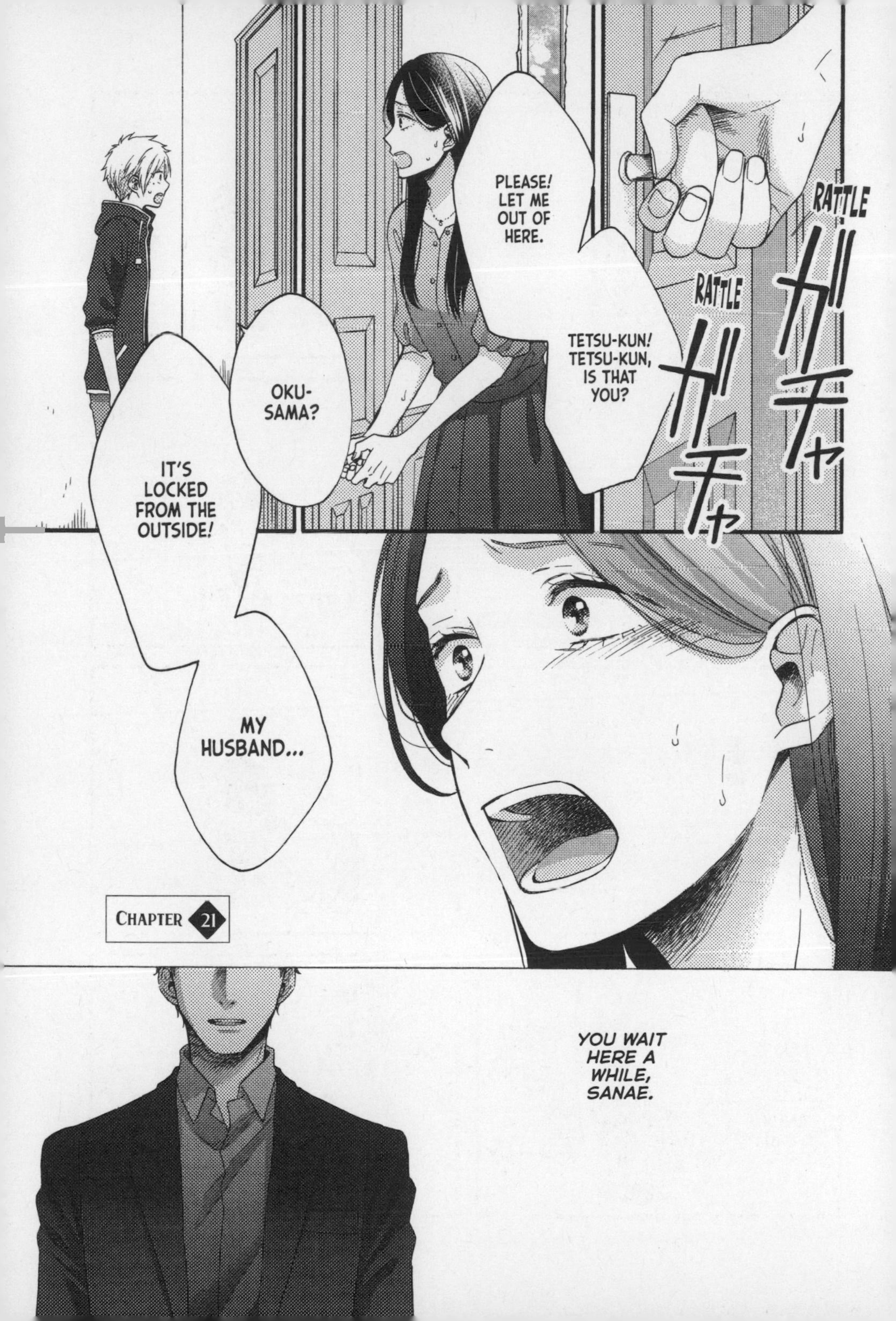

RATTLE
ガチャ
RATTLE
ガチャ
PLEASE! LET ME OUT OF HERE.
TETSU-KUN! TETSU-KUN, IS THAT YOU?
OKU-SAMA?
IT'S LOCKED FROM THE OUTSIDE!
MY HUSBAND...
CHAPTER 21
YOU WAIT HERE A WHILE, SANAE.

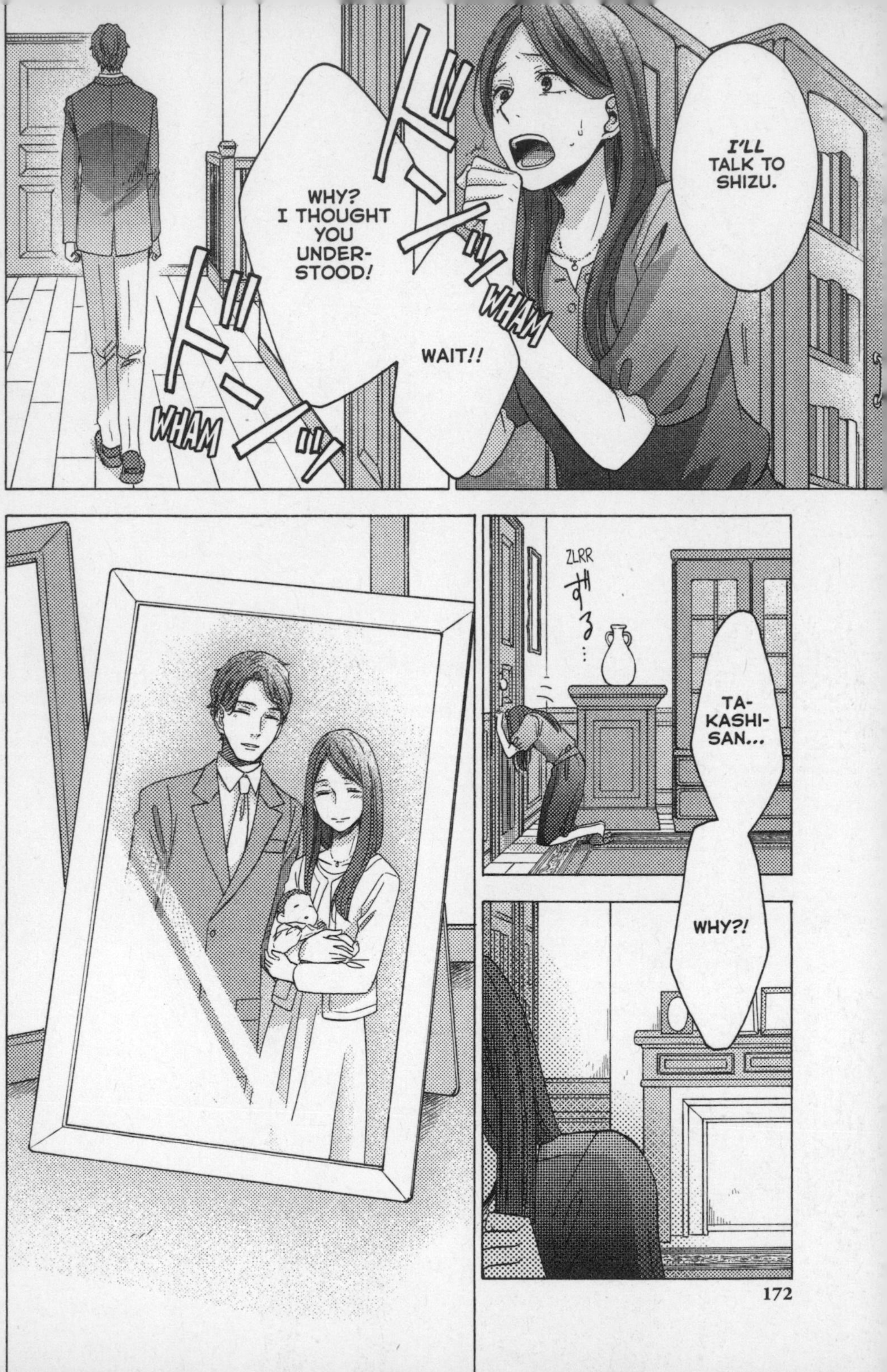
I'LL TALK TO SHIZU.
WHAM
WAIT!!
WHY? I THOUGHT YOU UNDER-STOOD!
WHAM
ZLRR
ずる…
TA-KASHI-SAN...
WHY?!

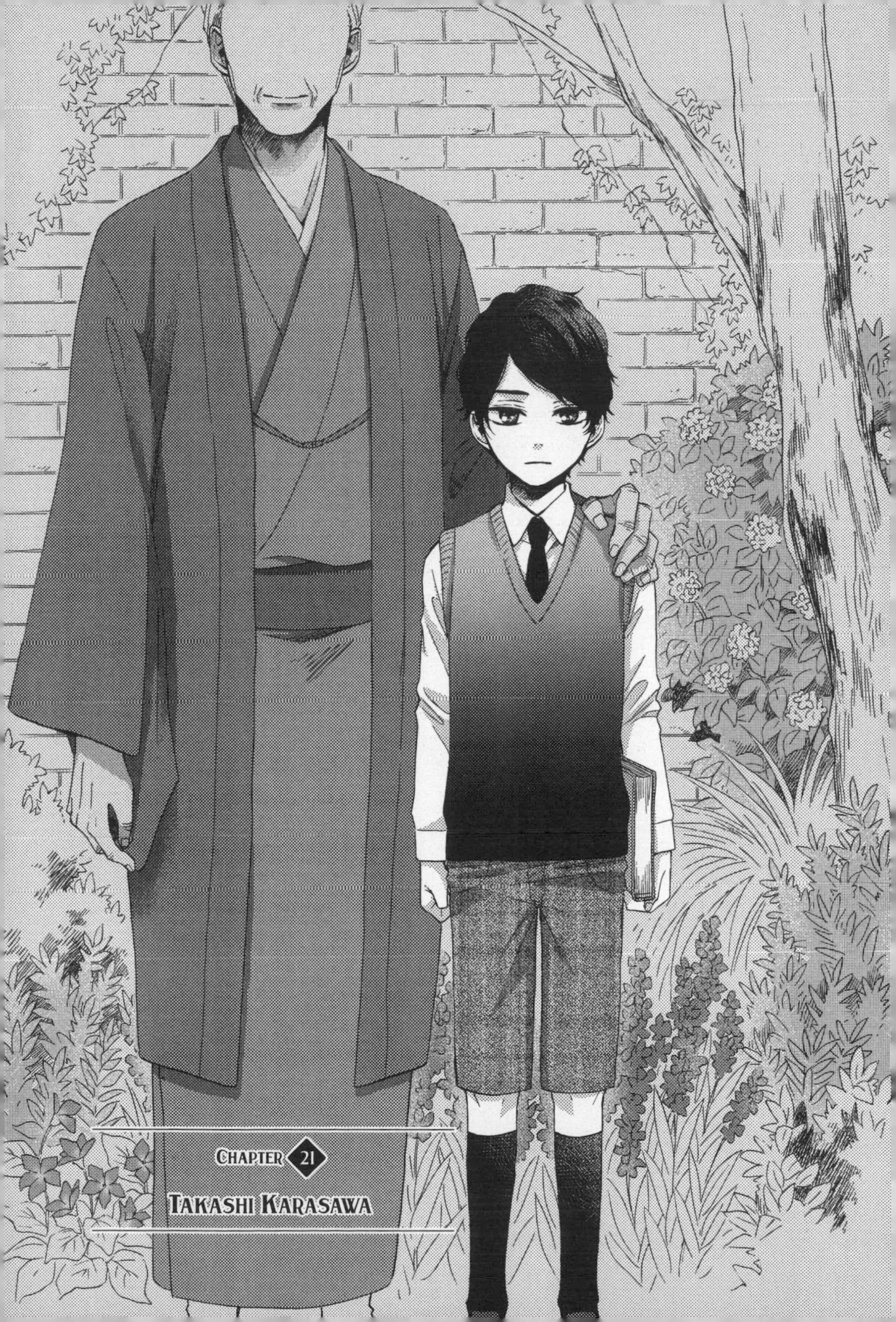
Chapter 21
Takashi Karasawa

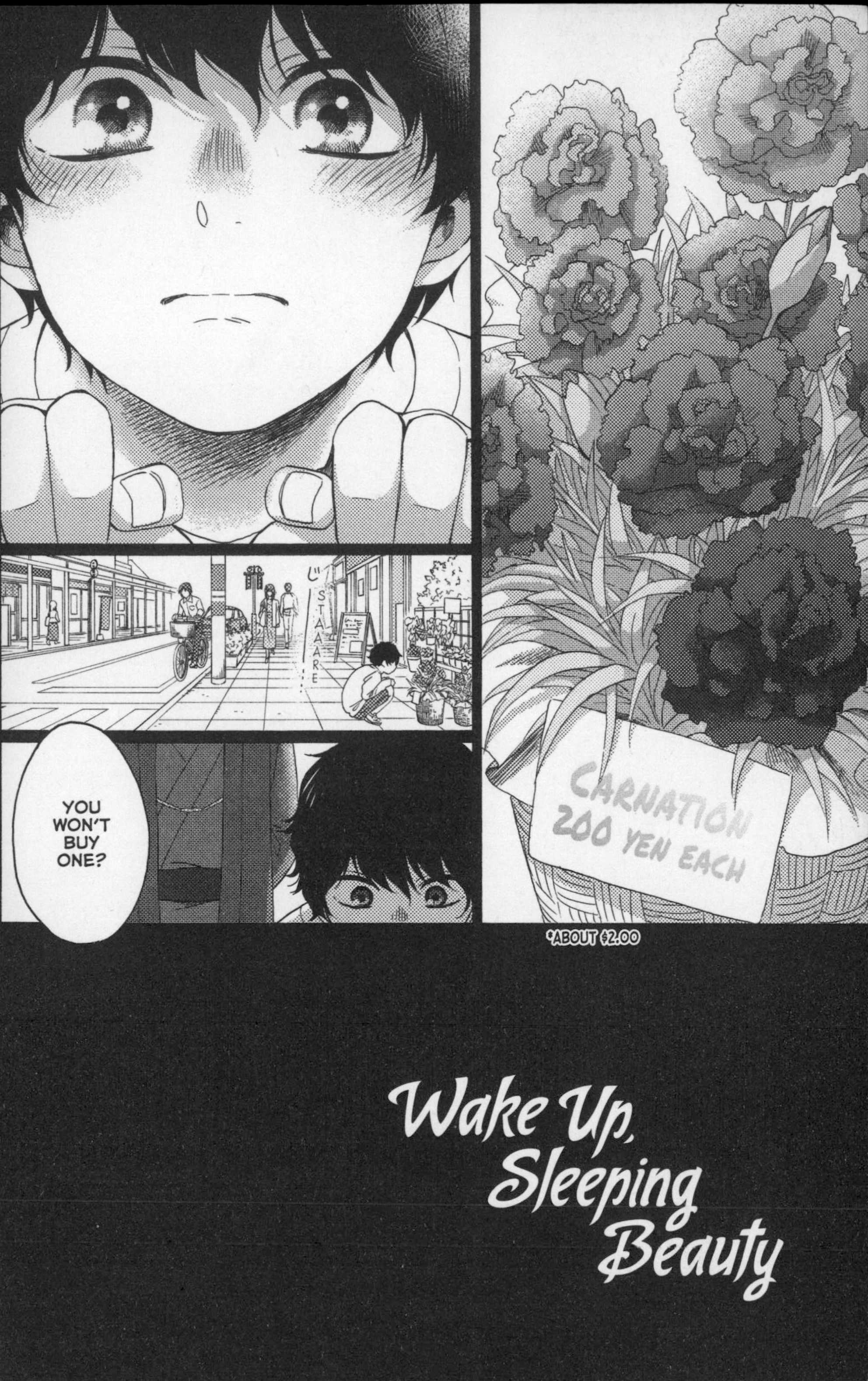
CARNATION
200 YEN EACH
じ
STAAARE
YOU WON'T BUY ONE?

*ABOUT $2.00

Wake Up, Sleeping Beauty

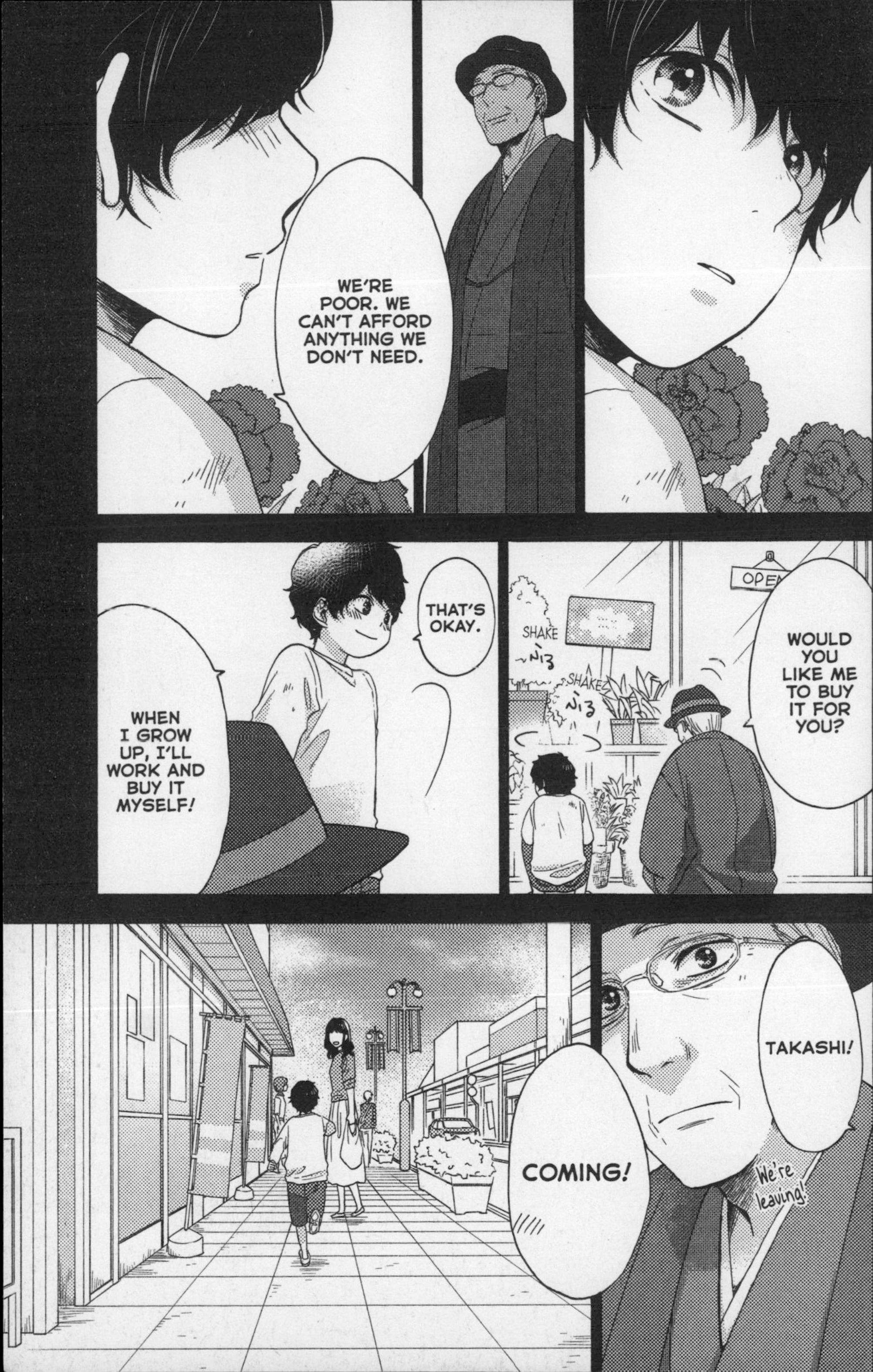
WE'RE POOR. WE CAN'T AFFORD ANYTHING WE DON'T NEED.
OPEN
WOULD YOU LIKE ME TO BUY IT FOR YOU?
SHAKE ぶる
SHAKES ぶる
THAT'S OKAY.
WHEN I GROW UP, I'LL WORK AND BUY IT MYSELF!
TAKASHI!
We're leaving!
COMING!

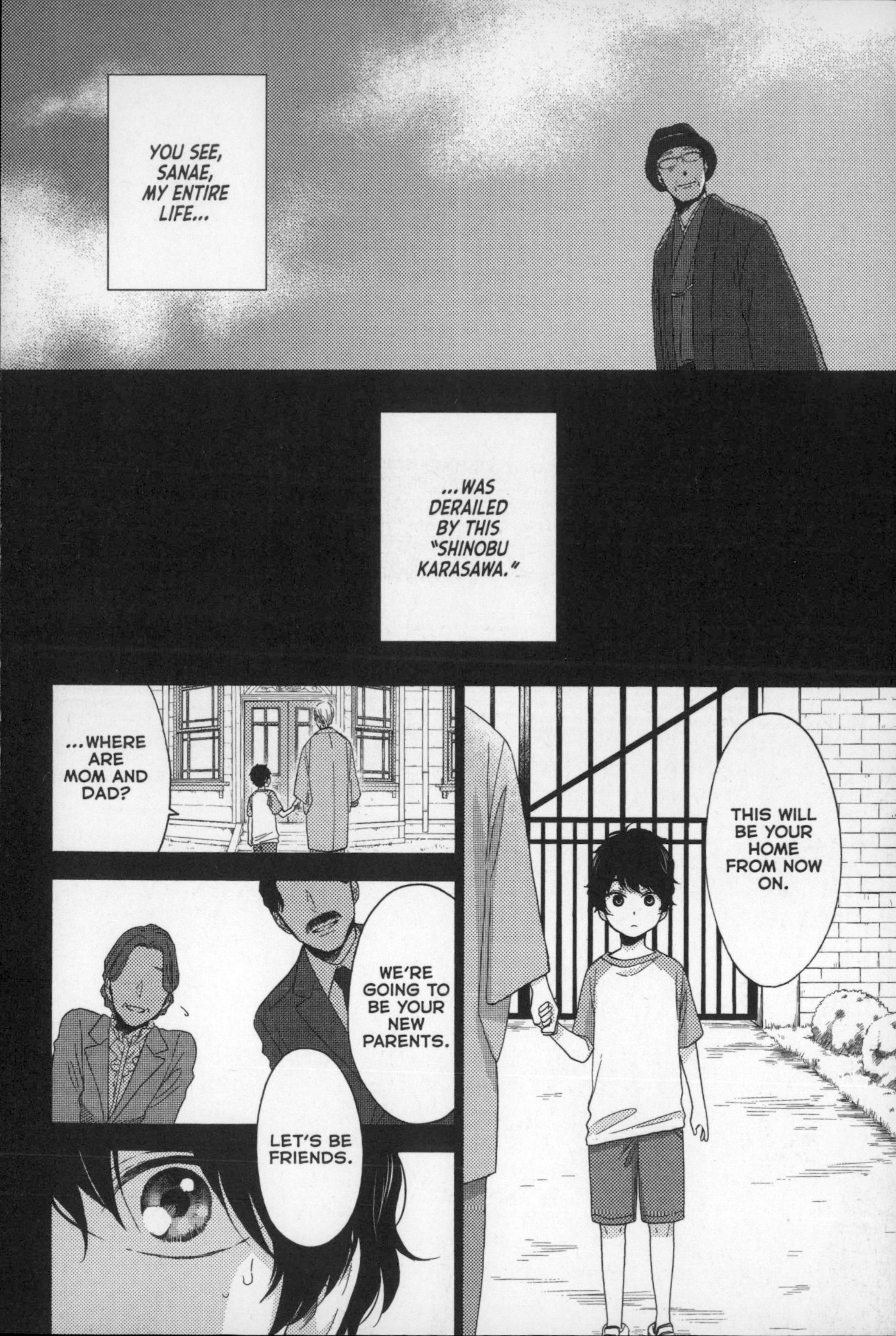
YOU SEE, SANAE, MY ENTIRE LIFE...
...WAS DERAILED BY THIS "SHINOBU KARASAWA."
THIS WILL BE YOUR HOME FROM NOW ON.
...WHERE ARE MOM AND DAD?
WE'RE GOING TO BE YOUR NEW PARENTS.
LET'S BE FRIENDS.

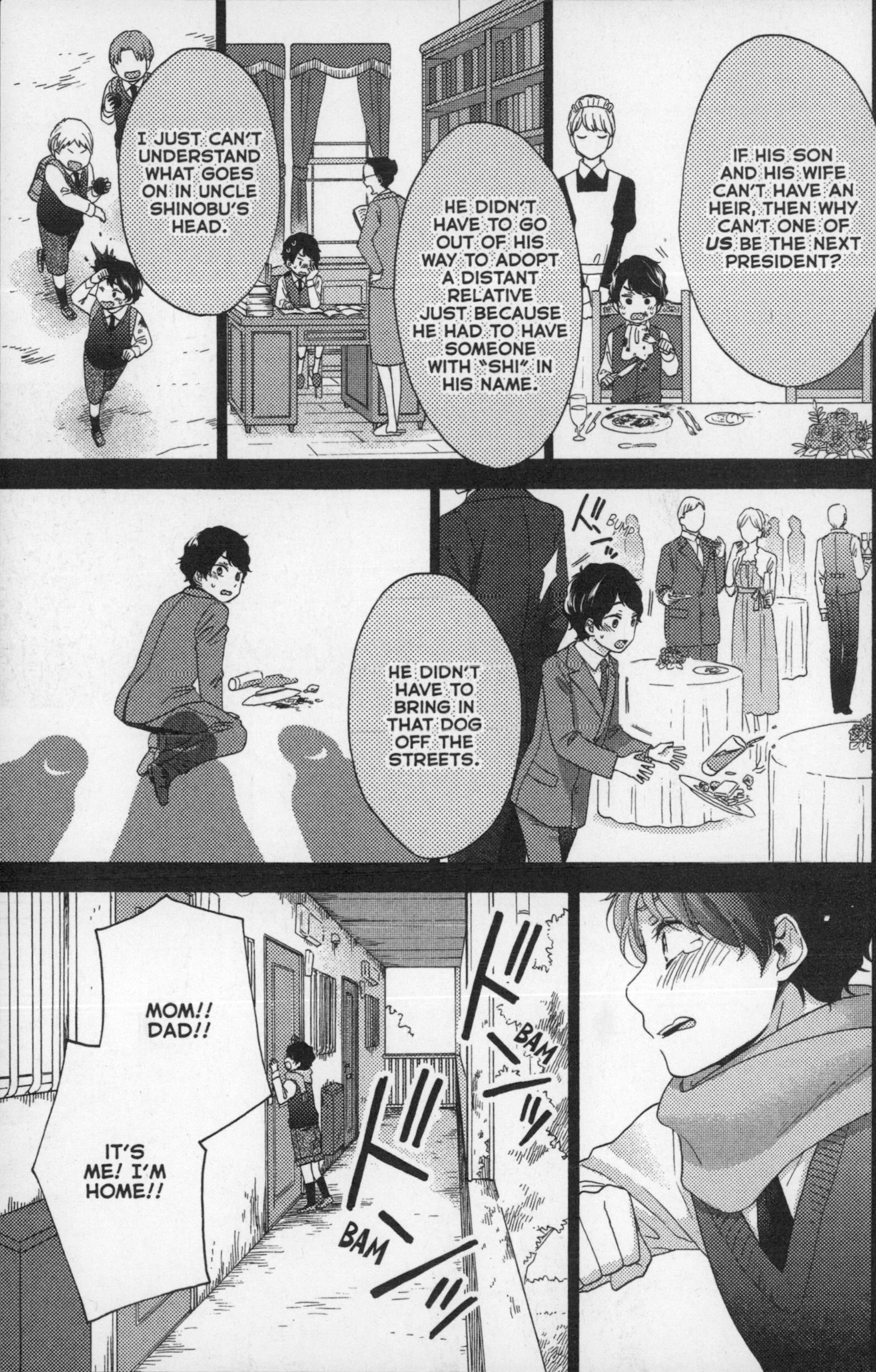
IF HIS SON AND HIS WIFE CAN'T HAVE AN HEIR, THEN WHY CAN'T ONE OF *US* BE THE NEXT PRESIDENT?
HE DIDN'T HAVE TO GO OUT OF HIS WAY TO ADOPT A DISTANT RELATIVE JUST BECAUSE HE HAD TO HAVE SOMEONE WITH "SHI" IN HIS NAME.
I JUST CAN'T UNDERSTAND WHAT GOES ON IN UNCLE SHINOBU'S HEAD.
BUMP
HE DIDN'T HAVE TO BRING IN THAT DOG OFF THE STREETS.
BAM
BAM
MOM!! DAD!!
IT'S ME! I'M HOME!!

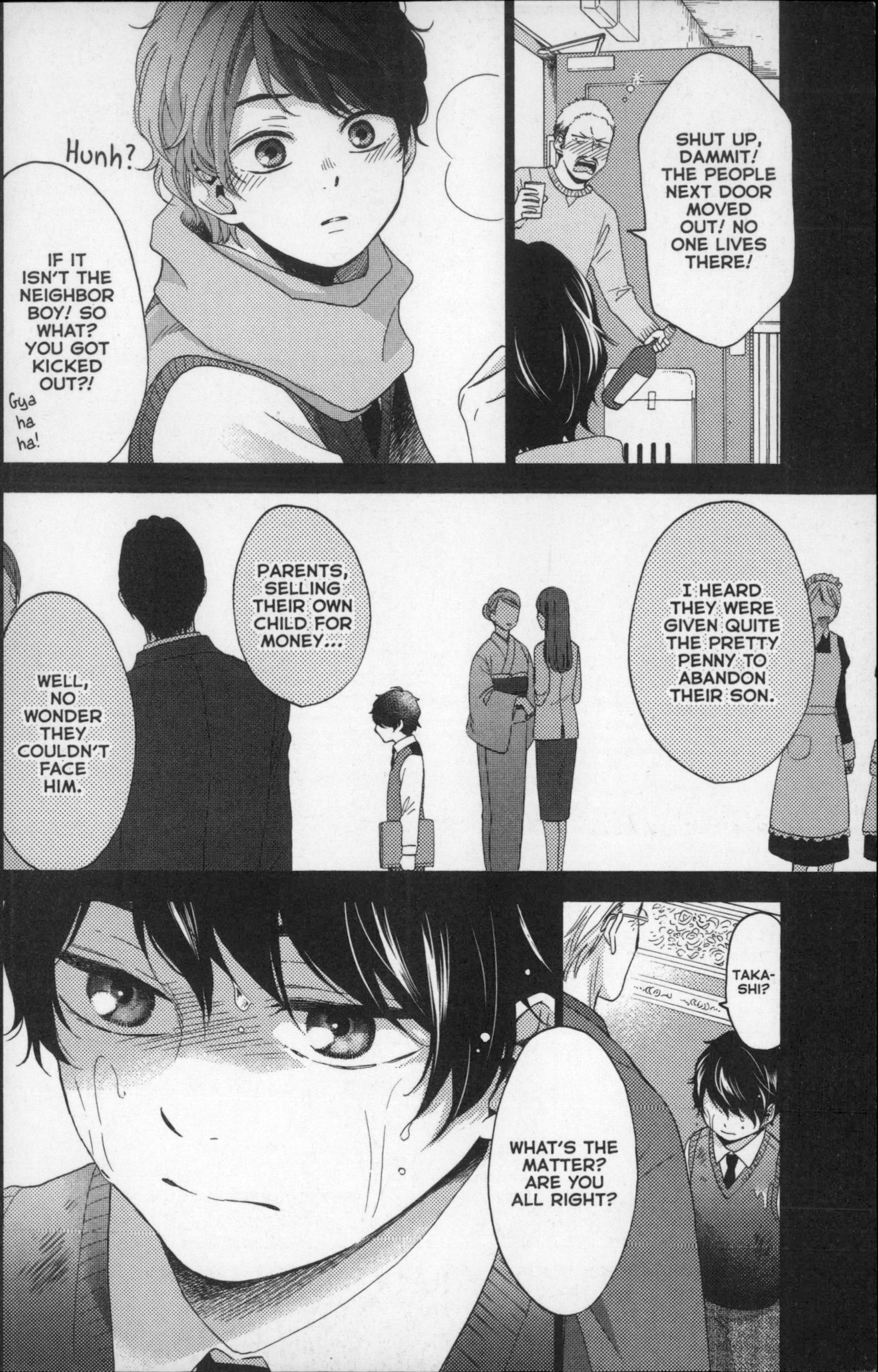
SHUT UP, DAMMIT! THE PEOPLE NEXT DOOR MOVED OUT! NO ONE LIVES THERE!
Hunh?
IF IT ISN'T THE NEIGHBOR BOY! SO WHAT? YOU GOT KICKED OUT?!
Gya ha ha!
I HEARD THEY WERE GIVEN QUITE THE PRETTY PENNY TO ABANDON THEIR SON.
PARENTS, SELLING THEIR OWN CHILD FOR MONEY...
WELL, NO WONDER THEY COULDN'T FACE HIM.
TAKA-SHI?
WHAT'S THE MATTER? ARE YOU ALL RIGHT?

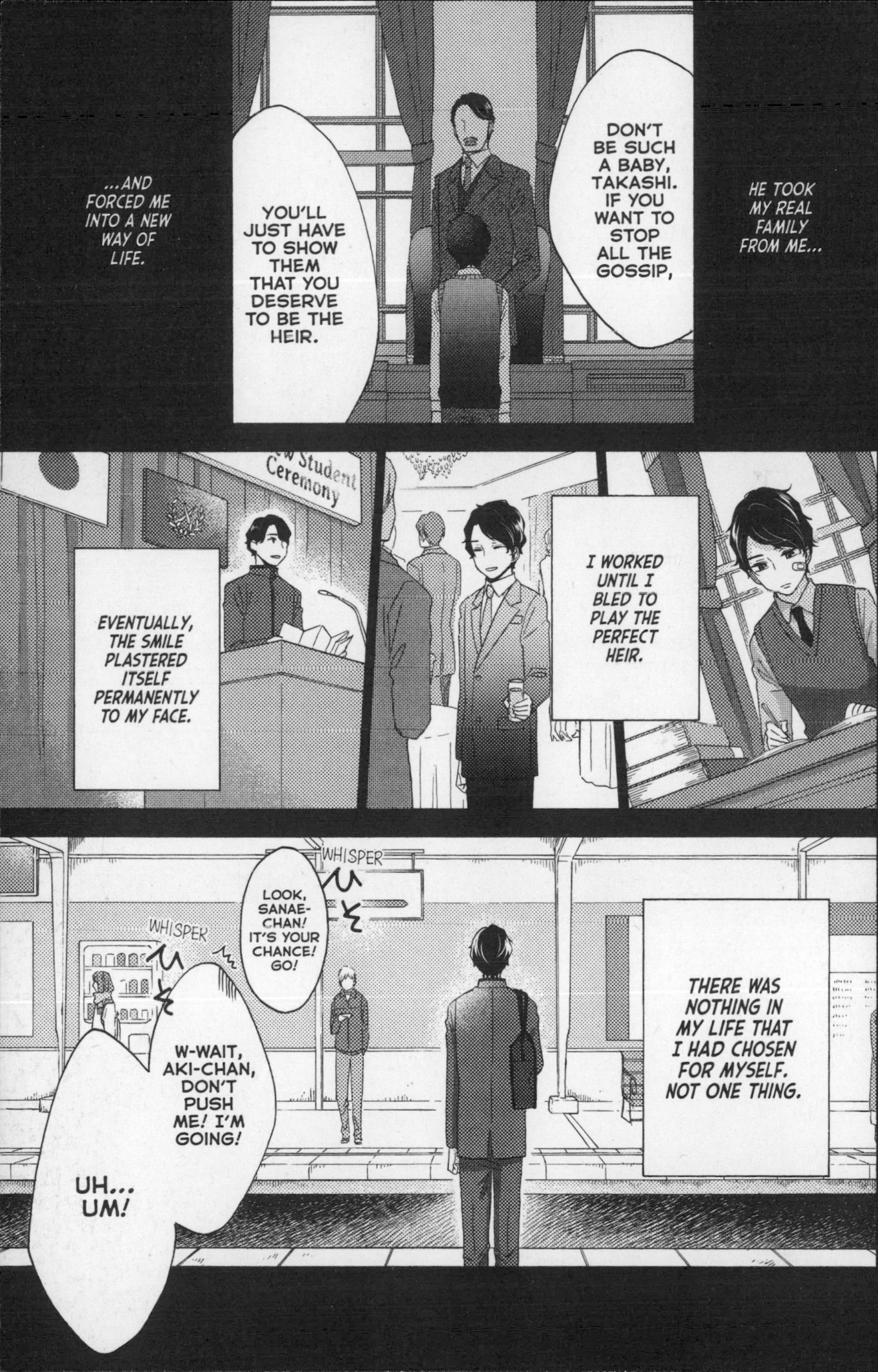
HE TOOK MY REAL FAMILY FROM ME...
DON'T BE SUCH A BABY, TAKASHI. IF YOU WANT TO STOP ALL THE GOSSIP,
YOU'LL JUST HAVE TO SHOW THEM THAT YOU DESERVE TO BE THE HEIR.
...AND FORCED ME INTO A NEW WAY OF LIFE.
I WORKED UNTIL I BLED TO PLAY THE PERFECT HEIR.
Student Ceremony
EVENTUALLY, THE SMILE PLASTERED ITSELF PERMANENTLY TO MY FACE.
THERE WAS NOTHING IN MY LIFE THAT I HAD CHOSEN FOR MYSELF. NOT ONE THING.
WHISPER
LOOK, SANAE-CHAN! IT'S YOUR CHANCE! GO!
WHISPER
W-WAIT, AKI-CHAN, DON'T PUSH ME! I'M GOING!
UH... UM!

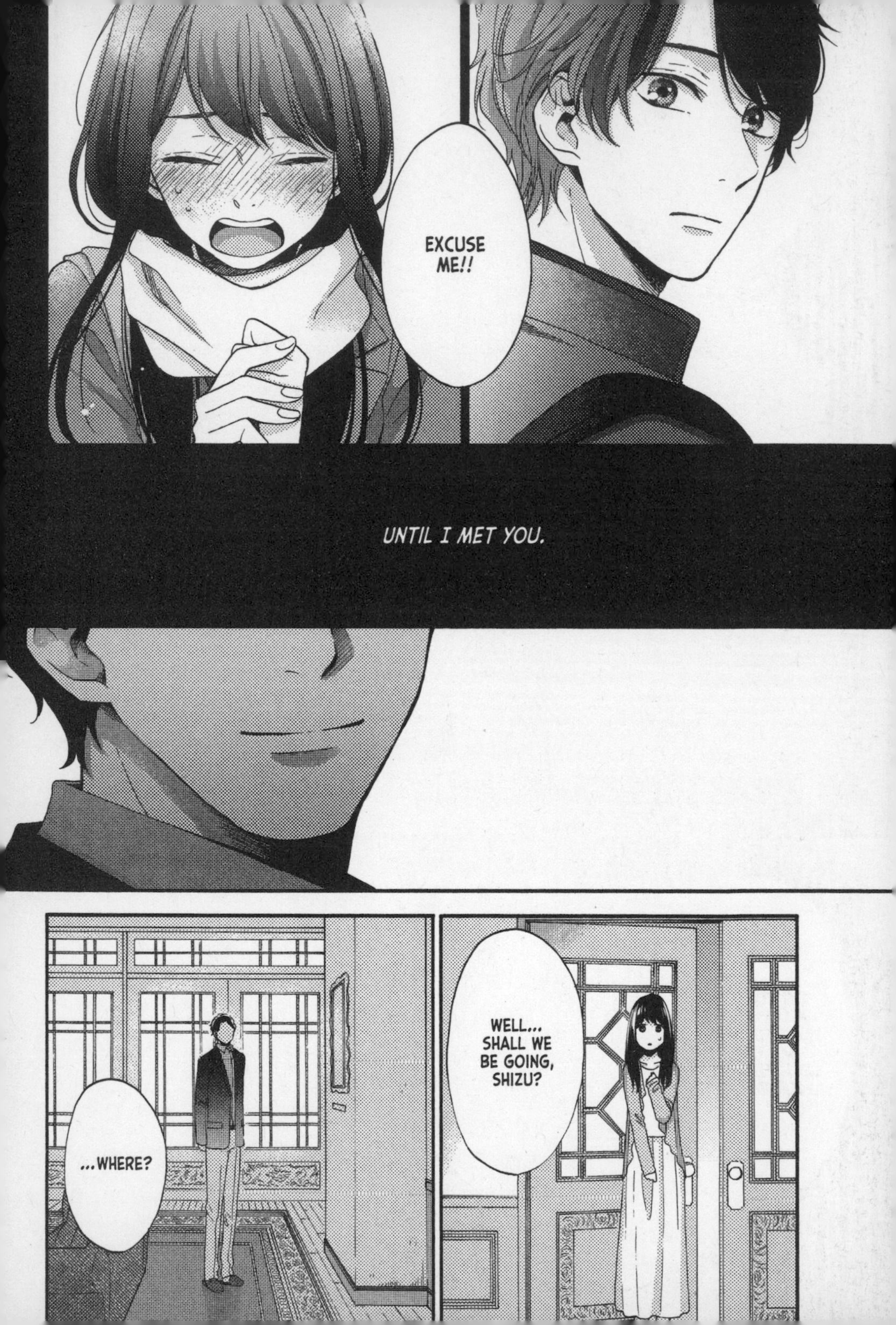
EXCUSE ME!!
UNTIL I MET YOU.
WELL... SHALL WE BE GOING, SHIZU?
...WHERE?

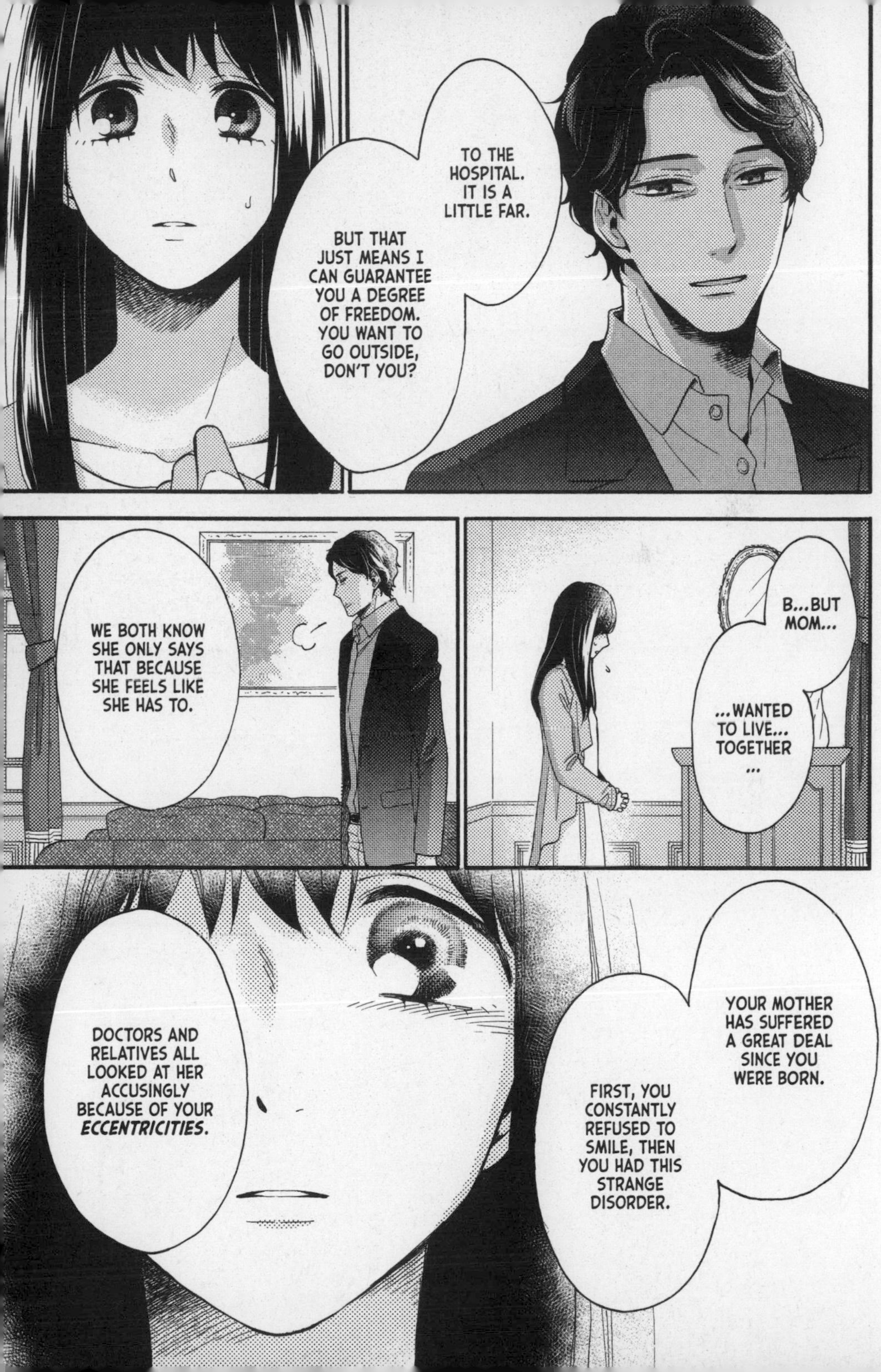
TO THE HOSPITAL. IT IS A LITTLE FAR.
BUT THAT JUST MEANS I CAN GUARANTEE YOU A DEGREE OF FREEDOM. YOU WANT TO GO OUTSIDE, DON'T YOU?
B...BUT MOM...
...WANTED TO LIVE... TOGETHER ...
WE BOTH KNOW SHE ONLY SAYS THAT BECAUSE SHE FEELS LIKE SHE HAS TO.
YOUR MOTHER HAS SUFFERED A GREAT DEAL SINCE YOU WERE BORN.
FIRST, YOU CONSTANTLY REFUSED TO SMILE, THEN YOU HAD THIS STRANGE DISORDER.
DOCTORS AND RELATIVES ALL LOOKED AT HER ACCUSINGLY BECAUSE OF YOUR *ECCENTRICITIES*.

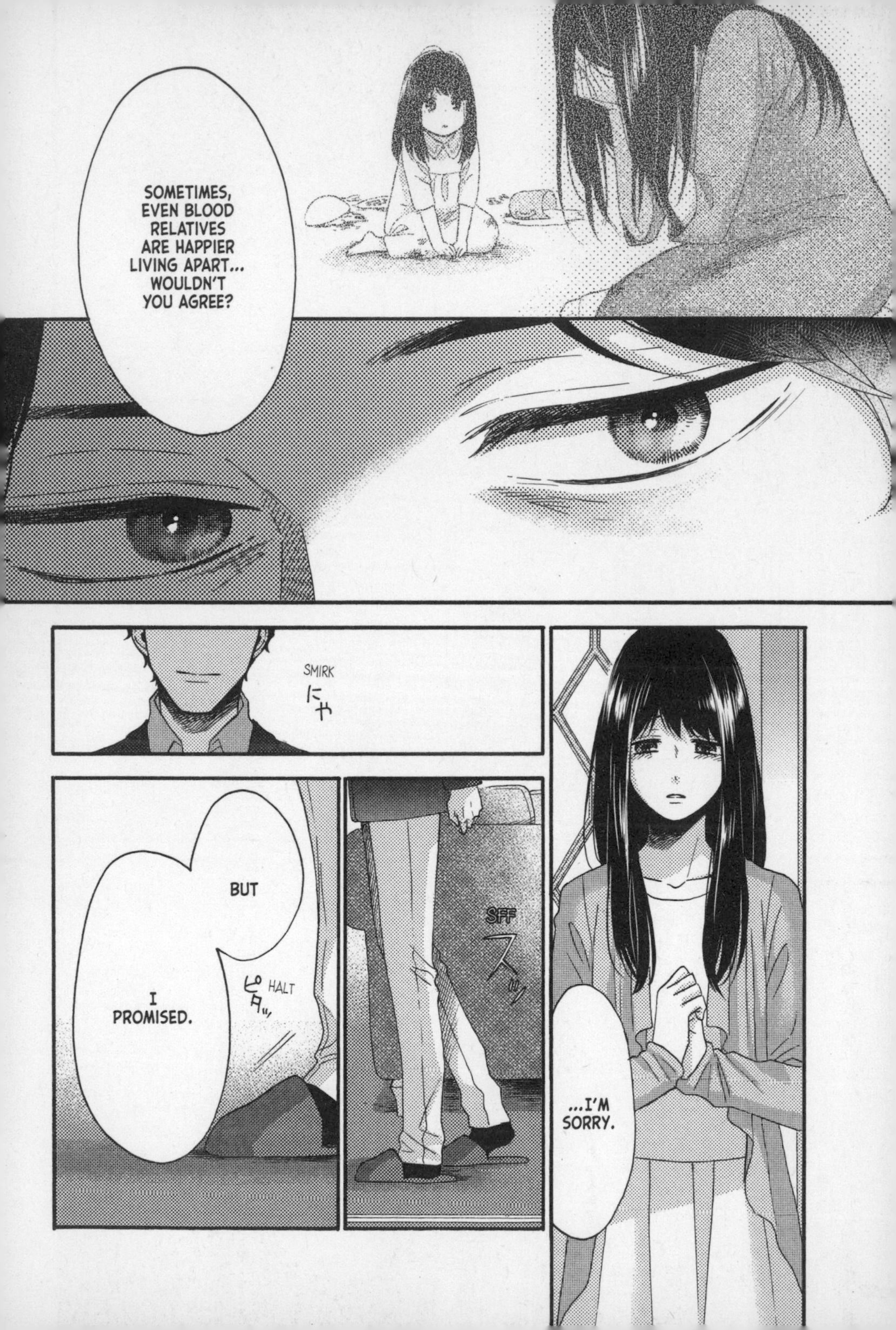
SOMETIMES, EVEN BLOOD RELATIVES ARE HAPPIER LIVING APART... WOULDN'T YOU AGREE?
...I'M SORRY.
SMIRK
にや
SFF
スッ
BUT I PROMISED.
HALT
ピタッ

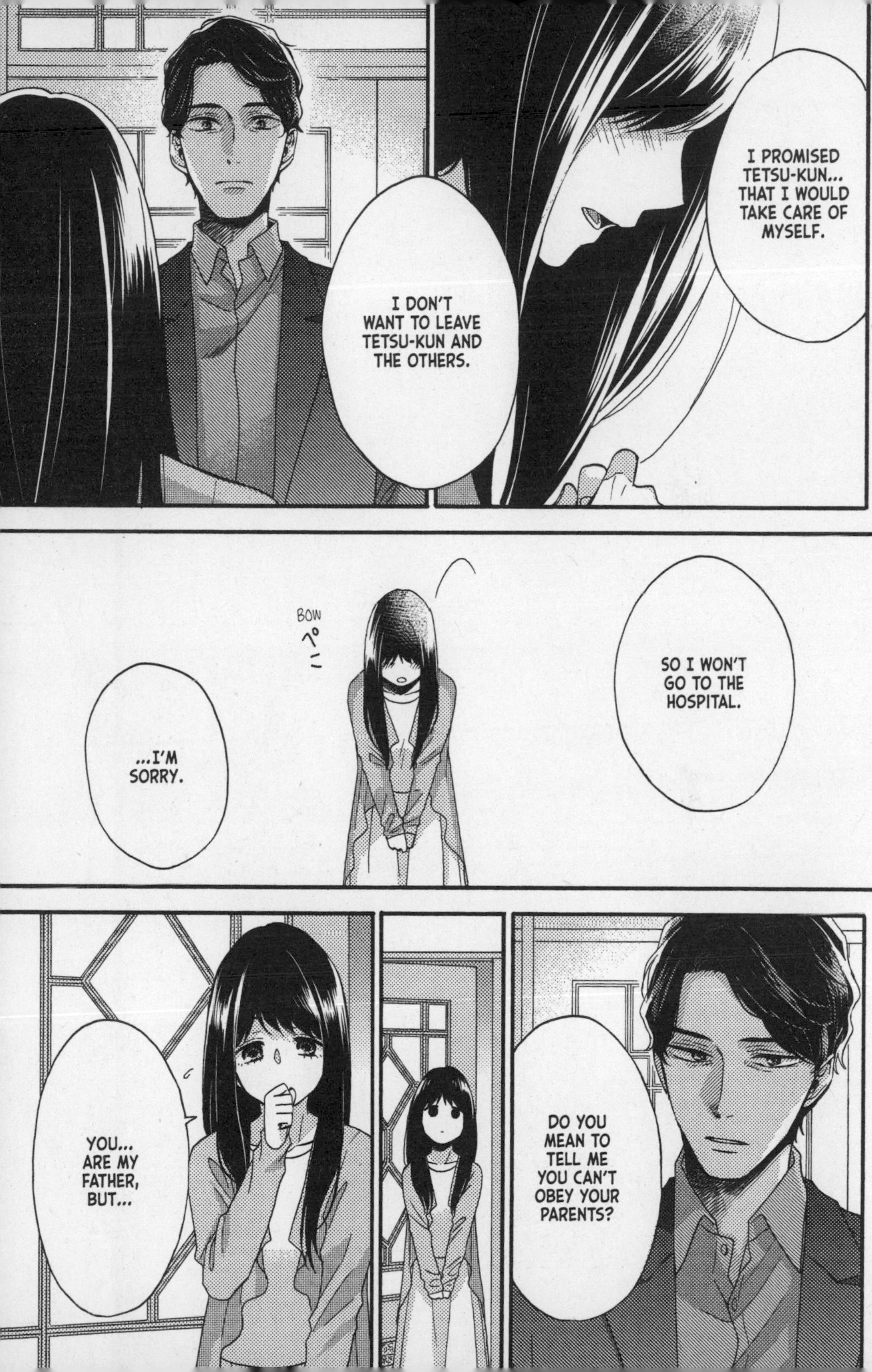
I PROMISED TETSU-KUN... THAT I WOULD TAKE CARE OF MYSELF.
I DON'T WANT TO LEAVE TETSU-KUN AND THE OTHERS.
SO I WON'T GO TO THE HOSPITAL.
BOW
ぺこ
...I'M SORRY.
DO YOU MEAN TO TELL ME YOU CAN'T OBEY YOUR PARENTS?
YOU... ARE MY FATHER, BUT...

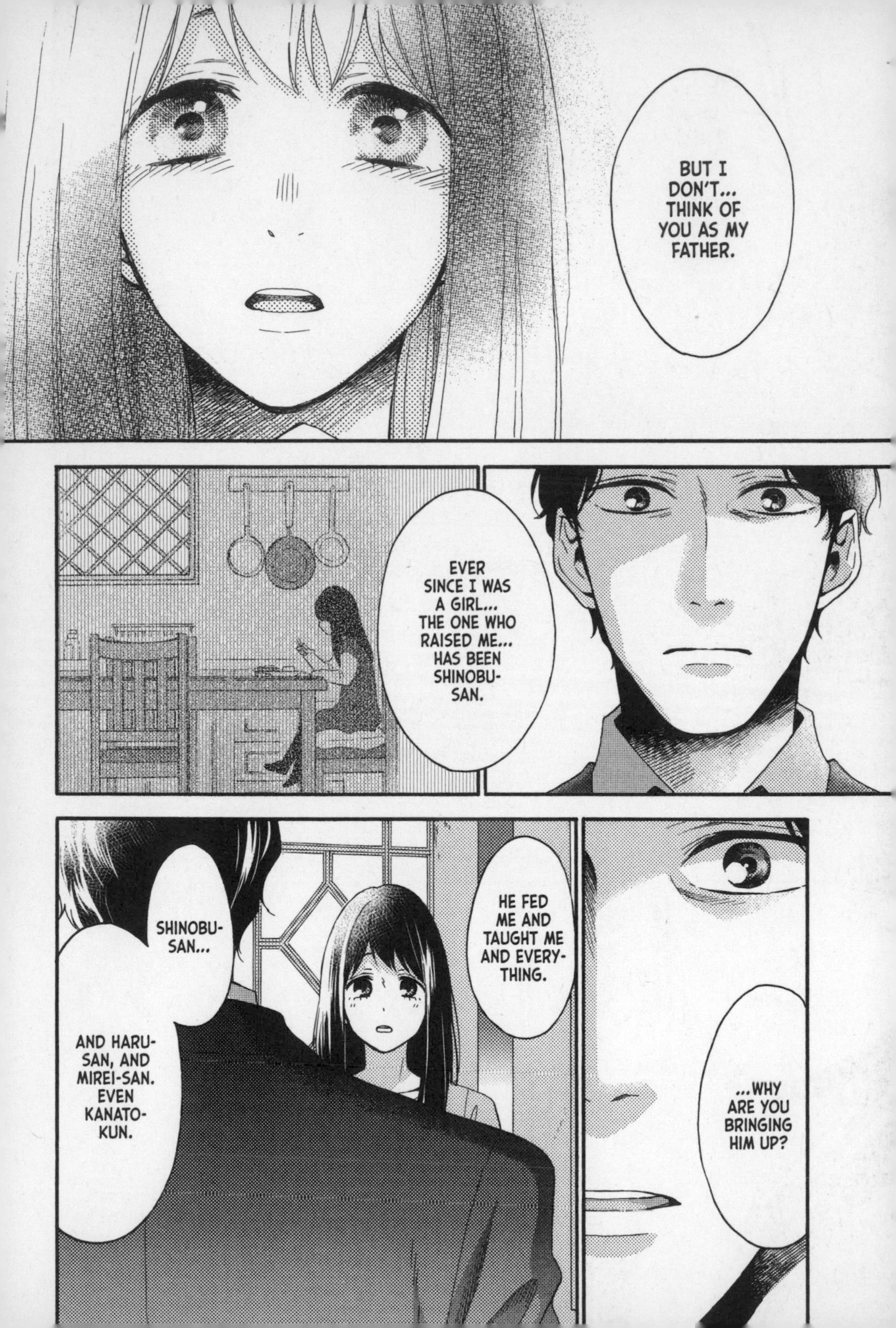
BUT I DON'T... THINK OF YOU AS MY FATHER.
EVER SINCE I WAS A GIRL... THE ONE WHO RAISED ME... HAS BEEN SHINOBU-SAN.
...WHY ARE YOU BRINGING HIM UP?
HE FED ME AND TAUGHT ME AND EVERY-THING.
SHINOBU-SAN...
AND HARU-SAN, AND MIREI-SAN. EVEN KANATO-KUN.

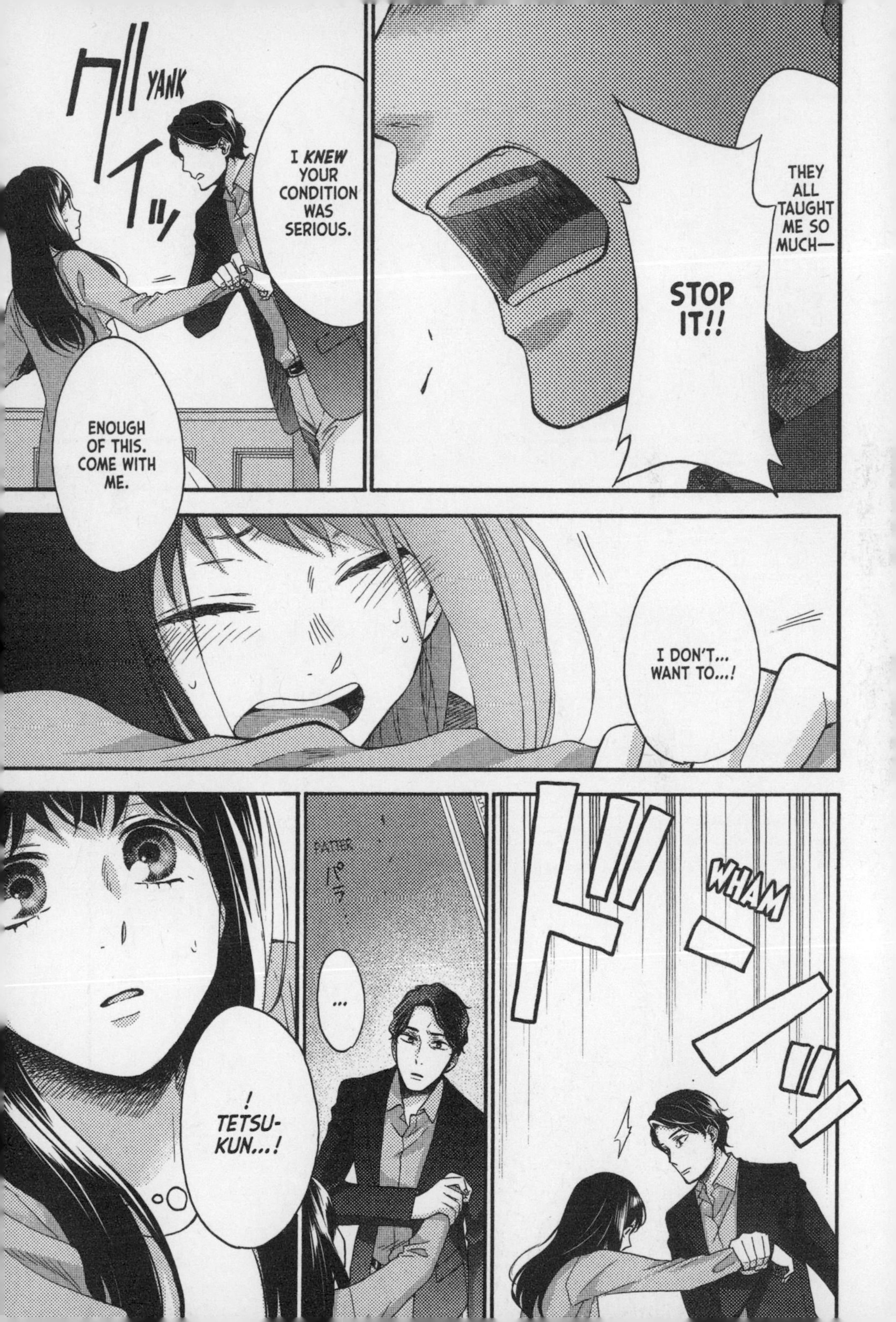
THEY ALL TAUGHT ME SO MUCH—
STOP IT!!
YANK
I *KNEW* YOUR CONDITION WAS SERIOUS.
ENOUGH OF THIS. COME WITH ME.
I DON'T... WANT TO...!
WHAM
PATTER
...
! TETSU-KUN...!

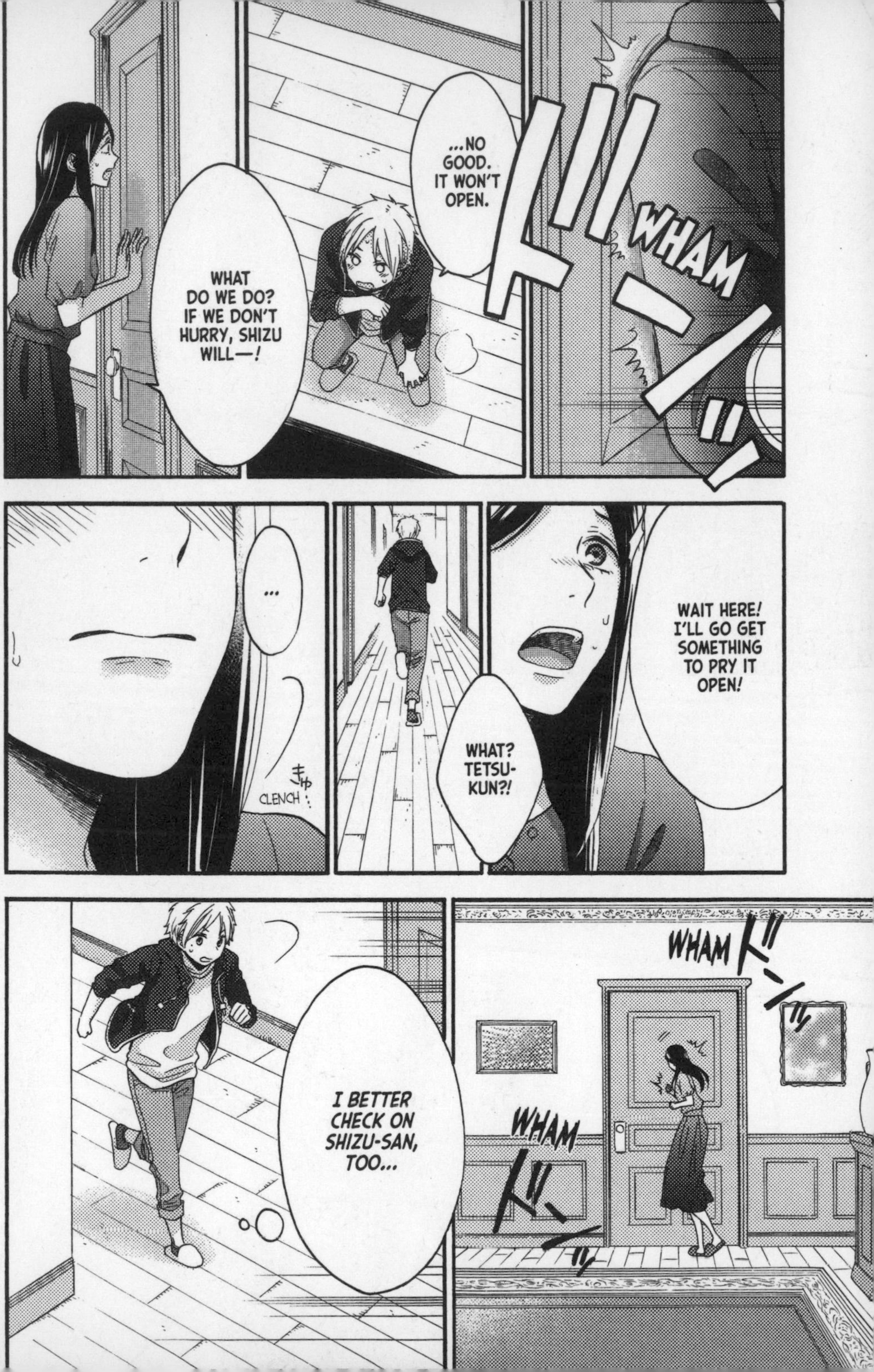
WHAM
...NO GOOD. IT WON'T OPEN.
WHAT DO WE DO? IF WE DON'T HURRY, SHIZU WILL—!
WAIT HERE! I'LL GO GET SOMETHING TO PRY IT OPEN!
WHAT? TETSU-KUN?!
...
CLENCH
WHAM
WHAM
I BETTER CHECK ON SHIZU-SAN, TOO...

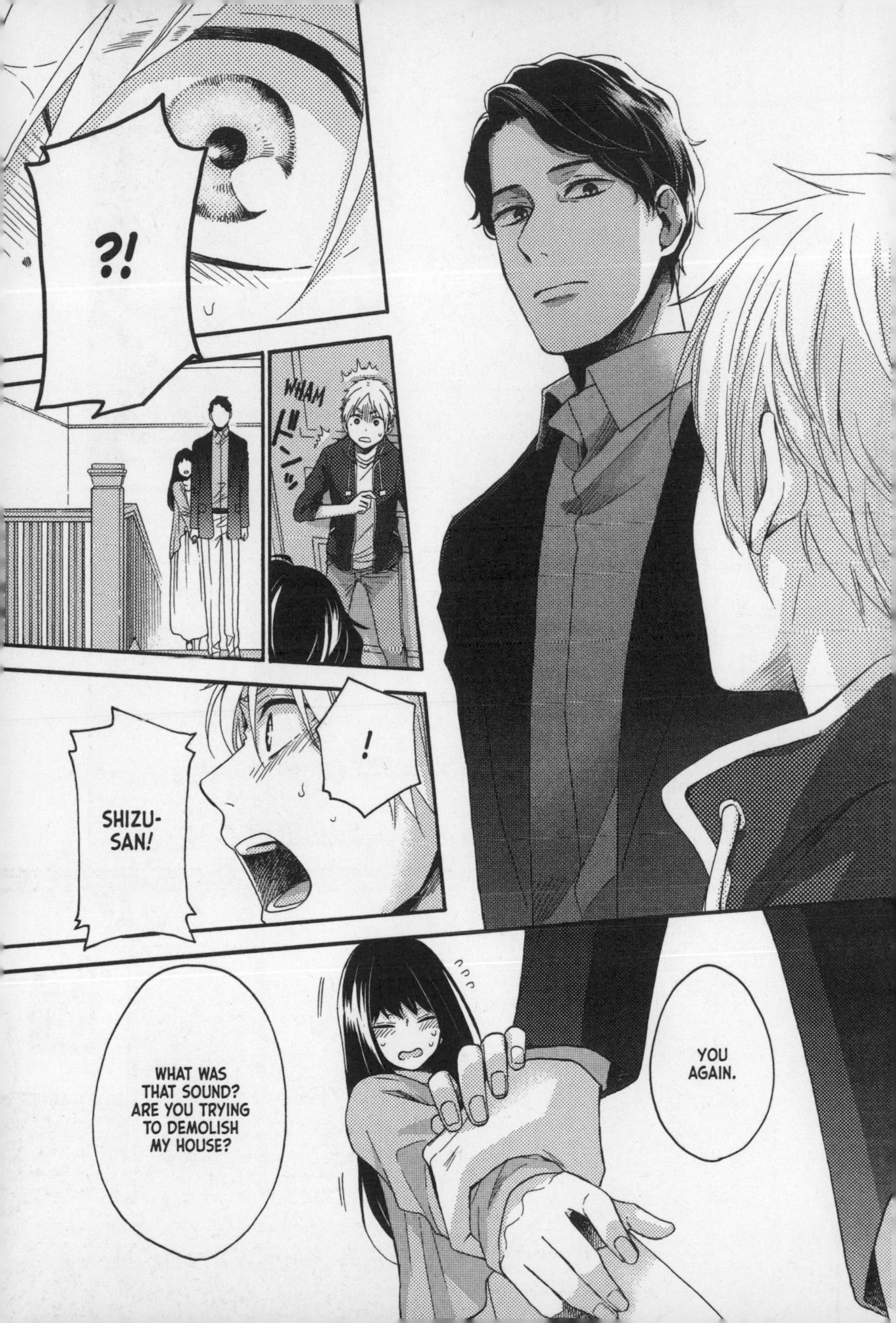
?!
WHAM
!
SHIZU-SAN!
YOU AGAIN.
WHAT WAS THAT SOUND? ARE YOU TRYING TO DEMOLISH MY HOUSE?

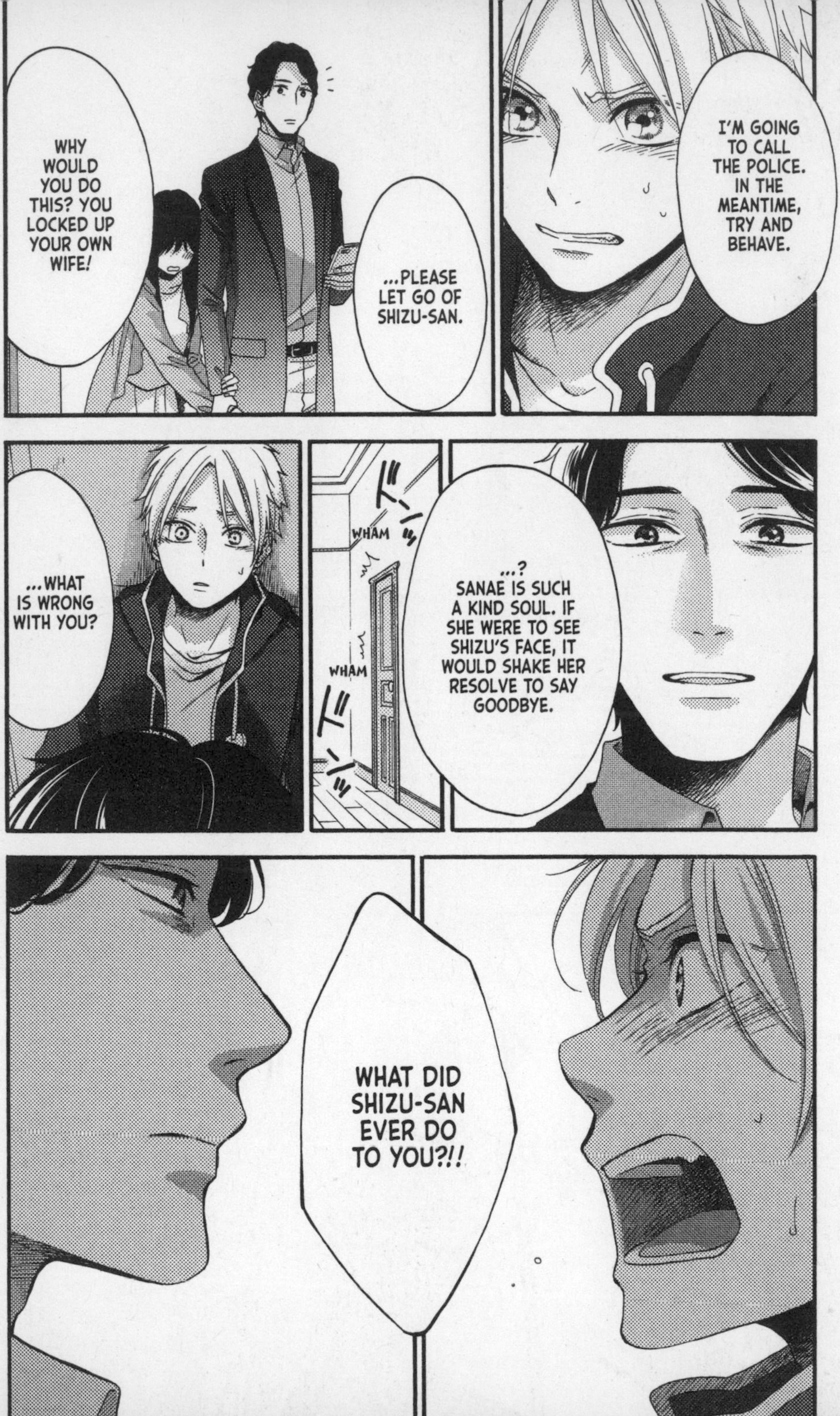
I'M GOING TO CALL THE POLICE. IN THE MEANTIME, TRY AND BEHAVE.
...PLEASE LET GO OF SHIZU-SAN.
WHY WOULD YOU DO THIS? YOU LOCKED UP YOUR OWN WIFE!
...? SANAE IS SUCH A KIND SOUL. IF SHE WERE TO SEE SHIZU'S FACE, IT WOULD SHAKE HER RESOLVE TO SAY GOODBYE.
WHAM
WHAM
...WHAT IS WRONG WITH YOU?
WHAT DID SHIZU-SAN EVER DO TO YOU?!!

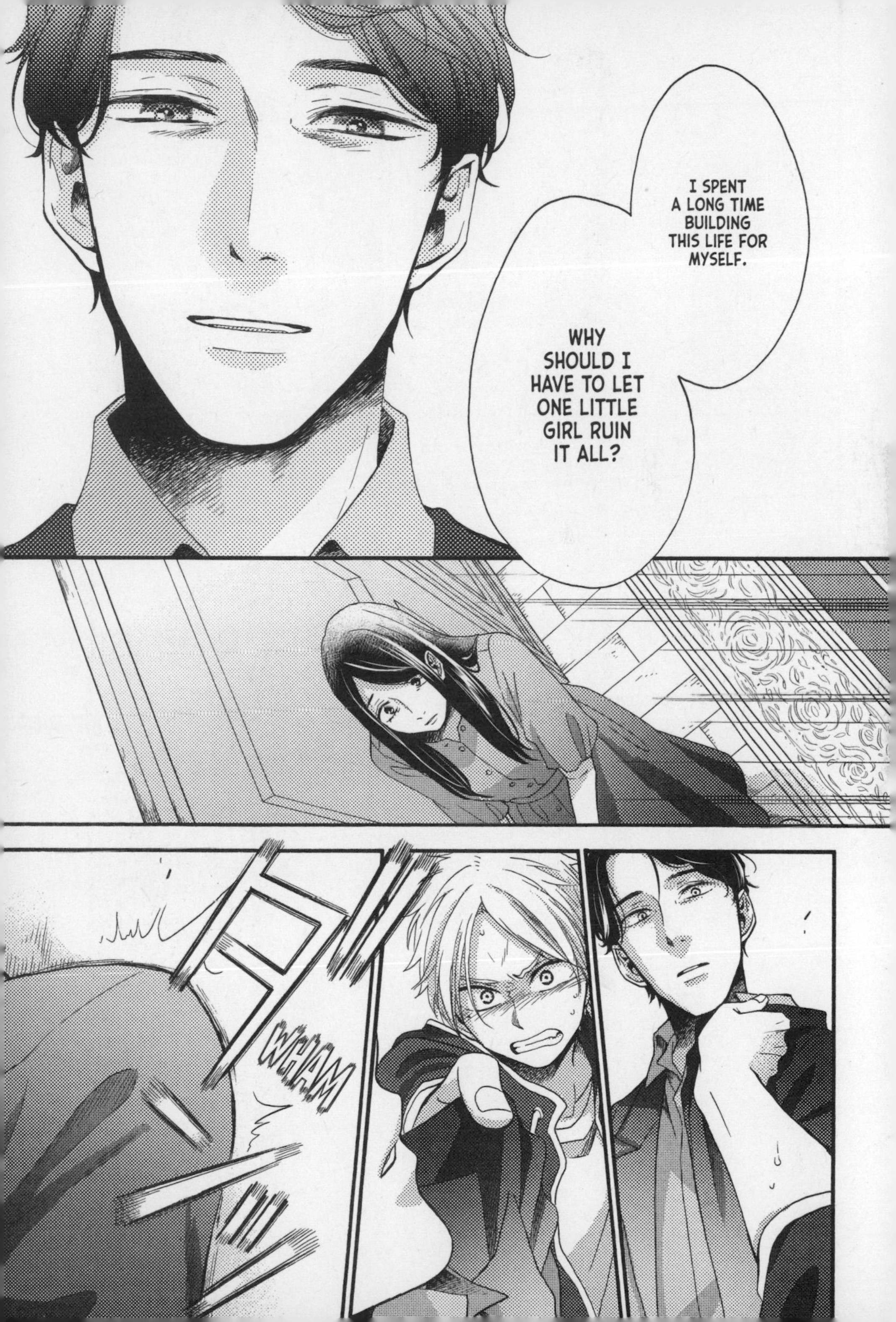
I SPENT A LONG TIME BUILDING THIS LIFE FOR MYSELF.
WHY SHOULD I HAVE TO LET ONE LITTLE GIRL RUIN IT ALL?
WHAM

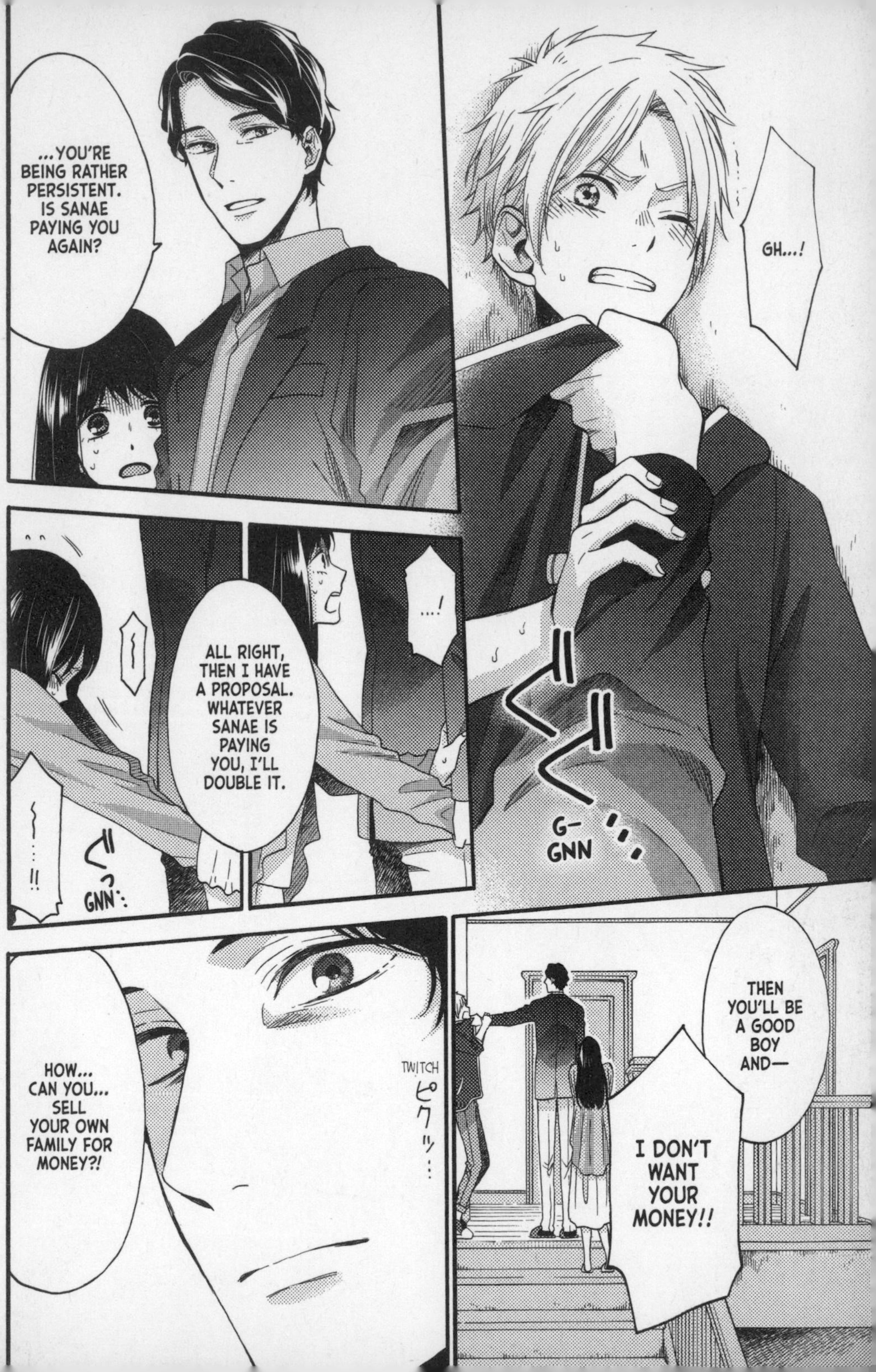
GH...!
G-GNN
...YOU'RE BEING RATHER PERSISTENT. IS SANAE PAYING YOU AGAIN?
...!
ALL RIGHT, THEN I HAVE A PROPOSAL. WHATEVER SANAE IS PAYING YOU, I'LL DOUBLE IT.
GNN
THEN YOU'LL BE A GOOD BOY AND—
I DON'T WANT YOUR MONEY!!
TWITCH
HOW... CAN YOU... SELL YOUR OWN FAMILY FOR MONEY?!

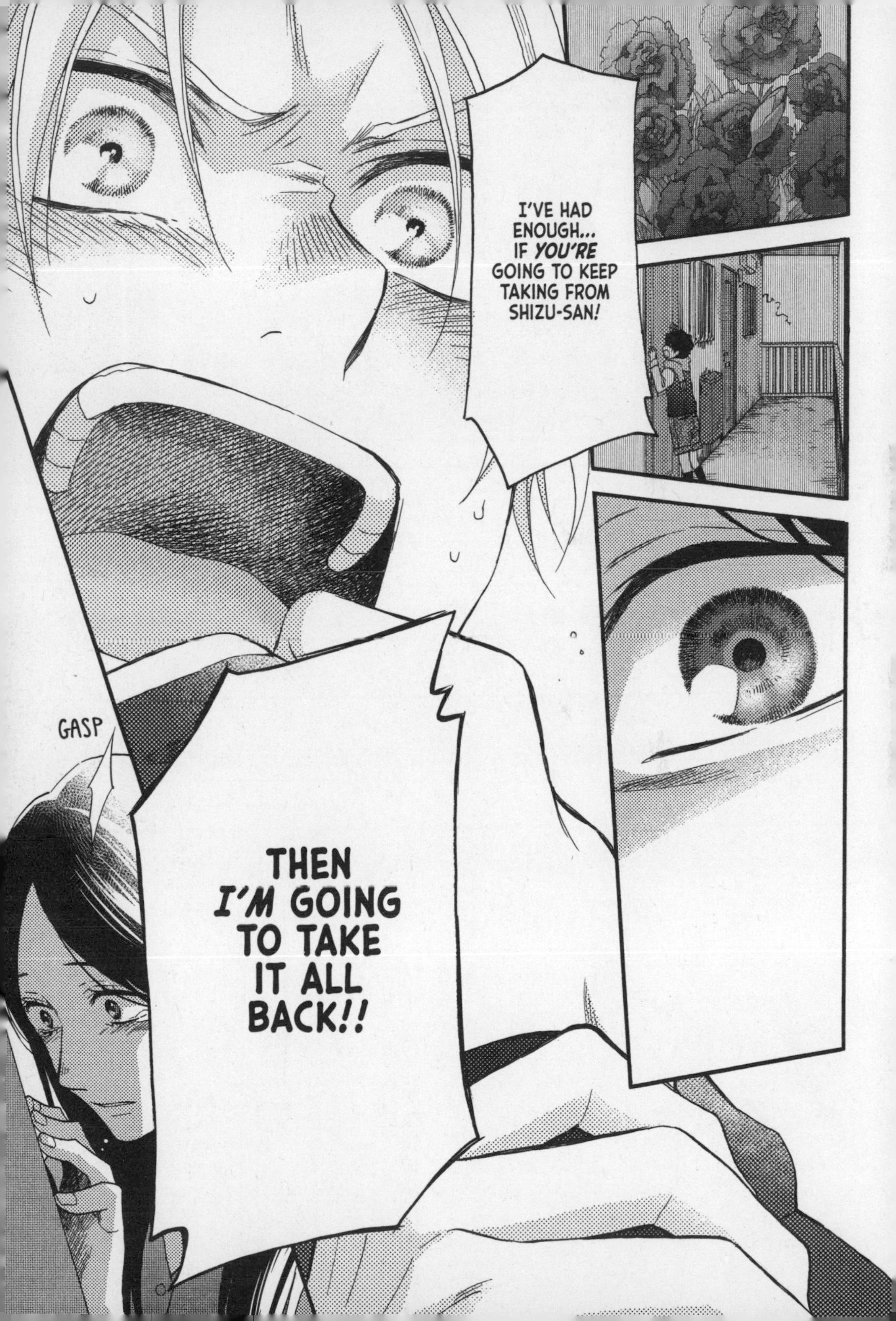
I'VE HAD ENOUGH... IF YOU'RE GOING TO KEEP TAKING FROM SHIZU-SAN!
THEN I'M GOING TO TAKE IT ALL BACK!!
GASP

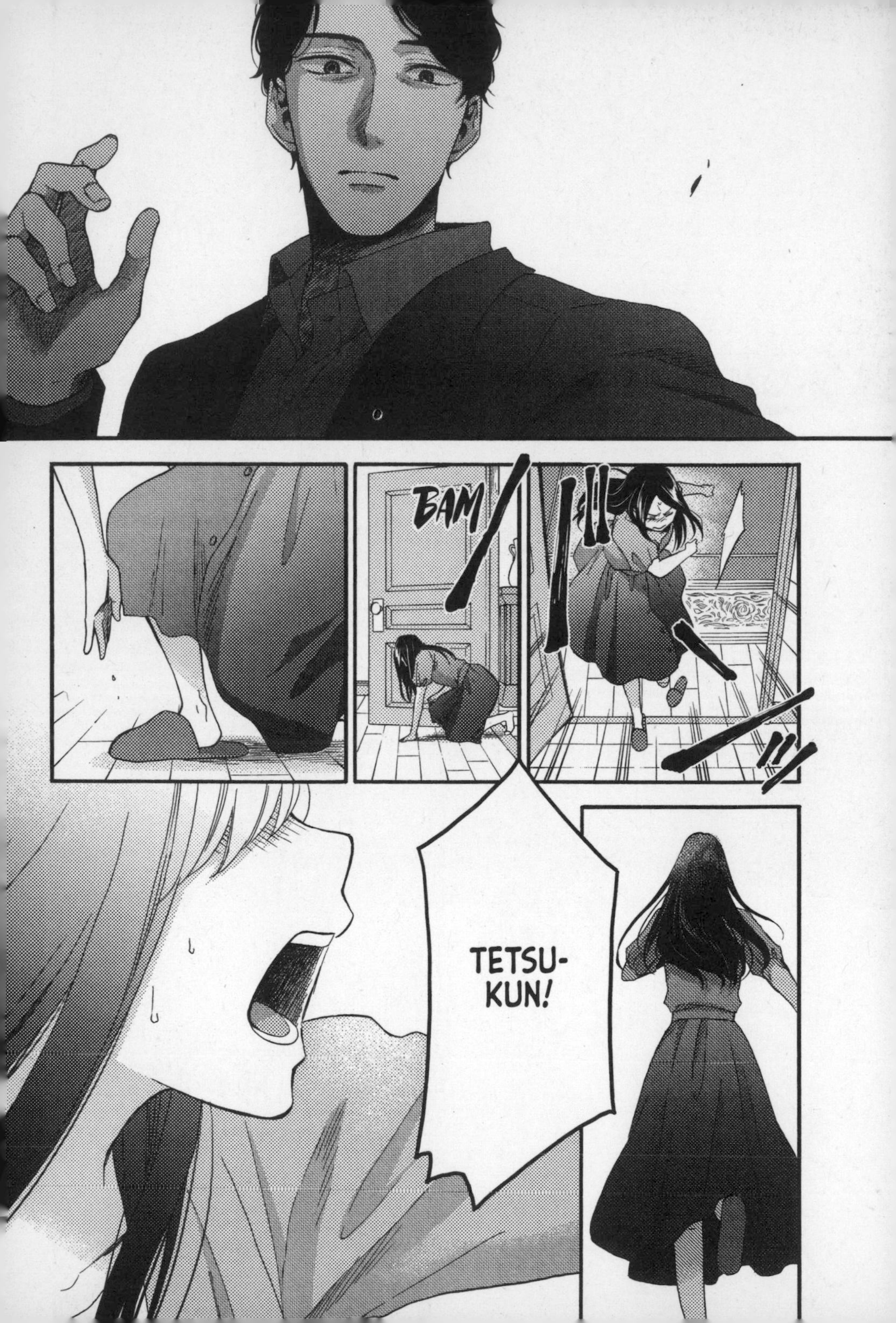
BAM
TETSU-
KUN!

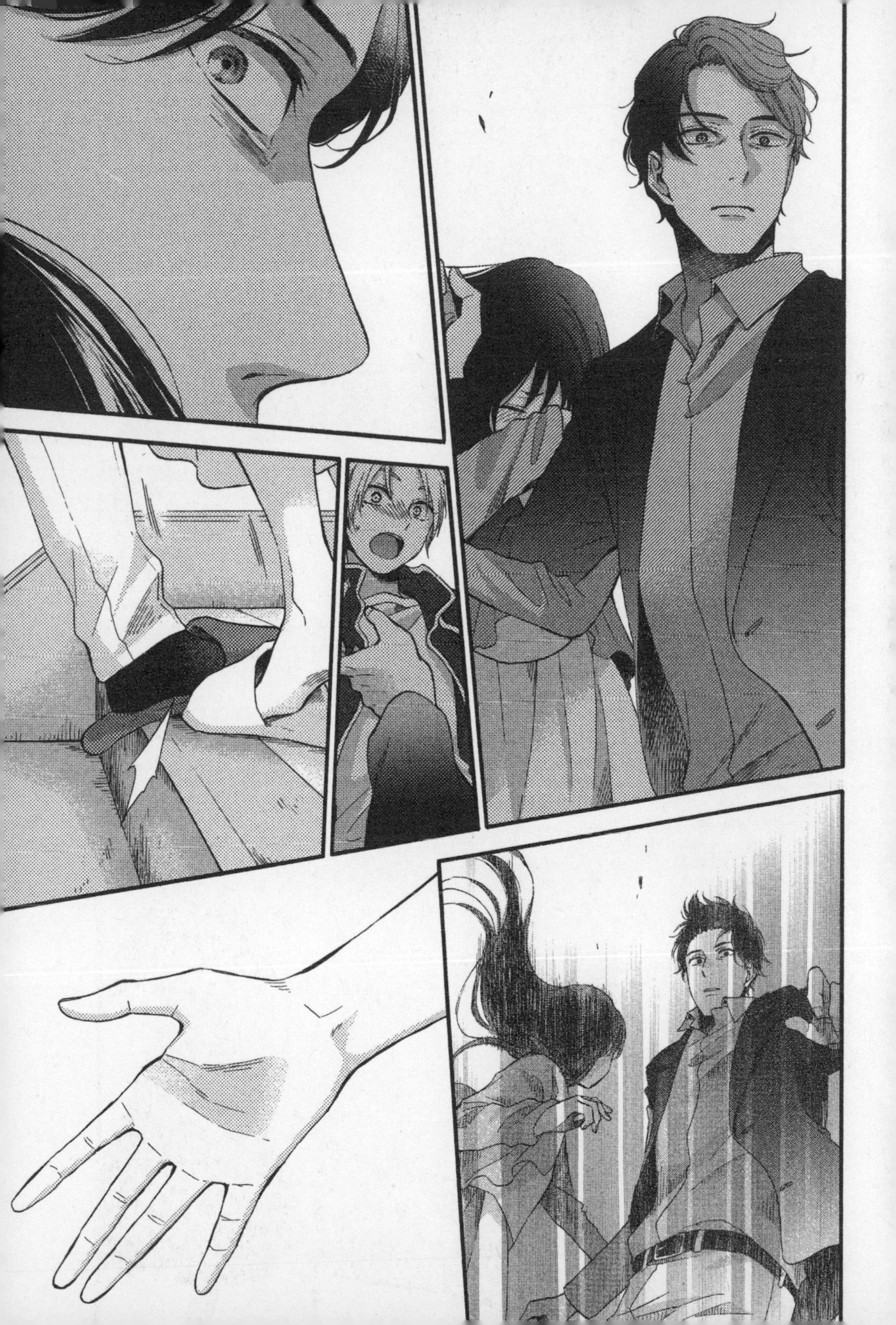

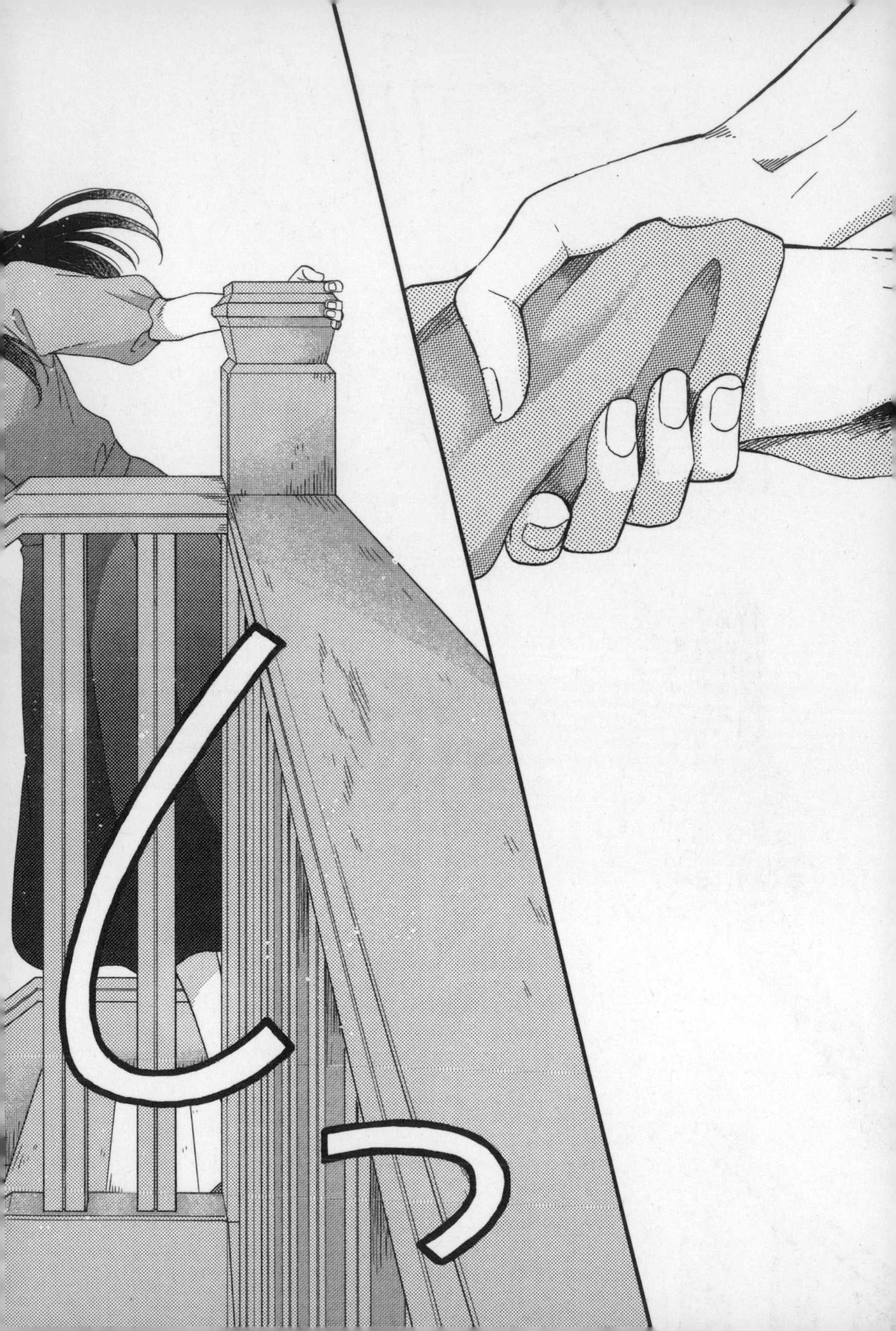
くっ

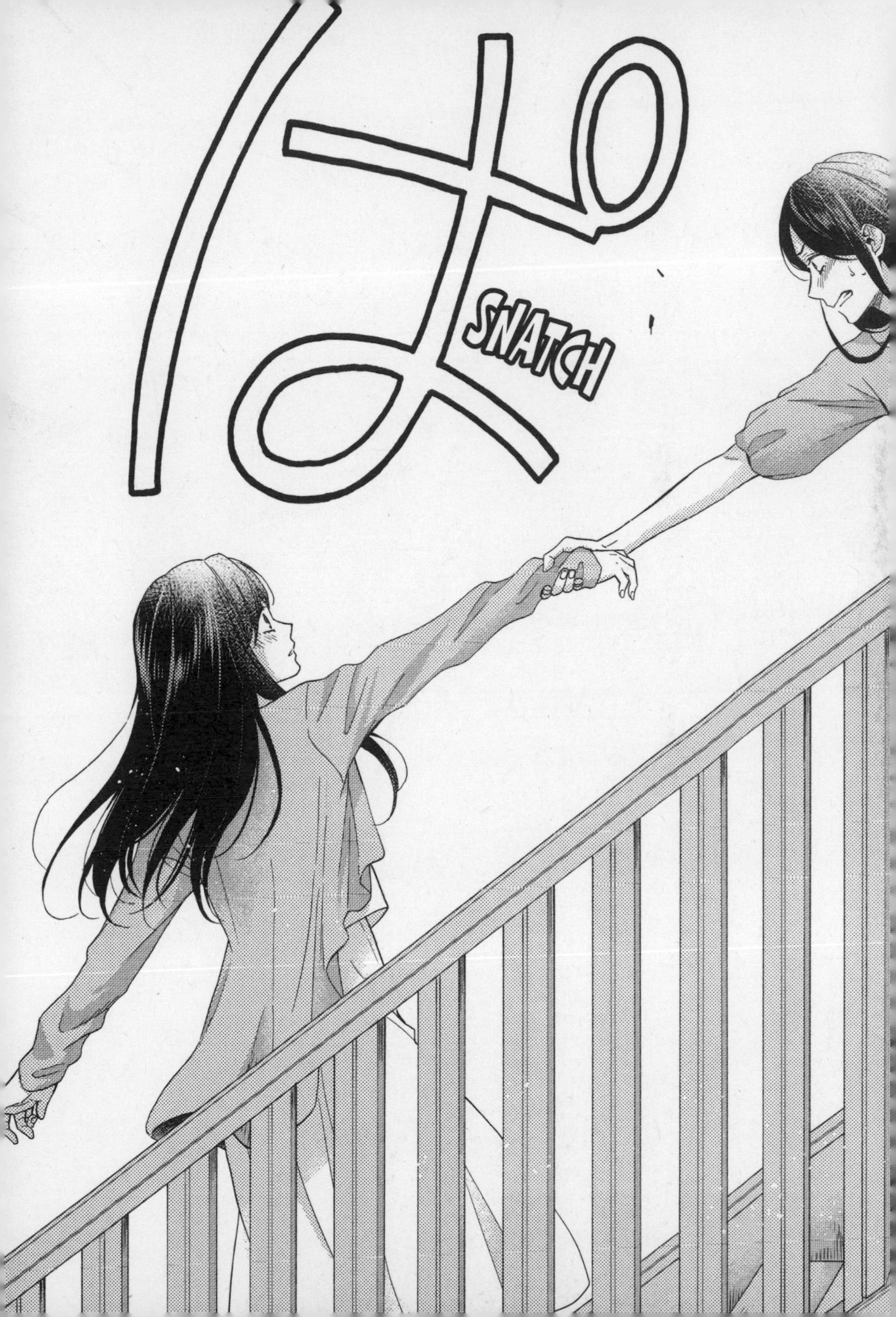
SNATCH

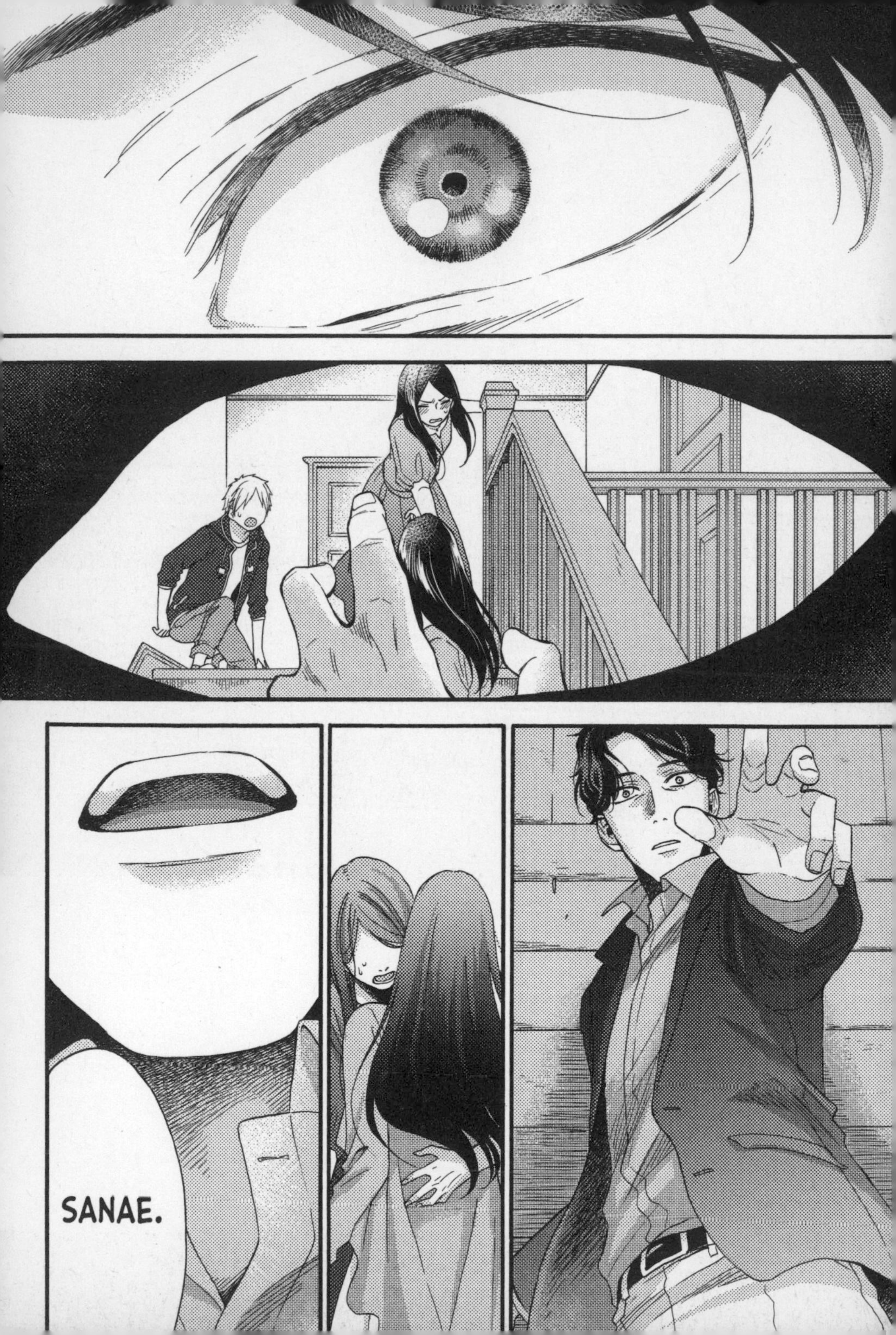
SANAE.

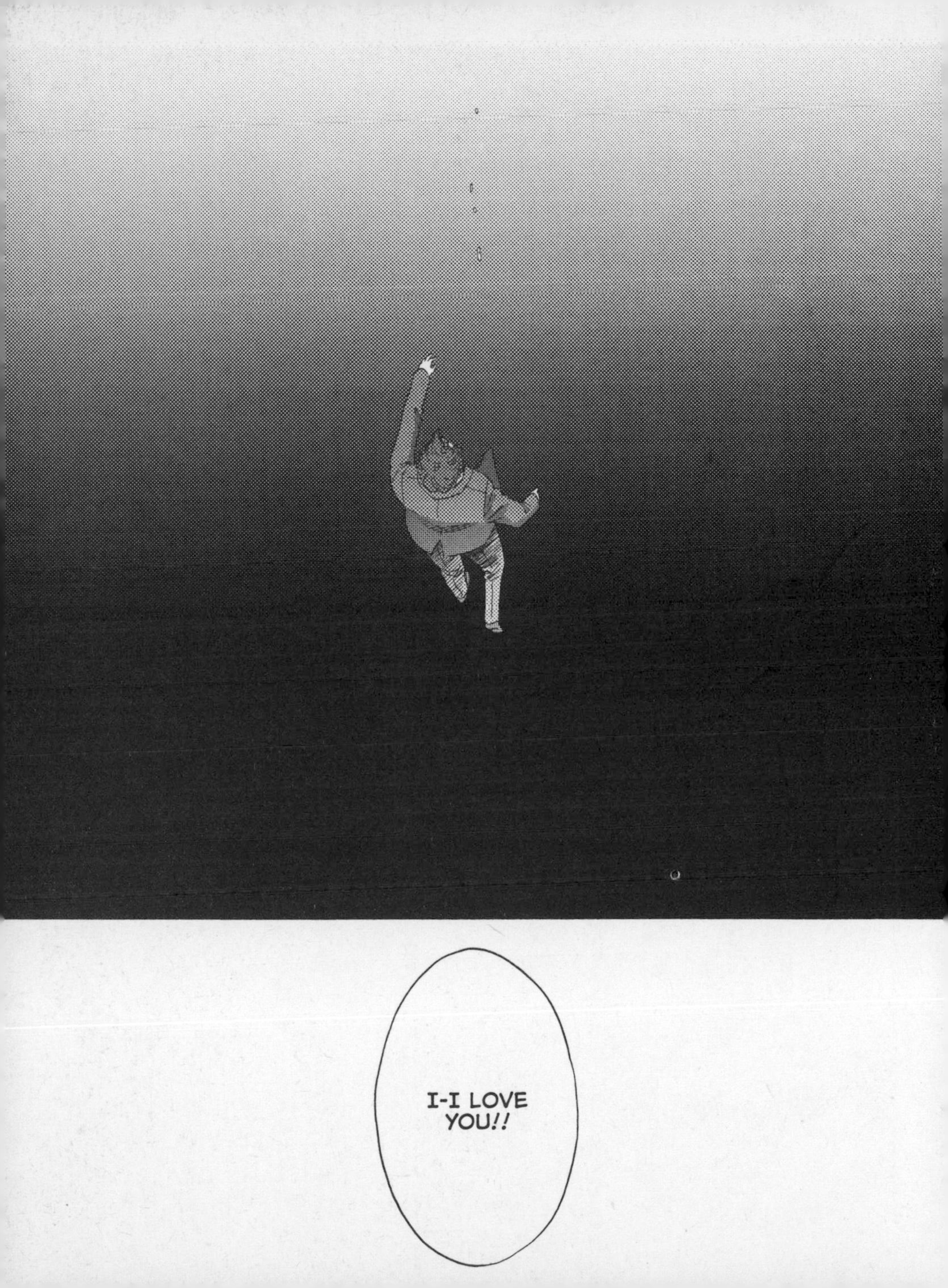
I-I LOVE YOU!!

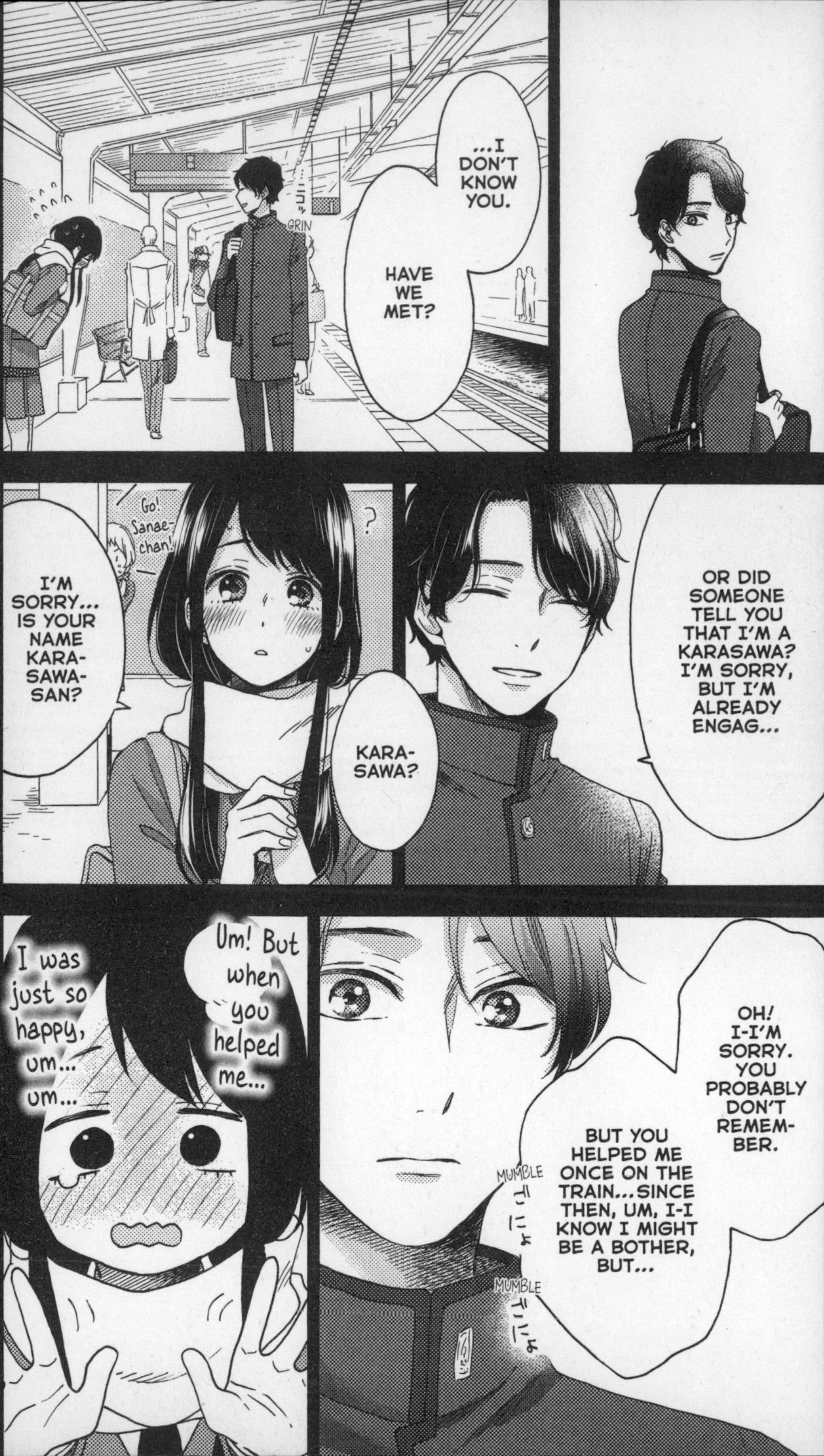

...I DON'T KNOW YOU.
HAVE WE MET?
GRIN
OR DID SOMEONE TELL YOU THAT I'M A KARASAWA? I'M SORRY, BUT I'M ALREADY ENGAG...
KARA-SAWA?
?
Go! Sanae-chan!
I'M SORRY... IS YOUR NAME KARA-SAWA-SAN?
OH! I-I'M SORRY. YOU PROBABLY DON'T REMEM-BER.
BUT YOU HELPED ME ONCE ON THE TRAIN... SINCE THEN, UM, I-I KNOW I MIGHT BE A BOTHER, BUT...
MUMBLE
MUMBLE
Um! But when you helped me...
I was just so happy, um... um...

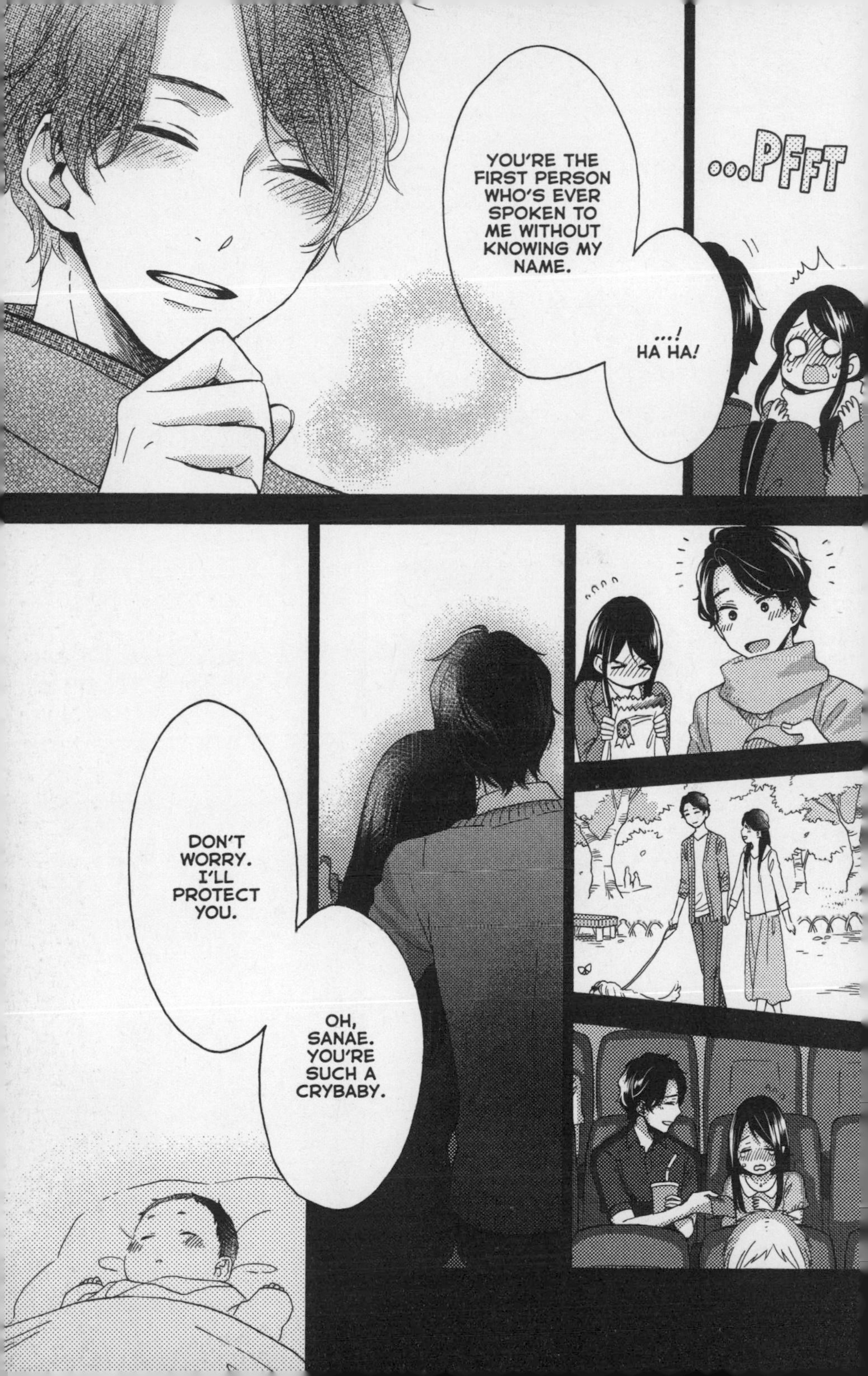
...PFFT
...! HA HA!
YOU'RE THE FIRST PERSON WHO'S EVER SPOKEN TO ME WITHOUT KNOWING MY NAME.
OH, SANAE. YOU'RE SUCH A CRYBABY.
DON'T WORRY. I'LL PROTECT YOU.

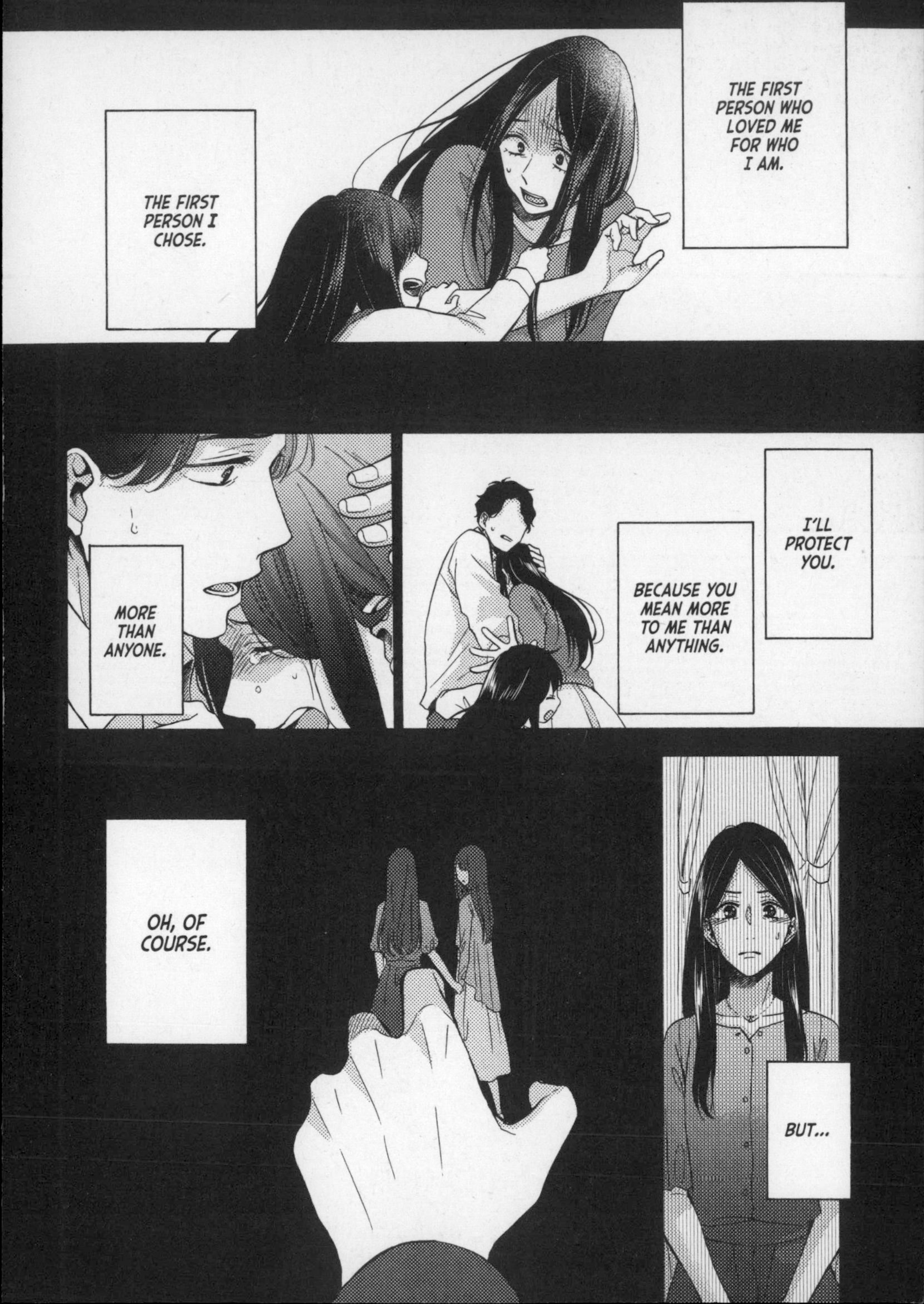
THE FIRST PERSON WHO LOVED ME FOR WHO I AM.
THE FIRST PERSON I CHOSE.
I'LL PROTECT YOU.
BECAUSE YOU MEAN MORE TO ME THAN ANYTHING.
MORE THAN ANYONE.
BUT...
OH, OF COURSE.

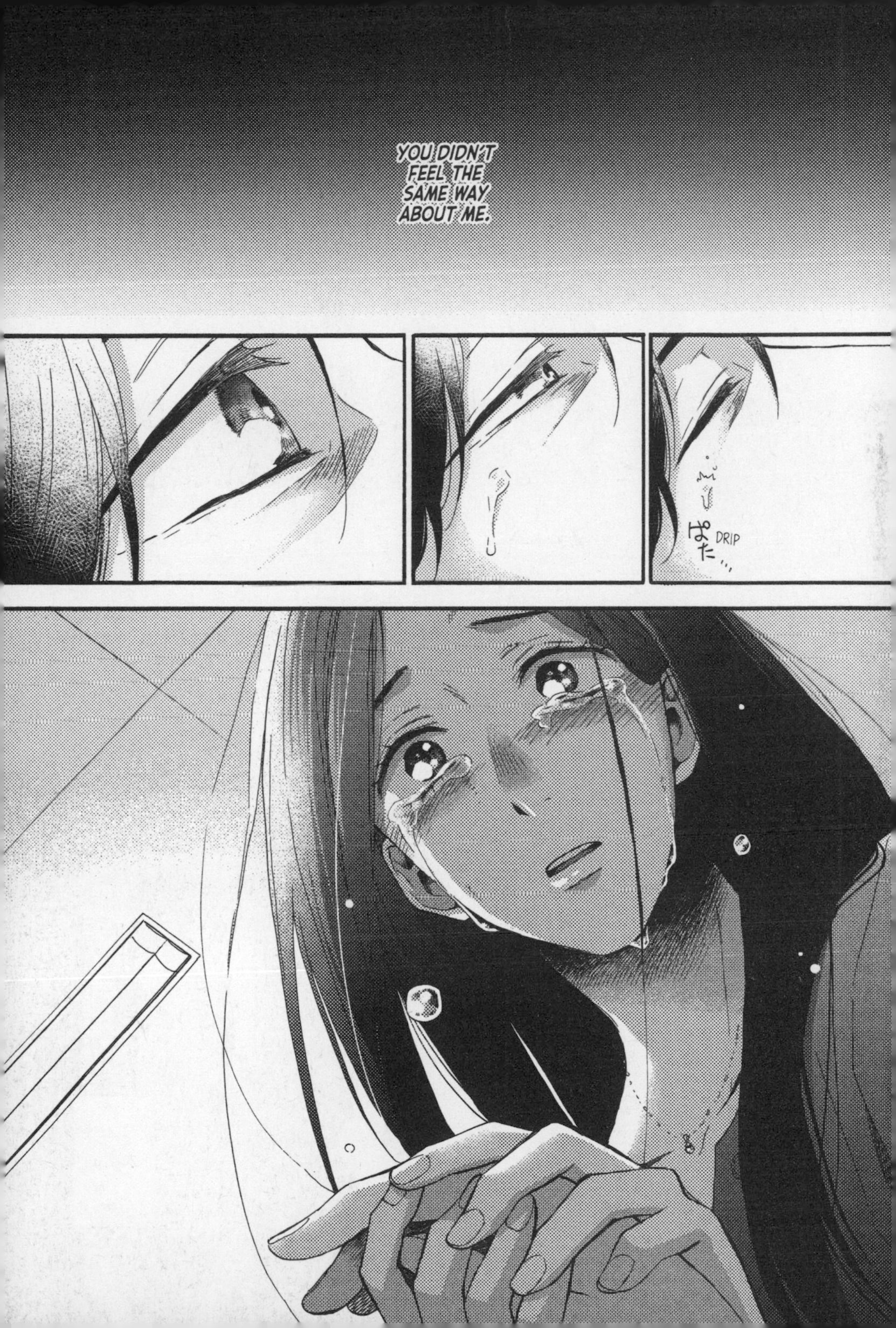
YOU DIDN'T FEEL THE SAME WAY ABOUT ME.
ぽた…
DRIP

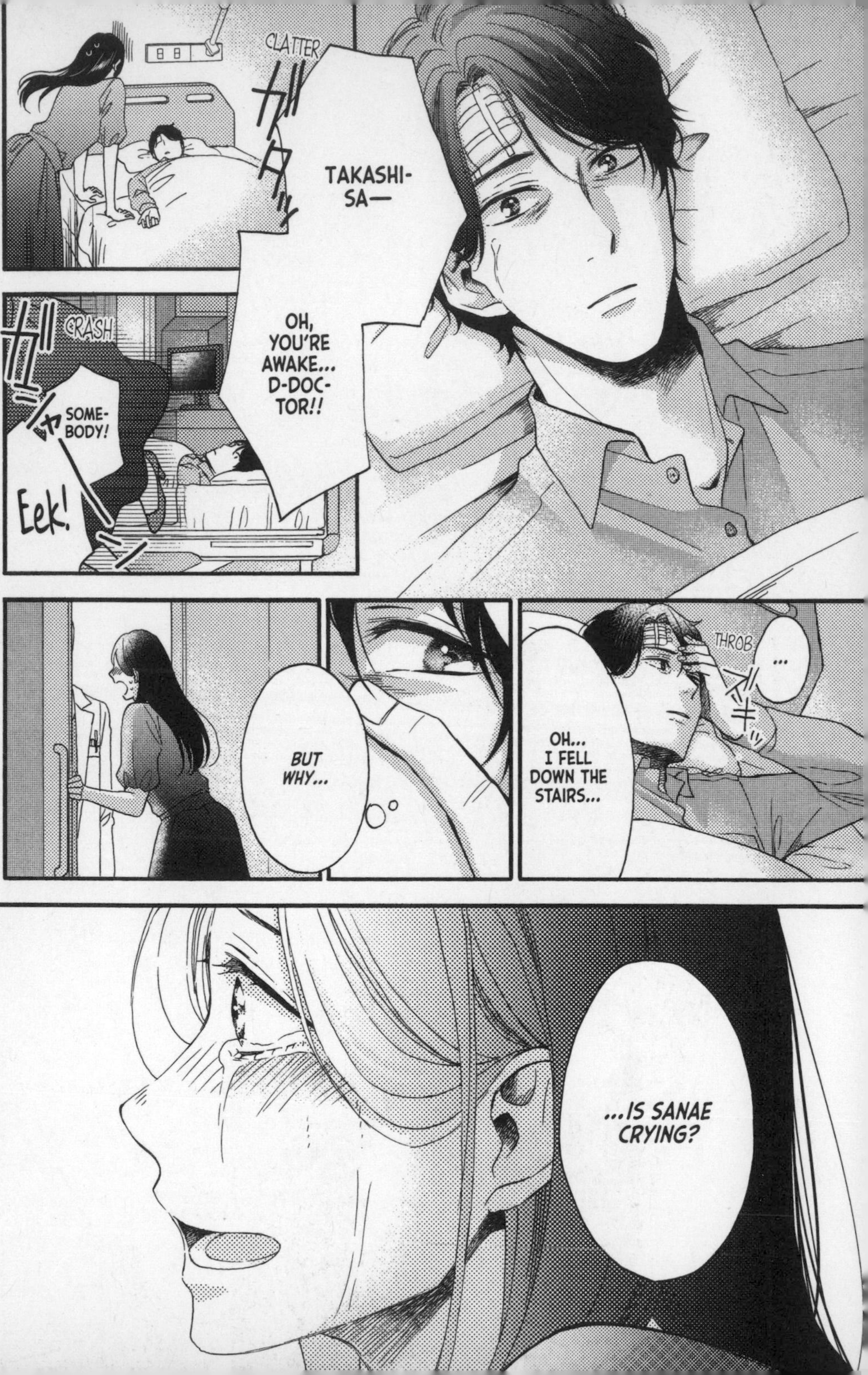

TAKASHI-SA—
OH, YOU'RE AWAKE... D-DOCTOR!!
CLATTER
CRASH
SOME-BODY!
Eek!
THROB
...
OH... I FELL DOWN THE STAIRS...
BUT WHY...
...IS SANAE CRYING?

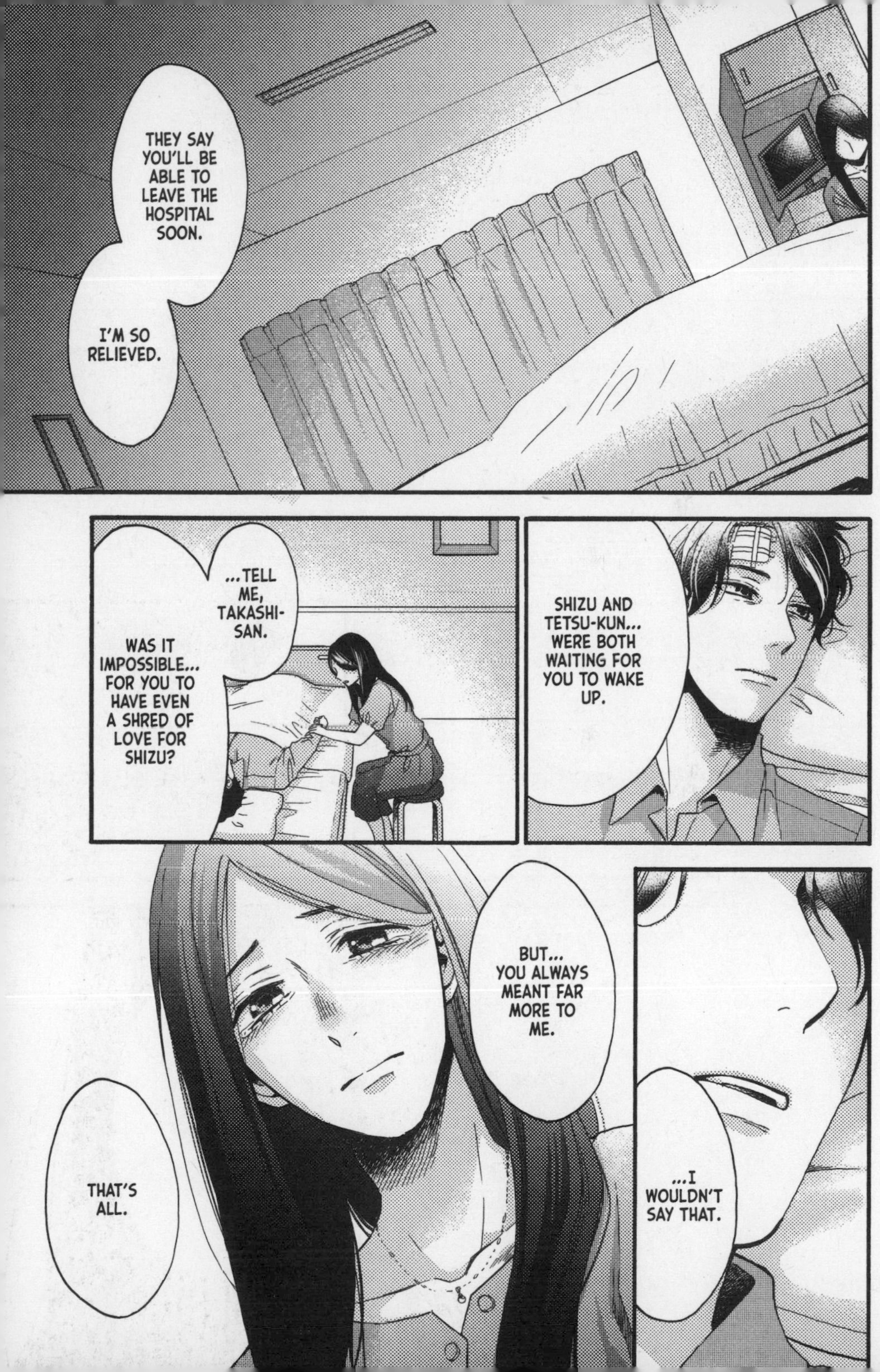
THEY SAY YOU'LL BE ABLE TO LEAVE THE HOSPITAL SOON.
I'M SO RELIEVED.
SHIZU AND TETSU-KUN... WERE BOTH WAITING FOR YOU TO WAKE UP.
...TELL ME, TAKASHI-SAN.
WAS IT IMPOSSIBLE... FOR YOU TO HAVE EVEN A SHRED OF LOVE FOR SHIZU?
...I WOULDN'T SAY THAT.
BUT... YOU ALWAYS MEANT FAR MORE TO ME.
THAT'S ALL.

I...

I WANTED YOU TO LOVE SHIZU JUST AS MUCH AS YOU LOVE ME.

I THINK THAT WHAT I REALLY WANTED... WAS FOR YOU TO HELP ME WORK THROUGH MY PROBLEMS, INSTEAD OF TAKING THEM ALL AWAY.

BECAUSE WE HAD HER TOGETHER... ME AND THE PERSON I LOVE.

SQUEEZE

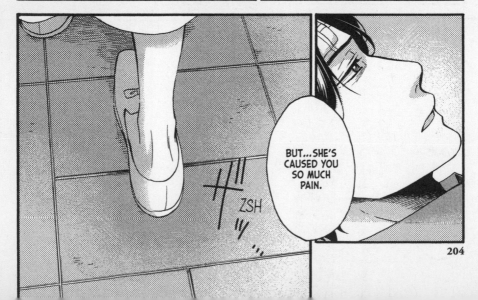

ZSH

BUT...SHE'S CAUSED YOU SO MUCH PAIN.

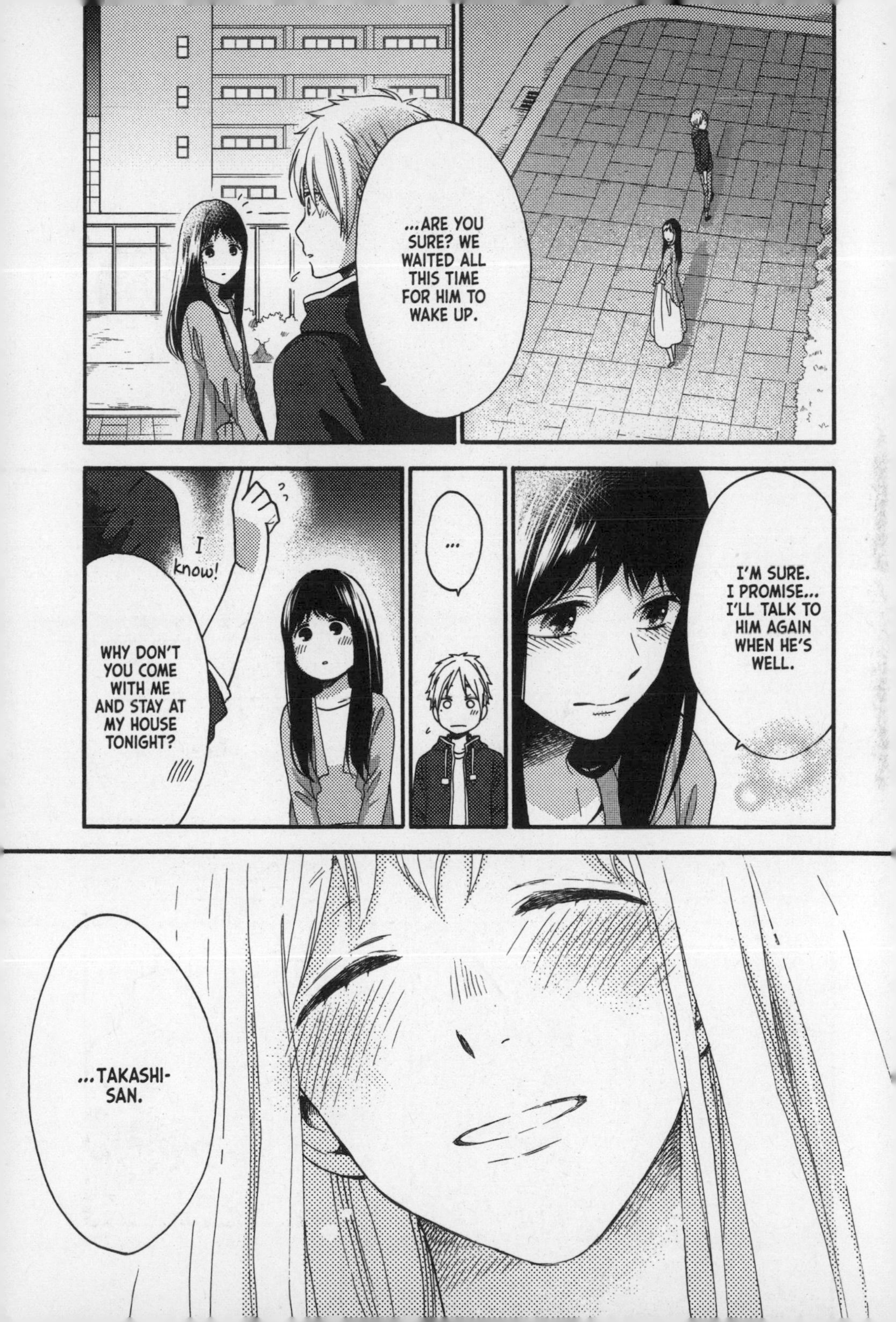
...ARE YOU SURE? WE WAITED ALL THIS TIME FOR HIM TO WAKE UP.
I'M SURE. I PROMISE... I'LL TALK TO HIM AGAIN WHEN HE'S WELL.
...
I know!
WHY DON'T YOU COME WITH ME AND STAY AT MY HOUSE TONIGHT?
...TAKASHI-SAN.

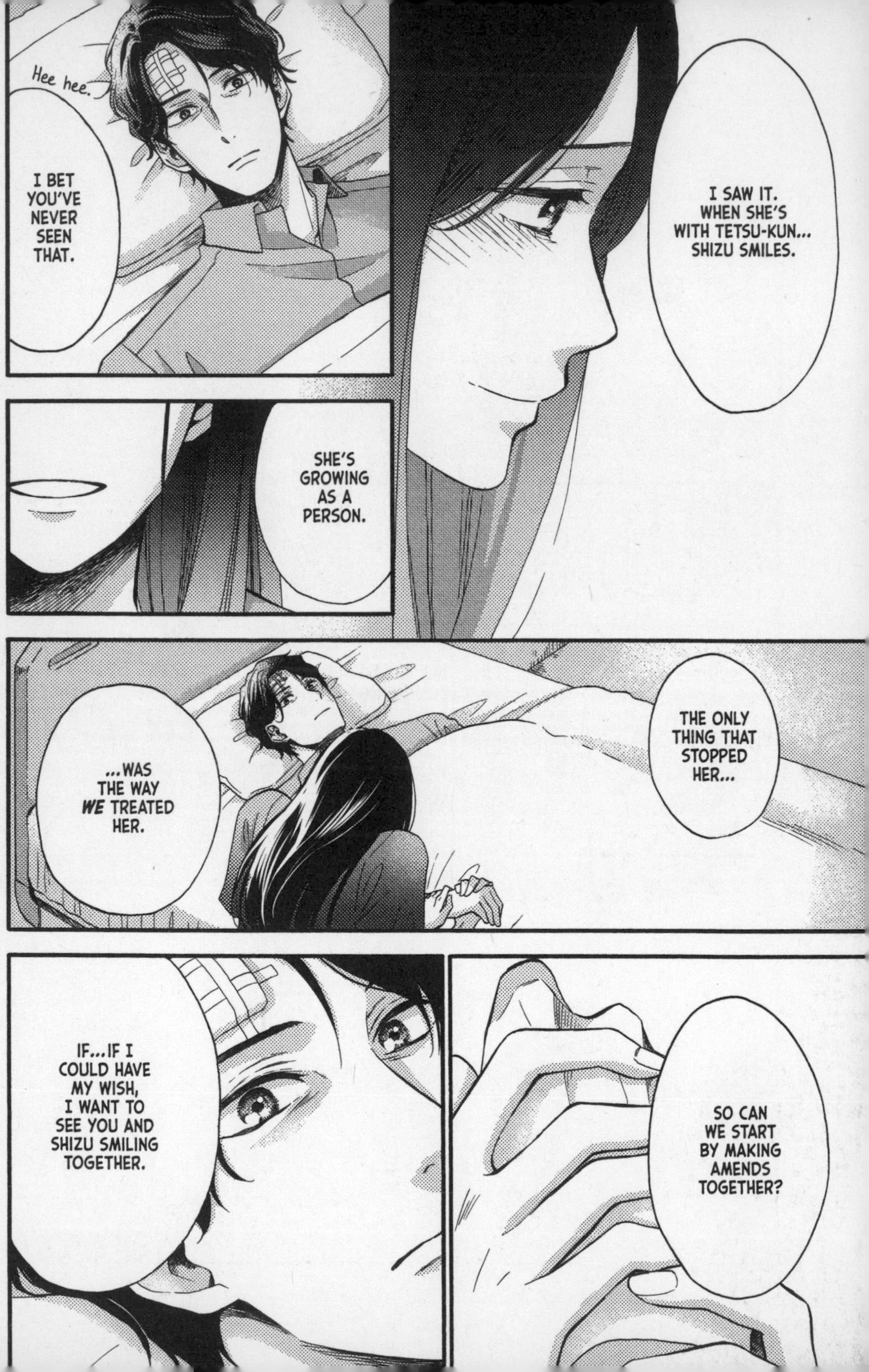
I SAW IT. WHEN SHE'S WITH TETSU-KUN... SHIZU SMILES.
Hee hee.
I BET YOU'VE NEVER SEEN THAT.
SHE'S GROWING AS A PERSON.
THE ONLY THING THAT STOPPED HER...
...WAS THE WAY *WE* TREATED HER.
SO CAN WE START BY MAKING AMENDS TOGETHER?
IF...IF I COULD HAVE MY WISH, I WANT TO SEE YOU AND SHIZU SMILING TOGETHER.

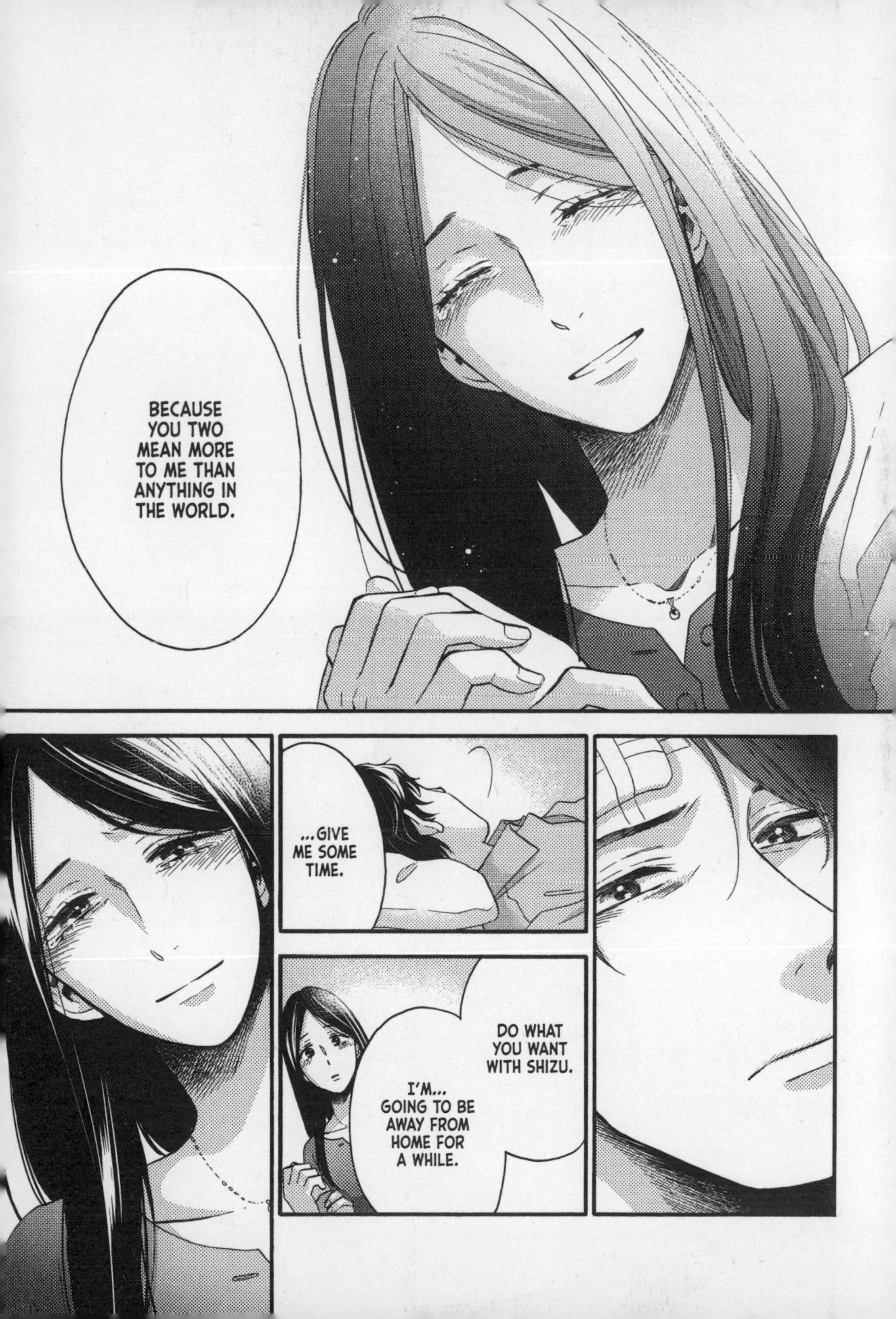
BECAUSE YOU TWO MEAN MORE TO ME THAN ANYTHING IN THE WORLD.
...GIVE ME SOME TIME.
DO WHAT YOU WANT WITH SHIZU.
I'M... GOING TO BE AWAY FROM HOME FOR A WHILE.

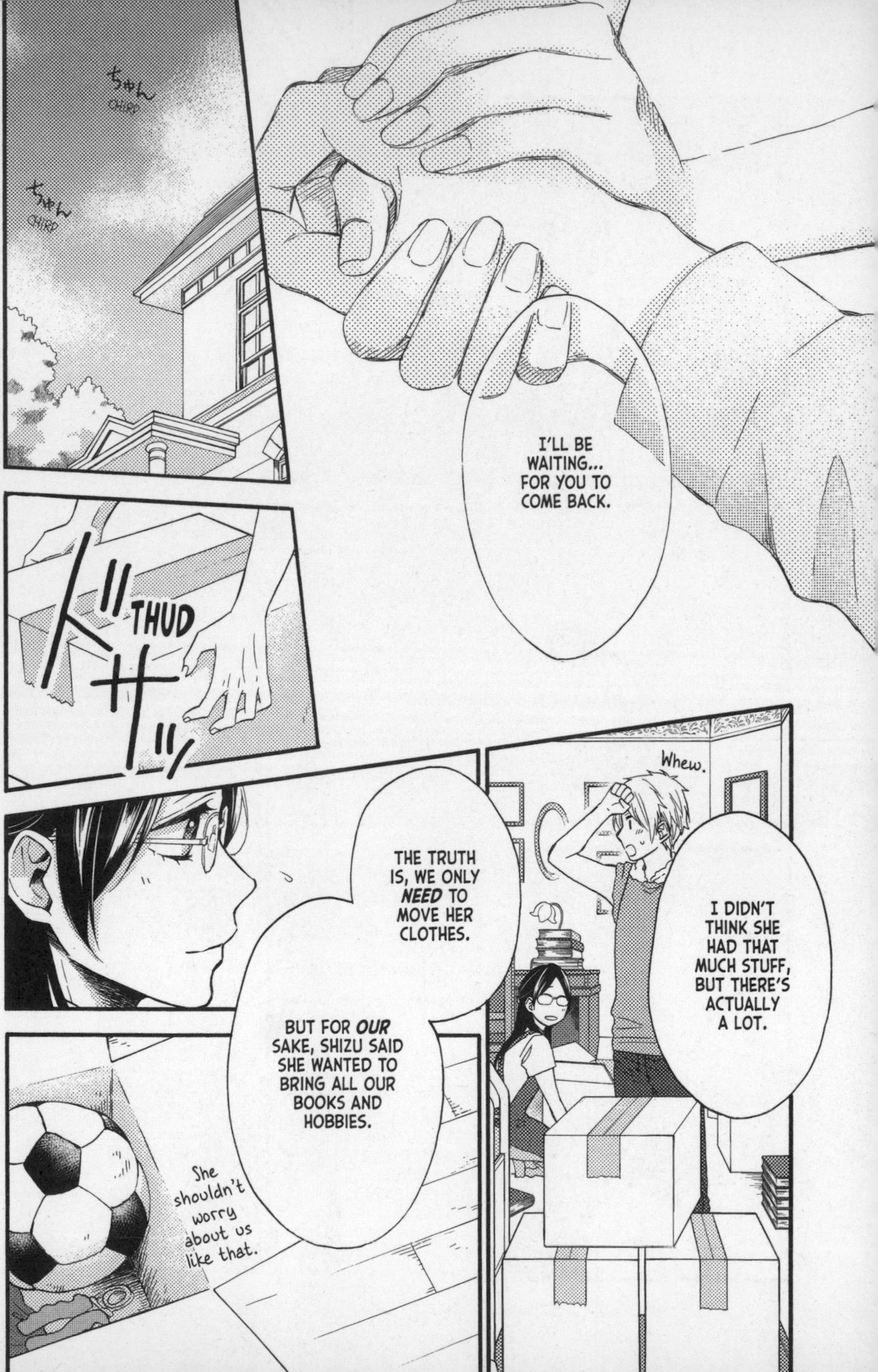
I'LL BE WAITING... FOR YOU TO COME BACK.
ちゅん CHIRP
ちゅん CHIRP
ドサッ THUD
Whew.
I DIDN'T THINK SHE HAD THAT MUCH STUFF, BUT THERE'S ACTUALLY A LOT.
THE TRUTH IS, WE ONLY *NEED* TO MOVE HER CLOTHES.
BUT FOR *OUR* SAKE, SHIZU SAID SHE WANTED TO BRING ALL OUR BOOKS AND HOBBIES.
She shouldn't worry about us like that.

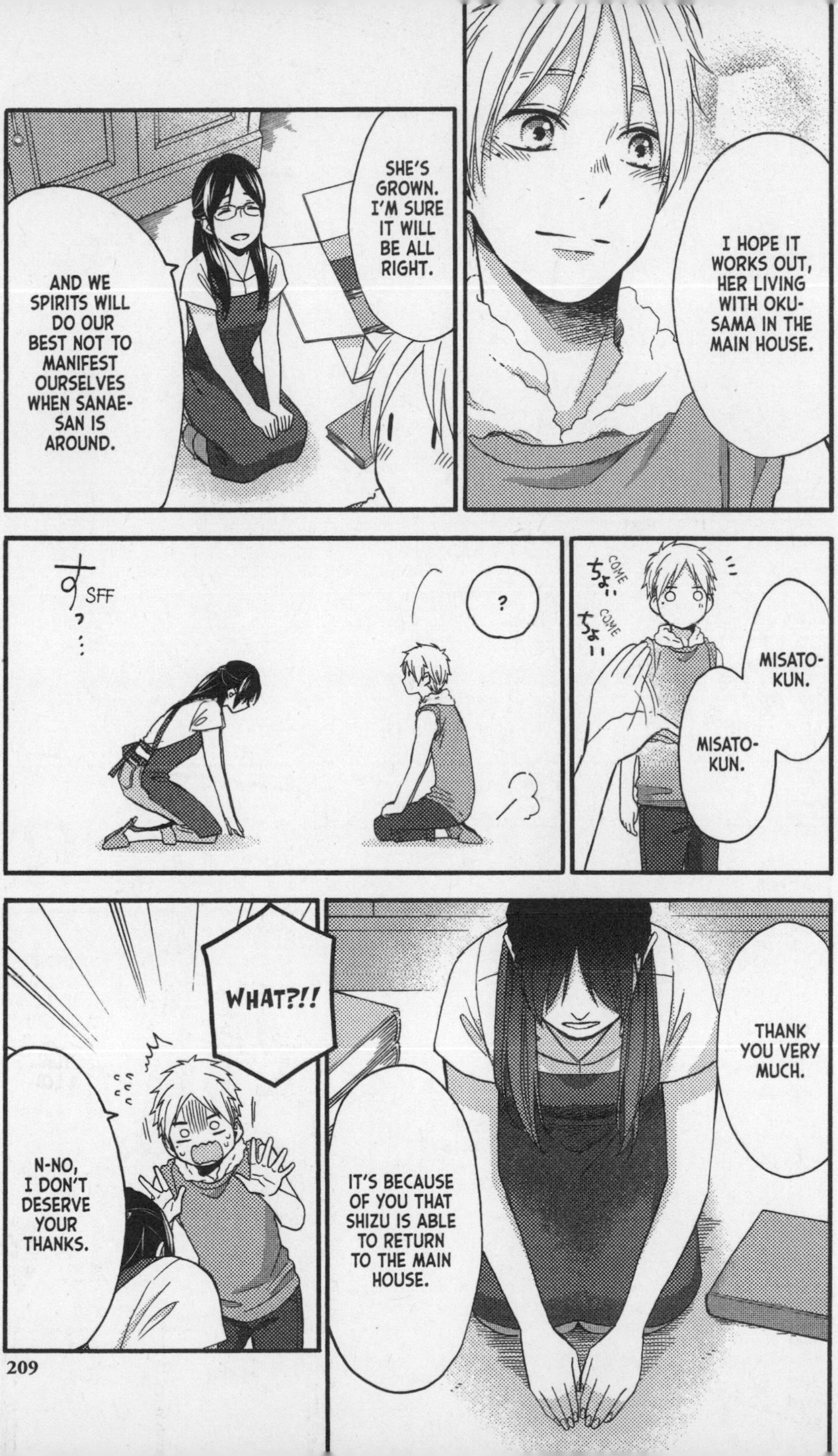
I HOPE IT WORKS OUT, HER LIVING WITH OKU-SAMA IN THE MAIN HOUSE.
SHE'S GROWN. I'M SURE IT WILL BE ALL RIGHT.
AND WE SPIRITS WILL DO OUR BEST NOT TO MANIFEST OURSELVES WHEN SANAE-SAN IS AROUND.
ちょい COME
ちょい COME
MISATO-KUN.
MISATO-KUN.
?
す SFF
っ…
THANK YOU VERY MUCH.
IT'S BECAUSE OF YOU THAT SHIZU IS ABLE TO RETURN TO THE MAIN HOUSE.
WHAT?!!
N-NO, I DON'T DESERVE YOUR THANKS.

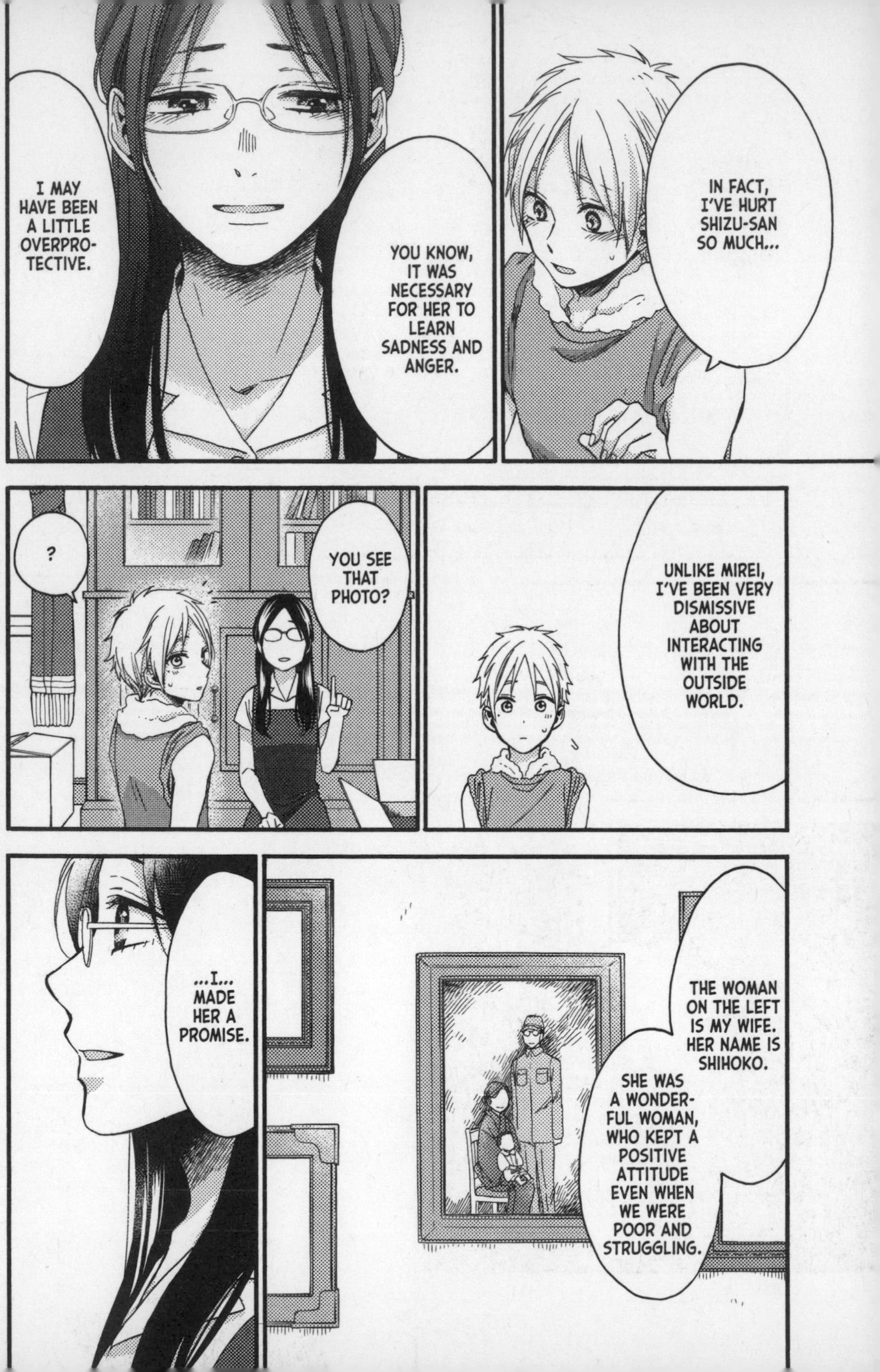
IN FACT, I'VE HURT SHIZU-SAN SO MUCH...
YOU KNOW, IT WAS NECESSARY FOR HER TO LEARN SADNESS AND ANGER.
I MAY HAVE BEEN A LITTLE OVERPROTECTIVE.
UNLIKE MIREI, I'VE BEEN VERY DISMISSIVE ABOUT INTERACTING WITH THE OUTSIDE WORLD.
YOU SEE THAT PHOTO?
?
THE WOMAN ON THE LEFT IS MY WIFE. HER NAME IS SHIHOKO.
SHE WAS A WONDERFUL WOMAN, WHO KEPT A POSITIVE ATTITUDE EVEN WHEN WE WERE POOR AND STRUGGLING.
...I... MADE HER A PROMISE.

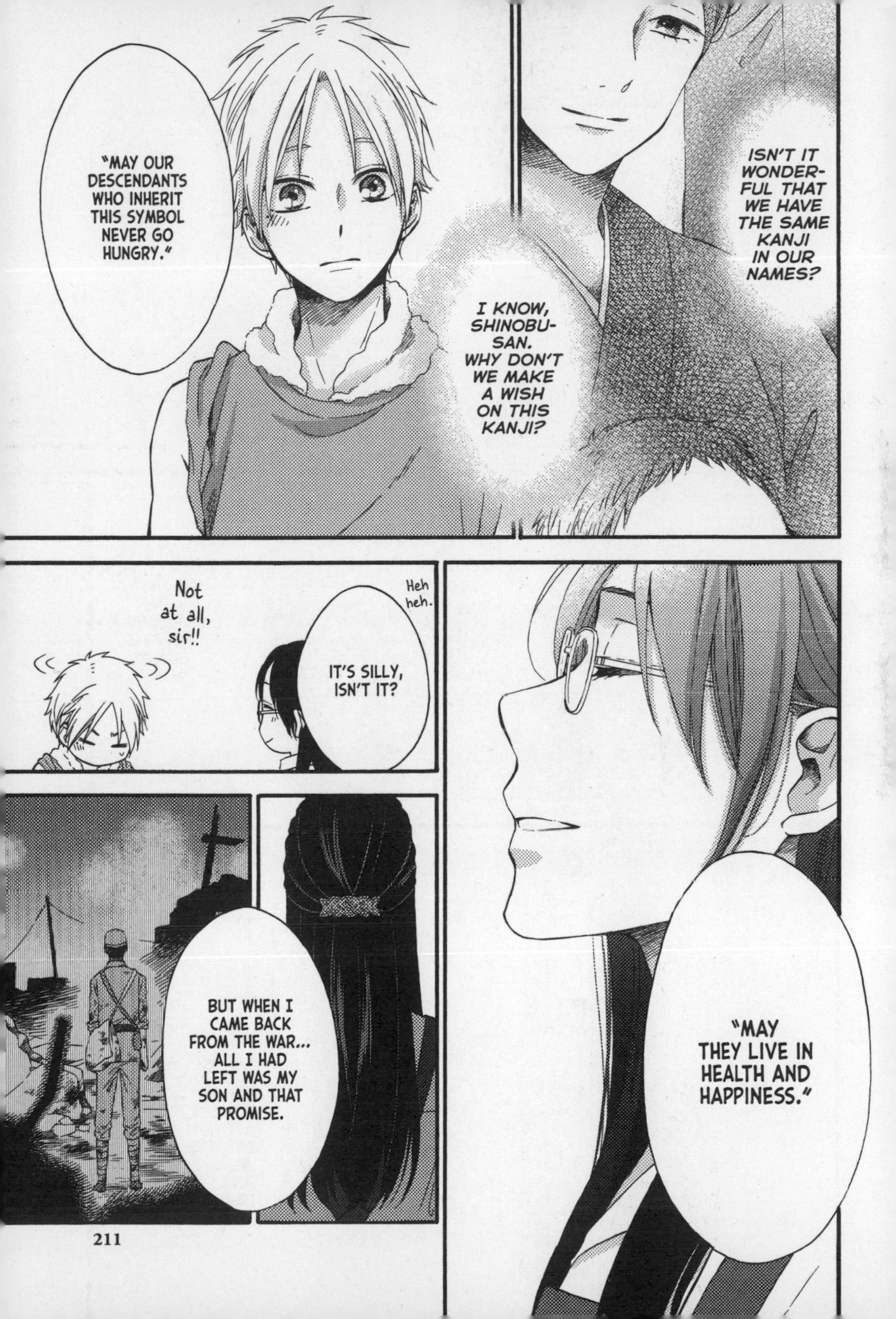
ISN'T IT WONDERFUL THAT WE HAVE THE SAME KANJI IN OUR NAMES?
I KNOW, SHINOBU-SAN. WHY DON'T WE MAKE A WISH ON THIS KANJI?
"MAY OUR DESCENDANTS WHO INHERIT THIS SYMBOL NEVER GO HUNGRY."
"MAY THEY LIVE IN HEALTH AND HAPPINESS."
Heh heh.
IT'S SILLY, ISN'T IT?
Not at all, sir!!
BUT WHEN I CAME BACK FROM THE WAR... ALL I HAD LEFT WAS MY SON AND THAT PROMISE.

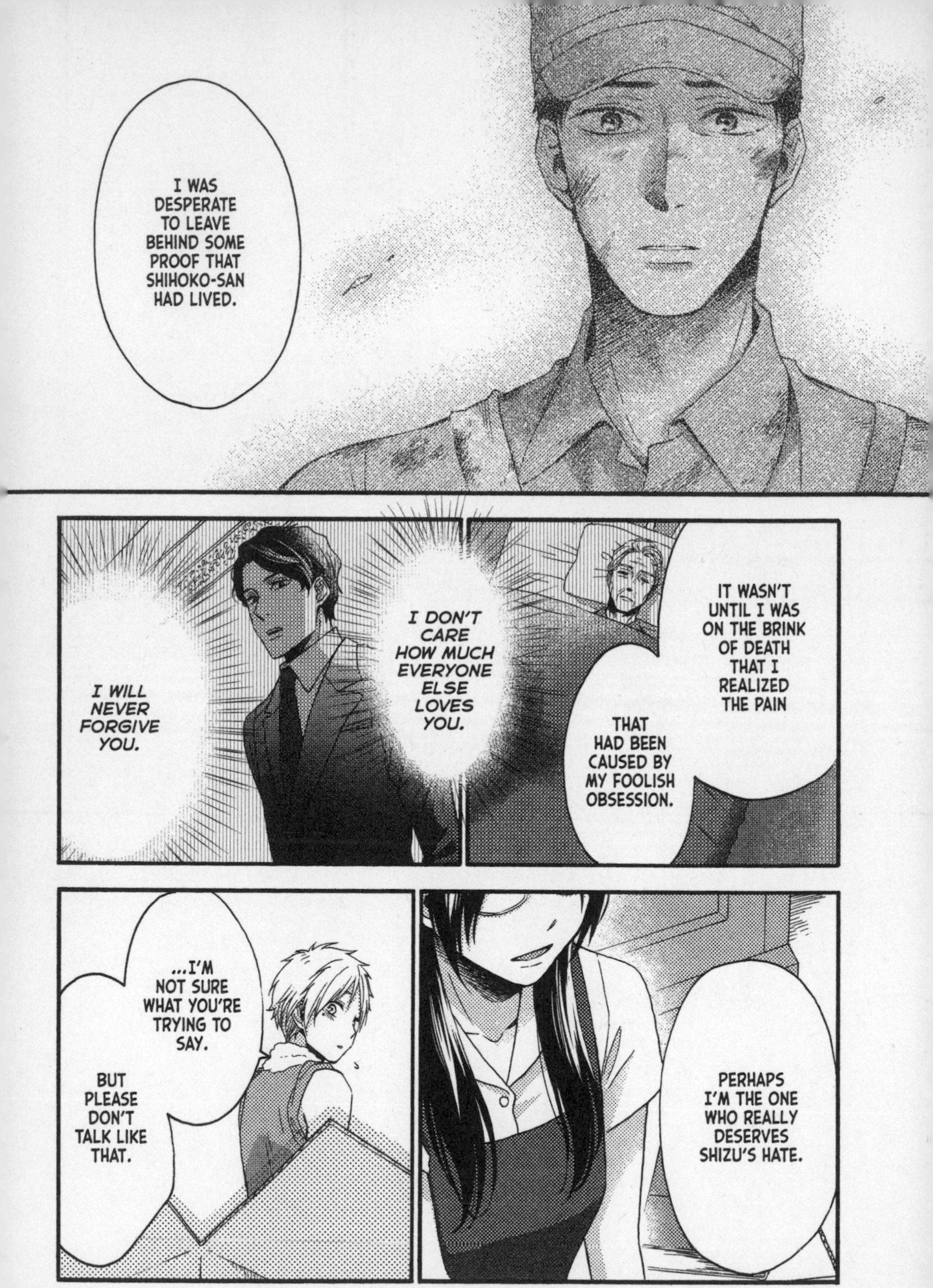
I WAS DESPERATE TO LEAVE BEHIND SOME PROOF THAT SHIHOKO-SAN HAD LIVED.
IT WASN'T UNTIL I WAS ON THE BRINK OF DEATH THAT I REALIZED THE PAIN
THAT HAD BEEN CAUSED BY MY FOOLISH OBSESSION.
I DON'T CARE HOW MUCH EVERYONE ELSE LOVES YOU.
I WILL NEVER FORGIVE YOU.
PERHAPS I'M THE ONE WHO REALLY DESERVES SHIZU'S HATE.
...I'M NOT SURE WHAT YOU'RE TRYING TO SAY.
BUT PLEASE DON'T TALK LIKE THAT.

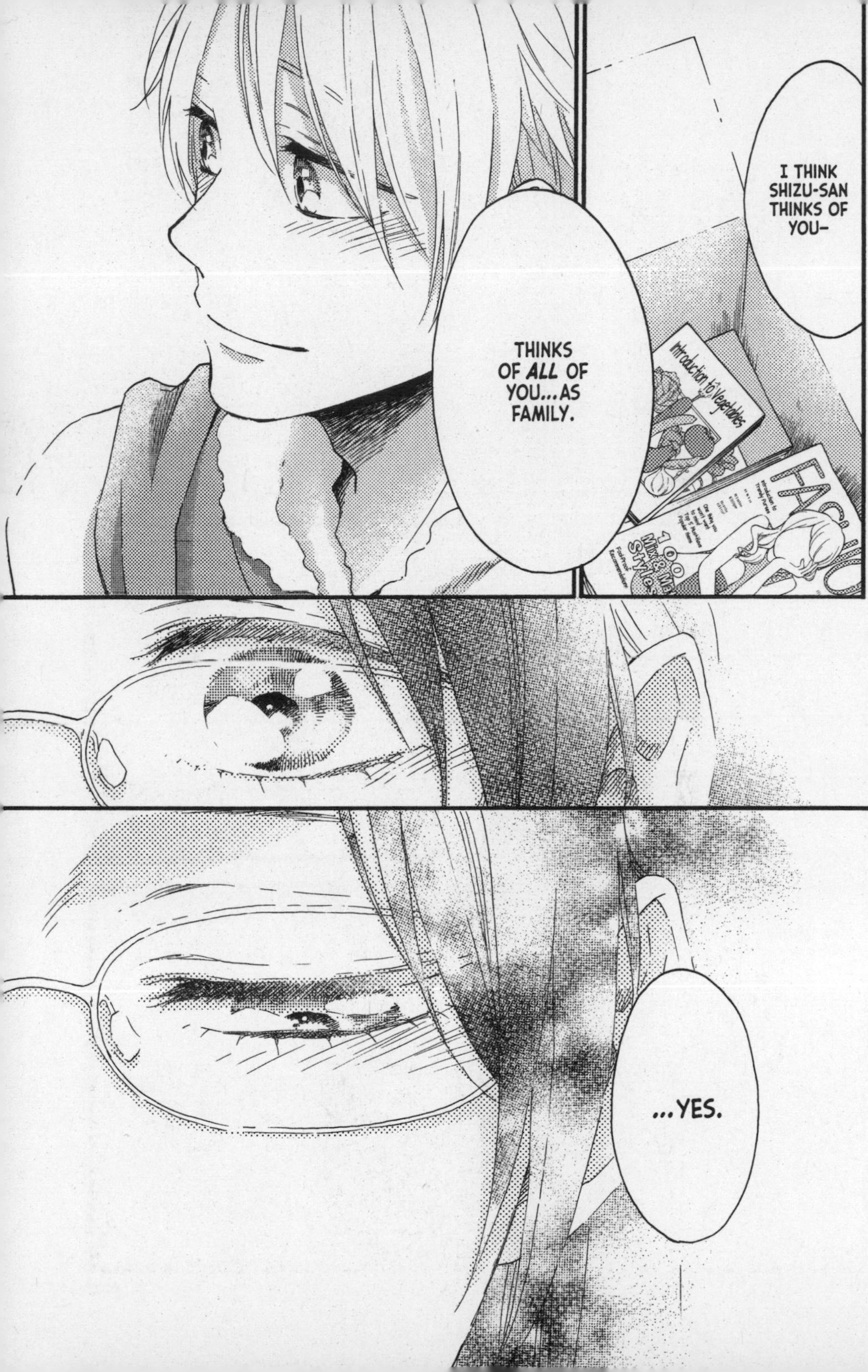
I THINK SHIZU-SAN THINKS OF YOU–
THINKS OF *ALL* OF YOU...AS FAMILY.
Introduction to Vegetables
...YES.

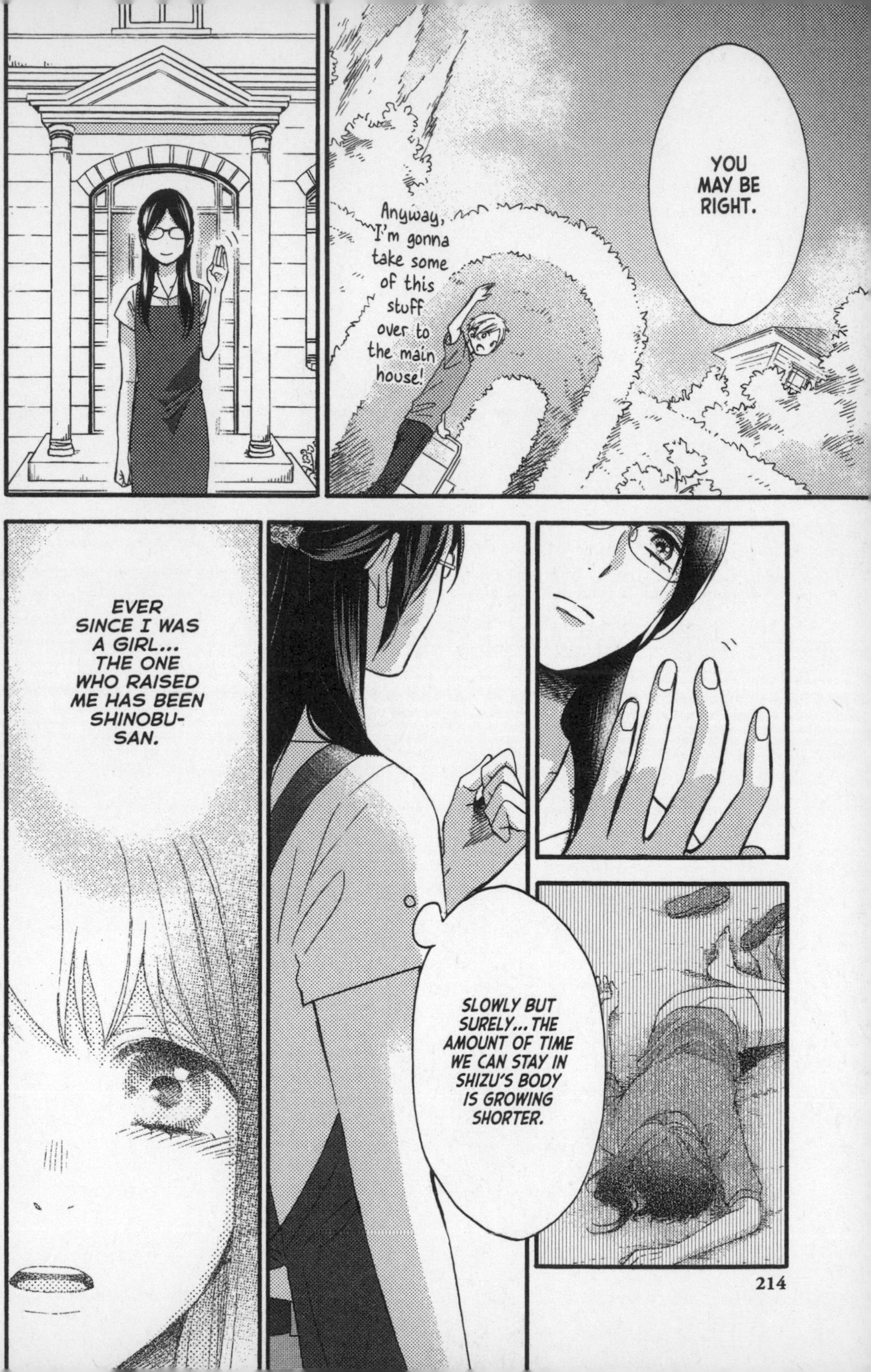
YOU MAY BE RIGHT.
Anyway, I'm gonna take some of this stuff over to the main house!
SLOWLY BUT SURELY... THE AMOUNT OF TIME WE CAN STAY IN SHIZU'S BODY IS GROWING SHORTER.
EVER SINCE I WAS A GIRL... THE ONE WHO RAISED ME HAS BEEN SHINOBU-SAN.

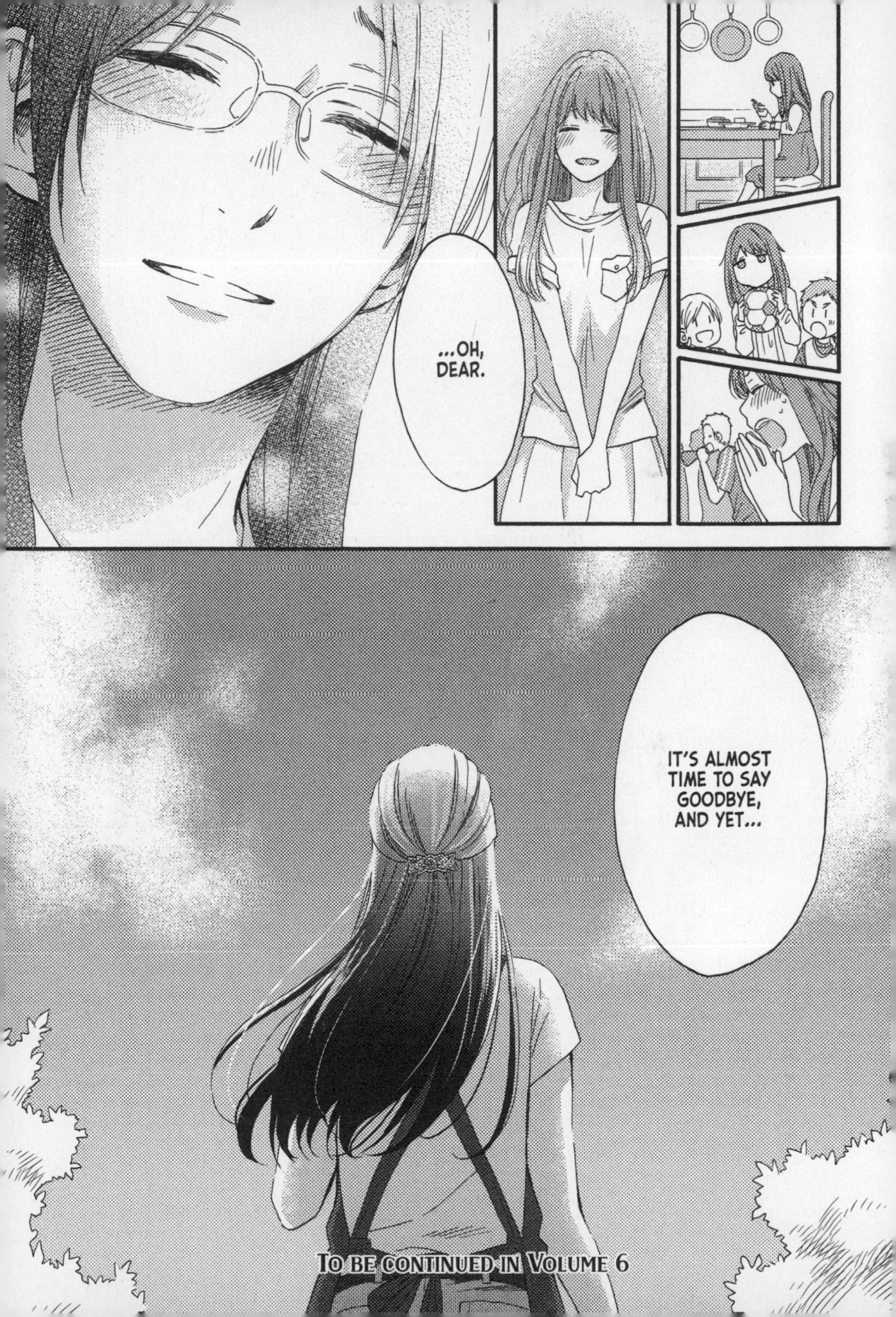
...OH, DEAR.
IT'S ALMOST TIME TO SAY GOODBYE, AND YET...
TO BE CONTINUED IN VOLUME 6

✷ Special thanks to ✷

- ✷ Kyonko-san
- ✷ Takematsu-san
- ✷ H.T-san
- ✷ Suzuki-san

- ✷ Kino-san
- ✷ Fumie Akuta-san
- ✷ My editor Y-san
- ✷ My family, friends, and former colleagues who are always supporting me.

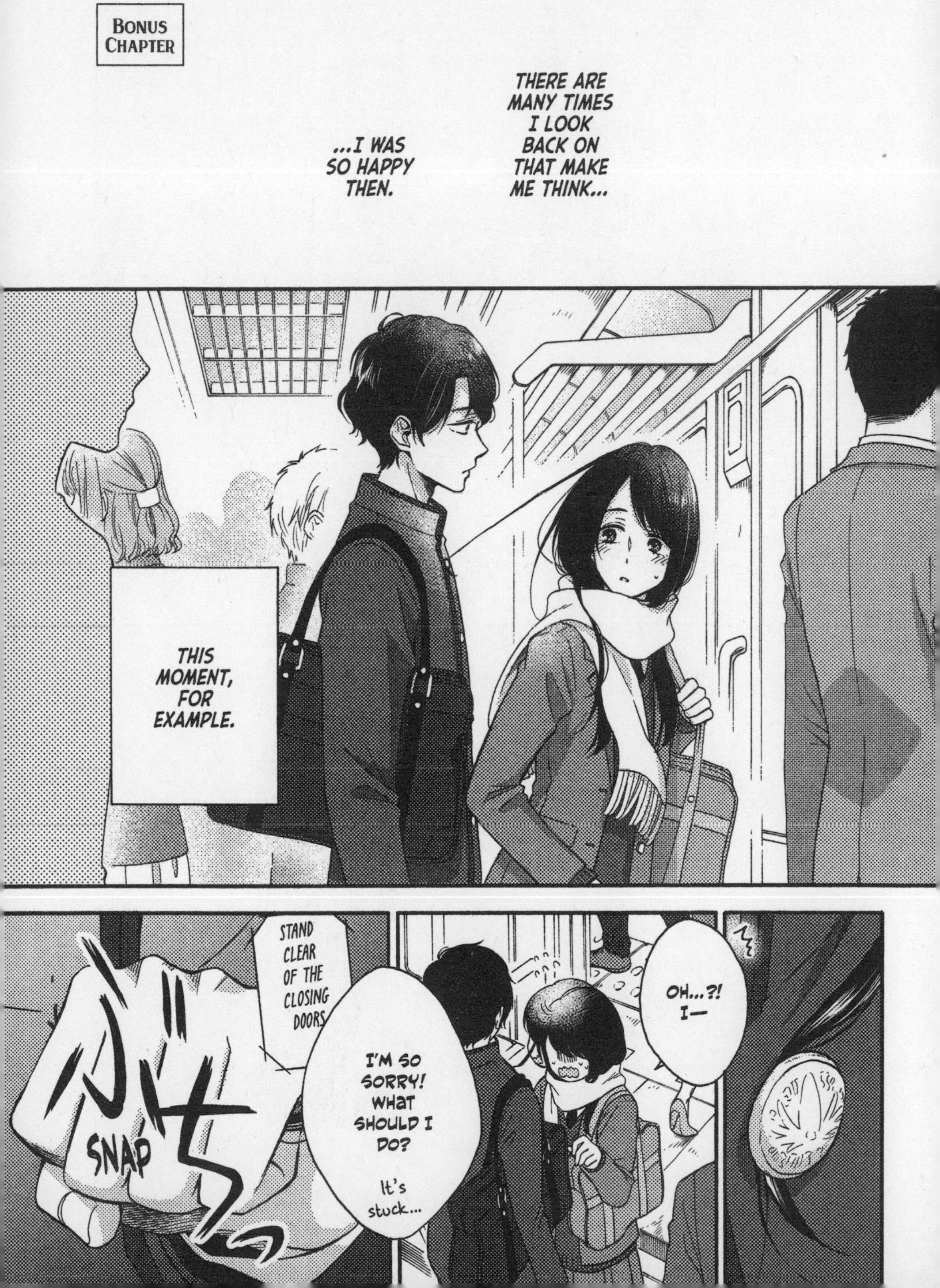
BONUS CHAPTER
THERE ARE MANY TIMES I LOOK BACK ON THAT MAKE ME THINK...
...I WAS SO HAPPY THEN.
THIS MOMENT, FOR EXAMPLE.
OH...?! I—
I'M SO SORRY! WHAT SHOULD I DO?
It's stuck...
STAND CLEAR OF THE CLOSING DOORS
SNAP

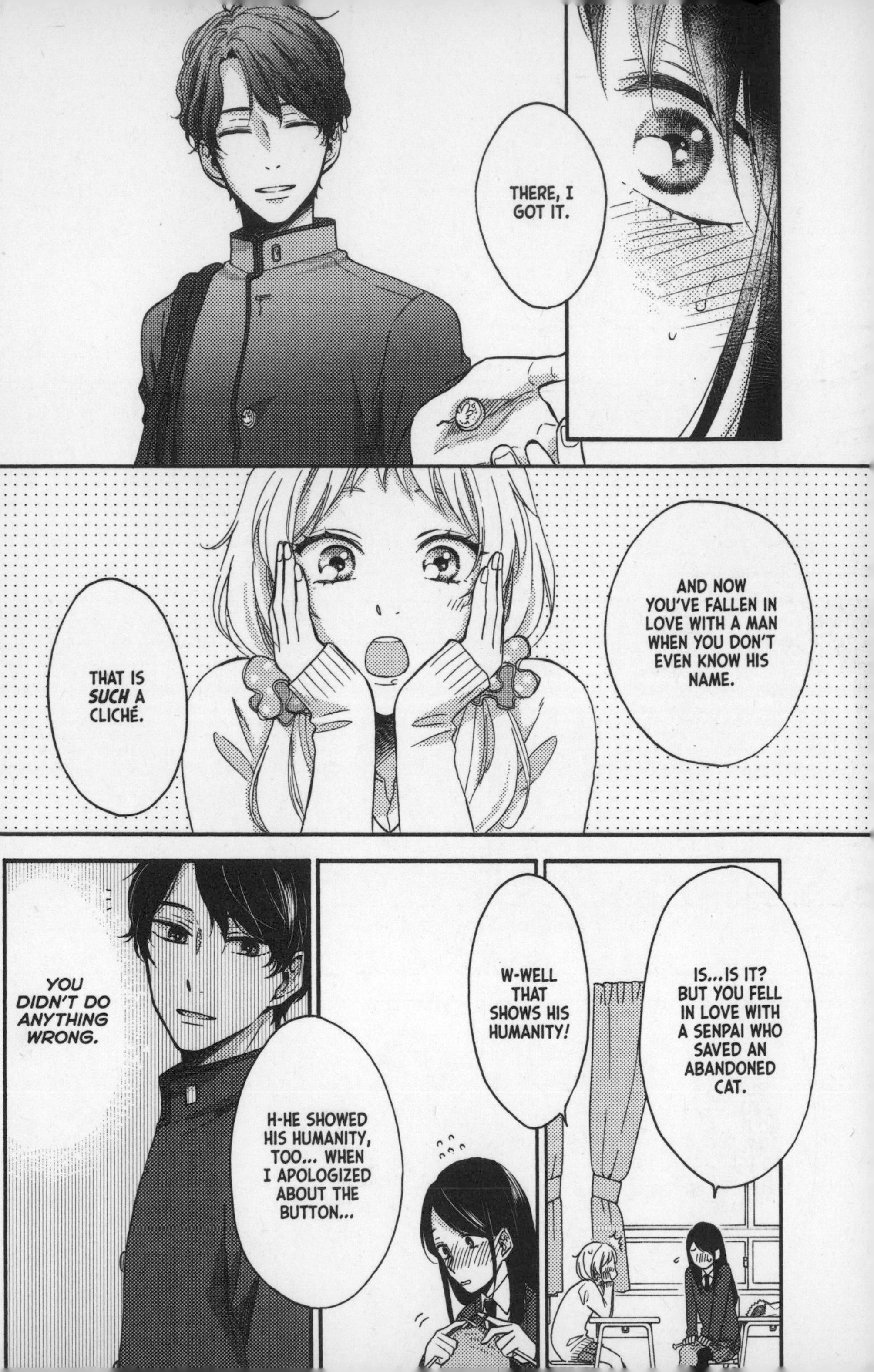
THERE, I GOT IT.
AND NOW YOU'VE FALLEN IN LOVE WITH A MAN WHEN YOU DON'T EVEN KNOW HIS NAME.
THAT IS *SUCH* A CLICHÉ.
IS...IS IT? BUT YOU FELL IN LOVE WITH A SENPAI WHO SAVED AN ABANDONED CAT.
W-WELL THAT SHOWS HIS HUMANITY!
H-HE SHOWED HIS HUMANITY, TOO... WHEN I APOLOGIZED ABOUT THE BUTTON...
YOU DIDN'T DO ANYTHING WRONG.

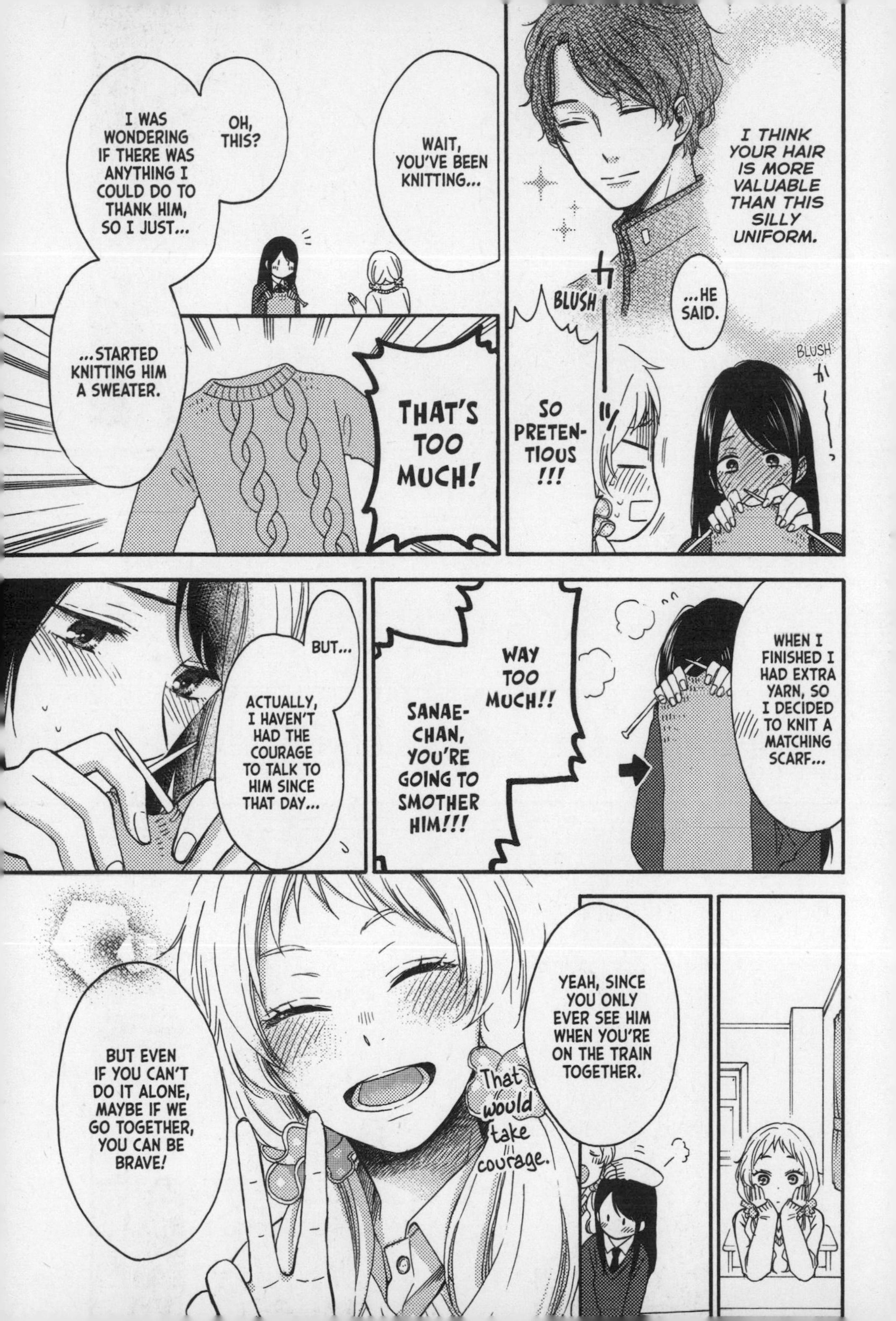
I THINK YOUR HAIR IS MORE VALUABLE THAN THIS SILLY UNIFORM.
...HE SAID.
BLUSH
BLUSH
SO PRETEN-TIOUS!!!
WAIT, YOU'VE BEEN KNITTING...
OH, THIS?
I WAS WONDERING IF THERE WAS ANYTHING I COULD DO TO THANK HIM, SO I JUST...
THAT'S TOO MUCH!
...STARTED KNITTING HIM A SWEATER.
WHEN I FINISHED I HAD EXTRA YARN, SO I DECIDED TO KNIT A MATCHING SCARF...
WAY TOO MUCH!!
SANAE-CHAN, YOU'RE GOING TO SMOTHER HIM!!!
BUT...
ACTUALLY, I HAVEN'T HAD THE COURAGE TO TALK TO HIM SINCE THAT DAY...
YEAH, SINCE YOU ONLY EVER SEE HIM WHEN YOU'RE ON THE TRAIN TOGETHER.
That would take courage.
BUT EVEN IF YOU CAN'T DO IT ALONE, MAYBE IF WE GO TOGETHER, YOU CAN BE BRAVE!

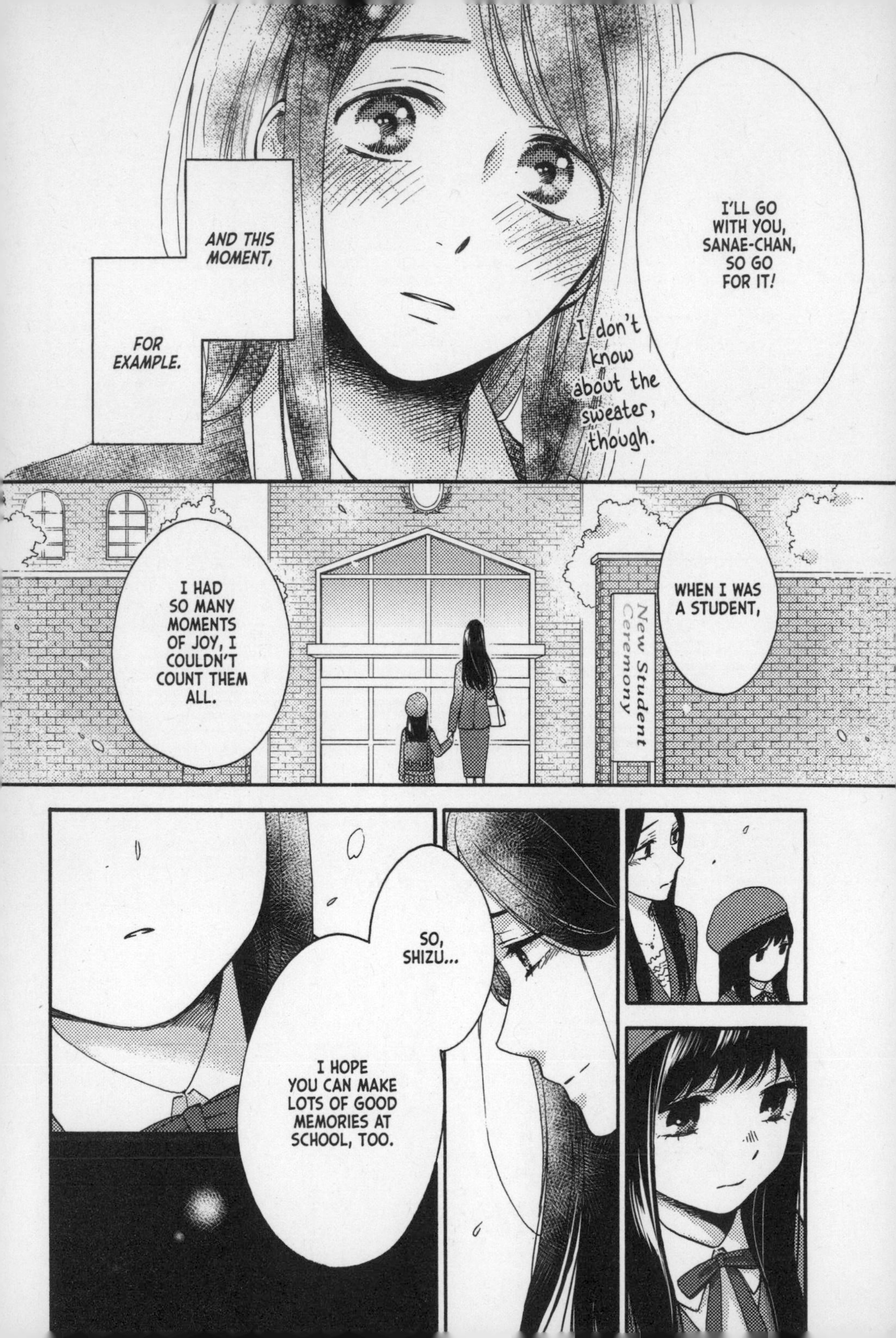
I'LL GO WITH YOU, SANAE-CHAN, SO GO FOR IT!
I don't know about the sweater, though.
AND THIS MOMENT,
FOR EXAMPLE.
WHEN I WAS A STUDENT,
New Student Ceremony
I HAD SO MANY MOMENTS OF JOY, I COULDN'T COUNT THEM ALL.
SO, SHIZU...
I HOPE YOU CAN MAKE LOTS OF GOOD MEMORIES AT SCHOOL, TOO.

Wake Up, Sleeping Beauty

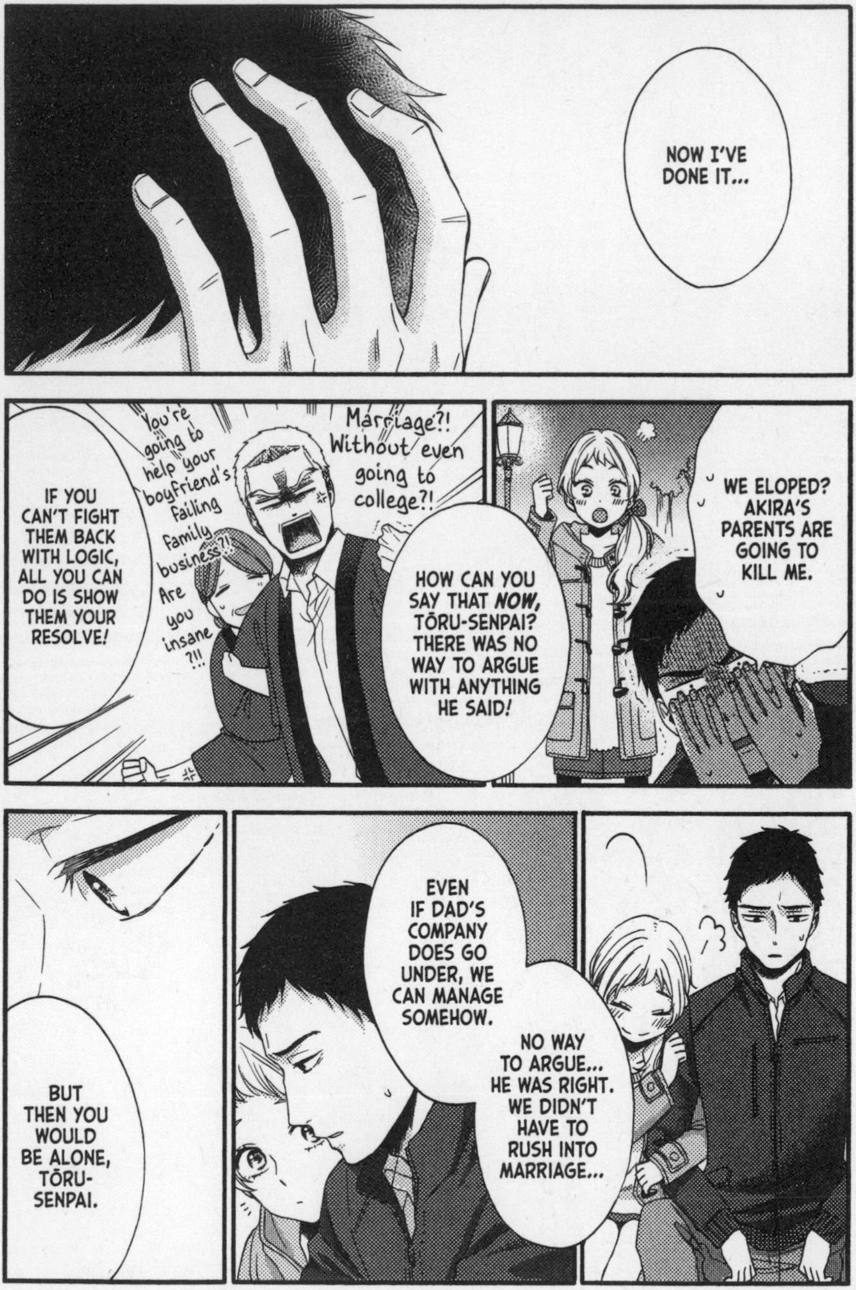
NOW I'VE DONE IT...
WE ELOPED? AKIRA'S PARENTS ARE GOING TO KILL ME.
HOW CAN YOU SAY THAT *NOW*, TŌRU-SENPAI? THERE WAS NO WAY TO ARGUE WITH ANYTHING HE SAID!
Marriage?! Without even going to college?!
You're going to help your boyfriend's failing family business?! Are you insane?!!
IF YOU CAN'T FIGHT THEM BACK WITH LOGIC, ALL YOU CAN DO IS SHOW THEM YOUR RESOLVE!
NO WAY TO ARGUE... HE WAS RIGHT. WE DIDN'T HAVE TO RUSH INTO MARRIAGE...
EVEN IF DAD'S COMPANY DOES GO UNDER, WE CAN MANAGE SOMEHOW.
BUT THEN YOU WOULD BE ALONE, TŌRU-SENPAI.

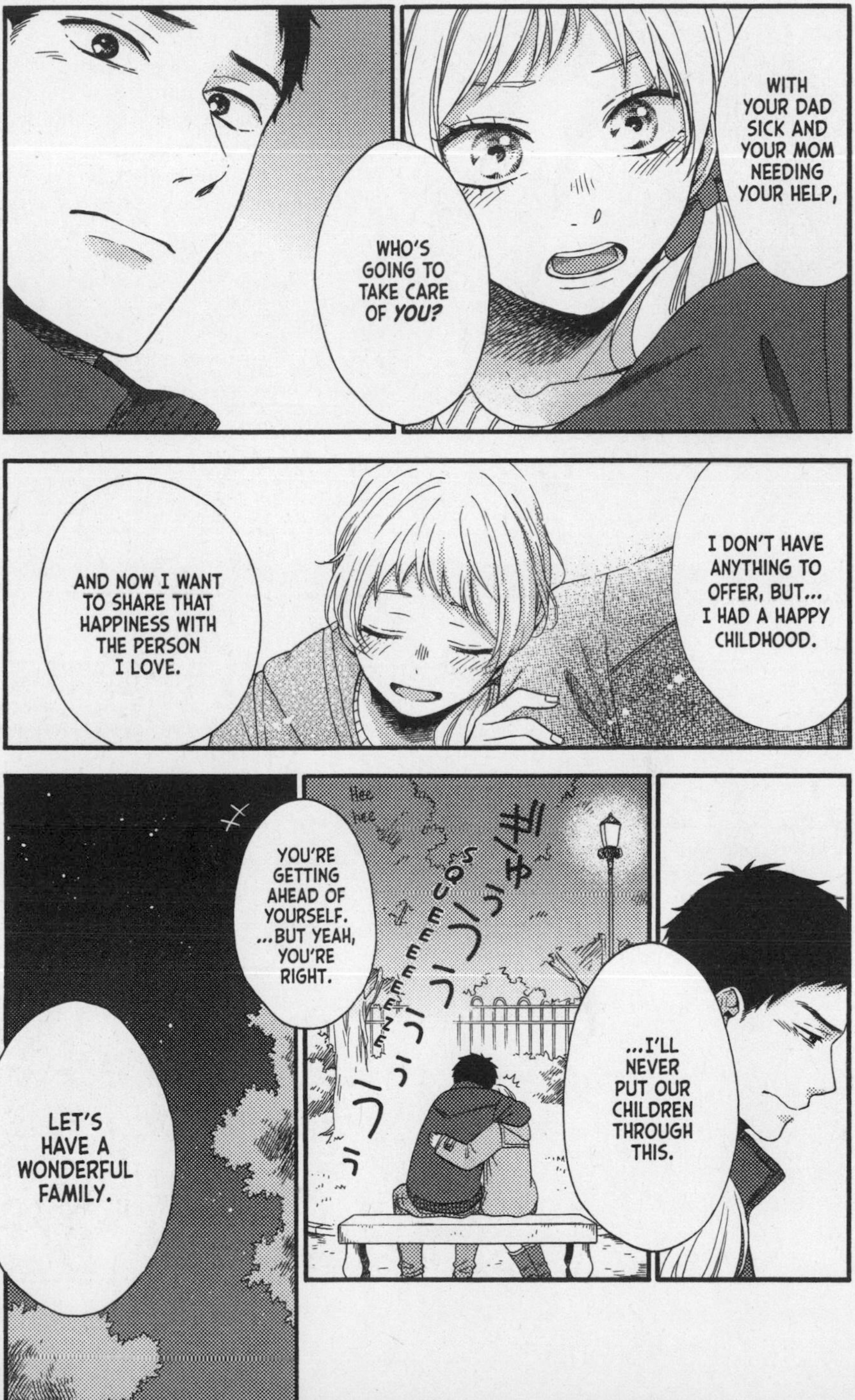
WITH YOUR DAD SICK AND YOUR MOM NEEDING YOUR HELP,
WHO'S GOING TO TAKE CARE OF *YOU?*
I DON'T HAVE ANYTHING TO OFFER, BUT... I HAD A HAPPY CHILDHOOD.
AND NOW I WANT TO SHARE THAT HAPPINESS WITH THE PERSON I LOVE.
...I'LL NEVER PUT OUR CHILDREN THROUGH THIS.
SQUEEEEEEZE
YOU'RE GETTING AHEAD OF YOURSELF. ...BUT YEAH, YOU'RE RIGHT.
Hee hee
LET'S HAVE A WONDERFUL FAMILY.

TRANSLATION NOTES

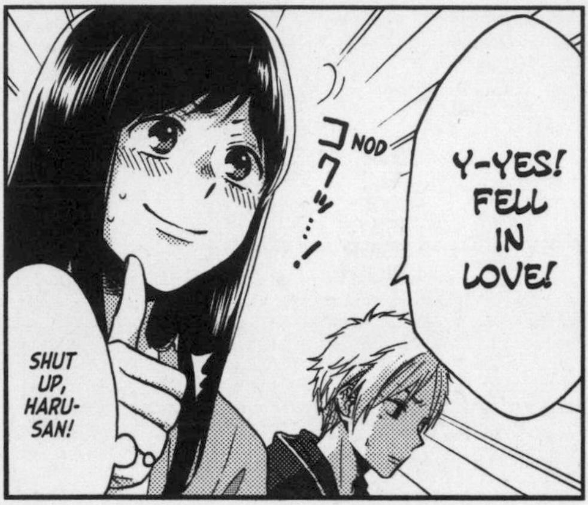
Y-YES! FELL IN LOVE!
コクッ…!
NOD
SHUT UP, HARU-SAN!

Y-Yes! Fell in love!, page 13
In the original Japanese, Harumichi says, in English, "Yes! Fall in love!" Whether or not he's trying to tell Tetsu's grandfather that Tetsu and Shizu are madly in love, he is referring to the Japanese comedy duo Fall in Love, famous for their one-minute love story sketches. Two people will talk under very ordinary circumstances, which will quickly escalate until they are madly in love. The sketch will always end with the pair saying, "Yes! Fall in love!"

***Otanko-nasu*, page 52**
Ryō uses a word that basically means Tetsu and her father are doing something she doesn't like, and therefore she thinks they are stupid. However, because the original word ends in *-nasu,* the Japanese word for "eggplant," a picture of the vegetable comes to Shizu's mind. In Japanese, *-nasu* is used often at the end of an insult, as are other vegetables.

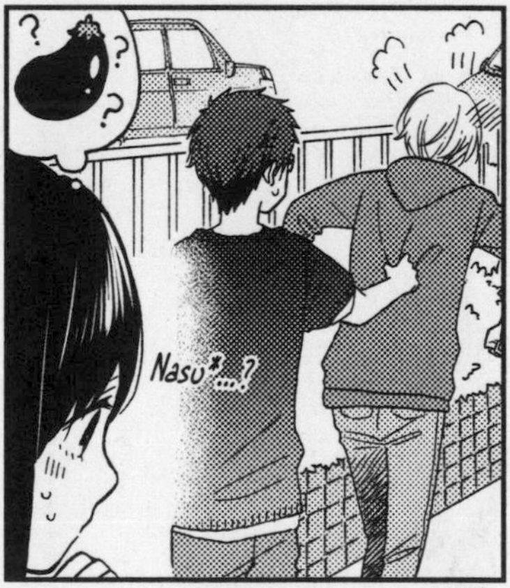
Nasu*...?

A good scare, page 85

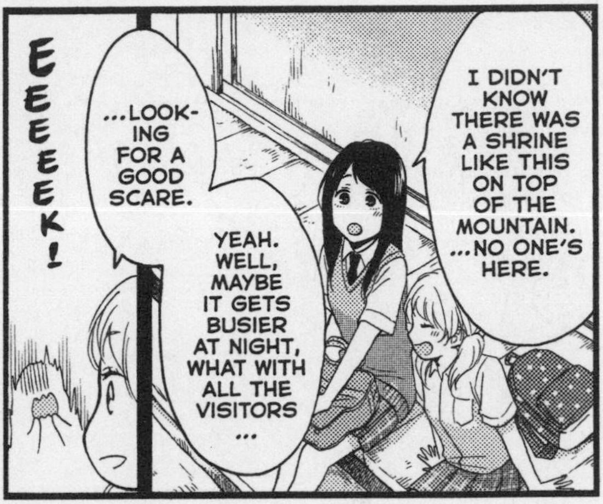
I DIDN'T KNOW THERE WAS A SHRINE LIKE THIS ON TOP OF THE MOUNTAIN. ...NO ONE'S HERE.
YEAH. WELL, MAYBE IT GETS BUSIER AT NIGHT, WHAT WITH ALL THE VISITORS ...
...LOOK-ING FOR A GOOD SCARE.
EEEEEK!

Specifically, the "good scare" comes in the form of a *kimo-dameshi,* or "test of courage." Young people will choose a frightening location, usually one with rumors of ghosts or that otherwise seems like a good place to run into something supernatural, and take turns walking a path through it alone or in pairs to see if they have the courage to make it all the way through. Sometimes other members of the group will dress up as ghosts and demons to improve the chances that something will go bump in the night.

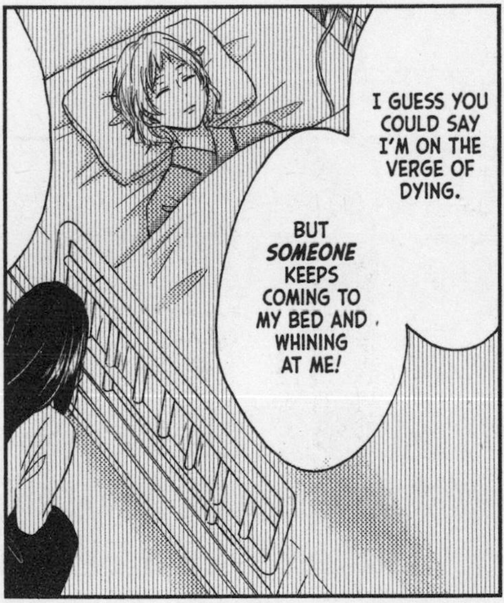
I GUESS YOU COULD SAY I'M ON THE VERGE OF DYING.
BUT *SOMEONE* KEEPS COMING TO MY BED AND WHINING AT ME!

On the verge of dying, page 131

In Japanese folklore, there is a belief that if a living person feels strongly enough about something or someone, their spirit will leave their body to do something about those feelings—for example, curse a love rival, or spend time with loved ones. In other words, a person doesn't have to be fully dead in order to wander this plane as a ghost, so Mirei's presence inside Shizu is not necessarily to be taken as evidence that she is on her way permanently out of this life.

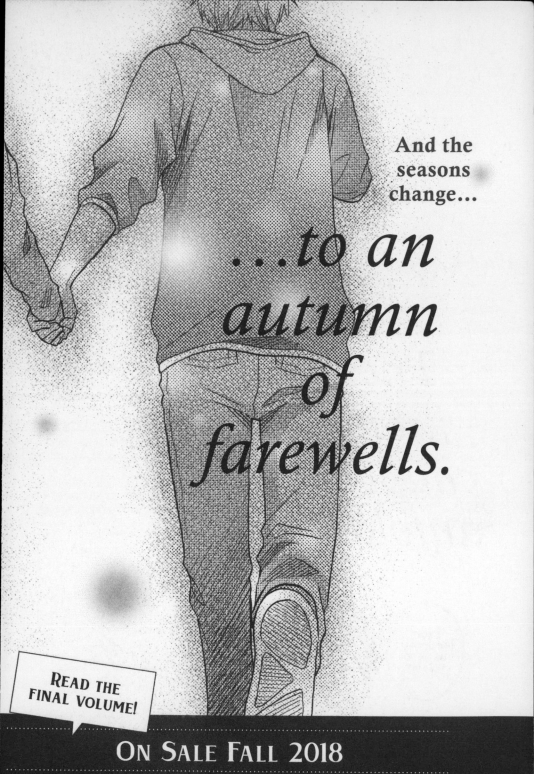

And the
seasons
change…

….to *an*
autumn
of
farewells.

READ THE
FINAL VOLUME!

ON SALE FALL 2018

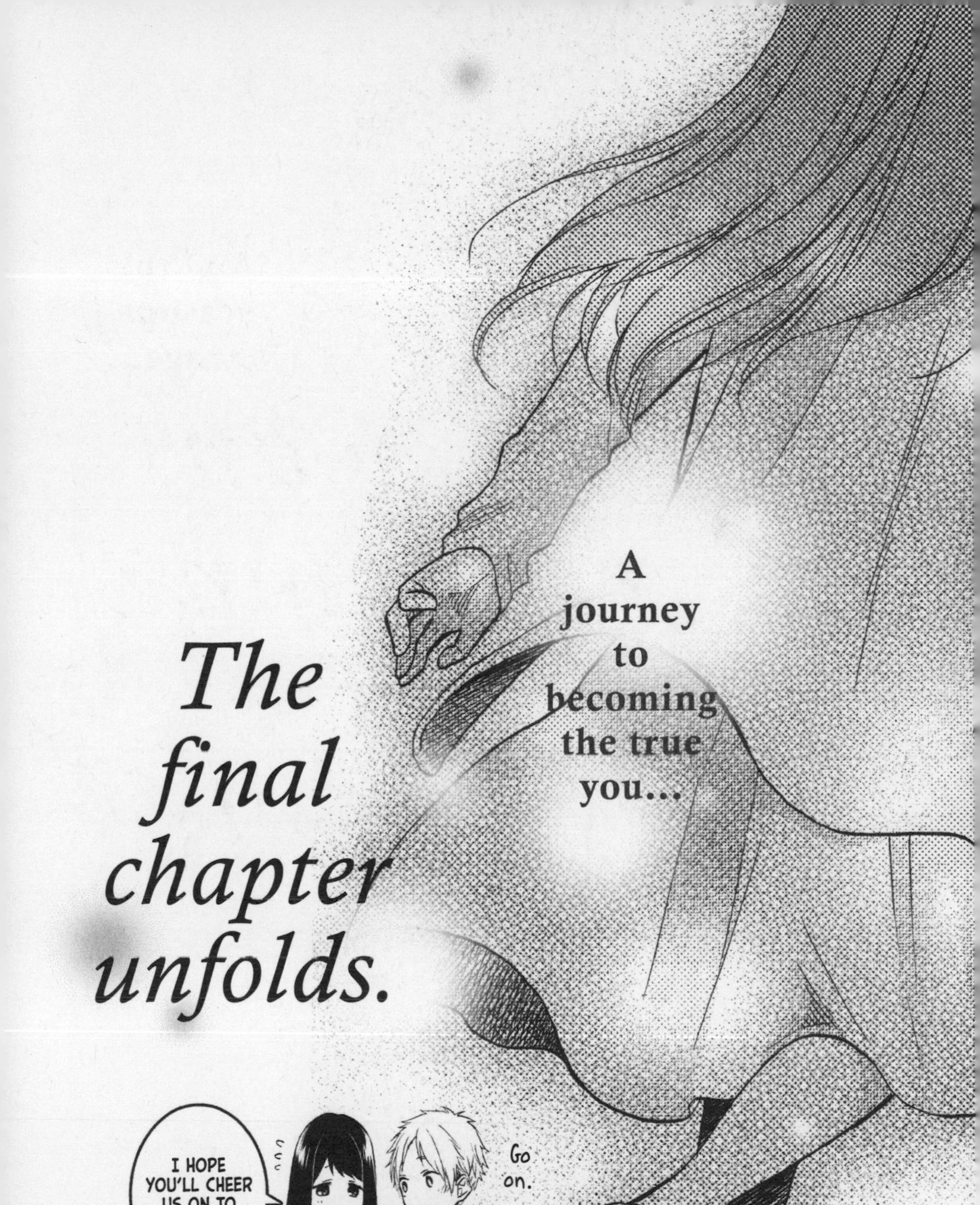
A journey to becoming the true you...
The final chapter unfolds.
Go on.
I HOPE YOU'LL CHEER US ON TO THE END!

Wake Up, Sleeping Beauty 6 (FINAL VOLUME)

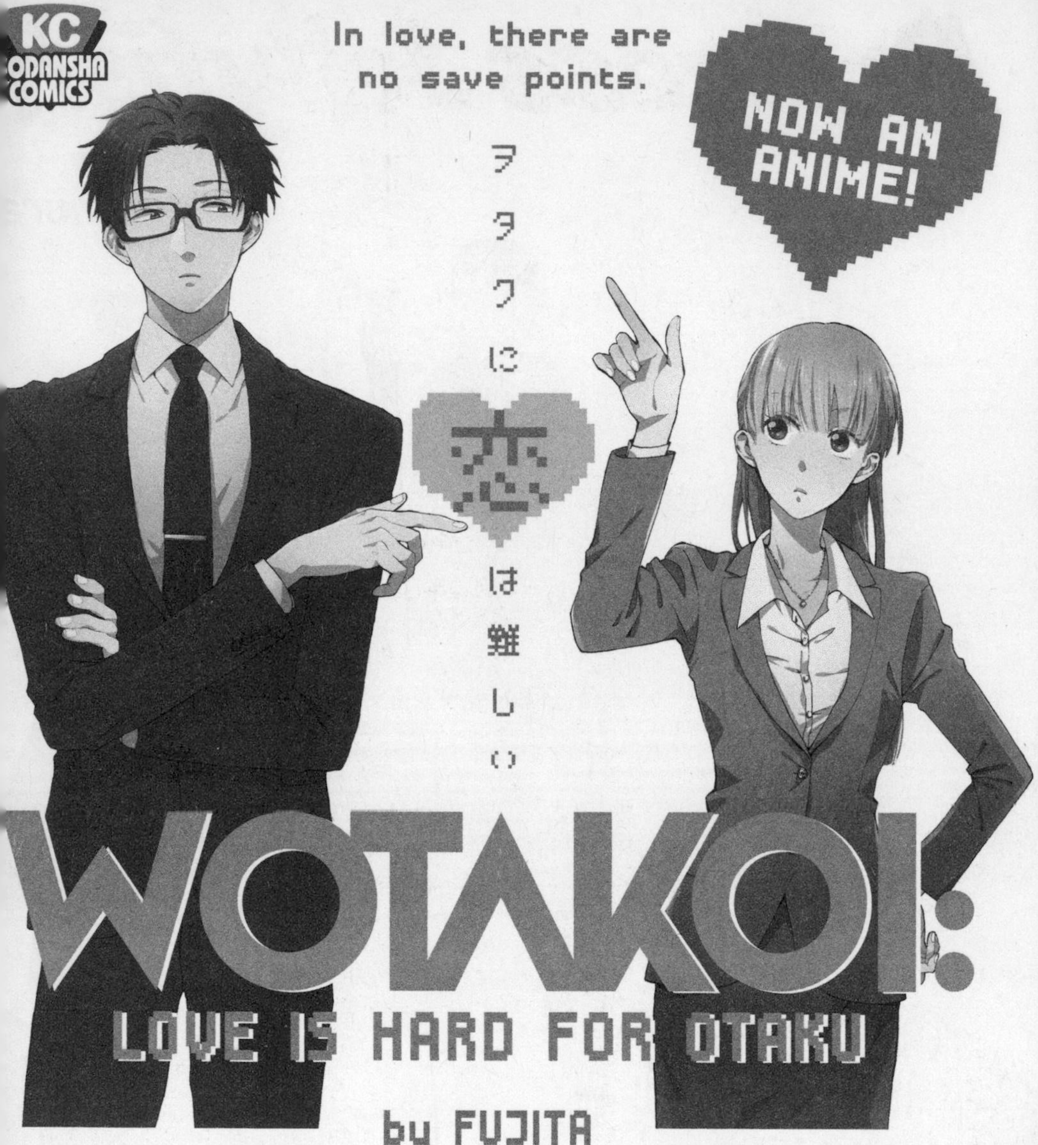
KC KODANSHA COMICS
In love, there are no save points.
NOW AN ANIME!
ヲタクに恋は難しい
WOTAKOI:
LOVE IS HARD FOR OTAKU
by FUJITA

Narumi has had it rough: Every boyfriend she's had dumped her once they found out she was an otaku, so she's gone to great lengths to hide it. At her new job, she bumps into Hirotaka, her childhood friend and fellow otaku. When Hirotaka almost gets her secret outed at work, she comes up with a plan to keep him quiet. But he comes up with a counter-proposal: Why doesn't she just date him instead?

Princess Jellyfish

Akiko Higashimura

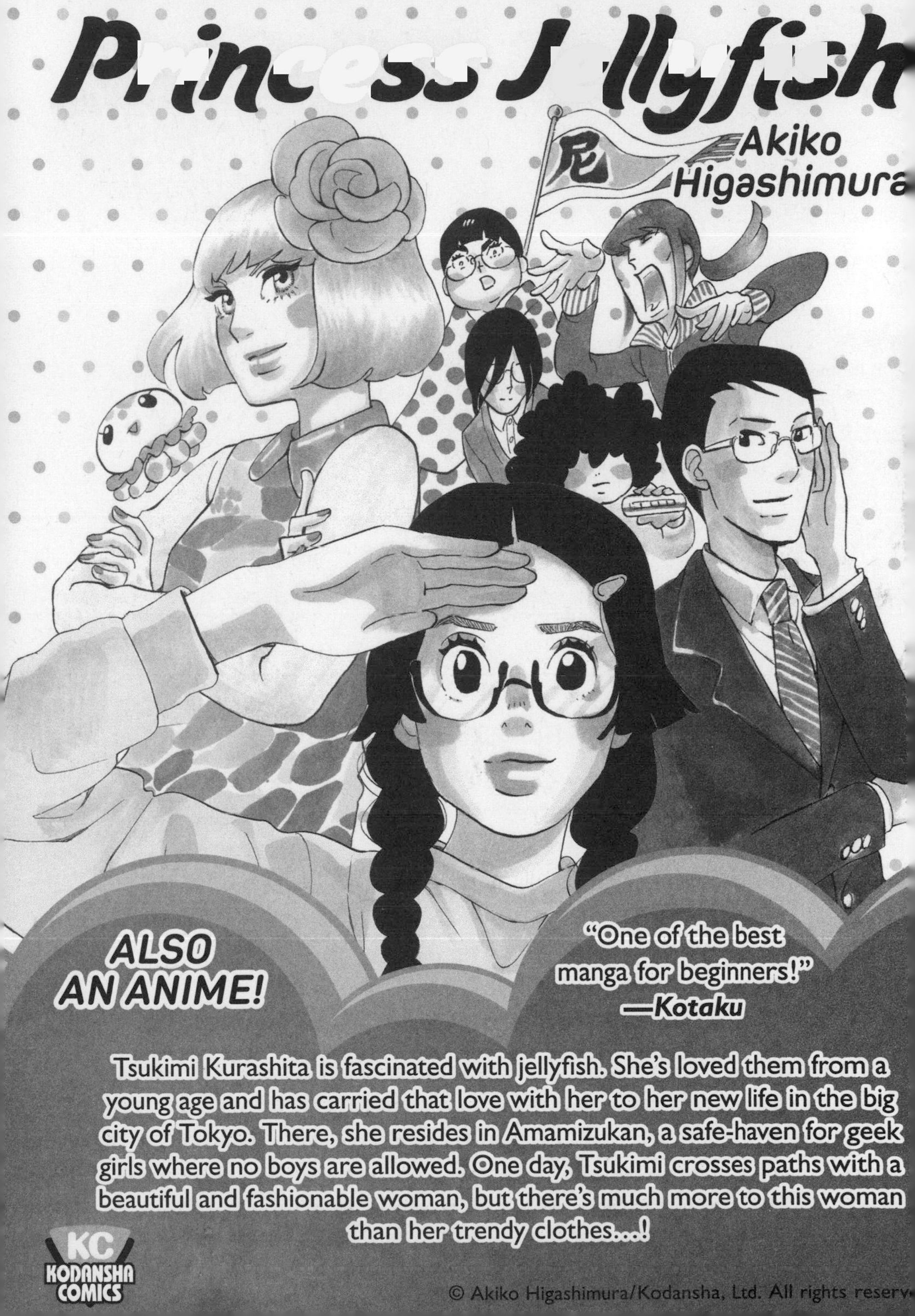

ALSO AN ANIME!

"One of the best manga for beginners!"
—*Kotaku*

Tsukimi Kurashita is fascinated with jellyfish. She's loved them from a young age and has carried that love with her to her new life in the big city of Tokyo. There, she resides in Amamizukan, a safe-haven for geek girls where no boys are allowed. One day, Tsukimi crosses paths with a beautiful and fashionable woman, but there's much more to this woman than her trendy clothes...!

KC KODANSHA COMICS

A Kodansha Comics Trade Paperback Original.

Published in the United States by Kodansha Comics,
an imprint of Kodansha USA Publishing, LLC, New York.

Publication rights for this English edition arranged through Kodansha Ltd., Tokyo.

First published in Japan in 2017 by Kodansha Ltd., Tokyo,
as *Ohayou, Ibarahime* volume 5.

Cover Design: Tomohiro Kusume (arcoinc)

ISBN 978-1-63236-591-0

Printed in the United States of America.

www.kodanshacomics.com

9 8 7 6 5 4 3 2 1

Translation: Alethea and Athena Nibley
Lettering: Lys Blakeslee
Editing: Haruko Hashimoto
Kodansha Comics Edition Cover Design: Phil Balsman